THE CAMBRIDGE COMPANION TO
# SPINOZA'S *ETHICS*

Since its publication in 1677, Spinoza's *Ethics* has fascinated
philosophers, novelists, and scientists alike. It is undoubtedly one
of the most exciting and contested works of Western philosophy.
Written in an austere, geometrical fashion, the work teaches us how
we should live, ending with an ethics in which the only thing good
in itself is understanding. Spinoza argues that only that which hinders us from understanding is bad and shows that those endowed
with human minds should devote themselves, as much as they
can, to a contemplative life. This Companion volume provides a
detailed, accessible exposition of the *Ethics*. Written by an interna-
tionally known team of scholars, it is the first anthology to treat
the whole of the *Ethics* and is written in an accessible style.

Olli Koistinen is professor of philosophy at the University of Turku
in Finland. He is the co-editor, with John Biro, of *Spinoza: Metaphysical Themes*.

T0370960

*The Cambridge Companion to*

# SPINOZA'S
# *ETHICS*

Edited by
Olli Koistinen
*University of Turku*

CAMBRIDGE
UNIVERSITY PRESS

CAMBRIDGE UNIVERSITY PRESS
Cambridge, New York, Melbourne, Madrid, Cape Town,
Singapore, São Paulo, Delhi, Tokyo, Mexico City

Cambridge University Press
32 Avenue of the Americas, New York, NY 10013-2473, USA

www.cambridge.org
Information on this title: www.cambridge.org/9780521618601

First published 2009
Reprinted 2011

*A catalog record for this publication is available from the British Library.*

*Library of Congress Cataloging in Publication Data*

The Cambridge companion to Spinoza's *Ethics* / edited by Olli Koistinen.
    p.  cm. – (The Cambridge companions to philosophy)
Includes bibliographical references and index.
ISBN 978-0-521-85339-2 (hardback) – ISBN 978-0-521-61860-1 (pbk.)
1. Spinoza, Benedictus de, 1632–1677. Ethica.  2. Ethics.  I. Koistinen,
Olli.  II. Title.  III. Series.
B3974.C36   2009
170 – dc22       2009010978

ISBN 978-0-521-85339-2 Hardback
ISBN 978-0-521-61860-1 Paperback

# Contents

# List of Contributors

DON GARRETT is professor of philosophy at New York University. He is the author of *Cognition and Commitment in Hume's Philosophy* and the editor of *The Cambridge Companion to Spinoza*.

SUSAN JAMES is professor of philosophy at Birkbeck College. She is the author of *Passion and Action: The Emotions in Seventeenth-Century Philosophy*.

CHARLES JARRETT is associate professor of philosophy at Rutgers-Camden. He is the author of *Spinoza: A Guide for the Perplexed*.

OLLI KOISTINEN is professor of theoretical philosophy at the University of Turku. He has co-edited *Spinoza: Metaphysical Themes* with John Biro.

MICHAEL LEBUFFE is assistant professor of philosophy at Texas A&M University. He is the author of *From Bondage to Freedom: Spinoza on Human Excellence* (forthcoming from Oxford University Press) and of articles on Spinoza and Hobbes.

MARTIN LIN is associate professor of philosophy at Rutgers University. He has published several articles on early modern philosophy, especially on Spinoza.

JON MILLER is associate professor of philosophy at Queen's University in Canada. His particular research interest is understanding how early modern philosophers received the ideas of the ancients.

ANDREAS SCHMIDT teaches philosophy at the Eberhard-Karls-Universtät Tübingen. He is the author of *Der Grund des Wissens. Zu Fichtes Wissenschaftslehren in den Versionen von 1794/95, 1804/II und 1812* and of *Göttliche Gedanken. Zur Metaphysik der Erkenntnis bei Descartes, Spinoza, Malebranche und Leibniz* (forthcoming).

PIET STEENBAKKERS is lecturer in the history of modern philosophy at the University of Utrecht and holder of the endowed chair of Spinoza studies at Erasmus University Rotterdam. He is a member of the international research team Groupe de recherches spinozistes, and he is currently involved in setting up a research project on Biblical Criticism and Secularization in the Seventeenth Century.

DIANE STEINBERG is associate professor of philosophy at Cleveland State University. She has published articles on Spinoza and is the author of *On Spinoza*.

VALTTERI VILJANEN is an Academy of Finland postdoctoral Fellow in the Department of Philosophy at the University of Turku. He obtained his Ph.D. on the concept of power in Spinoza's metaphysics and has published articles on Spinoza.

ANDREW YOUPA is assistant professor of philosophy at Southern Illinois University, Carbondale. His research focuses on Spinoza's moral psychology and ethical theory.

# Abbreviations

A. SPINOZA, BENEDICTUS DE (1632–77)

*Collected works* (for further details, see the bibliography):

> G = Spinoza. 1925. *Spinoza Opera.* 4 vols. Edited by Carl Gebhardt.
> C = Spinoza. 1985. *The Collected Works of Spinoza, vol. I.* Translated and edited by E. M. Curley.

The *Ethics:*
The *Ethics* was first published posthumously with the Latin title *Ethica Ordine Geometrico demonstrata* in Spinoza (1677b). Latin editions of the *Ethica* are included in Spinoza 1914 and G II. Widely used English translations of the *Ethics* are Edwin Curley's in C and Samuel Shirley's in Spinoza 2002. If not otherwise indicated, in this volume all translations of Spinoza's works are from C.

The first Arabic number specifies the part of the *Ethics*. The abbreviations following that numeral are as follows:

a = axiom
da = definition of the affects in the third part of the *Ethics*
app = appendix
c = corollary
d = definition (when not after a proposition number)
d = demonstration (when after a proposition number)
le = lemma
p = proposition
po = postulate
pref = preface
s = scholium

For example, 1p16c1 refers to the first corollary of the sixteenth proposition in the first part of the *Ethics*.

Other works:

> CM = *Metaphysical Thoughts (Cogitata Metaphysica).*

KV = *Short Treatise on God, Man, and His Well-Being* (*Korte Verhandeling van God, de Mensch, en des zelfs Welstand*).

TdIE = *Treatise on the Emendation of the Intellect* (*Tractatus de Intellectus Emendatione*).

TP = *Political Treatise* (*Tractatus Politicus*).

TTP = *Theological-Political Treatise* (*Tractatus Theologico-Politicus*).

Ep followed by an Arabic number specifies a letter in Spinoza's correspondence.

### B. OTHER SOURCES

AT = Descartes, René. 1996. *Œuvres*, publiées par Charles Adam et Paul Tannery, 12 Bde.

CSM = Descartes, René. 1985. *The Philosophical Writings of Descartes*. Volumes I and II. Translated by J. Cottingham, R. Stoothoff, and D. Murdoch.

CSMK = Descartes, René. 1991. *The Philosophical Writings of Descartes*. Volume III. Translated by J. Cottingham, R. Stoothoff, D. Murdoch, and A. Kenny.

# Introduction

Spinoza's *Ethics* is without doubt one of the most exciting and contested works in philosophy. The primary goal of this work written in the austere geometrical fashion is, as it was of the Ancients, to teach how we should live, and it ends with an ethics in which the only thing good in itself is understanding; only that which hinders us from understanding is bad; and beings endowed with a human mind should devote themselves, as much as they can, to a contemplative life. The purpose of the present volume is to provide a detailed and accessible step-by-step exposition of the *Ethics*; in this Introduction, we want to present the outlines of the reasoning behind Spinoza's rather uncompromising ethical intellectualism and briefly designate the particular topics discussed in the ensuing chapters.

It seems that any theory of good life inevitably makes some fundamental assumptions concerning what human beings are, and it can be seen as an important virtue of Spinoza's approach that these basic questions are tackled in a thorough and explicit manner. For Spinoza, to know what we are depends on knowing what the universe or God is, because Spinoza sees us as limitations in God or the universe. Our bodies have spatial limits and our understanding has limits in thought. In seriously thinking about our bodies, we have to conceive them as being embedded in a larger spatial whole, and in thinking about our minds, we clearly see that our intellects are limited, even defective. Thus, in thinking about our intellect, we by necessity form an idea of a more perfect intellect. However, that we are limited – both mentally and physically – by something larger suggests that in a sense we constitute this larger being and, thus, knowledge of this larger being gives knowledge of ourselves. Spinoza, then, adopts what is called a top-down strategy, which is explicated in the following passage:

And so they believe either that the nature of God pertains to the essence of created things, or that created things can be or be conceived without God – or what is more certain, they are not sufficiently consistent.

I

The cause of this, I believe, was that they did not observe the [proper] order of Philosophizing. For they believed that the divine nature, which they should have contemplated before all else (because it is prior both in knowledge and in nature) is last in the order of knowledge, and that the things that are called objects of the senses are prior to all. That is why, when they contemplated natural things, they thought of nothing less than they did of the divine nature; and when afterwards they directed their minds to contemplating the divine nature, they could think of nothing less than of their first fictions, on which they had built the knowledge of natural things, because these could not assist knowledge of the divine nature. So it is no wonder that they have generally contradicted themselves. (2p10s)

For Spinoza, knowledge of the infinite is, then, prior to knowledge of the finite; finite being is negation in the infinite. This kind of top-down strategy can be contrasted with Descartes's first-person point of view and his methodological scepticism, but, in fact, at least at one point in the *Meditations* Descartes holds a very similar view:

I clearly understand that there is more reality in an infinite substance than in a finite one, and hence that my perception of the infinite, that is God, is in some way prior to my perception of the finite, that is myself. For how could I understand that I doubted or desired – that is, lacked something – and that I was not wholly perfect, unless there were in me some idea of a more perfect being which enabled me to recognize my own defects by comparison? (CSM II, 31; AT VII, 46)

In the first two chapters of this book, entitled 'The Textual History of Spinoza's *Ethics*' and 'The Geometrical Order in the *Ethics*', Piet Steenbakkers scrutinizes the textual history of Spinoza's masterpiece, which reflects its contested and revered status, and its geometrical method, which is to a considerable extent responsible for that status. Devoting a section to each of its five parts, we now turn to explaining the main ideas of the *Ethics*.

### ETHICS, PART I

Part 1 of the *Ethics*, 'On God', is written very abstractly. One could see it as a tractate in cosmology investigating the nature of the world. The most important theses in the *Ethics*, Part 1, are the following three: (i) God necessarily exists; (ii) God is the only possible substance; (iii) everything follows from God by geometrical necessity. All these theses follow rather straightforwardly from Spinoza's ontology, which further develops Descartes's conception of the nature of reality. Thus, before these theses are investigated, a short exposition of Spinoza's ontology is required.

It is natural to think that the world consists of different individual things that are in mutual interaction. For example, the state and the form of a tree depend on various external factors. However, it also is natural to think that these ordinary things, trees and rocks, are themselves compositional objects, in the sense that they consist of smaller individual things, which in turn consist of smaller things, and so on. The existence of ordinary things is dependent on their parts. However, it is not implausible to claim that this kind of dependency on parts has to stop somewhere, that is, that there have to be simple things out of which all compositional things are ultimately composed. These simple things, it can be argued, have to be completely independent of all other things. Not only is their existence independent of any parts, but, moreover, they cannot have external causes for their existence, because it is natural to hold that when a thing comes to existence through external causes, these causes just arrange preexisting things so that they together compose a new thing. Moreover, it seems that simple things cannot be destroyed through external factors, because destruction through external causes can happen only if an external cause breaks the inner constitution of a thing. Finally, it seems that external causes cannot affect these simple things at all, because a thing can be affected only if it has an inner constitution that can be changed. This kind of independent things that lie at the basis of reality are traditionally called substances. In a certain sense, the existence of all other things is reducible to the ways or modes in which these simple substances exist. The independence of substances characterized above could be labeled *ontological independence*, and from this ontological independence it is a small step to what could be called *conceptual independence*. If a thing is completely independent of everything else and is able to exist alone, its nature, or what it is, cannot be dependent on anything else. Thus, all there is to know about an ontologically independent thing has to be in the thing itself, which means that the thing is conceptually independent.

In 1d3, Spinoza defines substance in terms of ontological and conceptual independence. Something is a substance just in case it *is in itself* and is *conceived through itself*, Spinoza says. Here the in-itself condition signifies ontological independence and the conceived-through-itself condition conceptual independence. Moreover, all other things are nothing but ways or modes of substances. Thus, Spinoza's conception of substance seems to differ in no way from the traditional conception; what makes his metaphysics so startling is the consequences he draws from that conception.

Spinoza argues that any possible substance has to exist by necessity, because nothing external can prevent a possible substance from existing (1p7d). This is an extremely interesting claim, and it is not quite clear whether Spinoza takes it as a self-evident truth – perhaps some background assumptions are needed. It is true that Spinoza endorses a version of the principle of sufficient reason. For Spinoza, this principle says not only that for the existence of a thing a cause is needed but also that the nonexistence of a thing requires a cause (1p11d2). One might, then, give the following indirect proof for the necessary existence of a possible substance s: suppose that s does not exist. From the independence of substances, it follows that nothing external to s can be the cause of the nonexistence of s. Thus, the cause of its nonexistence has to be somehow internal to s. But this can hold only if s has a contradictory nature; that is, only if s is not a possible substance. So we can conclude that any possible substance has to exist by necessity.

In 1d6, Spinoza defines God as a substance that has an infinity of attributes, each of which is infinite in its own kind. From this definition and from the necessary existence of any possible substance, it follows that God necessarily exists. However, the proof of the existence of God involves a difficulty that is absent from the proof of the necessary existence of substance. Even if it were granted that there have to be completely independent things, this is not enough to show that God, defined as a substance having an infinity of attributes, is possible. To understand the problem and Spinoza's solution to it, the notion of attribute has to be investigated. Let us first call the position that there are several independent things, that is, substances, which ground the existence of everything else, *substance pluralism* and Spinoza's view that only one such thing exists, *substance monism*. In substance pluralism the different substances have their own natures, that is, attributes that are responsible for the distinctness of the substances. Attributes are what could be called individuators, and so in Spinoza's substance monism it is assumed that all these distinct individuators, or individual natures, can be had by one thing (1p10s). However, this assumption is problematic, because it is not at all easy to understand how one thing can have several natures. But once the assumption is made, substance monism follows directly from the following three premises: (i) attributes are individuators; (ii) any possible substance exists by necessity; (iii) God, that is, a substance having all possible attributes, is possible. It is easy to show that substance monism really follows from these premises: suppose that besides God some other substance s exists. Because attributes are individuators, s must have an attribute that differentiates s from God. This, however, is impossible, because God has all possible attributes.

Spinoza's ontology and its relation to those of Aristotle and Descartes are considered in Valtteri Viljanen's chapter 'Spinoza's Ontology'. After having given a detailed overview of different interpretations of Spinoza's basic metaphysics, Viljanen emphasizes the importance of Spinoza's transition from considerations concerning concepts to propositions concerning real entities, the essence of which is causal power. Chapters by

Andreas Schmidt and by Jon Miller, 'Substance Monism and Identity Theory in Spinoza' and 'Spinoza and Stoics on Substance Monism', respectively, shed light on different aspects of Spinoza's monism. Schmidt pays close attention to different interpretations of Spinoza's argument for monism and he also considers the problem of how it is possible that Spinoza's God, a simple substance, has several natures or attributes. In Schmidt's interpretation, the key to the solution of this problem is to be found in Duns Scotus's concept of formal distinction. Schmidt also shows how Spinoza's view of the mind–body relation is partly based on monism. Jon Miller argues in his chapter that Spinoza's monism was not something he just borrowed from the Stoics. Whereas the Stoic arguments for monism rely on wholeness and teleology, Spinoza's monism follows from his theory of *per se* individuation.

For Spinoza, contingency is closely related to interaction. Only things that are in interaction can be said to have some of their features contingently. For example, we might be willing to say that a painted floor is only contingently brown, because brownness does not result from the nature of the floor. A necessarily existing substance, however, is in no interaction with other things, and thus all its properties somehow emanate from its inner nature; thus an independent thing completely determines itself (1p16 and 1p16d). Hence it seems that necessitarianism follows directly from substance monism.

However, Spinoza's modal theory has been a subject of a long controversy. Spinoza no doubt accepts the necessity of all truths, but it is not quite clear whether he accepts the absolute necessity of all truths. Truths about finite things have what is called relative necessity, or necessity by reason of cause (1p33s1), and it has been argued that this kind of necessity is consistent with contingency. In his chapter 'Spinoza on Necessity', Charles Jarrett discusses different interpretations of Spinoza's modal theory, reaching the conclusion that Spinoza has only one notion of necessity. Jarrett also compares Spinoza's ontological argument for the existence of God with that presented by Kurt Gödel.

### *ETHICS*, PART 2

In Part 2 of the *Ethics*, 'On the Nature and Origin of the Mind', Spinoza first gives content to the highly abstract metaphysics of Part 1. In the first two propositions Spinoza purports to prove that thought and extension are attributes of God. Even though the official demonstrations of these propositions are somewhat problematic, the scholium to 2p1, where Spinoza offers an alternative demonstration for thought's being an attribute of God, is illuminating. What Spinoza seems to claim there is that if we can conceive some property *F* so that it can be had to an infinite degree, then that property is an attribute. But because we can conceive a being that is infinite in respect of its power of thinking, thought is an attribute of God. In the same way, even though Spinoza does not do that, we could demonstrate that extension is an attribute of God: we can conceive a being that is infinite in its extension; therefore extension is an attribute of God.

The situation looks like this: God exists and is thinking and extended. One wonders whether these aspects of God are in any way related to each other. What does God think? At 2p3 Spinoza argues that God's thought is directed to himself. He can form the idea of his essence and of everything that flows from that essence. So he acquires the objects of thought from other attributes and because of his infinity in respect of thinking he is able to form an idea of everything. After this, Spinoza goes on to argue that the acts of thought (i.e., formation of ideas) are not caused by the objects thought about in these acts (2p5–p6). This means that God's intellect is not passive, but from his own infinite power of thinking God spontaneously thinks everything that it is possible to think about. This suggests a kind of parallelism between thought and extension; that is, that there are modes of thought that are purely mental that somehow represent the extended realm in such a way that the modes of thought do not have modes of extension, or modes of any other attributes, as their constituents. Thought does not borrow its content from other attributes.

However, there are reasons to think that this picture of parallelism cannot be accurate. One is tempted to endorse it because for Spinoza attributes are conceived through themselves (1p10). This is easy to read as a kind of conceptual independence, which suggests that any necessary tie between thought and what the thought is about is due not to the nature of these attributes but to some other force, as it were. We would like to suggest instead that the conceptual distinction is between the *acts of thinking* and *acts of extending*. God's infinite intellect does not think about a mode of extension because the mode is there, but the intellect affirms the mode's existence from its own power. The infinite intellect, however, obtains its objects from the extended realm. Without objects given to the intellect the intellect could not think about them, but the *act of thought* performed is due to God's infinite power of thinking and is in no way caused by the object. This is how thought–body unions come to be generated.

The aforesaid helps us to understand one of the most famous propositions of the *Ethics*, viz. 2p7 according to which '(t)he order and connection of ideas is the same as the order and connection of things.' From what has been said, it follows that God forms an idea of every thing. Moreover, he cannot form those ideas without the existence of the things the ideas are about. In 2p7, by 'order and connection' Spinoza means, as the proof makes evident, their causal order and connection. Read in this way, 2p7 says that if $x$ causes $y$, then the idea of $x$ causes the idea of $y$. Given what has been said above, it follows that if $x$ causes $y$, the idea of $x$ and the idea of $y$ exist. According to Spinoza's so-called causal axiom, 1a4, the idea of an effect cannot exist without the idea (knowledge) of its cause, which means that the idea of an effect depends on the idea of its cause. Thus, causal dependency between things is matched by dependency between the ideas of those things.

In 2p7s, Spinoza explains his position on the idea–object relation by claiming that in fact any idea and its object are one and the same thing but explained through different attributes. Even though identity theories in general are difficult to understand, what Spinoza says here is in conformity with what we have argued above. When an idea is seen as an act of thought, or a modification of a mind, it is explained through the attribute of thought; but an idea can also be seen as the object of the act of thought (*ideatum*). In this case, the idea is conceived through the attribute of the object.

After giving this kind of account of the relation between ideas and their objects, Spinoza begins his descent from God's mind to finite minds. Human beings are not substances because their nonexistence is conceivable; in this sense they are contingent. However, this does not contradict Spinoza's necessitarianism, because even though particular human beings are not necessary existents in the way substances are, it still holds, as we read Spinoza, that if a human being exists at a certain time, then it is absolutely necessary that he or she exist at that time.

For Spinoza, a human mind is an idea. It has to be an idea of an existent thing because the existence of the idea requires the existence of its object; and the object of the human mind has to be such that the changes in it result in changes, that is, perceptions, in the human mind (2p11–p12). But the only thing with which we have such direct acquaintance is what we call our body. Moreover, Spinoza goes on to deny that the mind could have some other object besides the body (2p13). The argument for this fascinating denial is a compelling one: suppose $X$ is not a body and is the object of your mind. Because everything that exists must have some effect, you should by 2p7 have ideas of the effects of that object; but Spinoza holds that you simply do not have ideas of such effects.

The picture drawn of the human mind and of the whole human being in Spinoza's top-down strategy can, then, be summarized as follows: a human being is generated by God's beginning to think an object that we call the human body. Because of this, all human minds are parts of the infinite intellect of God.

After this, Spinoza goes on to consider the nature of the human body and the natures of bodies in general (2p13). Once it is granted that the object of the human mind is the human body, this kind of investigation sheds light on the nature of mind. Spinoza's physics of the body has been much studied, and here we are satisfied to report how Spinoza uses the results of his physics in his epistemological considerations. What motivates Spinoza to give the basics of physics is that for him the body is the vehicle through which we are in contact with the world outside us – we can be affected by things outside us.

Having explicated the nature of human beings as mind–body unions, Spinoza begins to consider our status as knowers. Let us take an example that helps in understanding the situation Spinoza has left us with. Suppose Mary is looking out of the window and says that she sees or perceives a tree. Spinoza would claim that in this case Mary is having an idea the object of which she describes as a tree. The idea has begun to exist because of her contact with the external bodies. Stones do not have ideas of trees, not at least in the same way as we do, and, therefore, there is something special about Mary that makes this idea possible. It is partly due to her bodily structure that she has this idea of the tree. It is conceivable that somebody else, with a different bodily structure, would, due to this same external stimulus, have an idea whose object we would describe as a cow. The ideas we have depend on how we are affected by external things, and this depends partly on our intrinsic bodily nature. Mary has no direct distinct knowledge of the object of her idea, which she calls a tree, and is inclined to believe that the object of her idea exists in the external world the way she perceives it, even though the object in fact is an affection of her body. She sees the process in her body as a tree. A question worth posing is, what explains the fact that Mary, who has an idea of a process going on in her body, locates this object outside her body? Spinoza might want to give the following explanation. The process in Mary's body is an effect of something we call a tree. According to Spinoza's causal axiom 1a4, the idea of this process involves the idea of its cause, and, therefore, this idea of the process in her body is also an idea of something else. Thus, the mind's spreading itself onto external objects is part of the meaning of the causal axiom.

It is no wonder that because of this Spinoza believes that our sense perception gives us very inadequate and confused knowledge (2p28). When Mary perceives the tree, the causal flow from the tree and the input from her own body fuse together, and it is, on the basis of sense perception alone, impossible to separate these influences from each other and to have distinct knowledge of one's own contribution on the one hand and the contribution of the tree on the other hand. To obtain adequate knowledge of this would require that one could somehow step outside one's body and see the tree and its causal influence as they are. This helps us to understand Spinoza's characterization of inadequate knowledge at 2p11c:

[W]hen we say that God has this or that idea, not only insofar as he constitutes the nature of the human Mind, but insofar as he also has the idea of another thing together with the human Mind, then we say that the human Mind perceives the thing only partially, *or* inadequately.

The point here is that God has adequate knowledge of everything. But to have adequate knowledge of an external thing represented by our idea requires that one has direct knowledge of that external thing. However, our ideas in perception cannot reach beyond our bodies and, therefore, our knowledge of external bodies is inadequate. Moreover, because our bodies are constantly affected by other things, there is no possibility for us to acquire knowledge of our bodies as they are, but only as they are affected.

Even though through sense perception we can only have a distorted picture of reality, adequate knowledge is possible for human minds. Spinoza sees two routes open for reaching this kind of adequate cognition. The first one is affection-based and gives us common notions that function as the starting points of our reasoning process: we reach adequate ideas when it so happens that we are affected by external things in such a way that we come to think something that is in each and every thing, as it were. According to Spinoza, that which is equally in the part and in the whole is something that can only be adequately conceived (2p38). The thought behind this may be the following. In our example of Mary perceiving the tree, the idea refers outside its direct object, namely to its cause. But suppose that the tree somehow modified the perceiver so that there would be a perfect copy of that tree in her mind. In this case, to reach knowledge of the nature of the tree, there is no distance to be travelled. Thus, when something affects the mind through a common feature, the mind can begin to think of that feature and is able to have adequate knowledge of it (or perhaps more accurately, to form adequate knowledge on the basis of it). So the idea is that, via body, there is a way to adequate knowledge and to axioms that constitute the principles of reasoning in physics.

The second route to adequate knowledge is made possible through Spinoza's startling idea that the human mind possesses adequate knowledge of the essence of God (2p47). This is a rather surprising view, especially when contrasted to the inadequacy of our knowledge both of our minds and bodies. However, that there has to be this kind of adequate knowledge follows rather directly from Spinoza's basic metaphysical and ontological views. The reasoning seems to be the following. In the beginning of Part 1, it is made clear that substances are both ontologically and conceptually prior to everything else. Moreover, modes are conceived through their substances (1d5), and because besides substances (with their attributes) nothing but modes exist (1a1), it follows that any idea involves the idea of a substance. But in Spinoza's monism it holds that there is just one substance through which everything else is conceived. Thus, any idea involves an idea in which God is conceived through itself. However, Spinoza does not mean that in being conceived through itself, God is not being conceived *under* any of his attributes. Any identification, according to Spinoza, is property-based, which means that God has to be conceived under an attribute that the intellect perceives to constitute God's essence (1p10s). Thus, in order to have any idea, we must have an idea of an attribute of God, and thus of an essence of God. Even though this may sound strange, things become more understandable when attention is paid to what Spinoza thinks to be the attributes a human being participates in: thought and extension. My thought of a finite thinking thing necessarily treats that thing as limited by an infinite thinking thing, and any idea of a finite body necessarily sees that body as limited by an infinite space. Thus, any idea we have involves an idea of God under some attribute.

The abovesaid may be somewhat confusing, because it seems to go against experience that we should be constantly having ideas of God's infinite thought and infinite extension. However, this oddity is removable. In saying that any idea involves an idea of the essence of God, Spinoza means, as we interpret him, that on the basis of any idea, the mind can form a clear and distinct idea of God; in other words, any idea makes God cognitively accessible to a human being. Spinoza's panpsychism holds that a worm has an idea of its body and thus an idea that involves infinite extension, that is, extension as an attribute, but it would be rather absurd to say that the worm has a clear and distinct idea of God under the attribute of extension. What we have but the worm lacks is the power to realize and work out what the ideas of bodies involve. We have a sort of primordial understanding of space, which makes geometry and, Spinoza thinks, also the basics of physics possible for us to understand. Moreover, for Spinoza there is a kind of geometry of the mind. In this kind of geometry, we have to think of our own finite mental life as being embedded in God's infinite thought, of which we can also form adequate knowledge. Once we make the adequate knowledge of God's essence involved in all of our ideas clear and distinct, we are able to form new adequate knowledge; on that basis, we are able to deduce properties of God. Maybe the easiest way to clarify this is to consider the knowledge we have of geometry. A geometer does not need anything but the notion of infinite space to be able to see that certain fundamental axioms of space hold, and he or she is also able to understand what kind of individuals the space permits with respect to their geometrical form. This kind of knowledge – proceeding from the formal essences of the attributes of God to the essences of individual things – Spinoza calls intuitive knowledge, and it is not based on bodily affections (2p40s2).

After having explained the general nature of our possibility of acquiring knowledge and its scope, Spinoza begins to shift the focus. The common conception of human beings attributes to them a will. According to Descartes, the will plays a prominent role also in our cognitive life, that is, in the formation of beliefs. When we fall into error, the fault is ours: we accept those ideas of which we do not have a clear and distinct perception. However, Descartes claims that we can always withdraw judgment, at least when the ideas presented to the intellect are not clear and distinct. Spinoza sees the situation quite differently. In his world, there is no place for will as a separate faculty capable of making free choices (1p32, 1p32c1–c2). God's intellect could be called an intuitive intellect in which thinking of an object is creating it; God does not choose from a set of possible worlds which he is able to consider, but realizes everything that can fall under his infinite intellect. In the concluding propositions of Part 2, Spinoza wants to defend his view of the cognitive life as not involving a faculty of assenting and dissenting (2p48–p49). The key to this defence is Spinoza's thought that ideas are inherently judgmental. Every idea involves an affirmation (or denial) and thus, there is in principle no difference between having an idea and believing it. What Spinoza wants to show is that the affirmation and denial involved in ideas is what could be called the doxastic will of Descartes.

That there is no contracausal free will follows directly from the determinism of Part 1. Any supposed act of will follows from previous events and, therefore, nobody is able freely to decide whether to accept or reject an idea he or she is considering. Moreover, 3p2 and especially its scholium involve very subtle considerations concerning the freedom of mind–body agency. Spinoza's point there is to show that even though it appears to us that we do something, for example talk, from the free decision of the mind, that appearance is also due to our ignorance of the causes of our so-called free decisions. So Spinoza has to explain doxastic agency as not involving a commitment to the faculty of free will. The claim that the work of the will is already present in any of our ideas, however, faces the following objection. It is one thing to consider an idea that is in the intellect and another to accept or reject it. It is perfectly possible to consider the idea, *The number of stones in the world is even*, and withhold assent. Spinoza counters this objection by claiming that an idea that is not believed always requires ideas that are somehow stronger than and in conflict with the idea that is not believed. To take Spinoza's example, if a child imagines a winged horse and perceives nothing else, she cannot help believing that there is a winged horse in front of her (see 2p49s). So it is the perceptual situation of the child that determines which of her ideas amount to beliefs and which do not. The relation between ideas and beliefs in Spinoza can then be presented roughly as follows: if no perception is in conflict with an idea being a belief, the idea is a belief. Spinoza does not want to say that beliefs and ideas have the same extension, but that beliefs form a subclass of ideas.

In this volume, Spinoza's philosophy of mind and knowledge are examined in Diane Steinberg's chapter 'Knowledge in Spinoza's *Ethics*'. After considering the nature of the mind and its relation to the body, Steinberg analyzes justification, scepticism, and the relation between idea and belief in Spinoza. She also investigates Spinoza's famous threefold classification of knowledge. In 'Spinoza on Action', Olli Koistinen considers the nature of the mind–body relation and the role of the will in the formation of beliefs.

## *ETHICS*, PART 3

In Part 3, 'On the Origin and Nature of the Affects', Spinoza begins to construct his philosophical psychology, which forms a fundamental stage on the way to the theory of human happiness. In 3pref Spinoza proclaims:

The Affects, therefore, of hate, anger, envy, etc., considered in themselves, follow from the same necessity and force of nature as the other singular things. And therefore they acknowledge certain causes, through which they are understood, and have certain properties, as worthy of our knowledge as the properties of any other thing, by the mere contemplation of which we are pleased. Therefore, I shall treat the nature and powers of the Affects, and the power of the Mind over them, by the same Method by which, in the preceding parts, I treated God and the Mind, and I shall consider human actions and appetites just as if it were a Question of lines, planes, and bodies.

We believe that the reference to 'lines, planes, and bodies' should be taken very seriously: obviously, Spinoza wants to present a theory of emotions that proceeds with an exact method akin to that of geometry (see also especially 4p57s). The major challenge this project faces is that whereas geometry and such eternal things as God involve no change, we finite temporal beings undergo constant change due to the external causes that affect us. This does not keep Spinoza from holding that it is possible to present a rigorous theory of how we human beings feel and behave when we find ourselves in certain circumstances, necessarily modified in certain ways by external causes. In what follows, we aim to explicate the way in which Spinoza builds this part of his system.

Spinoza begins by giving us some basic definitions concerning finite causation and emotions. It is a central aim of his ethics to show us how to become as active as possible; and he claims 'that we act when something happens, in us or outside us, of which we are the adequate cause' (3d2), that is, when something happens of which we are the complete cause. In such a case, the effect can be understood clearly and distinctly as something that follows from our own nature alone. What, then, qualifies as action? This is a thorny question. As has been noted in the literature, it is uncertain whether we can be complete causes of *anything* that happens outside us: whenever we make something happen outside us, it seems inevitable that also something else is involved in the process, as we have seen when discussing Spinoza's theory of imaginative idea-forming processes. This makes it difficult to say whether there are any overt actions in Spinoza's strict sense. There may, however, be interpretative moves that offer us an unequivocal answer to this problem. Be this as it may, two points should be noted here (see 3p1). First, what may be called the acts of understanding or intellectual acts, such as forming an idea of a geometrical object on the basis of our adequate idea of extension and then inferring that this object must have certain properties, are, quite clearly, Spinozistic actions. Second, if something epistemically inadequate were to follow from our nature alone, then, as in such cases God forms his idea only insofar as he is modified by a modification that is us, he would have an inadequate idea, which, of course, would go against his omniscience. This means that the adequacy of God's thought is in certain cases produced through one finite human individual alone.

The third and final definition of Part 3 offers us Spinoza's explication of emotion:

By affect I understand affections of the Body by which the Body's power of acting is increased or diminished, aided or restrained, and at the same time, the ideas of these affections.

*Therefore, if we can be the adequate cause of any of these affections, I understand by the Affect an action; otherwise, a passion.* (3d3)

Here we encounter once again a dynamic notion, that of 'power of acting' (*agendi potentia*). By that notion, we would like to suggest, Spinoza refers to the part of our power that is exercised freely, that is, without being hindered by other finite causes. Emotions are fundamentally about changes in this kind of power. That the notion of force or power appears here is understandable given that we are modifications of God, an infinitely powerful being. Moreover, and most importantly, this idea underpins Spinoza's all-important *conatus* doctrine, which undeniably forms the very basis of all his subsequent theorizing concerning human emotions and happiness. According to the *conatus* doctrine, '[e]ach thing, to the extent it is in itself [*quantum in se est*], strives [*conatur*] to persevere in its being' (3p6, translation modified), and this essence is nothing less than the 'actual essence' of any finite individual (3p7). The derivation and meaning of this doctrine has been the subject of a lively discussion. Here it suffices to note that the striving in question is a form of power – power to resist at least all those factors that threaten an individual's actual existence.

The resulting view is a compelling one, offering us a uniquely elaborated theory of human existence that starts from the tenet that we are, in essence, dynamic entities or *strivers*, whose existence is determined by the relation our power has to the power of other finite things. From this point of departure, Spinoza constructs his revisionary theory of human action and motivation. Olli Koistinen offers a detailed discussion of this theory in his contribution; here it suffices to note the following. In 3p9s, Spinoza tells us that appetite is *conatus* 'related to the body and mind together', and when we are able to conceptualize what satisfies our appetite, we are desiring. Also, will is not a separate faculty, but our *conatus* as it is manifested as intrinsically judgmental volitions that endeavour to affirm the existence of our body. The same scholium contains a particularly weighty and famous passage:

> From all this, then, it is clear that we neither strive for, nor will, neither want, nor desire anything because we judge it to be good; on the contrary, we judge something to be good because we strive for it, will it, want it, and desire it.

This passage has been widely discussed; it seems to us that here Spinoza is articulating the basic idea of his theory of the good, which rejects invoking any ontologically preeminent final causes in explaining human behaviour. We will say more about Spinoza's theory of the good below, but already here we should appreciate the fact that, for Spinoza, our essence-originating striving determines what is good in the first place. Spinoza explains in 3p11s that apart from desire, there are also two other 'primary affects' or emotions: joy (or pleasure, *laetitia* in Latin) and sadness (or pain, *tristitia*). Joy is the mind's passing '*to a greater perfection*', whereas sadness is its passing '*to a lesser perfection*'. As we should expect given his definition of emotion, these changes in perfection can be stated in dynamic terms as increases and decreases in our power of acting (see, e.g., 3p15). There are thus real power-based criteria for designating certain changes as such that they enhance our perfection, others as such that they decrease our perfection. All the other emotions Spinoza goes on to analyze are modifications of the three primitive emotions, and in most cases they arise from the combination of different species of joy, sadness, and desire. It should be noted that here Spinoza is discussing passive emotions, but in 3p58–p59 he tells us that there are also emotions that are actions, and none of those can be species of sadness, only of joy or desire.

There are still two propositions we should discuss before taking a look at how Spinoza analyzes particular emotions, for these propositions reveal something fundamental about the *conatus* doctrine. In 3p12 and p13, Spinoza makes it clear that the good for which we strive amounts to more than just prolongation of our psychopsychical existence:

The Mind, as far as it can, strives to imagine those things that increase or aid the Body's power of acting. (3p12)

When the Mind imagines those things that diminish or restrain the Body's power of acting, it strives, as far as it can, to recollect things that exclude their existence. (3p13)

Strikingly, in the demonstrations of these claims, Spinoza takes it to follow solely from the *conatus* proposition of 3p6, or from 3p9, which is derived largely from 3p6, that finite things not only strive to maintain their present existence in whatever state that may happen but strive for joy, that is, for increase in the power of acting, and try to remove the causes of sorrow, that is, things that decrease the power of acting. Understandably, what licences Spinoza to infer these claims from 3p6 has been found somewhat puzzling. We think that the most promising way to justify this move is to draw attention, as some have done, to the fact that 3p6 says that finite things strive to persevere in their 'being' (*esse*) instead of their (present) state, which suggests that more is involved here than merely an essence's instantiation in actuality. We think the idea to be, roughly, that if a finite thing were completely uninfluenced by external causes, certain effects or properties would be brought about with the same kind of necessity that reigns between a geometrical figure's (e.g., a triangle's) essence and the properties that necessarily follow from that essence (e.g., the property of having the sum of the internal angles equal to two right angles). And this suggests that even though no finite real thing is ever uninfluenced by external causes, as long as the thing in question exists in actuality, there nevertheless is a *striving* to produce certain effects. This striving is the crucial individuating factor of finite things. To the extent that such a thing succeeds in producing effects determined by its own nature alone, it is exercising its power of acting; and when it is hindered from exercising its essential power freely, it strives to eliminate the hindering causes, that is, it strives to remove the sorrowful and promote the joyful things. In other words, when we are under passions, we do not strive only for prolonged existence but also for *increased* power of acting – just as 3p12 and p13 claim that we do.

With all this in place, we can see that Spinoza's challenge is to apply the model provided by geometrical objects, which do not undergo change, to the dynamics of actually existing temporal existents, which do undergo change. Meeting this challenge is by no means a small task; but Spinoza is convinced that it is possible to construct a rigorous science of emotions by showing how our emotions, as our properties, are brought about with the same ironclad geometrical necessity as everything else in nature, as our striving becomes modified by external causes. This conviction finds a fine articulation in the *Theological-Political Treatise*, published in 1670. There Spinoza teaches us that there will never

be a sovereign power that can do all it pleases. It would be vain to command a subject to hate one to whom he is indebted for some service, to love one who has done him harm, to refrain from taking offence at insults, from wanting to be free of fear, or from numerous similar things that necessarily follow from the laws of human nature. (TTP 17.1; Spinoza 2001, 185)

In this passage Spinoza is, of course, talking about passive emotions, that is, emotions that emerge partly due to external causes; and he seems to firmly believe that these, too, follow from our natures with the same kind of necessity as reigns in geometry. Especially later in Part 3 (see, e.g., 3p56d), Spinoza seems to refer to this by talking about different ways in which our nature is *constituted*.

There is neither space nor need for a thorough exposition of Spinoza's analysis and classification of emotions here. It suffices that we pick out a few examples typical of his approach. Let us begin with Proposition 3p19, because its demonstration cites almost exclusively propositions we are already familiar with. Here Spinoza reveals how certain emotions of sadness and joy arise:

He who imagines that what he loves is destroyed will be saddened; but he who imagines it to be preserved, will rejoice.

Dem.: Insofar as it can, the Mind strives to imagine those things that increase or aid the Body's power of acting (by p12), i.e. (by p13s), those it loves. But the imagination is aided by what posits the existence of a thing, and on the other hand, is restrained by what excludes the existence of a thing (by 2p17). Therefore, the images of things that posit the existence of a thing loved aid the Mind's striving to imagine the thing loved, i.e. (by p11s), affect the Mind with Joy. On the other hand, those which exclude the existence of a thing loved, restrain the same striving of the Mind, i.e. (by p11s), affect the Mind with Sadness. Therefore, he who imagines that what he loves is destroyed will be saddened, etc., Q.E.D.

Spinoza had defined love as 'nothing but *Joy with the accompanying idea of an external cause*' (3p13s). So the idea is quite plainly (and here we can already see the importance of the above discussed 3p12 and p13) that because we strive to increase our power of acting, we strive to keep in our minds those ideas of external objects that help us to increase our power, that is, ideas of objects we love because they give us joy. And when an idea of a joy-inducing thing is removed, our power of acting decreases, and hence we become saddened. Obviously, that these events are described in terms of power does nothing to diminish the necessity with which they take place.

To obtain a better grasp on how Spinoza proceeds in designating emotions, we may take the following example. In 3p13s, Spinoza says that by 'hate' he means '*Sadness with the accompanying idea of an external cause.*' The scholium of 3p24, in turn, defines 'envy' as '*Hate, insofar as it is considered so to dispose a man that he is glad at another's ill fortune and saddened by his good fortune*'. This term appears later in 3p35:

If someone imagines that a thing he loves is united with another by as close, or by a closer, bond of Friendship than that with which he himself, alone, possessed the thing, he will be affected with Hate toward the thing he loves, and will envy the other.

A complex architecture of these emotions leads, in the scholium of this proposition, to specifying 'jealousy' as '[t]his Hatred toward a thing we love, combined with Envy', 'which is therefore nothing but a vacillation of mind born of Love and Hatred together, accompanied by the idea of another who is envied.' Spinoza's long catalogue of brief definitions of emotions is located in the end of Part 3; in the chapter 'The Anatomy of the Passions', Michael LeBuffe examines in detail the catalogue and its philosophical underpinnings, pinpointing central problems pertaining to Spinoza's conception of desire and passive joy. Moreover, LeBuffe argues that Spinoza's catalogue should not be understood as an attempt to provide an exhaustive taxonomy of emotions, but as a useful compendium of those affects that are most relevant to his ethical project.

It is particularly revealing to take heed of the way in which Spinoza sees the relationship between his analysis and the common emotion descriptions. In 3p22s, he first explains what he understands by 'pity' and then adds, '[b]y what name we should call the Joy which arises from another's good I do not know.' But clearly the idea is that there is such an emotion. Late in Part 3, after having defined 'indignation', Spinoza remarks:

I know that in their common usage these words mean something else. But my purpose is to explain the nature of things, not the meaning of words. I intend to indicate these things by words whose usual meaning is not entirely opposed to the meaning with which I wish to use them. One warning of this should suffice. (da20exp)

The view is striking. Spinoza's analysis is supposed to explicate what kind of emotions, as our modifications, there *must be* as our natures are constituted in certain ways when we are affected by external causes. Finding the proper words for these emotions – and bridging the possible gap between his own and the common usage of terms – is a task of secondary importance. Obviously, Spinoza's contention is that his 'geometry of emotions' reveals the true nature of our psychological life, and can do this without starting from the common way of perceiving and talking about our emotions.

### *ETHICS*, PART 4

From Part 4 of the *Ethics*, 'On Human Bondage, *or* the Powers of the Affects', onward, Spinoza offers us his ethics proper. In 4pref, he tells us what he understands by perfection and imperfection, good and evil. The ontological status of these concepts has generated much discussion. *Prima facie*, Spinoza might be seen as saying that they are nothing real but 'only modes of thinking'. But even though perfection and good are not something built into the very ontological makeup of things, Spinoza is willing to retain these words. The key passage runs as follows:

But the main thing to note is that when I say that someone passes from a lesser to a greater perfection, and the opposite, I do not understand that he is changed from one essence, *or* form, to another. . . . Rather, we conceive that his power of acting, insofar as it is understood through his nature, is increased or diminished. (4pref)

The idea is, we would like to argue, that changes taking place in an individual's power of acting enable us to make well-founded judgments concerning perfection and goodness: to the extent a thing succeeds in exercising its power more freely than before, it can be said to become more perfect. Accordingly, defining good as 'what we certainly know to be useful to us' (4d1) means that to judge anything that aids us in freely using our power to be good is well-based. Keeping this and the connection between power and essence in mind, it follows that all this squares well with the aforementioned idea of 3p9s that it is nothing external to our essence but our essential striving (and what follows from it) that determines what is *judged* to be good. Spinoza defines 'the end for the sake of which we do something' (4d7) as appetite, that is, as our mental and bodily striving, and he seems to firmly believe that by these moves he has expunged everything teleological from his system.

Given all this, it should come as no surprise that Spinoza goes on to build his ethical theory in terms of power. The definition of virtue is especially revealing because in it we can clearly see the all-important – if also controversial – leap from the domain of descriptive metaphysics into that of ethics:

By virtue and power I understand the same thing, i.e. (by 3p7), virtue, insofar as it is related to man, is the very essence, *or* nature, of man, insofar as he has the power of bringing about certain things, which can be understood through the laws of his nature alone. (4d8)

The first eight propositions of Part 4 explain that as we all are limited parts of the whole of nature, there happens much in us which does not qualify as virtuous: we are always under passions, our limited power struggling with the power of external causes. These struggles determine the nature of our emotional life. Strikingly, in Spinoza's scheme of things, we have no other option but to fight power with power: 'An affect cannot be restrained or taken away except by an affect opposite to, and stronger than, the affect to be restrained' (4p7). The interconnectedness of ethics and psychology is emphasized by the thesis that it is only through our emotions that we are conscious of the ethically relevant changes in us (4p8); that which gives us joy (by helping our striving) is designated as good, that which saddens us (by hindering our striving) is designated as evil (it should be noted that to the extent that these emotions are passions and thus inadequate ideas, they can lead us astray from what is truly good or useful).

Spinoza's dynamism is not, however, without its intrinsic linkage to his intellectualism. Although an idea's truth or falsity is, as such, of no relevance to its strength (see 4p14–p15), Spinoza emphasizes that 'acting from virtue', that is, acting freely as determined by our own essential power alone, equals understanding, that is, forming adequate ideas, and those things that help us in understanding are with certainty good for us (4p23–p28). In the chapter 'Spinoza's Theory of the Good', Andrew Youpa considers different interpretations of what constitutes the ultimate good for Spinoza and defends an interpretation according to which human beings strive for eternal existence, not for the prolongation of their psychopsychical, temporal being.

Spinoza's position falls in line with the fact that, as we saw above, he has strong reasons related to God's omniscience to claim that causal adequacy must result in epistemic adequacy. But, of course, harmful external causes can keep us from understanding and activity. Understandably, then, Part 4 tells us how to achieve circumstances in which intellectual activities can flourish; and it soon becomes clear that Spinoza is far from recommending a reclusive life. He has already commented that '[t]o man . . . there is nothing more useful than man' (4p18s), and in 4p29–p37 he explains why this holds. Human beings are often torn by passions, but they can also lead a life of reason; and those who lead such a life know that the greatest good of all, knowing God, is shareable by everyone, not something that would thrust us against each other. Moreover, a rationally structured society can offer us many benefits that would otherwise be out of our reach. As a consequence, Spinoza estimates a well-ordered society as the best way to secure a harmonious life, fit for promoting our freedom, activity, and understanding. This is the line of thought behind 4p40, '[t]hings which are of assistance to the common Society of men, or which bring it about that men live harmoniously, are useful; those, on the other hand, are evil which bring discord to the State.' There is thus an important interconnection between Spinoza's political thought and his metaphysics. In the chapter 'Freedom, Slavery, and the Passions', Susan James shows how the *Ethics* can be seen as offering a comprehensive theory of freedom, which reflects and, most importantly, reveals the metaphysical underpinnings of the more restricted political freedom Spinoza defends in his *Theological-Political Treatise*.

After this, Spinoza indicates the ethical status of certain key emotions. Generally speaking, those emotions that arise from reason, from the free exercise of our power of acting, are good; and those things that decrease our power of acting are evil. To take one revealing – and perhaps striking – example: repentance cannot be a virtue (4p54), because it does not arise from reason, but from considering one's own lack of power, or how one's power of acting is restrained. There is, however, an important qualification: the moral worth of an emotion may depend on whether we are talking about a rational or a passionate human being. Spinoza makes clear that for those who are living and behaving from passions, such emotions as repentance, humility, hope, and fear may actually be *good* things (4p54s). They are the least of all evils, in a sense, because they can make those who live under passions form social contracts and behave, for a lack of a better word, decently. Of course, for rational human beings such passions are 'of no use' (4p58s). And we should bear in mind that there are things whose goodness can never be questioned: understanding, anything that helps us to achieve it, and everything we do and feel in virtue of our reason.

The rest of Part 4 is largely devoted to depicting the life of an ideally rational human being, or a 'free man'. Arguably, Spinoza does this in order to give us a paradigm – or as he puts it in 4pref, a model – of a finite but completely virtuous human existence. We can reflect upon our own life against this kind of model, which can offer us guidance and thus have the effect of making us more virtuous than before. 'Free man' is indeed an intriguing entity; for instance, he or she never acts deceptively, even when deception could save his or her life (4p72, 4p72s). Does this not go against the *conatus* doctrine? Here we should remember that Spinoza is talking about a human being 'insofar as he is free' (4p72d). Given this qualification, it may be considered, in fact, quite plain that nothing deceitful, or untrue, can arise from the free exercise of our power of thinking, that is, from our understanding.

### ETHICS, PART 5

The concluding part of the *Ethics*, 'On the Power of the Intellect, *or* on Human Freedom', is also admittedly the work's most difficult one, and there has been considerable disagreement over its worth and status. Spinoza's aim, however, is clear: to show us what to do to achieve freedom and happiness. Despite the fact that Spinoza eventually reaches a rather uncompromising intellectualist position, Part 5 opens in a more mundane spirit, by teaching us a set of techniques to gain control over our passive emotions. Although we cannot have absolute command over our emotional life and get rid altogether of the passions we undergo, these techniques can still help us to achieve a state in which passions 'constitute the smallest part of the Mind' (5p20s). In the chapter 'The Power of Reason in Spinoza', Martin Lin offers a detailed critical examination of Spinoza's remedies for passions, deeming Spinoza overly optimistic with regard to our appetite for rational inquiry. According to Lin, of the techniques Spinoza presents, only one does not rest on questionable assumptions: that in which reason forms associative links between useful maxims of life and circumstances to which those maxims can be applied. Here we would like to focus on the technique Spinoza himself regards as the best one: forming true knowledge of passions, which takes place as follows. Any passive emotion has a bodily state as its object. That state necessarily has features that are common to all physical things. As such common features can only be adequately conceived (by 2p38), there is no emotion 'of which we cannot form *some* clear and distinct concept' (5p4c, emphasis added). The idea seems to be that although this kind of idea-forming process does not altogether eradicate the original emotion, even a passive emotion (or its bodily object) offers us material for adequate ideas, the forming of which makes us more active than before. Moreover, certain deductive relations pertain between adequate ideas, and so Spinoza argues that there is 'the order of the intellect' governing adequate ideas (5p10). Thus, to the extent that we are capable of adequate thought, our minds are ordered according to the intellect, not according to 'the common order of Nature'. Rather strikingly but in keeping with his parallelism (2p7), Spinoza goes on to claim that this can give us 'the power of ordering and connecting the affections of the Body according to the order of the intellect' (5p1od).

Because in Part 2 of the *Ethics* Spinoza ties the human mind tightly to the actually existing body, it comes as a surprise that in the closing pages of the *Ethics* he begins to treat the human mind without relation to the body. The last sentence of 5p20s reads as follows:

So it is time now to pass to those things which pertain to the Mind's duration without relation to the body.

This is very puzzling because Spinoza's identity theory – even when presented in the way we have done here – seems to exclude any possibility of allowing the mind to exist without a relation to the body. Moreover, 5p23 only exacerbates these problems, for there Spinoza appears to allow a kind of eternity to the human mind:

The human Mind cannot be absolutely destroyed with the Body, but something of it remains which is eternal.

So the human mind, or part of it, survives bodily destruction. Moreover, the extent to which the mind is eternal seems to depend on what the human mind does during its embodied existence. The more one knows intuitively, the greater is the eternal part of one's mind.

Commentators have debated over the question of whether the immortality intended by Spinoza is personal or not. Personal immortality seems not to be in question, because memory needs an existing body, and for Spinoza memory is a necessary condition for being a person. So maybe a more fruitful question is whether Spinoza leaves room for individual immortality where the *self* as the subject of thoughts is independent of the existent body, or whether immortality for him does not mean more than that the *adequate ideas* a person has formed during his or her life are somehow eternal and thus continue to exist after the destruction of the actual body.

As several commentators have observed, what is important in Spinoza's theory of immortality, or mind's eternity, is his notion of formal essence. In the concluding chapter to this volume, 'Spinoza on the Essence of the Human Body and the Part of the Mind That Is Eternal', Don Garrett gives an illuminating interpretation of formal essence and its role in mind's eternity. For Garrett, it is of crucial importance that formal essences are infinite modes, and that any idea of a body requires the idea of the formal essence of that body. Because infinite modes are eternal, the very existence of a mind, as an idea of a body, requires an idea of something that is eternal. But from Spinoza's theory of mind–body identity it follows that these ideas of formal essences have to be eternal, too.

Spinoza does not clarify the notion of formal essence or the need for introducing it. One way to approach that notion, consistent with Garrett's interpretation, is as follows. For Spinoza there are an infinity of attributes. Embodied minds have bodies as their objects, whereas there is room also for other kinds of minds whose objects are not bodies but modes from some other attribute. The question is, how does a human mind find a particular body as its object when the power to think and the power to extend are independent of each other? If the human mind, that is, the idea of the body, were somehow caused by the body, then this kind of problem would not exist. But Spinoza denies this.

Spinoza seems to argue that the idea of the formal essence of a particular body is an *a priori* condition of there being an idea of that body as actually existing, and this paves the way for that idea being eternal. However, this seems to be rather far removed from any kind of individual immortality. In what way does God's eternally having an idea of the formal essence of a body contribute to the eternity of the human being whose actual existence consists in the actual, temporally limited body's being thought by God?

In the literature, several answers to the question just posed can be found. It seems that most scholars think that in his doctrine of the immortality of the soul, Spinoza does not have in mind any kind of individual immortality, that is, immortality of the thinking self. If this line of interpretation is correct, as it may well be, Spinoza endorses a rather moderate position. Moreover, it seems that in this kind of interpretation, the body should also have some kind of immortality, at least in the sense that the object of the eternal idea, which has to be a mode of extension, must be eternal – otherwise the eternal idea would lack an object. However, it seems that Spinoza does not accept such a symmetrical reading of the eternity of human beings. An alternative way to deal with this problem is to separate the actual mind of a human being from its self. In this reading, God as the thinking substance is formed by an infinity of selves doing the thinking. These selves are eternal, but before the actualization of the body they are, as it were, slumbering and waiting for the moment to affirm the actual existence of the body. Once they form the idea of the body, they begin to think. Moreover, this thinking has a twofold nature. On one hand, there is temporal thinking, which is directly related to the changing modifications of the body; on the other hand, the self that is, in a sense, activated through the affects of the body is able to become conscious of the eternal essence of God. This consciousness of the eternal essence of God is what we would like to call eternal thinking, which is an activity altogether beyond temporality, and it is a matter of degree. In sum, in this kind of interpretation, becoming more eternal means acquiring a perspective on the eternal with the help of the enduring body. The eternity of the self is not, for Spinoza, sempiternity or everlastingness, but is comparable to a timeless view. This kind of eternal view is something the self constructs in this temporal life through atemporal, intuitive cognition, and the more one does such thinking, the wider is the view one acquires, which, indeed, makes one more eternal.

Intuitive knowledge is closely connected to the intellectual love of God and ultimately to a state Spinoza calls blessedness. The reasoning underlying this is that in knowing things intuitively, the mind or the self understands. For Spinoza, understanding is by necessity tied to acting, and acting is something that in Spinoza's system is conceptually tied to pleasure. Moreover, in understanding, the subject, that is, the one who is doing the thinking, is conceiving him- or herself as the complete or adequate cause of the adequate ideas involved in the thought process and thus as the complete cause of the pleasure involved in that kind of thinking. Thus, the temporal process that makes the subject consider him- or herself *sub specie aeternitatis* leads by necessity to *self-love*, because love is, according to Spinoza, pleasure accompanied with the idea of that entity as the cause of the pleasure.

The self-love that is essentially tied to adequate thinking is also love of God. This may sound rather odd, because one might think that this kind of self-love cannot have several objects. The mind or the self has to consider itself as the complete cause of the pleasure; were the cause beyond the self, love towards oneself would have to be destroyed. However, for Spinoza, understanding what one is suffices for identifying self-love with the love towards God. The intellect of God is formed through all the finite intellects, and corresponding to any intellect there is a self. These selves are all embedded in God and constitute him. So when I love myself in adequate thinking, I love God for the simple reason that I am, to put it bluntly, a part of God. Moreover, the self-love I feel in adequate thinking is, for the same reason, God's loving himself:

The Mind's intellectual Love of God is the very Love of God by which God loves himself, not insofar as he is infinite, but insofar as he can be explained by the human Mind's essence, considered under a species of eternity; i.e., the Mind's intellectual Love of God is part of the infinite Love by which God loves himself. (5p36)

For Spinoza, this makes it possible to explain what is God's love towards human beings: it is just the self-love involved in all adequate thinking. God's infinite intellectual love towards himself is constituted by all the finite intellectual self-love of which we are capable. Thus, God cannot love himself with this infinite intellectual self-love without there being in God the finite entities endowed with intellectual self-love, and so God's loving himself is God's loving all men:

> From this it follows that insofar as God loves himself, he loves men, and consequently that God's love of men and the Mind's intellectual Love of God are one and the same. (5p36c)

There is one problem that Spinoza sees in the intellectual love of God. As we have seen, love for Spinoza is a kind of pleasure, and pleasure is a passage to a greater perfection. However, the intellectual love of God is eternal and, thus, cannot consist in a temporal process (i.e., in a passage). For this reason, Spinoza begins to speak of blessedness, which seems to be his substitute for a kind of eternal pleasure:

> If Joy [pleasure], then, consists in the passage to a greater perfection, blessedness must surely consist in the fact that the Mind is endowed with perfection itself. (5p33s)

Blessedness is, then, an atemporal eternal state. It is not a passage, but, and this should be appreciated, neither is it everlastingness. So there is no *durational* pleasure that does not consist in a movement towards greater perfection. Blessedness that is involved in the intellectual love of God is, then, an active affect that is the counterpart of durational pleasure in the world of change. This kind of intellectual love of God is, for Spinoza, an affect that cannot be taken away; there is simply nothing that can destroy it. It may be that human beings lead such lives that they are not conscious of God and do not relate what happens in the world to God, but Spinoza's point is that if somebody loves God, nothing can destroy that love. This kind of intellectual love that results from pure understanding is the highest good available to a human being. It contributes to our eternal survival and constitutes our blessedness. As a virtue, understanding is its own reward, something that is never done for the sake of anything else. Thus Spinoza arrives at a highly intellectualist position: there can never be any guarantee of true peace of mind and human happiness other than understanding.

# 1   The Textual History of Spinoza's *Ethics*

## I. THE PROBLEM STATED

Spinoza's *Ethics* has come down to us in a single version: the Latin text as it appears in the *Opera Posthuma*, published in Amsterdam in 1677, within a year after the philosopher's death. Spinoza himself had prepared the text for the press. He left a final version in his desk, and had given his landlord, Hendrik van der Spyk, and his friends (among them his publisher, the Amsterdam bookseller Jan Rieuwertsz) instructions to provide for its publication.

Summarized thus, the textual history of the *Ethics* would seem to be relatively simple and unproblematic. There are, however, some complications. To begin with, the process of writing the *Ethics* was not straightforward. Spinoza originally planned to present his philosophy in a plain, discursive (rather than geometrical) form. The original Latin text of this early work is lost, but a contemporary Dutch translation of this unfinished *Korte Verhandeling van God, de Mensch en Deszelvs Welstand* (*Short Treatise on God, Man and His Well-Being*) survives. He then decided to recast the material rigorously 'in geometrical order'. The conversion of the older text to the *Ethics* proceeded well until 1665. Then Spinoza slowed down the work on the *Ethics*, or perhaps suspended it altogether, in order to write his other masterpiece, the *Theological-Political Treatise*. After the publication of that work in 1670, Spinoza took up the *Ethics* again, though exactly when he did so is unclear. In 1675 he had finished the book and made preparations to have it printed, but then decided to postpone publication. It came out after he died in two versions: the Latin text of the manuscript in his desk was published in the *Opera Posthuma* and a Dutch rendering by the professional translator Jan Hendriksz Glazemaker appeared simultaneously in *De Nagelate Schriften van B.d.S.* ('The Posthumous Works of B.d.S.'). Glazemaker incorporated older Dutch versions of Parts 1 and 2, presumably made by Pieter Balling for the discussion of Spinoza's philosophy in a small circle of friends. The complications in the textual history of the *Ethics*, then, are due to the protracted and interrupted process of writing, the

26

precautions Spinoza and his friends had to take in publication, and divergences between the Latin and the Dutch texts. The present chapter will discuss the genesis of the text and its relationship to the *Short Treatise* (and, less prominently, the *Theological-Political Treatise*), the circumstances of its publication, and the Glazemaker translation. It will be concluded by a short survey of the subsequent editions of the text.

## 2. THE GENESIS OF THE *ETHICS*

Henry Oldenburg, secretary of the Royal Society, visited Spinoza in the summer of 1661, and wrote him a letter immediately upon his return to London, on 26 August (Old Style 16 August). This is the earliest surviving item of Spinoza's correspondence (Ep1). In September Spinoza sent Oldenburg a reply (Ep2) with an enclosure, now lost, in which he presented the basics of his theory of substance 'in geometrical fashion' (*more geometrico*). To the extent that this enclosure can be reconstructed,[1] it bears more resemblance to the geometrically presented first appendix 'On God' that Spinoza had attached to the *Short Treatise* than to the definitions, axioms, and propositions in the opening pages of the *Ethics*. A few months afterwards, in October, Oldenburg asked Spinoza to instruct him clearly and distinctly about the true and primary origin of things (Ep5). Spinoza did not answer until half a year later, at the end of a long letter (Ep6) that consisted practically in its entirety of the treatise 'On Nitre' (a commentary on Robert Boyle's *Tentamina quaedam physiologica* of 1661). Spinoza apparently felt that a clear and distinct account of the true and primary origin of things would far exceed the limits of a letter. Instead of giving an answer, he informed Oldenburg that he had written an entire work on the subject, and was transcribing and correcting that, as yet without any definite plans for publication. The work referred to in this letter is the *Short Treatise*. It is so close to the *Ethics* in scope and contents that it can only be considered a precursor of the latter work. The early exchange of letters between Spinoza and Oldenburg, then, shows that by April 1662, Spinoza had not yet embarked upon the arduous enterprise of unfolding his entire philosophy *ordine geometrico*. Yet he must have started that project, which eventually was to result in the *Ethics*, soon after that.

In February 1663, Simon Joosten de Vries wrote a letter to Spinoza reporting how a circle of the philosopher's friends met on a regular basis

---

[1] Wolf's annotations to Ep2, in Spinoza 1928, 371–3; Hubbeling 1977b; Hubbeling's annotations to Ep2 in Spinoza 1992, 435–8; Curley's annotations to Ep2 (C, 166–7), Saccaro del Buffa Battisti 1990 (reconstruction on 117–18).

in order to discuss his writings (Ep8). The references and quotations both in De Vries's letter and in Spinoza's reply (Ep9) indicate that what the friends had at their disposal was an early instalment of the *Ethics* rather than the *Short Treatise*. The discussion is about definitions, axioms, and propositions, again on the topic of substance and attributes. This time, however, the wording is close (albeit not identical) to what we find in the initial pages of the *Ethics* and markedly distinct from the appendix of the *Short Treatise*. From this we can infer that at some time between April 1662 and the winter of 1662–3 Spinoza decided to discard the first systematic exposition of his philosophy, the *Short Treatise*, in order to convert the material into an altogether different type of text that eventually developed into the *Ethics*. Because the instalment the friends had before them in February 1663 was already quite a sizable text, consisting of definitions, axioms, at least nineteen propositions, and several scholia, Spinoza must have started well before January 1663 or even before December 1662. We can only guess at Spinoza's exact motives for his rather drastic change of plan.

The most conspicuous difference between the *Short Treatise* and the *Ethics* is the thoroughgoing presentation of the latter in the geometrical order. Spinoza had used this format initially (in the *Short Treatise* and in the enclosure to Ep2) to elaborate a proof for the existence of God in connection with his notion of substance. This is still quite close to Descartes's (reluctant) application of the geometrical order in the Appendix to the Replies to the second set of Objections to the *Meditations*. In the *Ethics*, though, the geometrical presentation is no longer incidental: a comprehensive doctrine of metaphysics, psychology, and ethics is constructed on the groundwork of a restricted number of definitions and axioms. The methodological assumption underlying this edifice is that all modes of reality are ultimately contained in a single substance, God or Nature, from which they can be extracted and presented in a metaphysical deduction by systematically unfolding what is necessarily implied in this foundation. As Spinoza puts it in 1p16: 'From the necessity of the divine nature there must follow infinitely many things in infinitely many modes (i.e., everything which can fall under an infinite intellect).' The *Ethics* is a sustained attempt to unwrap the necessary implications of the nature of God for human blessedness.[2] This Olympian undertaking was to occupy Spinoza for the next thirteen or fourteen years. In late July or early August 1675 he wrote a letter to Oldenburg informing him that he had gone to Amsterdam in order to have the *Ethics* printed, but upon arrival he had decided to postpone publication because of the increasing hostility towards his

---

[2] See 2pref.

philosophy: theologians were plotting against him, and 'stupid Cartesians' tried to dissociate themselves from his opinions and writings (Ep68).

The title of the new exposition of his system, *Ethics*, occurs for the first time in a letter to Willem van Blijenbergh of 13 March 1665 (Ep23), but Spinoza also occasionally refers to it as 'my philosophy'.[3] That the writing of the *Ethics* took so many years was not due only to the ambitious range of the project. From Spinoza's correspondence it is clear that in the summer of 1665 he was also working on what he called 'a treatise on my views regarding Scripture' (Ep30) – the *Theological-Political Treatise*. That book came out early in 1670, so the actual writing of it must have occupied Spinoza from the summer of 1665 to the autumn of 1669.[4] If he did continue working on the *Ethics* as well in the meantime, he obviously could not proceed as quickly as before. But writing the *Theological-Political Treatise* also had its impact on the development of the philosophical views expounded in the *Ethics*. Already, before shifting his attention to the *Theological-Political Treatise*, Spinoza considerably expanded several aspects of his philosophy. This is most conspicuously the case in Parts 3, 4, and 5 of the *Ethics*. A letter from Spinoza to Johannes Bouwmeester of June 1665 (Ep28) shows that he was then working on a much longer version of Part 3. He told Bouwmeester that he would soon send him the third part of his *Philosophy*, which was turning out to be longer than he had thought, up to 'about the 80th proposition' (C, 396). Part 3 as we know it has no more than fifty-nine propositions. Evidently, the original *Ethics* was conceived as consisting of three parts. The division into what are now Parts 3, 4, and 5 belongs to a later stage of the composition of the work. This is confirmed by an emphatic reference to the *Ethics* by Spinoza's close friend Lodewijk Meyer in the epilogue to his *Philosophia Sacrae Scripturae Interpres* of 1666. There Meyer announced the imminent publication of a work by someone who would follow in Descartes's footsteps. It would deal with God, the rational soul, man's supreme happiness ('de Deô, Animâ rationali, summâ hominis felicitate'). This passage is often thought to refer to the *Short Treatise*. But as we have seen, Spinoza had already abandoned the idea of publishing that text by the end of 1662, if not earlier. Meyer's announcement, then, must refer to its successor, the

---

[3] For example Ep28 (Spinoza 2002, 841) and 76 (ibid., 948). In the early *Treatise on the Emendation of the Intellect* Spinoza systematically refers to '*mea Philosophia*' (§31 notes *k* and *l*, §36 note *o*, §41, §76 note *z*, §83; C, 17, 18, 20, 34). I subscribe to Mignini's hypothesis that the TdIE predates both the KV and the *Ethics*; this implies that 'my philosophy' denotes a projected work, rather than an existing text. KV certainly was Spinoza's first attempt to expound his entire 'philosophy'.

[4] See Steenbakkers forthcoming.

*Ethics*, which at that time was still divided into three parts, and which deals with the very subjects specified by Meyer: God, the human mind, and human blessedness.

Neither Spinoza's correspondence nor any external sources provide a clue to reconstructing the history of the *Ethics* between 1665 and 1675. The only certainty we have is that by the end of that period – roughly from the end of 1674 – copies of an apparently finished manuscript circulated among a select number of friends, among them Tschirnhaus and Schuller.[5] The letter to Bouwmeester and the announcement in Meyer's book indicate that by 1665 the *Ethics*, though still a work in progress, had developed into a substantial text; it even approached the point where publication began to come into view (at least, so Meyer thought.) After he published the *Theological-Political Treatise*, it took Spinoza another five years to finish his *Ethics*. It is impossible to determine exactly how Spinoza developed the final version out of the portions written up till 1665. The hypothesis I advance in the following paragraphs is therefore speculative. Before providing the details, I will here offer an outline of my argument. As I see it, from 1665 onwards Spinoza's attention was increasingly drawn towards social and political issues. It was the writing of the *Theological-Political Treatise* that made Spinoza aware of a serious hiatus in the first exposition of his philosophy: in the *Short Treatise*, society had only been the backdrop against which the dramatic struggle for liberation through philosophy was to take place – a backdrop that could not be ignored altogether,[6] but that was not deemed to require philosophical treatment in its own right. Spinoza's metaphysics and his doctrine of salvation had been there all along, ever since he began to give expression to his views (in the *Treatise on the Emendation of the Intellect* and the *Short Treatise*), but his philosophy developed, expanded, and matured as he responded to his environment. The *Short Treatise* hints that he started out as a somewhat esoteric, elitist thinker. He subsequently developed highly original theories of the mind and the passions, which finally allowed him to crown his philosophy with a robust political theory. It was only after finishing the *Ethics* that Spinoza could start writing the *Political Treatise*. This turn to a profound political awareness was, I think, the outcome of reflections upon the situation he found himself in. The *Theological-Political Treatise* contains – among many other layers – a meticulous analysis of the interaction between religion and politics as witnessed by Spinoza in the Netherlands in the 1660s. I will now try to corroborate this hypothesis in some more detail.

[5] Ep59, of 5 January 1675, Tschirnhaus to Spinoza, and the subsequent correspondence between Spinoza, Schuller, and Tschirnhaus.
[6] See KV 2.12.3.

That Spinoza's mature social and political thought is firmly rooted in the metaphysics expounded in the *Ethics* will not be a matter of controversy. After all, he explicitly claims to have shown what the foundations of society are (*civitatis quaenam sint fundamenta ostendi*), and then proceeds to say 'a few words about man's natural state and his civil state' (*pauca de statu hominis naturali, et civili*) (4p37s1.) In modern Spinoza scholarship, the connections between these admittedly rudimentary passages and the two treatises explicitly labeled 'political' – the *Theological-Political Treatise* and the *Political Treatise* – have received ample attention, a classic treatment being Alexandre Matheron's *Individu et communité chez Spinoza* (1988; originally published 1969). Spinoza's 'few words about the state of nature and the civil state' function as a hinge between the metaphysics of human nature – the human passions and their grounding in the *conatus*, the striving to persevere in one's being (3p6) – and a discussion of the meaning of such terms as good and evil, just and unjust, sin and merit. These are 'extrinsic' notions; that is, they receive their meaning from the consent of people in the civil state: in the state of nature, nothing can properly be said to be just or unjust (4p37s2). The nature of men, their specific *conatus* to preserve themselves, gives rise to the dynamic process of interaction that explains why there is a society rather than the deadlock of a war of all against all. And it is by living in a society that human beings ratify, as it were, normative terms such as honourable and disgraceful, just and unjust, sin and merit. In order to realize what is new about this in the *Ethics*, we should note that although the same concept of *conatus* and an early version of the theory of the human passions both already occur in the *Short Treatise*,[7] that early work offers no theory of society, not even an elementary one such as the sketch in *Ethics* 4, p37s2. Pierre-François Moreau (1990) has pointed out that the common view of Spinoza's alleged lack of interest in politics up to 1665 may be in need of some qualification, and he rightly cites *Short Treatise* 2.18 as a counterexample. The case is indeed an interesting one, as Spinoza converted the contents of this particular chapter into the memorable concluding paragraph of 2p49s. In the *Ethics*, that paragraph is precisely the very first adumbration of a theory of social life. I quote some striking parallels. This is from the *Ethics*:

It remains now to indicate how much knowledge of this doctrine is to our advantage in life. We shall see this easily from the following considerations: [...]

[Third] This doctrine contributes to social life [*ad vitam socialem*], insofar as it teaches us to hate no one, to disesteem no one, to mock no one, to be angry at no one [...]

---

[7] *Conatus* (the Dutch term is *poginge*): KV 1.4; passions: KV 2.3–17.

[Fourth] Finally, this doctrine also contributes, to no small extent, to the common society [ad communem societatem] insofar as it teaches how citizens are to be governed and led, not so that they may be slaves, but that they may do freely the things that are best. (2p49s; translation modified)

Here are the corresponding passages in the *Short Treatise*:

Of the advantages of the preceding[8]
... Third, in addition to the true love of one's fellow man which this knowledge gives us, it disposes us so that we never hate him, or are angry with him, but are instead inclined to help him and bring him to a better condition....

Fourth, this knowledge also serves to further the commonwealth [tot bevordering van 't gemeen Best], for through it a judge will never be able to favor one more than another, and being required to punish one in order to reward the other, he will do this with insight, so as to help and improve the one as much as the other. (KV 2.18; C, 127–8)

In both cases the context is Spinoza's exposition of his doctrine that free will is an illusion. But he insists that this thoroughgoing determinism, rather than doing away with ethics, will in fact greatly advance moral and social behaviour. It is worthwhile to have a closer look at the different wording of the two texts. In the *Ethics*, observing the rule that one should not hate nor despise anyone[9] is said to contribute to social life (vita socialis), whereas in the *Short Treatise* it is associated with true love of (or charity towards) one's fellow man (de ware liefde des naasten). This is in line with the generally more religiously tinged idiom of the *Short Treatise*. The fourth item in the *Ethics* broaches the issue of rational government; in that perspective, the doctrine of the will greatly contributes ad communem societatem. As the occurrence of cives in the same sentence indicates, Spinoza here uses the word societas loosely as an equivalent of civitas. The Dutch counterpart in the *Short Treatise* is ambiguous: 't gemeen Best is generally interpreted as 'the common Good'.[10] But the Dutch word (a calque of res publica; now spelt gemenebest) currently means 'commonwealth', in the sense of 'body politic', rather than 'common wealth' (or 'common weal'), in the sense of 'the common good'. In the seventeenth century the word was rarely used in Dutch, and the senses 'commonwealth', 'state', 'common good' tended to be conflated.[11] In view of the parallel passage in the

[8] Caption supplied from the Table of Contents (*Register der Hooftdeelen*).
[9] Spinoza offers this injunction as many as eight times throughout his works: in addition to the two passages under scrutiny here, it is also to be found (in varying formulas) in 3pref, 4p50s, 4p73s; TP 1.1, 1.4; Ep30.
[10] Thus Curley, C, 491, and many other translators.
[11] In de Vries (ed.) *Woordenboek der Nederlandsche Taal*, entry 'Gemeenebest'.

*Ethics*, however, it seems likely that *'t gemeen Best* here renders *communis societas* or a close equivalent, possibly *res publica*. Intriguingly, the *Short Treatise* cites an impartial judge rather than rational government as a profitable consequence of this doctrine.[12] This has no match in the *Ethics* – the only occurrence of *judex* there in 4p63s2 does not appear to be connected. It is noteworthy that in the *Ethics* the third item in the list of advantages – the injunction not to hate nor despise anyone – contains an incorrect cross-reference: *ut in Tertia parte ostendam*, 'as I will show in Part 3'. But in fact the reference is to Propositions 35 and 50 of Part 4 – the wrong number is a remnant of the stage when the *Ethics* was still planned as a triptych. Summing up: the undeniable but flimsy social perspective in the *Short Treatise* is taken up again in the *Ethics* but then as a prelude to a proper discussion in Part 4. The foundation of society as Spinoza analyses it in *Ethics* Part 4 is absent from the *Short Treatise*.[13]

After 1665, then, the original Part 3 of the *Ethics* was gradually transformed into three final parts. It is precisely in those parts that the discrepancies from the *Short Treatise* are most palpable. Looking at the *Ethics* in its final form we can observe, I think, three major transformations, all of which were somehow already implied in the basic metaphysics that Spinoza had had from the beginning.

The first innovation is a new theory of *imaginatio*, the first kind of knowledge.[14] With this powerful tool, Spinoza is able to account for the way the affects work, physically and psychologically. This elaborates Spinoza's fundamental tenet that body and mind are a unity. The *imaginatio* is then accounted for as the kind of knowledge that incorporates the experience of an individual human body. In the *Short Treatise*, the imagination is still presented – in agreement with the Cartesian view – as fictitious knowledge, set over against the pure intellect. In the *Theological-Political Treatise* Spinoza begins to rehabilitate the *imaginatio*, when he employs the concept to provide explanations for prophecy, the belief in miracles, and revealed religion.

---

[12] Neither here nor elsewhere does Spinoza offer a further explanation of why the judge's impartiality is so essential for the commonwealth, but compare Hobbes's eleventh law of nature (in *Leviathan*, chapter 15): without equity, controversies can only be determined by war, and consequently a partial judge will cause war.

[13] The *Short Treatise* invites comparison with the *Ethics*, because the latter was manifestly written as a mature elaboration of the former. The case is quite different for the *Treatise on the Emendation of the Intellect*: this is so different in scope from the *Ethics* that the absence of any interest in society (apart from the very general remark in §14) is inconsequential for a study of Spinoza's philosophical development.

[14] For a fuller treatment of the imagination, see Steenbakkers 2004.

Spinoza's second innovation is a refined and powerful theory of the passions, including a systematic inventory and analysis of the forty-eight most important affects, as well as a therapy to remedy the damage they may cause. This is an elaboration of Spinoza's view that everything in nature, even such apparently chaotic and disturbing phenomena as the passions, follows with inexorable necessity from the divine substance. In the *Short Treatise*, the theory of the passions is still basically Cartesian in outlook, constructed as it is upon Descartes's *Passions de l'âme* of 1649. Here, too, his rethinking in the *Theological-Political Treatise* of the emotional foundation of human life and its profound implications for religion and politics must have made him aware of the shortcomings of his earlier views.

The third and final innovation is a new view of the essentially social existence of human beings. This is an elaboration of his doctrine of the relative autonomy of individual modes. The *conatus sese conservandi* also functions as a principle of individuation; that is to say, it is used by Spinoza to account for the infinite variety of modes in nature and their particular essences.[15] Assemblages of bodies may be increasingly complex, and yet all can be considered as individuals:

> If we proceed in this way to infinity, we shall easily conceive that the whole of nature is one Individual, whose parts, i.e., all bodies, vary in infinite ways, without any change of the whole Individual. (2p13le7s)

This flexible notion of individuality allows Spinoza to consider single human beings as individuals, but also, if that is appropriate, the group, class, nation (3p46), or species to which they belong. This is one of the elements of his view on people as fundamentally social. Another element is Spinoza's view of reason as common to all human beings: people may be divided by passions but they are united by rational insight.[16]

These three innovations are closely connected. In the *Short Treatise* social existence is merely an unpleasant fact of life. In the *Ethics*, however, it receives pride of place. There even is a specific mechanism of interaction between human beings that generates a particular set of affects. Imagining affects to be at work in other people will give rise to similar or otherwise related affects in ourselves.[17] This sparks off a complicated series of interactions, thus creating strong social ties already at the emotional level. Here we see the merging of imagination (the ability to imagine other people's feelings), affectivity, and social ties.

---

[15] Yet this individuality is only relative: an individual is a composite assembly of bodies that behaves like a single body with respect to its environment (definition of 'individual' in the excursus between 2p13 and 2p14).

[16] See 4p34, 4p35, 4p37s1.

[17] 3p27 ff.

In the *Ethics*, Part 4 Spinoza elaborates this social aspect: he there argues that the force whereby a human being persists in existing is limited and infinitely surpassed by the powers of nature as a whole. This weakness can be strengthened only by cooperation between people under the guidance of reason. In fact, this is what constitutes the *civitatis fundamenta*.[18]

When Spinoza finished his *Ethics* in 1675, Dutch society around him had changed dramatically. In the year 1672, the Dutch Year of Disaster, the brothers De Witt had been lynched in The Hague not far from the house where Spinoza lived. His *Theological-Political Treatise* had been banned; he could not publish his *Ethics* for fear of persecution. It looks as though Spinoza had to go through the experience of writing the *Theological-Political Treatise* before he found the right perspective to finish his *Ethics*. There are also some textual indications for this hypothesis. The prophets Moses and Jesus, so conspicuously present in the *Theological-Political Treatise*, occur in the *Ethics* only towards the end of Part 4 (the prophets in 4p54s, Moses and Jesus in 4p68s). The geometrical presentation of the *Ethics* does not allow any references to external authorities: its synthetic argument requires that all propositions are derived from definitions, axioms, and preceding propositions. When Spinoza included the references to the prophets Moses and Jesus he did so by way of illustration rather than to invoke authorities. Still their occurrence in that context is unusual and is, I think, to be explained as reflecting Spinoza's immersion in the issues of the *Theological-Political Treatise*.

### 3. OPERA POSTHUMA

Publishing the *Ethics* was a precarious undertaking. Spinoza himself put the manuscript away in 1675, and when his friends did publish it in the *Opera Posthuma*, they took safety measures to cover their activities. The book appeared without the publisher's name (Rieuwertsz), without mentioning the place of publication (Amsterdam), and with the philosopher's name abbreviated to 'B.d.S.' In the correspondence, references to people who were still alive were generally avoided and many factual allusions were discreetly suppressed. This covertness makes it difficult to determine who the editors were and what they did with the manuscripts they had at their disposal. I have reconstructed the story of the editing of Spinoza's *Ethics* in detail elsewhere (Steenbakkers 1994, Chapter 1). This section summarizes these findings.

---

[18] 4p37s1; G II, 236.25–6.

On the twenty-first of February, 1677, Spinoza died in The Hague. Within a matter of days his publisher, the Amsterdam bookseller Jan Rieuwertsz, received a writing box that contained unpublished writings and correspondence of the philosopher. Some nine months after Spinoza's death and burial, in December 1677, the manuscripts in the box had already been published, under the title *B.d.S. Opera Posthuma*.[19] The Dutch translation, *De Nagelate Schriften van B.d.S.*, was realized in the same period.[20] In less than a year's time, then, the Latin texts of Spinoza's posthumous works had been edited and translated into Dutch; moreover, both versions had been prepared for the press and printed, making quarto volumes of some eight hundred and seven hundred pages, respectively. We owe this remarkable achievement to the circle of Spinoza's friends. Their joint efforts in the realization of these publications constitute the editorial history of the *Opera Posthuma* and *De Nagelate Schriften*. For their involvement clearly exceeded the merely technical task of preparing the manuscripts for the press: both versions show traces of deliberate editing. Their approach is characterized by a familiarity with the philosopher and his works, a command of the languages involved, and a strategy that may conveniently be summarized in the motto *caute* (for example, the interventions in the letters). The editors derived their guidelines at least in part from preparations Spinoza himself had made.

Spinoza's friends divided the editorial labour between them. Some addressed themselves to the task of preparing the texts for the Latin edition, the *Opera Posthuma*. At least four people are to be considered as in some way involved in this: Lodewijk Meyer, Johannes Bouwmeester, Georg Herman Schuller, and Pieter van Gent. Others were in charge of its Dutch counterpart, *De Nagelate Schriften*. Here three names present themselves: Jarig Jelles, Jan Rieuwertsz, and Jan Hendriksz

---

[19] The communication by Stolle and Hallmann that the Amsterdam edition of the *Opera Posthuma* was a reprint of an earlier edition published in The Hague immediately after Spinoza's death (Freudenthal 1899, 224; Freudenthal and Walther 2006, I, 85) must be due to a misunderstanding. No traces of an earlier edition survive, nor does the information square with the story of the transmission of the *Opera Posthuma* as we can reconstruct it. There is no reason to doubt the indications that Spinoza's manuscripts were at once shipped to Rieuwertsz. (To be sure, an *Opera Omnia* did come out in 1677, but this is merely a collection consisting of extant editions of the separate works then in print, *Descartes' 'Principles of Philosophy'*, TTP, and *Opera Posthuma*, with a specially printed general title page. See Gerritsen 2005, 253.)

[20] A facsimile reprint of the *Opera Posthuma* is now available in the series Spinozana, published by Quodlibet in Macerata, Italy. There is as yet no facsimile reprint of *De Nagelate Schriften*, but a fulltext edition is scheduled to be available online by 2009 on www.dbnl.org/basisbibliotheek.

Glazemaker.[21] Jelles wrote the preface and Meyer translated and edited that for the Latin book. An important task was to decide which texts were to be included. Surely there cannot have been any hesitations about the *Ethics*: the friends knew Spinoza wanted them to publish it. The *Political Treatise* did not present any real problems either. It was a mature and well-balanced work, and Letter 84 clearly showed that Spinoza himself would have published it – if only he had had the time to finish it. Some of the letters had already been divulged in manuscript form with the author's consent and support. The correspondence did create practical problems, though: the items to be included had to be collected, selected, and edited, and correspondents had to be protected. These matters had to be agreed upon by the editors. But the real moot points between the friends were the *Treatise on the Emendation of the Intellect* and the *Compendium Grammatices Linguæ Hebrææ*, the concise Hebrew grammar that Spinoza left (and which was included in the *Opera Posthuma*, but not in *De Nagelate Schriften*). Schuller and his friend Tschirnhaus had a particular interest in the unfinished *Treatise on the Emendation of the Intellect*. In his correspondence with Leibniz, Schuller asserted that he had persuaded the other friends to publish all of Spinoza's works – not just the *Ethics*. There may well be truth in his claim.

Apart from the selection of the texts, there were other tasks. For the *Opera Posthuma* the editors drew up an *Index Rerum*. It looks as though the separate title page for the *Ethics* in the *Opera Posthuma* was rearranged so as to make it more sophisticated and coherent. This involved moving the hallowed phrase *ordine geometrico demonstrata* to the subtitle. The Dutch version of that title page is probably a more literal rendering of Spinoza's original wording. In addition, the editors regularized spellings, punctuation, accents, and the use of capitals throughout the books. The 'trimmings' or outer apparel of the geometrical order – numerals, cross references, full or truncated endings of the demonstrations – also required editorial attention. Apparently they were not treated consistently and unequivocally in Spinoza's manuscript, and the editors of the *Opera Posthuma* and *De Nagelate Schriften* handled them in different ways.

Which text did the editors have to work on? When Spinoza went to Amsterdam in 1675 to get his *Ethica* published he probably had someone

---

[21] For biographical details on Meyer, Bouwmeester, Jelles, Rieuwertsz, and Glazemaker, see the entries in the *Dictionary of Seventeenth and Eighteenth-Century Dutch Philosophers* (Akkerman 2003, Steenbakkers 2003a, 2003b, van Bunge 2003b, Visser 2003). Van Gent and Schuller are dealt with in Steenbakkers 1994, 35–63.

fair-copy the text according to his instructions and under his supervision. After he decided to abandon his plans, he took the fair copy back to The Hague with him and put it away for future publication. This was the copy sent to Rieuwertsz immediately after Spinoza's death. There must also have been an autograph version (Schuller mentioned it to Leibniz), but that was presumably not used in the preparation of the edition. All manuscripts are now lost; we have only the text as it was printed in 1677.

## 4. THE DUTCH TRANSLATIONS

Perhaps the greatest quandary in the textual history of the *Ethics* is the occurrence of numerous divergences, in Parts 1 and 2 only, between the Latin text as found in the *Opera Posthuma* and its Dutch counterpart in *De Nagelate Schriften*. The first scholar to offer a systematic analysis of this phenomenon was the Dutch poet J. H. Leopold. In his study *Ad Spinozae Opera Posthuma* (1902, 57), he stated that a scholarly edition of the *Ethics* should take into account a careful analysis of all the discrepancies between the two versions.[22] This was an overt criticism of the edition of Van Vloten and Land (1882), who only occasionally mentioned the Dutch translation in their apparatus. Leopold had wanted to make a new critical edition himself, but he never brought that project to fruition. The injunction to base a new edition on a comparison of the Latin and Dutch versions was taken to heart by Carl Gebhardt, in his 1925 edition of *Spinoza Opera*. Gebhardt, however, gratuitously assumed that the differences reflected two distinct drafts of the first two parts of the *Ethics*. He was convinced that throughout his life Spinoza had incessantly been polishing his texts, up to his death.[23] As a result, so Gebhardt thought, various manuscript versions circulated, and the two printed texts ultimately go back to two different stages, *De Nagelate Schriften* showing an earlier state of composition than the *Opera Posthuma* (G II, 340–42). Though ill founded, Gebhardt's supposition unfortunately became quite influential. That Spinoza wrote successive versions of the *Ethics* has been disproved by Fokke Akkerman (1980, 95–101).[24] Akkerman's explanation for the discrepancies is that

---

[22] Leopold 1902, 57. Leopold's book is in Latin. The most important section of this essential text is accessible in a French translation: Leopold 2005. See also Akkerman 1991.

[23] G IV, 369; cf. G II, 317.

[24] Akkerman 1980, 95–101. Yet Gebhardt's fallacious theory is still to be found in the work of several scholars. Bernard Rousset, for instance, published two articles (1985 and 1988) in which he claimed he could reconstruct the two different versions and even identify passages that Spinoza inserted afterwards (a third layer, that is), in the period 1675–7.

when Spinoza started sending instalments of the *Ethics* to the circle in Amsterdam, one of his friends – probably Pieter Balling[25] – translated these texts into Dutch. He got as far as Parts 1 and 2, and a few pages of Part 3.[26] These are the portions of the text where the Dutch version of *De Nagelate Schriften* markedly deviates from the Latin in the *Opera Posthuma*. When Glazemaker was hired to produce a translation in 1677 he was given the parts Balling had already translated. Glazemaker integrated these into his own Dutch text. The differences reflect the discussions in the Amsterdam circle. A fascinating illustration is the second axiom of Part 2. The Latin simply reads '*Homo cogitat.*' In *De Nagelate Schriften*, this is expanded to 'De mensch denkt; of anders, wy weten dat wy denken.' ('Man thinks; or, to put it differently, we know that we think.') As Akkerman has shown, the expansion does not come from Spinoza himself (let alone from an earlier version, as Gebhardt supposed) but from a gloss provided by the circle of friends. Their source for it was a Dutch translation by Glazemaker of Descartes's *Principles of Philosophy* 1§8, where Glazemaker followed the French translation of Picot, who had enriched Descartes's *cogito* argument with the phrase 'nous sçauons certainement que nous pensons.' The gloss was duly recorded in Balling's manuscript and thus eventually found its way to Glazemaker's translation of the *Ethics*.[27]

Akkerman's conclusion is that a critical edition of the *Ethics* must be based rigorously on the *Opera Posthuma* and that readings from *De Nagelate Schriften* can only be adopted when there is reason to assume that the editors of the *Opera Posthuma* made mistakes. All other differences should be relegated to the critical apparatus. This is also the approach Akkerman and I follow in our forthcoming critical edition of the text.[28]

A phenomenon that has sometimes invited scholars to speculate about a Latin version of the *Ethics* different from the one printed in the *Opera Posthuma* is the abundance of Latin marginal glosses in *De Nagelate Schriften*. As I have argued elsewhere (Steenbakkers 1997), this was a common practice in Dutch translations of the sixteenth and seventeenth centuries. There was a strong purist tendency to include Dutch neologisms in translations, and marginal glosses in the original language were added in order to give the reader a clue to the technical term the neologism was intended to convey. By the time *De Nagelate Schriften* were printed, the habit had become mechanical: Latin equivalents were

---

[25] Akkerman 1980, 152–60. For Balling's biography, see van Bunge 2003a.
[26] We do not know when Balling died: his wife is referred to as a widow in 1669. At any rate, it appears that he was no longer available for translating the instalments in 1665, for that is when Spinoza asked Bouwmeester to translate Part Three.
[27] Akkerman 1980, 145–6; cf. 97–9.
[28] To be published in the series *Spinoza Œuvres*.

routinely given in the margins without consulting the original texts. This accounts for the many lapses and discrepancies between the Latin terms found in the margins of *De Nagelate Schriften* and the text of the *Opera Posthuma*. None of these will justify an intervention in the Latin text.

### 5. THE EDITIONS OF THE *ETHICS*[29]

For 125 years, the printed version of the *Ethics* as it features in the *Opera Posthuma* was to remain the only edition of the Latin text. As a result of the great German debates on Spinoza at the end of the eighteenth century, the so-called *Pantheismus-Streit*, there was a new demand for the philosopher's texts. The first complete edition of Spinoza's works (1802–3), *Benedicti de Spinoza Opera Quae Supersunt Omnia*, by H. E. G. Paulus, was in fact an uncritical reprint of the original seventeenth-century editions. Paulus, who did have the competence to make a scholarly edition, apparently only saw it as his task to make the texts available again in print; there is no critical apparatus, no justification of his editorial choices, no discussion of any textual problems. Paulus did not even put into effect the list of errata in the *Opera Posthuma*. The great merit of his edition is that it made Spinoza's texts available to German philosophy at a crucial moment of its development: this is the edition read by Fichte, Schelling, Hegel, and Schopenhauer, and it formed the basis of many comments and translations.

In 1830, A. F. Gfrörer published *Benedicti de Spinoza Opera Philosophica Omnia*. This is basically a corrected reprint of Paulus's edition and it suffers from the same weaknesses as its precursor. It seems that Gfrörer's edition only had a limited circulation. It was hardly noticed outside Germany. The same is true for Carl Riedel's *Renati des Cartes et Benedicti de Spinoza Praecipua Opera Philosophica*. Apart from Spinoza's *Ethics*, his edition included Descartes's *Meditations*, Spinoza's *Treatise on the Emendation of the Intellect* and *Political Treatise*, and a treatise written neither by Descartes nor Spinoza: *De Jure Ecclesiasticorum Liber Singularis* by an unidentified author with the pseudonym Lucius Antistius Constans. Riedel's Spinoza texts simply reproduce the edition by Paulus without Gfrörer's corrections.

The most important edition in Germany in the nineteenth century, with a very wide circulation, was that of Karl Hermann Bruder: *Benedicti de Spinoza Opera Quae Supersunt Omnia* (three volumes, 1843–6). It

---

[29] For a more detailed account, see Steenbakkers 2007, which furnishes all bibliographical details. This is a survey of the editions of Spinoza's works in Germany in the nineteenth century, but it thereby covers most of the editorial work done with regard to Spinoza.

went through several reprints, even in the twentieth century, though all are dated 1843–6. Bruder did go back to the original seventeenth-century texts, but still reproduces some of Paulus's errors. Many commentators and translators worked from this *Opera* edition. Bruder's edition was more or less copied by Hugo Ginsberg for his *Die Ethik des Spinoza im Urtexte* (1874), an undistinguished and uninteresting publication.

With the publication of *Benedicti de Spinoza Opera Quotquot Reperta Sunt*, edited by J. van Vloten and J. P. N. Land in 1882–3, Spinoza scholarship entered a new phase.[30] They were the first editors to provide the texts with an (admittedly slender) apparatus and they took the original editions for their starting point. In the first printing, the presentation of the texts has been carefully executed. Unfortunately, the subsequent printings ([2]1895, [3]1914) are increasingly inferior, each adding new misprints to the ones copied from the preceding.

It is only with the monumental critical edition of Carl Gebhardt (1925, reprinted 1972) that Spinoza's texts are carefully presented again. As we have seen, however, his edition of the *Ethics* is marred by the erroneous assumption that Spinoza wrote two different versions. Gebhardt offers the readings of these alleged versions partly in the text, partly in the *Textgestaltung*, a mixture of commentary and apparatus. As yet there is no truly critical edition of the *Ethics*. The forthcoming edition in the series *Spinoza Œuvres* is intended to fill that gap.

[30] Land was the first scholar to do serious philological research on Spinoza. Apart from his editorial work, he published several articles on textual issues; Land 1882 deals with the text of the *Ethics*.

# 2 The Geometrical Order in the *Ethics*[1]

## I. PHILOSOPHY IN GEOMETRICAL GUISE

Anyone who opens a copy of Spinoza's *Ethics* will immediately be struck by its unusual layout, modelled on the classic geometry textbook: the *Elementa geometrica* of Euclid (ca. 300 B.C.E.). Starting from a few definitions and axioms, propositions are derived by means of deduction and this continues until the entire philosophical system, from its metaphysical foundations up to an elaborate theory of human bondage and liberation, has been unfolded. Rather than offering a discursive elaboration of the argument, Spinoza breaks it down to a sequence of definitions, axioms, propositions, and proofs. To this basic framework he adds a variety of elucidations in the shape of comments (scholia), prefaces, and appendices. Though all of these elements serve as links in the chain (and may therefore be invoked in the subsequent reasoning), the elucidations are written in a looser style. Here Spinoza occasionally steps aside in order to comment on his own argument.[2] By furnishing these scholia himself, he departs from his model: explanatory comments were added to Euclid's textbook only in later ages.

It is mainly as an oddity that the Euclidean layout of the *Ethics* has won historical fame. In view of the high esteem in which mathematics has generally been held, this is remarkable. Apparently philosophy, by the mere act of donning the classical costume of Euclidean geometrical discourse, does not acquire the incontrovertible and scientific aura of its mathematical model. What philosophy, thus formulated, does share with mathematics is the appearance of inaccessibility. Plato is

---

[1] In this contribution I summarize (with corrections and updates) material presented in Chapter 5 of my *Spinoza's* Ethica *from Manuscript to Print* (Steenbakkers 1994, 139–80).

[2] Gilles Deleuze (1968, 317–18; 1981, 42–3) even goes so far as to suggest that the *Ethics* was written twice simultaneously: he sees the scholia as a reduplication of the arguments set forth in the propositions, composed in a different key and register. Similarly, Efraim Shmueli (1980, 209) considers the appendices, prefaces, and scholia as 'eminently nongeometric' parts.

said to have put a notice over his porch: 'Let no one ignorant of geometry enter.'[3] Readers of the *Ethics* usually find its geometrical layout
intimidating. Thus Friedrich Nietzsche (1886, 1.5, end) ridiculed the
hocus-pocus of the mathematical form with which Spinoza armoured
and masked his philosophy, and Henri Bergson (1934, 142) even compared the terrifying effect of this machinery with that of a dreadnought
battleship. Spinoza himself was aware of the potentially deterrent effect
of the *ordo geometricus*, as 3pref testifies:

For now I wish to return to those who prefer to curse or laugh at the Affects
and actions of men, rather than understand them. To them it will doubtless
seem strange that I should undertake to treat men's vices and absurdities in the
Geometric style, and that I should wish to demonstrate by certain reasoning
things which are contrary to reason, and which they proclaim to be empty,
absurd, and horrible.

Apparently Spinoza saw the style of presentation as an integral part of
the theory of human salvation he develops in the *Ethics*. Yet because it
put off so many readers, we may raise the question why exactly he went
to such great lengths in order to present his philosophy geometrically. In
this chapter, I will try to provide an answer in two steps. First, is the *ordo
geometricus* merely the layout of the *Ethics*, or is the term equivalent to
'method', and if so, what are we to understand by 'method'? Second, is
the geometrical order intimately connected with Spinoza's philosophy,
or is it rather its external shape, with little or no direct relevance for the
philosophical content?

## 2. FORM AGAINST METHOD

There is a vast amount of literature on the *ordo geometricus*. In the
last forty years or so there have been, broadly speaking, two schools of
thought in Spinoza scholarship about the use of the geometrical order:
one that sees it as nothing but an exterior form, and one that emphasizes
the close links between form and content. These different traditions are
connected with the names of two great Spinoza scholars, Harry Aus-
tryn Wolfson and Martial Gueroult. Wolfson (1934 I, 38–44) outlined
the descent of the *ordo geometricus* by enumerating a host of Greek,
scholastic, and Jewish philosophers. Speaking of his own historiograph-
ical vantage point, he stated, 'As for Spinoza, [ . . . ] if we could cut up
all the philosophic literature available to him into slips of paper, toss
them up into the air, and let them fall back to the ground, then out of

---

[3] The anecdote is too late to have a serious claim to authenticity (Gilbert 1960, 88).
The earliest sources for it are sixth-century commentators on Aristotle.

these scattered slips of paper we could reconstruct his *Ethics*' (Wolfson 1934 I, 3). This reduction of Spinoza's philosophy to a jigsaw puzzle (the term is Wolfson's own) of fragmentary classical, scholastic, and rabbinic influences has been severely criticized in later Spinoza research – more particularly in the French reception of Spinoza, which is strongly determined by Martial Gueroult's (1968, 1974, 1977) monumental commentary. The latter (1968, 442) had qualified Wolfson's approach as a pitiful venture, 'une gageure affligeante'.[4] This qualification is not altogether fair, because it fails to take into account the extraordinary erudition and depth of Wolfson's study, but then the image of the jigsaw puzzle appears to be an embarrassment even to admirers of his work.[5] Gueroult upheld a close connection between geometrical disposition and the philosophical system of Spinoza. His views have been widely supported, especially in France and Italy. The discussion of the *ordo geometricus* has since been a debate between two currents of thought, one of them following Wolfson's line of interpretation, and the other Gueroult's.

Scholarly research is by no means limited to Spinoza's use of it: the subject has been extensively examined in general terms and with respect to other authors, too.[6] Notwithstanding the manifold differences

---

[4] Gueroult does, for that matter, acknowledge Spinoza's indebtedness to tradition (Gueroult 1974, 480), but he tends to overemphasize the assumed affinity to Hobbes.

[5] For example, Curley 1988, x–xi.

[6] The fundamental monographs on the *ordo geometricus* at large are those by De Vleeschauwer (1961), De Angelis (1964b), Schüling (1969), Arndt (1971), and Engfer (1982). For the primary sources Engfer and Schüling provide the best bibliographical information. Some further general studies are those by Bredvold (1951), Tonelli (1959 and 1976), De Angelis (1964a), Arndt (1980), Freudenthal (1980), and Staal (1986 and 1988). Because most studies of Spinoza's philosophy contain some remarks on what is commonly referred to as his 'geometrical method', a full bibliography is unattainable here. The following selection presents publications that either are dedicated primarily to Spinoza's *ordo geometricus*, or have exerted a marked influence on its reception: Scholz (1863), Von Dunin Borkowski (1910, 398–416), Brunschvicg (1923, 260–78), McKeon (1930), Wolfson (1934 I, 3–60), Moorman (1943), Scarpellini (1954), Brunt (1955), De Lucca (1967), Hubbeling (1967, 1977a, 1977b, 1980), Gueroult (1968, 25–37; 1970; 1974, 467–87), De Dijn (1971, 295–395; 1973; 1974; 1975; 1978a; 1978b; 1986), Rice (1974), Mark (1975), Biasutti (1979, 197–233), Robinet (1980), Shmueli (1980), Curley (1986, 1988), Savan (1986), Cassirer (1994, vol. 2 [1907], 73–125), and Schuhmann (2004). More recent works that concentrate on Spinoza, mathematics, and the geometrical order are Kaplan (1998), A. V. Garrett (2003) Audié (2005), Barbaras (2007), and Brissoni (2007). Not primarily concerned with the *ordo geometricus* but valuable for its remarkable treatment (from a mathematician's point of view) of geometrical and formal aspects of the *Ethics* is Parrochia 1993. The geometrical order is discussed in connection with other authors, or with related issues, by De Vleeschauwer (1932), Iwanicki (1933), Risse (1962; 1970, 14–293, 582–638), Crapulli (1969), Röd (1970), De Dijn (1983), Hubbeling (1983), Schuhmann (1985), Petry (1986), Prins (1988), Bunge (1990), Schildknecht (1990, 85–122), and Vermij (1991).

between these studies, virtually all seem to agree that the geometrical (or mathematical)[7] order is to be understood as a *method*, rather than as a *form*. It is, however, expedient to distinguish between Spinoza's method on the one hand, and the geometrical form he gave to some of his writings on the other, even though – as we shall see presently – the two are interrelated.

Method, as a technical term, has a history of its own in early modern philosophy and science. Although the term is classical, it is only in the Renaissance that it begins to occupy a central position in reflections on the advancement of knowledge. Characteristic of this modern notion of method is that it is thought of as comprehensive, as against the multifarious classical and medieval methods. (Arndt 1971, 15; Biasutti 1979, 201.) In his monograph on *Renaissance Concepts of Method*, Neal Gilbert (1960, 66) summarizes the Renaissance view of method as follows:

An art is brought into method by being presented in short, easily memorized rules set forth in a clear manner, so that the student may master the art in as short a time as possible. In order to qualify as methodical, the rules of an art require to be disposed in a certain order. Thus method is almost synonymous with art . . . , but it is distinguished from it by the fact that it facilitates or speeds up the mastery of the art.

For our subject it is relevant to note the close links between codification of rules, didactic purpose, and textbook layout. Although perhaps never completely shedding these didactic undertones, the term method gradually acquires a decidedly heuristic meaning. This development reaches its apogee in the work of Descartes. In the *Discourse on the Method* of 1637, he presents his project of 'a method whereby, it seems to me, I can increase my knowledge gradually and raise it little by little to the highest point allowed by the mediocrity of my mind and the short duration of my life' (CSM I, 112; AT VI, 3). And in Rule 4 of the earlier *Rules for the Direction of the Mind*, we find this definition: 'By "a method" I mean reliable rules which are easy to apply, and such that if one follows them exactly, one will never take what is false to be true or fruitlessly expend one's mental efforts, but will gradually and constantly increase one's knowledge till one arrives at a true understanding of everything within

---

[7] Mathematics is of course not identical to geometry, and the terms are not interchangeable, but in this context they tend to be blurred: Euclidean geometry for a long time was the height of exact mathematical reasoning (cf. Crapulli 1969, 13). From the perspective of the history of science, though, it is now commonly held that mathematics only began to take off by turning towards algebra, and away from the geometry of Archimedes and Euclid (see, for example, Kline 1972, 391–2). The mathematical revolution already began in the sixteenth century (Whitrow 1988), but it is not until much later that it is denoted as a turn towards algebra.

one's capacity' (CSM II, 16; AT X, 371–2). What made the Cartesian concept of method revolutionary and ensured its success (and imitation) is not primarily its content, but its heuristic thrust: 'one must go back as far as the Greeks to find a spirit of inquiry so penetrating and so philosophical' (Gilbert 1960, 228). For an understanding of Spinoza's notion of method, we must take into account the crucial Cartesian development of this theme. It is in this climate that Spinoza's conception of method is to be situated. His treatise on method *par excellence* is the early, unfinished *Treatise on the Emendation of the Intellect*. Spinoza there gives the following description of method proper:

the true Method is the way that truth itself, or the objective essences of things, or the ideas (all those signify the same) should be sought in the proper order. Again, . . . Method is not the reasoning itself by which we understand the causes of things, much less the understanding of the causes of things; it is understanding what a true idea is by distinguishing it from the rest of the perceptions; by investigating its nature, so that from that we may come to know our power of understanding and so restrain the mind that it understands, according to that standard, everything that is to be understood; and finally by teaching and constructing certain rules as aids, so that the mind does not weary itself in useless things. From this it may be inferred that Method is nothing but a reflexive knowledge, or an idea of an idea; and because there is no idea of an idea, unless there is first an idea, there will be no Method unless there is first an idea. So that Method will be good which shows how the mind is to be directed according the standard of a given true idea. (TdIE §§ 36–8; C, 18–19)

The notion of method as reflexive knowledge or an idea of an idea is original, but the emphasis on directing the mind in the search for truth and on issuing rules shows that Spinoza is indebted to Descartes, too. Now the *Treatise on the Emendation of the Intellect* unequivocally favours geometry as a model (as the geometrical examples elsewhere in the text illustrate). Moreover, it sets down the requirement of presenting the philosophical system deductively, with God (the cause of all things) as its starting point:

As for order, to unite and order all our perceptions, it is required, and reason demands, that we ask, as soon as possible, whether there is a certain being, and at the same time, what sort of being it is, which is the cause of all things, so that its objective essence may also be the cause of all our ideas, and then our mind will . . . reproduce Nature as much as possible. For it will have Nature's essence, order, and unity objectively. From this we can see that above all it is necessary for us always to deduce all our ideas from Physical things, or from the real beings, proceeding, as far as possible, according to the series of causes, from one real being to another real being, in such a way that we do not pass over to abstractions and universals, neither inferring something real from them, nor inferring them from something real. (TdIE § 99; C, 41)

Nevertheless, the treatise nowhere underpins the *ordo geometricus* as the proper mode of exposition for this deduction. The *Short Treatise* does start from God and thence deduces the rest of the philosophical system.[8] Although this deduction is not carried out *more geometrico*, I think it would be difficult to maintain that the philosophical reasoning of the *Short Treatise* fails to meet the standard set in the *Treatise on the Emendation of the Intellect*. Spinoza eventually deemed the expository form of the *Ethics* more appropriate for his system. This does not, however, alter the fact that at one stage of the development of his thought he experimented with a systematic deduction of his philosophy from God in a nongeometrical fashion. In fact, the method as set forth in the early *Treatise* leaves room for the geometrical order in the exposition, but does not in any way dictate or privilege its use to the exclusion of other expository modes. On the level of method, then, the eventual form of the exposition is as yet wholly undecided.

### 3.  ANALYSIS AND SYNTHESIS

Already in Euclid's days, the concepts of analysis and synthesis were employed to denote well-defined and complementary methods in geometry, as their occurrence in Book 13 of the *Elements* testifies.[9] It is, however, worth noting that 'the analysis and synthesis of geometry, although never quite lost from sight in the commentaries, do not emerge into the full light of day until the late sixteenth century, when they quickly became the common property of philosophers as well as scientists. Previous to this time they tend to be blurred and lend themselves to identification with all sorts of other kinds of "analysis" or "synthesis"' (Gilbert 1960, 34–5). In the seventeenth and eighteenth centuries the concept of method is determined by the central position of the twin concepts analysis and synthesis (Arndt 1980, 1313). For our purpose it is the Cartesian reception of these notions that is relevant. The *Meditations* had been published in 1641 together with a number of objections by some reputed scholars and Descartes's replies. Spinoza knew this work well. In the second series of objections (CSM II, 92; AT VII, 128), Mersenne had urged Descartes to rearrange the conclusion of the *Meditations* in the Euclidean fashion, *more geometrico*, with the help of some definitions, postulates, and axioms. In his response, Descartes complies with this request by adding as an appendix 'Arguments proving the existence of God and the distinction between the soul and the body

---

[8] For a refutation of the alleged hiatus in the beginning of the text, see Mignini's comment in his 1986 edition of Spinoza's KV, 394 ff.

[9] See the translation by Heath of Euclid (1956 [1908], Vol. 3, 442).

arranged in geometrical fashion [*Rationes Dei existentiam & animae a corpore distinctionem probantes, more geometrico dispositae*]' (CSM II, 113; AT VII, 160–70). The proofs are preceded by an explanation of the 'twofold manner of demonstration', namely analysis and synthesis:

Analysis shows the true way by means of which the thing in question was dis-covered methodically and as it were *a priori*. . . . Synthesis, by contrast, employs a directly opposite method where the search is, as it were, *a posteriori* (though the proof itself is often more *a priori* than it is in the analytic method). It demon-strates the conclusion clearly and employs a long series of definitions, postulates, axioms, theorems, and problems. (CSM II, 110–11; AT 156)

Here Descartes closely follows the Alexandrian mathematician Pappus.[10] A more extended treatment of these terms along the same lines is to be found in Antoine Arnauld and Pierre Nicole (1970, Part 4, chapters 2 and 3, 368–77).[11] Analysis or *resolutio* is reasoning back from effects to causes, or the gradual reduction of complex and obscure propo-sitions to the simplest propositions. Synthesis or *compositio* is the con-trary movement: from causes to effects, or from definitions, axioms, and the like to conclusions. Analysis is the scientific procedure actu-ally applied in practice, and if in geometry its results may afterwards be expounded synthetically, as the Greek geometricians were wont to do, this does not mean that synthesis is valid or even possible in other branches of science or philosophy. For Descartes, analysis is not only the appropriate scientific method of research, but also the genuine and best way of expounding the results (CSM II, 111; AT VII, 156).

For Spinoza method, as set forth in the *Treatise on the Emendation of the Intellect*, involves both moments. First, there is an analytical move to establish the unknown true idea that can serve as our starting point, yardstick, and guideline. The most perfect method will start from the idea of a most perfect being.

If this is to be done properly, the Method must, first, show how to distinguish a true idea from all other perceptions, and to restrain the mind from those other perceptions; second, teach rules so that we may perceive things unknown according to such a standard; third, establish an order, so that we do not become weary with trifles. When we came to know this Method, we saw, fourth, that it will be most perfect when we have the idea of the most perfect Being. So in the beginning we must take the greatest care that we arrive at knowledge of such a Being as quickly as possible. (TdIE § 49; C, 22)

---

[10]  Cf. Engfer 1982, 127–8.
[11]  Cf. Tonelli 1976, 185–6. There is an explicit acknowledgement to Descartes in Arnauld and Nicole's footnote to Chapter 2 (368).

Once the starting point has been found, the movement will rapidly take another direction; in what Spinoza calls the second part of his method (TdIE § 91), reasoning goes from what is clear and simple to what is obscure and complex, and this is where the synthetic geometrical order comes in. In order to understand things, says Spinoza in his *Descartes' Principles of Philosophy*,

we shall have to devise such principles as are very simple and very easy to know, from which we may demonstrate how the stars, earth and finally all those things that we find in this visible world, could have arisen, as if from certain seeds – even though we may know very well that they never did arise in that way. For by doing this we shall exhibit their nature far better than if we only described what they now are.... We only ascribe seeds to things fictitiously, in order to get to know their nature more easily, and in the manner of the Mathematicians [*Mathematicorum more*], to ascend from the clearest things to the more obscure, and from the simplest to the more composite. (C, 295; G I, 226–7)

Although we must make allowances for the fact that the wording and the conceptual framework here owe much to Descartes's *Principles*, of which Spinoza's text is an adumbration, the passage links up rather neatly with the views propounded in the *Treatise on the Emendation of the Intellect*. Summing up, Spinoza's *method* cannot be reduced to either the analytic or the synthetic procedure: he uses the term to cover both moments.

### 4. SPINOZA'S FOUR EUCLIDEAN TEXTS

Spinoza employed the geometrical form four times in his works.[12] There are two short annexes: an enclosure to Ep2 (to Oldenburg, September 1661),[13] and the first of the two appendices to the *Short Treatise*.[14] Later Spinoza offered a geometrical elaboration of parts of Descartes's *Principles of Philosophy*. This was already a sizeable text, covering some

---

[12] That is, if we limit ourselves to purely formal criteria. There are of course quite a few other passages in Spinoza's works where the argument has a distinctly mathematical flavour. An interesting borderline case is Ep34, to Johannes Hudde, consisting solely of a demonstration of the unity of God.

[13] The enclosure is lost but can be reconstructed fairly accurately from the ensuing correspondence. It is thought to have consisted of three definitions, four axioms, three propositions, and a scholium.

[14] The appendix contains seven axioms, four propositions with their proofs, and a corollary. There is no agreement on the chronology of Spinoza's two oldest geometrically fashioned writings nor on their internal relationship: Saccaro del Buffa Battisti (1990) judges the enclosure to Letter 2 to be older than the appendix to the KV, contrary to Hubbeling (1977a) and Mignini (in the commentary to his edition of Spinoza's KV, 773–85).

ninety pages.[15] But the really monumental application is the geometrical presentation of the *Ethics*, the undisputed pinnacle of the genre,
which takes up as many as three hundred pages.

Apart from being geometrically expounded, there is nothing that *all*
these four texts have in common. Yet there are several parallels to be
drawn. The two earliest of them, the enclosure to Ep2 and the first
appendix to the *Short Treatise*, illustrate that Spinoza (like Descartes
in the *Second Replies*) initially employed the *ordo geometricus* exclusively for proofs of God's existence. The enclosure for Oldenburg and
Spinoza's adumbration of the *Principles of Philosophy* are akin in that
both have a didactic, explanatory orientation. We do not have a cue to
establish the exact status of the first appendix to the *Short Treatise*. It is
clear, however, that it anticipates the geometrical design of the *Ethics*,
although still closely related to the philosophical positions developed in
the *Short Treatise*.[16]

What is striking is that three of the texts under consideration are
paraded as being set forth 'in the geometrical manner'. Only in the case
of the appendix to the *Short Treatise* is such an explicit reference to
the *mos* or *ordo geometricus* lacking. The *Principles* and the *Ethics*
expose their geometrical character in their subtitles: *more geometrico
demonstratae* and *ordine geometrico demonstrata*.[17] That these labels
refer to the formal framework of definitions, axioms, propositions, and
proofs is shown by the following scholium:

With these few words I have explained the causes of man's lack of power and
inconstancy, and why men do not observe the precepts of reason. Now it remains
for me to show what reason prescribes to us, which affects agree with the rules
of human reason, and which, on the other hand, are contrary to those rules. But
before I begin to demonstrate these things in our cumbersome Geometric order,
I should like first to show briefly here the dictates of reason themselves, so that
everyone may more easily perceive what I think. (4p18s)

And the scholium concludes thus: 'These are those dictates of reason
which I promised to present briefly here before I began to demonstrate

---

[15] Spinoza's geometrical version of the *Principles of Philosophy* is incomplete: he
rewrote only the first two parts and a fragment of Part Three. The book was published in that unfinished form. It consists of definitions, axioms, and propositions
with proofs, as well as prefaces (to parts 1 and 3), corollaries, scholia, and lemmas.
We are well informed about the origins, background, and evolution of this work,
owing to Letters 9, 12A, 13, and 15 of Spinoza's correspondence, and to the preface
by Lodewijk Meyer that precedes it.

[16] Cf. Mignini, in his edition of Spinoza's KV, 773–85.

[17] Spinoza usus *mos* and *ordo* without distinction: *ordo geometricus* in the *Ethics'*
subtitle, and 4p18s, *mos geometricus* in the subtitle of *Descartes' Principles of
Philosophy* and in 3pref.

them in a more cumbersome order.' From Spinoza's own point of view, then, the scholia are asides, standing outside the framework of the geometrical exposition. That exposition is called *prolixus*, long-winded, because in it no steps can be skipped: even the seemingly obvious must be explicitly enunciated.[18] Spinoza also explicitly presents the enclosure he sent to Oldenburg as set forth geometrically: 'I can think of no better way of demonstrating these things clearly and briefly than to prove them in the Geometric manner [*more Geometrico*] and subject them to your understanding. So I send them separately with this letter and await your judgment regarding them' (Ep2; C, 166).

Summing up: when qualifying three of his four geometrical texts as 'set forth in the geometrical manner' or 'geometrical order', Spinoza unmistakably has in mind the Euclidean *layout* of these texts.

## 5. FORM AND METHOD: INTERFERENCES

So far I have argued that the synthetic way in which Spinoza expounds his philosophy in the *Ethics* is not identical with his method, because for him that term covers analysis as well as synthesis. On the other hand, there are also interferences between form and method.

To begin with, Spinoza's own terminology oscillates. It seems to me that it is in particular the key notion of *ordo* that interferes with 'method', because it can denote a very wide range of orderly dispositions or arrangements, varying from a simple orderly enumeration to the law-governed pattern of nature as a whole. *Methodus* is not unequivocal either. The word itself occurs only twice in the *Ethics*.[19] In both cases, Spinoza unmistakably means the geometrical form of the exposition. In 3pref, he initially uses *mos geometricus* – expressing his intention to deal geometrically with men's vices and shortcomings – and afterwards calls this the method: 'Therefore, I shall treat the nature and powers of the Affects, and the power of the Mind over them, by the same Method by which, in the preceding parts, I treated God and the Mind, and I shall consider human actions and appetites just as if it were a Question of lines, planes, and bodies' (3pref.).

Apart form terminology, there is a further link between geometrical order and method. As we have noted, Spinoza initially reserved the geometrical mode of exposition for proofs of the existence of God. In

[18] In the prolegomenon to *Descartes' Principles of Philosophy* Spinoza says that the geometrical mode of discourse is prolix due to its step-by-step approach, when he justifies his decision not to reduce Cartesian doubt to the mathematical order. He wants his readers to have an overall view of these matters, as in a picture.

[19] 4p40s1, beginning, and 3pref, at the very end.

this respect, he followed Descartes's single application of the *ordo geometricus*. Such proofs have enjoyed a special status in the history of philosophy since Anselm of Canterbury first propounded his ontological argument for the existence of God in the *Proslogion* (ca. 1077). Anselm's proof was taken up again by Descartes, and subsequently by Spinoza and Leibniz. It became part and parcel of modern philosophy: discussion of it has continued well into the twentieth century.

The early modern period was characterized by a turn towards mathematics, whose most spectacular effect has been the revolution in natural sciences. In connection with the natural sciences, the well-known image employed by Galilei in *Il saggiatore* of 1623 is often referred to:

Philosophy is written in that great book that lies permanently open before our eyes – I mean the universe – but it can be understood only after we have learned to understand the language and the characters in which it is written. It is written in mathematical language, and its characters are triangles, circles and other geometrical figures. Without these means it is impossible, humanly speaking, to understand a word; without them, we wander in vain through an obscure labyrinth. (Galilei, *Opere* 6, 232; my translation)

The radiation of mathematics affected not only the natural sciences, but every intellectual activity that had scientific aspirations – theology included.[20] The proof for the existence of God was evidently considered a suitable case for mathematization, a procedure to which its independence of any empirical prerequisites certainly contributed. Descartes and (in his wake) Spinoza and Leibniz were fascinated by the ontological argument for God's existence and provided geometrically arranged versions of it. In the process, the ontological proof for the existence of God came to occupy a central position: whereas it was one among several possible proofs for Anselm and the scholastics, it became the keystone of the construction of rationalist philosophical systems: it is indispensable for an *a priori* demonstration of the correspondence between thought and reality.[21]

Part One of Spinoza's *Ethics* deals with God. His concept of God serves as the foundation for the subsequent deductive construction of the entire philosophical system.[22] This development rests on two essential steps: the first is the identification of God with Nature (1p14 and 1p15) and the second the perfect coincidence of the order of things and

---

[20] Cf. Risse 1970, 137–43.

[21] For these views I am indebted to Röd's fine monograph on the ontological argument (1992).

[22] Strictly speaking, of course, the *Ethics* (unlike the *Short Treatise*) does not actually begin with God, but with the notion of substance, from which the notion of God is constructed in the course of the first fourteen propositions.

the order of ideas (2p7). The two arguments are, of course, interwoven: because the one substance – an eternal and infinite being that is called God or Nature – can be considered under the attribute of extension and under the attribute of thought, it follows that their order and connection in both cases must be one and the same. Consequently the world has an orderly arrangement, and can therefore in principle be known. Because God is the immanent cause of all things (1p18), the deduction by means of rational thought of the systematic connection of things from God's nature is not a merely conceptual construct, but will reflect the state of affairs in reality.[23] Once again, *ordo* is the keyword. Spinoza states explicitly that the correct philosophical order, neglected by previous thinkers, must begin with the nature of God, 'because it is prior both in knowledge and in nature' (2p10s2).

Seen from this perspective, the application of the *ordo geometricus* finds its ultimate justification in Spinoza's concept of God. The rational, geometrical form matches the systematic arrangement of nature and is thus its appropriate expository mode. This, then, constitutes an important link between form and philosophical method, touching a crucial methodological issue, namely the guarantee that reality can be known.

## 6. MATHEMATICS, RHETORIC, AND PHILOSOPHY

In the appendix that concludes the first part of the *Ethics*, Spinoza attacks the notion that the world has been equipped for the benefit of mankind. Those who choose to stick to this view are forced to explain away all sorts of misery and distress. This can be done, for example, by arguing that the ways of the gods are inscrutable: 'So they maintained it as certain that the judgments of the Gods far surpass man's grasp. This alone, of course, would have caused the truth to be hidden from the human race to eternity, if Mathematics, which is concerned not with ends, but only with the essences and properties of figures, had not shown men another standard of truth' (1pref.). This passage makes it sufficiently clear that for Spinoza mathematics was of paramount importance for human knowledge and salvation. Even if he did not provide an explicit theoretical underpinning, the application of the geometrical order to his *Ethics* shows that it must have been much more to him than just a fashionable and arbitrary apparel.

According to the influential commentary of Wolfson, the geometrical order was nothing but an exterior literary form, chosen by Spinoza for didactic purposes and for the high prestige mathematics enjoyed.[24] In

---

[23] Cf. De Dijn 1973, 759–60.
[24] Wolfson 1934 I, 32–60, especially 53–7.

this interpretation, the geometrical form is cut off completely from the contents of Spinoza's philosophy. But for a seventeenth-century philosopher, firmly rooted in the rhetorical tradition, the choice of a literary form is not neutral or arbitrary. Spinoza did not write the *Ethics* in the form of, for example, a didactic poem, a dialogue, or a series of meditations. In his own view the subject matter – in which the endless concatenation of all that exists is unfolded in its global coherence – must have required precisely this literary form.

Spinoza was not the first to apply the geometrical order to philosophy. A comprehensive and richly documented survey of the vicissitudes of the geometrical order up to the middle of the seventeenth century is to be found in Hermann Schüling's pioneering study of 1969, *Die Geschichte der axiomatischen Methode im 16. und beginnenden 17. Jahrhundert*.[25] Seventeenth-century philosophy since Descartes is characterized by its penchant for mathematics, but this was the outcome of a long-term development. Thus the ground was prepared for the Cartesian position that all knowledge is to be measured against the certainty of mathematics. Thus, Spinoza could build upon a long tradition, and his application of the geometrical order to the composition of the *Ethics*, though certainly a remarkable *tour de force*, was not an innovation.[26] The result, however, is unrivalled – a class of its own. Many authors take it for granted that the *Ethics* is difficult of access on account of its Euclidean layout. Yet this is by no means self-evident, for it may be argued that the *Ethics*, on the contrary, has an uncommonly open structure, due to its explicit, step-by-step exposition. This enables its readers to follow the argument and check the author's proofs, as it were, in instalments. Thus, several modern commentators have turned to the formal aspects of Spinoza's reasoning and tried to assess its strengths and amend its weaknesses.[27] That this is possible at all is, in my opinion, one of the often neglected assets of the *ordo geometricus*. Another aspect that deserves more attention than it has received so far is the obvious connection that Spinoza himself perceived between the joy (in a strong, Spinozistic sense) of doing mathematics and the philosophical 'therapy' he developed in the *Ethics*. The point has recently been made by Françoise Barbaras: what the Euclidean mathematician experiences when gradually disclosing the 'universal ballet of proportion' is an

---

[25] In spite of its title, which suggests a restricted scope, the work deals with the 'prehistory' (that is, with Antiquity and the Middle Ages), too.

[26] Kaplan's (1998, 28) forced attempt to present Spinoza as the first philosopher who *really* applied the geometrical method to philosophy fails to convince.

[27] For example, the publications of Friedman (1974, 1976, 1978) and Jarrett (1978).

unequalled joy.[28] It is only in this way that geometry could become the model for Spinoza's philosophy. To get back to my initial question: the geometrical order is not an external shape, with little or no direct relevance for the philosophical content, but is intimately connected with Spinoza's philosophy.

[28] Barbaras 2007 is entirely dedicated to the topic; see quotation 190.

# 3    Spinoza's Ontology

In the opening definitions of the *Ethics* Spinoza mentions three kinds of basic entities, *substance*, *mode*, and *attribute*, after defining which he is quickly on the way to building his metaphysical system. In what follows, I present the basics of Spinoza's ontology[1] and attempt to go some distance toward clarifying its most pertinent problems. I start by considering the relationship between the concepts of substance and mode; my aim is to show that despite his somewhat peculiar vocabulary there is much here that we should find rather familiar and intelligible, as Spinoza's understanding of these matters harks back to the traditional distinction of substance and accident, or thing and property. After this I move on to fitting the concept of attribute into Spinoza's conceptual architecture, and then examine the implications concerning real existents and causation that Spinoza sees these fundamental conceptual commitments as having. The most startling of these implications is of course his monism, according to which there is only one substance. Through this examination it becomes clear that it is only when Spinoza makes the transition from considerations concerning concepts to existential claims that the collision with what was previously commonly accepted becomes inevitable.

## I. SUBSTANCE AND MODE

Right at the beginning of the *Ethics*, Spinoza states his definitions of substance, attribute, and mode:

By substance I understand what is in itself and is conceived through itself, i.e., that whose concept does not require the concept of another thing, from which it must be formed. (1d3)

By attribute I understand what the intellect perceives of a substance, as constituting its essence. (1d4)

---

[1] Ontology is the study of the general nature of being, or the most basic features of what exists; as such, it is something found already in Aristotle, in his discussion of 'being as being' (see, e.g., *Metaphysics* IV).

By mode I understand the affections of a substance, *or* that which is in another through which it is also conceived. (1d5)

Attributes pose some time-honoured and thorny interpretative problems, but we can leave them aside for now and focus on the relationship between substance and mode.

That substances are in and conceived through themselves, whereas modes are in and conceived through another, clearly implies that substances hold some kind of ontological and epistemological priority over modes. But what kind of priority? For someone proceeding 'in geometric order' it is of course of the utmost importance that the basic building blocks – definitions and axioms – are clearly stated and cogent. Spinoza obviously thinks that his definitions of substance and mode are precisely that, but it would be hard to claim that they are – at least for us – particularly transparent in their meaning. As a consequence, it is difficult to form an opinion concerning their adequacy. However, if we remain alive to certain key features pertaining to the philosophical landscape of Spinoza's times, his treatment of substance and mode starts to make sense; in fact, I would claim that he does not pack anything particularly controversial into his definitions. Here, as so often, two of Spinoza's most important philosophical sources make their presence felt: Descartes, who arguably was Spinoza's most influential predecessor, and the Aristotelian scholastic tradition, which still dominated much of Western thought in the seventeenth century.

As we have seen, a substance is 'what is in itself', whereas a mode is an affection of a substance, which, according to Spinoza, means that a mode 'is in another'. The fundamental question would thus seem to concern *what it means to be in itself or in another*. I would like to argue that here Spinoza offers us his understanding of the classic distinction between substance and accident. In the Aristotelian tradition, an accident is an entity that cannot exist on its own but needs something (ultimately a substance) to serve as a subject in which it exists; accidents are thus said to *inhere* in subjects, whereas substances are entities that *subsist*. Although scholastic debates concerning substances and different kinds of accidents are complicated, it still seems possible to define the difference roughly as follows: accidents are dependent on the substances in which they inhere, but substances are not similarly dependent on their accidents. What individuates substances, makes them the entities they are, is not accidents, but certain basic features constituting their essences; more to the point, substances do not exist in subjects and thus they occupy an ontologically privileged position. For instance, yellow is an accident and can only exist, ultimately, in a substance, let us say in Garfield the cat; Garfield himself, in contrast, does not exist in any other subject.[2] Moreover, consider how strongly the wording of 1d3 and 1d5 echo the following passage from Thomas Aquinas's *Summa Theologiae* (I, 29.2, resp.): '[T]hose things subsist which exist in themselves, and not in another.' Spinoza's 'being in itself' and 'being in another' would thus seem to track rather faithfully the traditional Aristotelian distinction between subsistence and inherence.

The aforementioned Peripatetic framework can be found practically unscathed in the thought of such an innovator as Descartes, who in the first part of the *Principles of Philosophy* (henceforth PP) discusses the meaning of the terms important for our purposes.[3] Much attention has been directed to the fact that he starts by emphasizing the causal independence of substances in Proposition 51 – which is a point to which we will return later – but the governing assumption underpinning much of what Descartes says is that there are things, that is, substances, in which some other entities – Descartes refers to them variably as attributes, qualities, modes, and properties – inhere. In this connection, at least the following passages are especially noteworthy. First, the French version of the *Principles* contains a supplement to the just-mentioned proposition, and in it Descartes notes that apart from substances, there are 'qualities' or 'attributes', which 'are of such a nature that they cannot exist without other things' (PP 1.51; CSM I, 210). Second, he claims that 'we cannot initially become aware of a substance merely through its being an existing thing', but the presence of a substance can easily be inferred from the perception we have of some of the attributes the substance possesses (PP 1.52; CSM I, 210; see also PP 1.63; CSM I, 215). Third, in his explication of what is meant by 'modal distinction' (PP 1.61; CSM I, 214), Descartes notes that modes inhere in substances, and he repeats this later. Finally, in the second set of replies, Descartes begins the definition of substance by saying that it is the term that 'applies to every thing in which whatever we perceive immediately resides, as in a subject' (CSM II, 114; see also the Sixth Meditation, CSM II, 54).

It seems to me that Descartes's view can be expressed using only the terms Spinoza later adopts, by saying that modes and attributes inhere in substances; modes are determining properties which make change

---

[2] Aristotle's *Categories* (1a16–3b23) is here the most important original source (see also *Metaphysics* 1017b10–25); for a very illuminating discussion of these matters, to which I am here indebted, see Carriero 1995, 245–7. Likewise Charles Jarrett (1977b, 84–5) draws attention to the fact that Spinoza's way of understanding the relationship between substance and mode matches the Aristotelian idea of accidents inhering in a substance. See also Bennett 1984, 55–6; Steinberg 2000, 8–10.

[3] For discussions emphasizing the close relationship between Spinoza's ontology and that of Descartes, see Curley 1988; Koistinen 2002; Della Rocca 2008.

possible, whereas attributes are properties that remain constant during a finite substance's existence (see PP 1.56; CSM I, 211–12; see also PP 1.64; CSM I, 215–16); among the attributes there is always one that is principal, that which constitutes nothing less than the substance's essence (PP 1.53; CSM I, 210). Interestingly, this part of the *Principles* makes it, to my mind, rather clear that Descartes really *is* conceiving the conceptual framework involving substances, essences, and different kinds of (necessary and non-necessary) accidents in a remarkably non-Aristotelian fashion. However, he is not radical to the extent of discarding the basic traditional tenets concerning inherence; he obviously accepts the idea that modes or properties inhere in substances, whereas substances do not inhere in anything – they need only the ordinary concurrence of God in order to exist (PP 1.51, French edition; CSM I, 210).[4]

When Spinoza says that substances are in themselves whereas modes are in another, he is thus respecting the traditional way of conceiving things and their properties: there are those things, namely substances, that do not exist in anything else but are ontologically self-supporting; and there are those things, namely modes or modifications – Spinoza's gloss for accidents – that exist in, or inhere in, something, namely substances.[5] I think that we should recognize the fact that nothing more and nothing less is put forward at this stage; most importantly, as has been observed,[6] the definitions at hand do not contain any causal notions. It is thus understandable that Spinoza takes himself to be entitled to hold, without offering any further proof, that modes are affections of substance (1d5). And as it is an axiom for him that '[w]hatever is, is either in itself or in another' (1a1), he feels entitled to arrive at the conclusion that 'outside the intellect there is nothing except substances and their affections' (1p4d). It thus seems not improper to say that the only entities in Spinoza's ontology classifiable as *things* are substances and modes.

Spinoza's definitions, as noted above, contain not only claims concerning being in itself or being in another, but also the corresponding claims that what is in itself is 'conceived through itself' (1d3) and that what is in another is also conceived through that (1d5). In other words, a

---

[4] Indeed, Descartes contends that if we tried to consider modes 'apart from the substances in which they inhere, we would be regarding them as things which subsisted in their own right, and would thus be confusing the ideas of a mode and a substance' (PP 1.64; CSM I, 216).

[5] This is the way in which Pierre Bayle already read Spinoza; for Bayle's objections against Spinoza, see n. 49. For Edwin Curley's important objection against interpreting modes as properties, see n. 48.

[6] See especially Carriero 1995, 261; but also Koistinen 1991, 14.

mode does not merely inhere in a substance; it is also conceived through that substance. What, exactly, is at stake here?

It is well founded to claim, as John Carriero (1995, 248–50) does, that the way in which conceivability is treated in 1d3 and 1d5 reflects the definitional priority Aristotelians considered substances to have over accidents: a definition reveals the essence of the thing defined, and the definition of an accident must refer to something other than the accident, namely the subject in which the accident in question inheres, whereas a substance is definable without reference to anything external to the substance. So when Spinoza elucidates his claim that a substance is conceived through itself by saying that a substance's 'concept does not require the concept of another thing, from which it must be formed' (1d3), he can be regarded as proceeding broadly along traditional lines. The only problem with this interpretation is that conceiving a thing through understanding its definition seems to be a rather adequate and intellectual way of forming an idea of the thing; as Carriero notes, he is discussing 'a full characterization of an accident'.[7] But Spinoza's definitions do not say anything about the adequacy of the conceiving in question; and later (2p45, 2p45d) he makes it clear that *any* idea we may form, regardless of its level of adequacy or intellectual sophistication, of *any* finite mode involves the concept of something else, namely of the attribute that constitutes the essence of the substance in which the mode inheres.

Even if we grant that 1d3 and 1d5 echo certain Aristotelian doctrines, Descartes still seems to play a much more important role here.[8] The crucial passage of the *Principles* reads:

A substance may indeed be known through any attribute at all; but each substance has one principal property which constitutes its nature and essence, and to which all its other properties are referred. Thus extension in length, breadth and depth constitutes the nature of corporeal substance; and thought constitutes the nature of thinking substance. Everything else which can be attributed to body presupposes extension, and is merely a mode of an extended thing; and similarly, whatever we find in the mind is simply one of the various modes of thinking. *For example, shape is unintelligible except in an extended thing; and motion is unintelligible except as motion in an extended space; while imagination, sensation and will are intelligible only in a thinking thing. By contrast, it*

---

[7] Carriero 1995, 250.

[8] Carriero 1995, 250 argues rightly that 'Descartes's view is not completely novel' because it reflects the Aristotelian idea of definitional priority. A truly important element in Descartes's approach that I have not been able to locate in any of his predecessors is the idea that there are only two basic properties, of which other properties are modifications and through which those other properties are conceived. On this, see also Gueroult 1968, 60–63.

*is possible to understand extension without shape or movement, and thought without imagination or sensation, and so on;* and this is quite clear to anyone who gives the matter his attention. (PP 1.53; CSM I, 210–11, emphasis added)

In other words, no body or idea can be conceived without conceiving extension and thought, respectively. Here we encounter the notion of attribute; I examine it below, but for present purposes it suffices to note that there are things that do not require anything other than themselves to be conceived, and things the conceiving of which always involves conceiving something else. Obviously, then, Spinoza is treading on well-established grounds when he claims substances to be conceived through themselves, modes through another; this is just his way of formulating the conceptual priority traditionally given to substances over properties. Hence the preliminary conclusion we can draw is that Spinoza's definitions of substance and mode do not contain anything controversial; these basic premises could not easily be rejected by his contemporaries.[9] Substance is a self-supporting and conceptually independent entity, mode an entity that inheres in a substance through which it is also conceived.[10] All this means that Spinoza can be said to operate with a basic idea that could hardly be more accessible: whenever we think of something, we are thinking of some *thing* (i.e., a substance), but that thing must always be a thing of some *kind*, it cannot be without some qualities, properties, or characteristics (i.e., modes).

[9] I would thus agree not only with Carriero (1995) but also with William Charlton (1981, 509–11), who explicates Spinoza's position by invoking PP 1.53 and ends up defending the view that Spinoza's concept of substance is in line with that of Aristotle and Descartes; see also Steinberg 2000, Ch. 2. Although I agree with the claim of Curley (1988, 11–12) that there is nothing in 1d3 and 1d5 Descartes would find objectionable, I would not find it preferable, as Curley does, to understand the relationship between mode and substance 'not as the inherence of a property in its subject, but as the relation of an effect to its cause' (Curley 1988, 31; see also 1969, Ch. 1). Moreover, I would disagree with Harry Wolfson (1934 I, 61–78), who contends that although Spinoza's understanding of substance is in line with the tradition, he is offering a new way of understanding mode; and, finally, I would not be ready to endorse the view put forward by Gueroult in one passage, that the notions of being in itself and in another should be translated in terms of causality (Gueroult 1968, 63), although it is not clear how strong the "translation" suggested here ultimately is (for discussion, see Carriero 1995, 254–5).

[10] Clearly, there is a close connexion between inherence and conception. As Don Garrett (1990, 107) puts it, Spinoza's way of deducing the claim that there is nothing apart from substances and modes (in 1p4d) from 1d3, d5, and a1 'suggests that Spinoza understands "a is in b" and "a is conceived through b" as mutually entailing, either through their own meaning, or through the mediation of one or more axioms.' If a mediating axiom is needed, 1a4 is to my mind an especially strong candidate for such (Garrett considers also 1a6). See also Curley 1969, 15–18, 163.

## 2. ATTRIBUTE

The third fundamental ontological concept that receives its own definition in the opening pages of the *Ethics*, that of attribute, complicates
matters considerably. Recall that an attribute is 'what the intellect perceives of a substance, as constituting its essence' (1d4). We can ten-
tatively characterize attributes along the lines suggested by Jonathan
Bennett (1984, 61), as basic ways of being.[11] The historical context of the
concept is not hard to locate: the notion matches the Cartesian notion
of principal attribute or property 'which constitutes its [the substance's]
nature and essence' (PP 1.53; CSM I, 210). Now, as 'human being' was
traditionally defined as 'rational animal', the property of being rational could be said to 'constitute the essence' of any human being. As
a consequence, 1d4 would quite naturally be read as saying no more
than that there are certain properties that count as essential to a thing,
properties so fundamental to a substance that conceiving that substance
apart from them is simply impossible.[12] Here, however, interpretative
challenges begin to crop up: if a substance is conceived through itself,
how can it not be conceived apart from an attribute? These worries are
exacerbated if we take a look at 1p10 and its scholium, where Spinoza
does not hesitate to claim – solely on grounds of 1d3 and 1d4 – not only
that attributes are conceived through themselves but that 'each being
must be conceived under some attribute' (1p10s). This means, obviously,
that any substance must be conceived under some attribute. But would
all this not give conceptual priority to attributes over substances, thus
conflicting with the conceptually preeminent and independent position
just assigned to substances?

One approach to these problems is to identify substances with attributes.[13] Apart from solving the problem of how a substance can be conceived both through itself and through its attribute, there are passages
that taken at face value rather straightforwardly confirm this position:
in 1p4d, for instance, Spinoza contends that 'there is nothing outside

---

[11] 'An attribute for Spinoza is a *basic way of being* – a property which sprawls across
everything on one side of the dualist split, and nothing on the other side' (Bennett
1984, 61).

[12] The status of attributes would thus appear to resemble the status of things that
Aristotelians considered to be, as Carriero (1995, 246) puts it, 'too closely bound
up with' the things they are predicated of for the relation of inherence to apply:
'[W]ithout his [Socrates's] humanity, there would be no "him" for anything to exist
in' (Carriero 1995, 247). This points towards understanding attributes, as Carriero
(1995, 252) does, as definitions of essence.

[13] At least Gueroult (1968, 47–50) and Curley (1969, 16–18) endorse this approach,
and Jarrett (1977a, 451–2) reconstructs from Spinozistic premises an argument for
the identity of substance and attribute.

the intellect through which a number of things can be distinguished from one another except substances, *or* what is the same (by d4), their attributes, and their affections'.[14] This approach, however, encounters the following problem: Spinoza holds that 'it is far from absurd to attribute many attributes to one substance' (1p10s), so if we think that substances are identical with attributes, how can a substance with many attributes be *one* substance and not many substances, in fact an aggregate of substances? Although arguments have been put forward to solve this problem,[15] it seems that substances cannot be simply identified with attributes; this move threatens the high demands of unity Spinoza sets for substances (see 1p12, 1p13). I think it is fair to say that Spinoza cherishes the idea that one substance can have many attributes while being perfectly unified, completely free of all division.

How, then, should the relationship between a substance and its attribute be understood? I believe that Olli Koistinen's (1991, 18–24) answer to these questions is the best one available. Koistinen accepts that the concept of substance and its attribute must be identical, but observes that somewhat surprisingly this does not entail, for Spinoza, that a substance would be identical with its attribute. This is so, Koistinen suggests, because ideas are active affirmations, that is, propositions that always predicate properties of something, and we can regard the idea of a certain substance whose essence is constituted by a certain attribute, let us say $E$, as a proposition that predicates $E$ of the substance in question. Thus a proposition 'Substance is $E$' – or, more exactly, 'Something is $E$'[16] – expresses the absolutely primitive ontological feature of Spinoza's system. That is, substances and attributes are as it were inextricably fused together: the above proposition is not only the concept of the substance in question but also the concept of the attribute in question, that is, of $E$. There can be no idea of a substance without an idea of an attribute, and the idea of an attribute always contains the idea of a substance. That the above-mentioned complex proposition reveals the foundation of Spinoza's ontology explains how the *concepts* of substance and attribute can be identical while substance and attribute still remain distinct *entities*. And because the concepts of substance and

---

[14] Consider also 'God is eternal, *or* all God's attributes are eternal' (1p19) and 'God, *or* all of God's attributes, are immutable' (1p20c2).

[15] See especially Curley 1969, 78; 1988, 29–30.

[16] As Koistinen (1991, 23) observes, the proposition 'Something is $E$' would be of a more accurate form, as the proposition 'Substance is $E$' might be seen as already presupposing knowledge of substance; in Koistinen's words, what makes the former 'proposition a proposition about $s$ [substance] must be a feature of the predicate "is $E$". Since attributes are essences, the proposition "Something is $E$" cannot be about any other individual but $s$'.

attribute are identical, that it can be said that a substance is conceived both through itself and through its attribute poses no threat to the tenet that the concept of a substance – and thus also of an attribute – does not refer to or involve any other concept, making it conceptually independent.

But even if this were right and solved the problem of how a substance may be conceived both through itself and through its attribute, there is still another famous problem plaguing Spinoza's doctrine of substance and attribute: how are we to understand the claim that one substance may have many attributes, each truly predicable of a substance, and each constituting the essence of the substance? One approach to this problem is to take attributes to be ways in which an intellect can know a substance, which introduces an element of subjectivity to attributes.[17] It can even be argued that this is in fact something Spinoza quite explicitly says, because he defines attributes as 'what the *intellect perceives of a substance*, as [*tanquam*] constituting its essence' (1d4, emphasis added).[18] There would thus be no special problem in one substance having many attributes: one and the same object can of course be perceived in many different ways, and Spinoza's claim would simply be that there are certain basic ways in which a substance can be perceived, and he calls these basic ways attributes. However, emphasizing the subjective element pertaining to attributes risks, I think, making Spinoza too much of an idealist. On the whole, attributes certainly are depicted as something very objective, real, or actual – hardly something whose existence would depend on a perceiving subject[19] – and certain passages are especially difficult to reconcile with any kind of subjectivist interpretation of attributes.[20] Thus I would argue that the reference to 'the intellect'

[17] Scholars who may be seen as proponents of this overall approach hold differing views on the nature and role of the subjective element. For a strong form of subjectivism, according to which attributes are subjective concepts invented by the mind and do not have independent existence, see Wolfson 1934 I, 142–57; for more moderate views, which do not regard attributes as inventions of the mind, see Eisenberg 1990, 1, 11–12; Carriero 1994, 634–5.

[18] That the word *tanquam* in 1d4 can be translated both as 'as' and 'as if' has been important for the debate concerning the status of attributes ('as if' would arguably speak for the subjective interpretation). On this, see n. 21.

[19] Note that Spinoza holds any intellect to be 'only a certain mode of thinking' (1p31d); on this, see also Gueroult 1968, 50.

[20] I agree with Jarrett (1977a, 447–8; 2007, 55) that 1p20d is such a piece of text:

God (by p19) and all of his attributes are eternal, i.e. (by d8), each of his attributes expresses existence. Therefore, the same attributes of God which (by d4) explain God's eternal essence at the same time explain his eternal existence, i.e., that itself which constitutes God's essence at the same time constitutes his existence. So his existence and his essence are one and the same, Q.E.D.

in 1d4 is there because a substance can only be known under some attribute, as an entity of some basic kind; but we perceive attributes as constituting the essence of a substance simply because those attributes really *do* constitute the essence of a substance.[21] An essence of a substance can be perceived as constituted in many different ways, but not in just any way.

Still, if we take attributes to be objective features constituting nothing less than the essence of a substance, is it not problematic to claim that one substance can have many attributes? It is an intriguing fact that Spinoza shows at most extremely mild concern about this. The important 1p10s, as we have seen, asserts that it is 'far from absurd to attribute many attributes to one substance', but the scholium is not as enlightening as one might wish on the question of the relationship between substance and attribute.[22] The beginning of the scholium reads:

From these propositions it is evident that although two attributes may be conceived to be really distinct (i.e., one may be conceived without the aid of the other), we still can not infer from that that they constitute two beings, *or* two different substances. For it is of the nature of a substance that each of its attributes is conceived through itself, since all the attributes it has have always been in it together, and one could not be produced by another, but each expresses the reality, *or* being of substance. (1p10s)

The propositions referred to in the beginning ('[f]rom these propositions it is evident') are presumably 1p9 and 1p10. The former contends that it is 'evident from' 1d4 that reality and being correlate with the number of attributes of a thing; the latter says that attributes are conceived through themselves. The foremost aim of 1p10s is obviously a negative one, namely to show that from the fact that attributes are really distinct it does not follow that each attribute must constitute a thing of its own; this is an important point, given the Cartesian doctrine that each substance can have only one principal attribute.[23] Spinoza's idea

---

Moreover, propositions 1p21–p23 describing 'what follows from the absolute nature' of attributes and thus, obviously, assigning causal efficacy to attributes (on this more below) fit poorly, to my mind, with an interpretation according to which attributes are only subjective ways of perception. Consider also 1p9, 2p1, and 2p2.

[21] Alan Donagan (1988, 70) argues, correctly and based on Martial Gueroult (1968, 428–61), that 'what the intellect perceives' cannot mean 'what the intellect (possibly) falsely perceives'; as Donagan puts it, 'Spinoza himself treats his definition as implying that attributes really are what the intellect perceives them to be.'

[22] Note also that even though this question has haunted his readers for ages, Spinoza discusses it in a *scholium*; that is, he does not seem to feel the need to offer a more "official" proposition and demonstration for his stand.

[23] The topic is also discussed in Spinoza's correspondence; see Ep8 and Ep9.

here may well be, as Michael Della Rocca has argued, that no attribute, say $E$, can offer grounds for a substance not to have some other attribute, say $T$, because then a fact about $T$ – that it is not possessed by a certain substance – would be explained by $E$; but then something concerning $T$ would be conceived through $E$, and this would go against $T$'s status as an attribute, that is, as something that is conceived solely through itself (there is hence what Della Rocca calls a *conceptual barrier* between attributes, which in this kind of case would be violated).[24] In any case, the scholium under scrutiny does not shed much positive light on our present question; and having established the negative claim, Spinoza appears to see it as plainly unproblematic to hold that, just as we are fundamentally both mental and physical creatures, a substance can be for instance both thinking and extended.[25] In other words, the scholium's explicit concern is to show that Spinoza's stand does not present a radical departure from what was commonly thought in his times – it is something even Cartesians should allow – but the all-important underlying view obviously is that a substance can be conceived under many different aspects, can have several objective essential features, many basic ways of being. Moreover, as 'each being must be conceived under some attribute' (1p10s), this applies to modifications as well: they must always be conceived under some attribute, which means that they must be modifications of some objective feature of a substance.

There is one absolutely focal contention concerning attributes that we have not yet discussed: the claim that substances cannot share attributes, or, as Spinoza puts it, '[i]n nature there cannot be two or more substances of the same nature *or* attribute' (1p5). This proposition receives a detailed demonstration:

If there were two or more distinct substances, they would have to be distinguished from one another either by a difference in their attributes, or by a difference in their affections (by p4). If only by a difference in their attributes, then it will be conceded that there is only one of the same attribute. But if by a difference in their affections, then since a substance is prior in nature to its affections (by p1), if the affections are put to one side and [the substance] is considered in itself, i.e. (by d3 and a6), considered truly, one cannot be conceived to be distinguished from another, i.e. (by p4), there cannot be many, but only one [of the same nature *or* attribute], Q.E.D.

Leibniz is, of course, most often identified as the classic thinker championing the principle of the identity of indiscernibles; but it is clear that

---

[24] Della Rocca 2002, 18, 28–9.
[25] The relationship between attributes and substance has been further explicated with the help of the Scotist doctrine of formal distinction; see Schmidt's contribution in this volume.

in 1p4, on which 1p5d is partly based, Spinoza is relying on a version of that principle.[26] All along he seems to assume that if there is no feature with regard to which two things differ from each other, they must be identical; so if there are to be two distinct things, there must be something with regard to which they differ. Understandably, attributes and modes are the only candidates for entities that can be used to distinguish substances from each other. I think Spinoza's argument is easier to grasp by first considering the passage concerning affections. The crucial and often asked question is, what licenses Spinoza to put the affections 'to one side' when considering substances? Given what we found in the previous section, the case is in a sense rather straightforward: by remarking that 'a substance is prior in nature to its affections', Spinoza is reminding us that distinguishing a substance by its modes would amount to a situation in which a substance is individuated by and conceived through something external to it (i.e., external to its essence); this would be at odds with the very definition of substance, which, as we have seen, characterizes a substance as a self-supporting entity, and one that does not require anything external to be conceived. Moreover, on this point Spinoza is in accordance with more or less the entire Western tradition.[27]

So two substances cannot be distinguished from each other by their modes, and we are left with attributes to do the job. Spinoza remarks briefly that if substances were distinguished 'only by a difference in their attributes, then it will be conceded that there is only one of the same attribute.' In other words, if we take any attribute, say $E$, it is evident that if both substance $s$ and substance $z$ have $E$, it cannot be $E$ that differentiates $s$ and $z$ from each other; thus, given the identity of indiscernibles, $s$ and $z$ must be identical. Any (putative) case of attribute sharing between two distinct substances is on closer inspection a case of substance identity – and so, Spinoza thinks, he can confidently assert that no two or more substances can have the same attribute.

[26] See Bennett 1984, 66; Garrett 1990, 98–100; Steinberg 2000, 12; Della Rocca 2002, 13–14; 2008, 47.

[27] Here I would wholeheartedly agree with Carriero (1995, 251), who contends, '[a]s would have been obvious to a contemporaneous reader of the *Ethics*, to make a substance depend on its accidents for its individuation would be to make a substance depend on its accidents for its existence, a dependence that is incompatible with its status as a substance.' Moreover, the type of approach presented by Willis Doney (1990, 37) and Della Rocca (2002, 14–17) strikes me as particularly apt: were two substances distinguished by their modes, the substances would have to be conceived through their modes; but this cannot be, given that substances are entities conceived through themselves. For more discussion, see Gueroult 1968, 118–20; Charlton 1981, 514–15; Bennett 1984, 67–9; Curley 1988, 17–19, 145; Garrett 1990, 73–83.

Here, however, Spinoza appears to be on less solid ground than with
regard to modes: as has often been noted, the argument seems to go
through only if we make an un-Spinozistic assumption, for otherwise
it cannot escape an important objection that goes all the way back
to Leibniz.[28] Namely, why could not $s$ and $z$ share $E$ and differ with
regard to some other attributes, so that $s$ would have $E$ and $T$, $z$ have
$E$ and $X$? There would, then, be a way to distinguish $s$ from $z$ based on
their attributes even though they shared $E$, and this would undermine
Spinoza's argument: it would be valid on the assumption that there are
only one-attribute substances, but this, as we have seen, is not enough
for Spinoza's purposes, and he holds dear the idea that one substance can
have many attributes. We should note that even though this objection of
considerable force is rather easy to state, it is uncertain whether Spinoza
recognized it. In what follows, I first try to explicate why he might not
have, thinking that 1p5d could handle the above objection, and then
present another, and probably better, argument that is designed to do
the same thing.

In general, Spinoza seems to think that essences are highly individual,
unique to their possessors. Consider the following definition, which,
despite the great importance of its *definiendum*, comes as late as the
beginning of Part 2 of the *Ethics*:

I say that to the essence of any thing belongs that which, being given, the thing
is [NS: also] necessarily posited and which, being taken away, the thing is necessarily [NS: also] taken away; or that without which the thing can neither be
nor be conceived, and which can neither be nor be conceived without the thing.
(2d2)

The claim that an essence 'can neither be nor be conceived without'
its possessor is the most surprising ingredient in this definition, and
it can shed light on Spinoza's mindset in 1p5d. Given it, there cannot
be two distinct things of the same essence; and as attributes constitute
essences, Spinoza is led to think that it is impossible for two substances
to share an attribute, because whenever there is an attribute constituting
an essence, we have a particular substance without which the attribute
could not exist.[29] As we have seen, Spinoza is at pains to show, in
1p10s, that there is nothing dubious about claiming that one and the
same substance can have as essential attributes both, say, $E$ and $T$. The
relation between essences and attributes is tight enough for it to go

---

[28] The objection is located in Leibniz 1969, 198–9. For expositions and evaluations of
    this objection, see Bennett 1984, 69–70; Curley 1988, 15–16; Garrett 1990, 83–101;
    Della Rocca 2002, 17.

[29] At least Koistinen (1991, 13–14) puts forward this kind of reading of 1p5d.

against the doctrine of attributes constituting – whatever may be the exact meaning of this – individual essences to claim that $s$ can have $E$ and $T$, while $z$ has $E$ and $X$: if $E$ constitutes the essence of $s$, it cannot also constitute the essence of $z$ distinct from $s$, because $s$ and $z$ would, then, have the same essence and thus be identical. In 1p8s2, the no-shared-attribute thesis receives another argument, which is in line with this line of thought: without leaning on anything previously said, only on the linkage between definitions and essences,[30] Spinoza claims that because the definition that expresses the nature of the substance does not involve 'any certain number of individuals,' there can be only one substance 'of the same nature'. The idea thus seems to be that any essence pertains to one individual only, and so, if an attribute constitutes an essence, we see that there can only be single substance of a particular nature, and there is nothing to be distinguished, no several substances left to share an attribute.[31] This, then, would block the above objection to 1p5d.

Even if the present argument were what Spinoza really has in mind, it is only as strong as its point of departure, his definition of essence (2d2). The problem with the idea of individual essence is that it would have a hard time convincing any dedicated Cartesian. Thought and extension are principal attributes that constitute the essences of their possessors, but it would seem strange, especially for Cartesians, to claim that there is anything individual about them, or that an attribute could not be or be conceived without a certain substance; on the contrary, they appear to be quite easily shareable by many substances.[32] Perhaps Spinoza could say in rebuttal (relying on a widely accepted seventeenth-century way of conceiving essences and the definitions that express those essences) that as both attributes and definitions express essences, and definitions

---

[30] There appears not to be anything idiosyncratic in Spinoza's way of understanding definitions as expressions of essences; cf. Mercer 2001, 227.

[31] A similar argument has been put forward by Koistinen (1993, 149): '[A]ttributes for Spinoza are those properties that make individuation through itself possible and for that reason they must be non-relational individuating properties which means that they cannot be shared by several substances: they are individual essences – rejected by all things except their bearer.' For other arguments turning on the close connection between essence and attribute, see Allison 1987, 52–3; Donagan 1988, 70–71; for criticism of Allison's and Donagan's positions, see Garrett 1990, 89–93. For a line of argument against Leibniz's criticism that turns on the traditional tenet of the simplicity of God's nature, see Carriero 1994, 631–4 and Schmidt's contribution in this volume.

[32] In correspondence, Henry Oldenburg expresses his sentiments in a clear manner: 'Against the first I hold that two men are two substances and of the same attribute, since they are both capable of reasoning; and thence I conclude that there are two substances of the same attribute' (Ep3; Spinoza 1995, 65).

do not involve any number of individuals, even a Cartesian has to admit that only one particular kind of individual can be constituted by each attribute. However, it is unclear how convincing this argument is.[33]

There is, however, another argument, presented recently by Della Rocca in Spinoza's defence, and one that is partly based on the same material as the previous one. The starting point of this argument is that Spinoza accepts the claim that '[e]ach attribute of a substance, independently of any other attribute of that substance, is sufficient for conceiving of that substance.'[34] This certainly seems to be a plausible claim in the Spinozistic framework, and Della Rocca gathers a convincing body of evidence that Spinoza really does endorse it; among other things, when Spinoza's definition of attribute (1d4) is combined with his definition of essence (2d2), the claim follows.[35] Now, given this, it is well grounded to maintain that there cannot be cases in which for instance $s$ has $E$ and $T$, and $z$ has $E$ and $X$, for then $s$ could not be conceived solely through $E$, that is, as the substance that has $E$, because this would not be enough to distinguish $s$ from $z$; instead, $s$ would have to be conceived as the substance with $E$ and $T$, and this would mean that the concept of a certain substance with $E$ would require not only the concept of $E$ but also the concept of $T$, and would thus be partly conceived through $T$.[36] But this would violate the conceptual barrier between the attributes: conceiving a substance with a certain attribute would depend on conceiving some other attribute. Thus, the conceptual independence of attributes

---

[33] For criticism of this argument, see Bennett 1984, 69–70. A more convincing way to defend Spinoza's position is, however, available. As Koistinen (1993) maintains, not only Descartes but also Kant and Frege hold that 'substances cannot be individuated or thought about directly' (p. 144), and Spinoza joins their company when he claims that 'each thing must be conceived under some attribute' (1p10s); and because it holds that if all things were individuated through something else, an infinite regress would follow (p. 142), 'we have to individuate at least one thing with the help of a property which is non-relational (qualitative, intrinsic) and identifying. But it is not conceivable that this property could be anything else but the essence of the thing' (p. 145). Thus, 'individual essences make individuation possible' (p. 146), and an argument for the no-shared-attribute thesis relying on attributes as individual essences is on rather strong grounds.

[34] Della Rocca 2002, 18.

[35] Della Rocca 2002, 19. Della Rocca (2002, 20–21) argues that it is also entailed by Spinoza's claim that attributes express the reality of the substance (E1p10s), for Spinoza accepts the assertion that 'x expresses y if and only if x is sufficient for conceiving of y' (Della Rocca 2002, 20).

[36] Later Della Rocca presents his view as follows: '[I]f a substance has more than one attribute, each attribute by itself must enable us to conceive of the substance, and this can be the case only if each attribute that a substance has is unique to that substance. Thus Leibniz's scenario is ruled out' (Della Rocca 2008, 49).

guarantees that the kind of situations depicted in the objection cannot occur.[37] An argument put in epistemological terms thus seems to fare better than one based on the doctrine of individual essences.

We can sum up the offerings of these examinations as follows. Spinoza adheres quite closely to traditional lines of thought with regard to the concepts of substance and mode: substance is a self-supporting and conceptually independent entity through which are conceived the modes that inhere in it. Attribute too is defined in a Cartesian fashion, as that which constitutes the essence of a substance; but Spinoza departs from Descartes in asserting not only that one substance can have many attributes but also that substances cannot share attributes. Both claims certainly bring with them complex issues, but as we have seen, Spinoza is not left without resourceful arguments for his position. In any case, it can be said that in defining the basic concepts of his ontology Spinoza is treading rather familiar ground, and it is difficult to regard the novelties concerning the relationship between substance and attribute as presenting any truly radical departure from the tradition; as we shall see, it is not so much these basic conceptual issues pertaining to ontology as certain theorems Spinoza draws from them that so alarmed his contemporaries.

### 3. EXISTENCE AND CAUSALITY

It is noteworthy how little, in a sense, has thus far been achieved: despite all the conceptual moves made, it has not yet even been established whether any such entities as substances, modes, or attributes really exist.[38] Claims concerning real existence appear only when Spinoza hooks the notions of substance, attribute, and mode up with causal notions, which – strikingly – are missing from 1d3–d5.[39] This is when his unique philosophical system begins to quickly take shape.

The seventh proposition of the opening part of the *Ethics* makes the crucial existential claim concerning substances and can serve as a vantage point from which to examine the way in which Spinoza moves from purely conceptual considerations to existential ones. The proposition states,

---

[37] Della Rocca 2002, 17–22.

[38] 'Man thinks' (2a2) is an axiom in the *Ethics*, so there seems to be a path open to a *cogito* argument for the existence of the thinking subject. However, Spinoza makes no move to take it.

[39] As Carriero (1995, 261) perspicaciously puts it, '[t]here may, indeed, be some fairly quick routes from being a substance to being causally independent (as, for example, the alternative demonstration to IP6C testifies), but we shouldn't lose sight of the fact that there is distance to be traveled.'

[i]t pertains to the nature of a substance to exist (1p7),

and it is proved as follows:

A substance cannot be produced by anything else (by p6c); therefore it will be the cause of itself, i.e. (by d1), its essence necessarily involves existence, *or* it pertains to its nature to exist, Q.E.D. (1p7d)

Now, before considering the overall validity of the argument, we may note that it may in fact take two routes, corresponding to the two ways in which 1p6c – the corollary stating the causal independence of substances – can be demonstrated. The quicker route is the more interesting one for our purposes; according to it, adding merely the following axiom to the notion of substance is needed to show that a substance is *causa sui*:

The knowledge of an effect depends on, and involves, the knowledge of its cause. (1a4)

Now, whatever the exact meaning of this axiom – it is not clear what kind of knowledge Spinoza here has in mind – it enables Spinoza to argue that if a substance had an external cause, it would be conceived through that cause; and because this would violate the 'what is conceived through itself' claim of 1d3, a substance cannot be produced by anything else and is thus, according to Spinoza, the cause of itself. There is, then, an exceedingly quick route from the conceptual independence of substances to a fundamental causal claim.[40] If conceiving things requires conceiving their causes (as 1a4 says), everything conceptually independent must be causally self-sufficient.[41]

The obvious and often repeated objection to 1p7 is that even if a substance cannot be produced by anything external to it, it does not follow that it necessarily exists – it only follows that if a substance exists, the cause of that existence must lie within it. Spinoza seems to think that

[40] The longer route goes via 1p5: because substances cannot share an attribute (1p5), they do not have anything in common (1p2) and so (by 1p3) one cannot be the cause of the other; because the only external thing that could produce a substance is another substance (from 1d3, 1d5, and 1a1), a substance cannot be produced by anything else. It should be noted that also 1p3d invokes 1a4.

[41] It should be noted that, as Don Garrett (2002, 136) has convincingly shown, inherence implies, for Spinoza, causation, and for the following reason. Spinoza endorses (this is indicated by the way in which he uses 1d3, 1d5, and 1a1 in 1p4d) the doctrine that 'If y is *in* x, then y is conceived through x' (p. 136; on this see n. 10); and because he also accepts (by 1a4) that 'If y is conceived through x, then y is caused by x' (p. 136), we reach what Garrett dubs the 'Inherence Implies Causation Doctrine': 'If y is *in* x, then y is caused by x' (p. 137). This doctrine, Garrett (p. 137) points out, 'when applied to the definitions of *mode* and *substance*, entails both that every mode is caused by the substance that it is *in* and that every substance is self-caused'.

because everything must be caused either by external causes or by itself, and because in the case of a substance external causes are ruled out, the only option is that it is self-caused, which, by 1d1, means that it must exist already by its own essence; thus, given such an essence, the entity in question must exist. Nevertheless, it may surely be pressed: on what grounds can it be claimed that such an essence is given?

The following observations help to answer this question. Spinoza demonstrates the claim 'God, *or* a substance consisting of infinite attributes, each of which expresses eternal and infinite essence, necessarily exists' (1p11) in several ways, and the one I would regard as the most important demonstration contains a line of argument revealing Spinoza's conception of the principle of sufficient reason that can be used to defend 1p7. *Ethics* 1p11d2 starts by maintaining, '[f]or each thing there must be assigned a cause, *or* reason, as much for its existence as for its nonexistence.' In other words, there must be a sufficient reason not only for the existence but also for the nonexistence of anything. That reason, Spinoza continues, must be located either inside or outside of the thing in question, and because in the case of God – who is a substance – it cannot be outside of it, the reason for the existence or nonexistence of God must be found in God's essence. Now, the only possible reason for the latter would be that God's essence is contradictory, like that of a square circle; and because this cannot be, God's essence can only be the cause or reason for God's existence; thus God necessarily exists. As has been pointed out by Don Garrett (1979, 209–10), this line of argumentation applies to any substance whatsoever, because each one of them seems to have a noncontradictory essence.[42] Thus the idea behind 1p7 could be spelled out as follows. Substances are causally isolated entities (by 1d3 and 1a4); hence, given the principle of sufficient reason, only a substance's essence can be the cause or reason either for its existence or for its nonexistence; but not for nonexistence, for this would mean that the essence in question was contradictory and the substance an unthinkable, self-denying nonthing – such as a square circle. As there can be no reason for the nonexistence of the substance, there must be one for its existence, and that reason can only be its essence itself; thus that essence involves existence, that is, a substance is *causa sui*.

So, when we add to 1p7d Spinoza's version of the principle of sufficient reason, together with the assumption that a substance cannot

---

[42] I thus think Garrett (1979, 208) is right in claiming that '[t]he second proof of Proposition XI, we now see, is simply a more explicit formulation of the argument which is needed to justify Proposition VII, but made for the special case of God rather than the general case of substance(s).' It should be noted, however, that this generates the widely discussed problem – one that I do not examine here – of on what grounds can Spinoza claim that only one God with an infinity of attributes exists, rather than many substances with, say, one attribute.

have a contradictory nature, we arrive at a valid argument. In particular, the commitment to the principle of sufficient reason is contentious indeed; but neither of the additional premises is easy to reject, especially for Spinoza's contemporaries, who would not be particularly strongly inclined to deny the conclusion, either: as noted above, Descartes *starts* by holding that a substance is a causally independent entity when he contends, '[b]y *substance* we can understand nothing other than a thing which exists in such a way as to depend on no other thing for its existence' (PP 1.51; CSM I, 210). And there is probably much that a good Aristotelian could find acceptable in this way of understanding a substance; any substance, even a created one, is to a certain important extent independent of other things.[43] Spinoza shows acquaintance with this when he writes in his early *Treatise on the Emendation of the Intellect*, '[i]f the thing is in itself, *or*, as is commonly said, is the cause of itself' (TdIE § 92); characteristically, however, in the *Ethics* he gives an argument for the move from ontological and epistemological independence to causal independence and the necessary existence that results from it.

Thus, granted certain additional premises, Spinoza has succeeded in covering the distance from mere conceptual considerations to contentions concerning real existence. The claim of 1p11, that God necessarily exists, was of course a cornerstone of traditional philosophical theology, so there is nothing unacceptable about that; the claim of 1p7, that any substance must be a necessary existent, admittedly sounds strange and suspiciously strong,[44] but it is still close enough to the Cartesian conception of substance so that when it is left to its own devices, it is difficult to say what to think about it; perhaps it may be mitigated, somewhat as Descartes does in PP 1.51, to fit the traditional picture? But Spinoza is not ready to make any such concessions, and so is led to a collision of the greatest magnitude, long in the making, with traditional philosophical theology: 'Except God, no substance can be or be conceived' (1p14). I do not here discuss in detail the way in which Spinoza proves his monism;[45] briefly stated, the argument is that

---

[43] On this, see Carriero 1995, 247.

[44] Oldenburg certainly saw the threat posed by Spinoza's position:

> With regard to the second I consider that, since nothing can be the cause of itself, we can scarcely understand how it can be true that 'Substance cannot be produced, nor can it be produced by any other substance.' For this proposition asserts that all substances are causes of themselves, that they are each and all independent of one another, and it makes them so many Gods, in this way denying the first cause of all things. (Ep3; Spinoza 1995, 65)

[45] For more on Spinoza's monism and its derivation, see Miller's and Schmidt's contributions in this volume.

as God, the being with all the attributes, necessarily exists and as substances cannot share attributes, there can be no other substances besides
God.

From the claim that there is only one substance, it is – given Spinoza's
understanding of substance and mode – only a stone's throw to 1p15,
'[w]hatever is, is in God, and nothing can be or be conceived without God', which demotes a plethora of things – horses, chairs, human
beings – from substances to modes of the one substance. There has been
considerable discussion as to how we should conceive finite things as
God's modes. Proposition 1p16, '[f]rom the necessity of the divine nature
there must follow infinitely many things in infinitely many modes',
along with others, such as 1p25, make it clear that some kind of causal
relation obtains between God-substance and his modes;[46] but based on
the preceding discussion, it is also evident that finite modes inhere in
God, just as 1p15 says they do.[47] Indeed, we should be clear as to where
Spinoza's radicalism lies: in the claim that the substance–property relationship obtains between God and finite things,[48] not in the claim that

[46] For my attempt to explicate this relationship, see Viljanen 2008b.
[47] Much of the discussion has revolved around Curley's (1969) claim that modes do
not inhere in substances as properties, but that the relationship between substance
and modes is exclusively one of (efficient) causation; but I would agree with Jarrett
(1977b, 92–3) and Carriero (1995, 254–6) that already the way in which 1p15 (that
concerns inherence) and 1p16 (that concerns causality) differ from each other (they
are proved differently and have differing deductive progeny) strongly suggests that
there are two different relations, inherence and causation, at work in Spinoza's
system. However, for recent criticism of this view, see Della Rocca 2008, 67–8.
[48] Curley presents a powerful objection against this line of interpretation:

> Spinoza's modes are, prima facie, of the wrong logical type to be related to substance
> in the same way Descartes' modes are related to substance, for they are particular
> things (*E* Ip25C), not qualities. And it is difficult to know what it would mean to
> say that particular things inhere in substance. When qualities are said to inhere
> in substance, this may be viewed as a way of saying that they are predicated of it.
> What it would mean to say that one thing is predicated of another is a mystery
> that needs solving. (Curley 1969, 18)

> Now, I think that finite modes can be predicated of God; and, of course, Spinoza
> speaks of finite modes as things. Obviously, much here hinges upon what kind
> of entities, in the end, one takes Spinozistic finite modes to be. Bennett presents
> an interpretation that makes 'particular extended things adjectival on regions of
> space' (Bennett 1984, 95); according to this view, there is no problem in claiming
> the relation of a subject and a predicate – or a thing and a property – to hold
> between the one extended substance and its modes (see especially Bennett 1984,
> 93). Jarrett (1977b, 85) maintains that the difficulty presented by Curley 'can be
> solved by distinguishing inherence from predication'; and Carriero (1995) rejects
> Curley's objection similarly on the grounds of the fact that in Aristotelianism, the
> distinction between *what can be said of a subject* and *what cannot be said of a
> subject* is orthogonal to the distinction between *what exists in a subject* and *what*

both inherence and causation are at play in that relationship. In a widely endorsed Aristotelian view, substances cause those properties they necessarily have (the so-called *propria*), and these properties inhere in their causers.[49]

Finally, I would like to point out certain claims Spinoza draws from God's causal efficacy – claims that can shed light on the way in which substance, mode, and attribute should be conceived. Now, because God is, in virtue of his essence, the cause of himself (1p11) and of all things (1p16), Spinoza claims his essence to be power (1p34). This brings us back to attributes: as they too are conceived through themselves, they must be causally efficacious in a way that differs rather clearly from what the Cartesian conception of attributes seems to imply. There are passages in the late correspondence in which Spinoza delineates the difference between his and Descartes's conceptions of the attribute of extension:

[F]rom Extension as conceived by Descartes, to wit, an inert mass, it is ... quite impossible to demonstrate the existence of bodies. For matter at rest, as far as in it lies, will continue to be at rest, and will not be set in motion except by a more powerful external cause. For this reason I have not hesitated on a previous occasion to affirm that Descartes' principles of natural things are of no service, not to say quite wrong. (Ep81; Spinoza 1995, 352)

---

*does not exist in a subject*; according to Carriero, '[i]f we keep these distinctions separate, there is no immediate barrier to counting particular things as accidents' (Carriero 1995, 256).

[49] In his *Historical and Critical Dictionary* of 1697, Pierre Bayle interprets Spinozistic modes as properties of substance and famously levels a series of criticisms against Spinoza. Three objections raised by Bayle and taken up by Curley (1969, Ch. 1) have been the subject of recent discussions (see Jarrett 1977b; Carriero 1995; Nadler 2008). (1) If modes are God's properties, because there is change in modes, God cannot be immutable; (2) because modes can be predicated of God, it follows that God is the subject of contradictory terms (e.g., if both Peter and Paul are God's properties and Peter denies what Paul affirms, God both denies and affirms the same thing); (3) if modes are God's properties and the modes, e.g., human beings, commit evil acts, it is ultimately God who is evil. A thorough exposition of the ways in which Spinoza could answer these accusations would take us too far afield, but the following brief points can be made in his defence. (1) From the adequate point of view, that is, *sub specie aeternitatis*, everything follows, as in geometry, from God's nature as it does, from eternity to eternity, and hence God is immutable; (2) if God *modified as* Peter denies something that God *modified as* Paul affirms, Bayle's formulation of contradiction, that 'two opposite terms' are 'truly affirmed of the same subject, *in the same respect*, and at the same time' (Bayle 1965, 309, emphasis mine), is not violated (see Jarrett 1977b, 87; Carriero 1995, 263; Nadler 2008, 60); (3) evil is nothing positive but only something that we imaginatively, and hence inadequately, attribute to things (see especially Ep19, but also Curley 1969, 13; Carriero 1995, 266–73; Nadler 2008, 60).

With regard to your question as to whether the variety of things can be demon-strated a priori solely from the conception of Extension, I think I have already made it quite clear that this is impossible. That is why Descartes is wrong in defining matter through Extension; it must necessarily be explicated through an attribute which expresses eternal and infinite essence. (Ep83; Spinoza 1995, 355)

There is thus something seriously wrong in the way Descartes under-stands extension: he does not acknowledge the fact that extension, like any attribute, expresses God's essence. The crux of this criticism seems to be that the Cartesian conception of attributes fails to take into account that substance, or Nature, is something essentially dynamic in character. In light of the preceding discussion, these contentions make sense: a substance causing itself and an attribute doing the same just means that the primitive state 'something is $E$' is realized solely by the constituents involved in that state. So we can say both that a substance is self-caused and that an attribute is self-caused; and by this causal power are brought about all the modes as well. As we have seen, a sub-stance cannot be conceived other than under some attribute, but all the ways in which the substance can be conceived – all the ways in which its nature is constituted – involve causal power; that much is certain. Being in itself, or subsistence, equals power to exist (cf. 1p11d3). All this suggests, I think, that the Spinozistic God can be characterized as an absolutely infinite power, producing all existents as determined by essence-constituting attributes, which makes attributes God's powers as it were, fundamental manifestations of the one basic power.[50] In conso-nance with this – indeed, due to it – the backbone of Spinoza's theorizing concerning human existence is based on the idea that striving (conatus) – which is undoubtedly something dynamic in character – 'to persevere in being' forms the very essence of our actual existence (3p7). In other words, as all finite things are modifications of the intrinsically dynamic God-nature, human beings as well are, in Spinoza's framework, beings of power striving for their own kind of existence.[51]

[50] Already H. H. Joachim (1901, 65) sees 'attributes as "lines of force," or forms in which God's omnipotence manifests its causality to an intelligence', and A. Wolf (1974 [1927], see especially 19, 22–4) draws attention to Spinoza's identification of God's essence with power and emphasizes the dynamic character of attributes. More recently, Sherry Deveaux (2003, 334) underscores that 'an attribute is a dif-ferent way in which absolutely infinite and eternal power is expressed', and Della Rocca (2003, 225) maintains that 'extension conceived as inherently dynamic is, for Spinoza, an attribute.' The powerful or active nature of God and attributes is widely recognized in French Spinoza scholarship; for classic interpretations, see Gueroult 1974, 188–9; Matheron 1988 (1969), 13; Deleuze 1997 (1968), 90–95, 198–9. For my analysis of the concept of power, see Viljanen 2008a, especially 99–101.

[51] For my detailed argument for this conclusion, see Viljanen 2008a.

## 4. CONCLUSION

At the beginning of the *Ethics* we find Spinoza operating the way he is inclined to, drawing momentous conclusions from relatively uncontentious – or at least not easily rejectable – definitions and axioms. This, of course, makes sense: should he begin with unusual and unbelievable contentions, his arguments expressed in geometrical fashion, regardless of their sophistication, would hardly have any force. Proceeding by way of certain innovations concerning the relationship between substance and attribute, Spinoza then arrives at his monism, in which the things around us are not only effects but modes of the single substance. Understandably enough, this ontological upheaval is not without its ethical implications: in the ensuing theorizing concerning human happiness, wherever it may eventually lead us, the fact that we are all modifications of an intrinsically powerful God-nature should never be lost from sight.[52]

[52] I would like to thank Olli Koistinen, John Carriero, Juhani Pietarinen, Arto Repo, and Hemmo Laiho for many constructive comments and criticisms concerning this essay.

# 4  Substance Monism and Identity Theory in Spinoza

Spinoza is famous – or rather notorious – for his contention that there is only one substance, namely God. Everything else is but a mere property of this substance, that is, a property of God. Spinoza presents this view in 1p14: 'Except God, no substance can be or be conceived'. Now, it is certainly an interesting question whether or not the proof that Spinoza adduces for this claim is valid. But even if it is, the reader may still be at a loss. For the premises of this proof are by no means evident or uncontroversial. No shrewd Aristotelian or Cartesian would have any trouble denying their truth and replacing them with other principles more suitable for their own purposes.[1] So the question about Spinoza's *motive* for his substance monism still remains. One might approach the question by pointing out that in his *Principia Philosophiae* Descartes defines 'substance' in such a way that only God could possibly be a substance in the strict sense.[2] Descartes, however, is unwilling to draw the conclusion that there is after all only one substance. He instead maintains the ambiguity of the term 'substance'; in a weaker sense it can just as well be applied to creatures of God, viz., to *res cogitans* and *res extensa*, both of which depend on nothing apart from God.[3] Spinoza, one could argue, is more consistent here: he avoids this ambiguity and uses 'substance' in a univocal sense. Monistic consequences follow immediately from

---

[1] Or so it seems. For a different view see Viljanen's contribution in this volume.

[2] 'By *substance* we can understand nothing other than a thing which exists in such a way as to depend on no other thing for its existence. And there is only one substance that can be understood to depend on no other thing whatsoever, namely God. In the case of all other substances, we perceive that they can exist only with the help of God's concurrence" (*Principles of Philosophy* 1.51; AT VIII/1, 24; CSM I, 210).

[3] 'Hence the term "substance" does not apply *univocally*, as they say in the Schools, to God and to other things; that is, there is no distinctly intelligible meaning of the term which is common to God and his creatures.... But as for corporeal substance and mind (or created thinking substance), these can be understood to fall under this common concept: things that need only the concurrence of God in order to exist' (*Principles of Philosophy* 1.51–2; AT VIII/1, 24–5; CSM I, 210).

this move.[4] But this is surely not sufficient to explain the *motive* for Spinoza's monism, for why should a univocal use of the term 'substance' be preferable? Why not acknowledge degrees of substantiality? In looking for Spinoza's motive it will be advisable to pay closer attention to the *consequences* of his monistic thesis. For instance, monism provides him with a simple and ready explanation for why our clear and distinct ideas are always (and even necessarily) true: these ideas are ultimately divine ideas, and hence are *identical* to what they represent. In addition to this epistemological advantage, substance monism offers new perspectives on the relationship between body and mind. If there is only one, divine substance and if we retain the Cartesian dictum that the difference between thinking and extension is irreducible, then it is natural to regard them as different attributes of one and the same substance. If this idea can be fleshed out in a consistent way, an attractive nonreductive identity theory of the mind–body relationship could be developed – from the very same resources that would explain the necessary truth of our clear and distinct ideas.

In the first part of this chapter I will outline Spinoza's proof for substance monism in Part 1 of the *Ethics* and argue that Spinoza makes implicit use of the scholastic premise that God is absolutely simple. This, however, will lead to an intricate problem that already bothered the scholastic philosophers: how can divine simplicity be compatible with the multiplicity of divine attributes? In the second part of this chapter I will contend that this problem can be solved by means of the concept of a 'formal distinction' as it can be found in Duns Scotus, and I will suggest that a similar concept is at work in Spinoza's theory. In the third part I will finally try to outline how Spinoza applies the solution of this theological problem to his philosophy of mind in order to develop his theory of the mind–body relationship.

## I. THE ARGUMENT FOR SUBSTANCE MONISM

Spinoza assumes that nothing has being apart from 'substances' and 'modes', for, as he says in an axiom, '[w]hatever is, is either in itself or in another' (1a1). But what is in itself is a substance (1d3), and what is in another is a mode (1d5). In addition, Spinoza's ontology contains 'attributes'. Attributes are essential properties of substances. As essential properties they are constitutive of the substances that they

---

4  See for example Feuerbach 1847 [1833], 300–316. Feuerbach even sees a contradiction here in Descartes: it is impossible that something (*res extensa, res cogitans*) can be 'conceived through itself' and at the same time be dependent on something else for its existence. This argument, however, already presupposes Spinozistic premises concerning the relation between causality and conception.

characterise, and therefore Spinoza does not mention them separately in his list: if a substance is given, the attributes are given without further ado. We will even see later that substances are *identical* to their attributes. Modes are properties of substances, too, but they are only accidental properties; that is, they are not constitutive of the substances in which they inhere, and in this sense they can be said to be distinct from them.[5] They relate to attributes as determinates do to determinables. Spinoza's concepts of substance and attribute have been the subject of a lively debate, but it seems to me that there is, in fact, nothing especially surprising in Spinoza's classification of what there is; it is part and parcel of the standard Cartesian ontology.[6]

What is surprising, however, is that Spinoza contends that that there can be only one substance, that is, God. For this contention Spinoza offers a proof that comprises two steps. In the first step (1p1–p8), it is shown that there can be at most one substance per attribute; that is, there cannot be several substances that have the same attribute in common. In the second step (1p9–p14), it is shown that there is only one substance for all attributes. Spinoza's argument for the first thesis reads as follows:

If there were two or more distinct substances, they would have to be distinguished from one another either by a difference in their attributes, or by a difference in their affections (by p4). If only by a difference in their attributes, then it will be conceded that there is only one of the same attribute. But if by a difference

---

[5] The fact that modes are accidental properties will be of some importance for the interpretations of 1p5. However, some might object that according to 1p16 the modes follow from the definition (and hence from the essence) of the substance. This suggests that the modes are essential properties or parts of the essence of the substance. This cannot be right, however, as becomes evident in 2p10, where Spinoza argues as follows: (1) $x$ belongs to the essence of $y$ only if the definition of $y$ (expressing that without which $y$ neither can be nor be conceived) includes $x$ – *and vice versa*. (2) Now the definition of a mode includes God (whose mode it is and on whom it depends), *but not vice versa*: the definition of God does not include the modes; he can be conceived without them. (3) Therefore, God, according to the definition given above, does not belong to the essence of a mode. What is crucial for us is step (2): God can be conceived without modes; the modes are therefore accidents of God, not essential properties. If Spinoza asserts that they follow from the essence of God, this can only mean that they are *propria* of God: *necessary* properties that are, however, not contained in the definition or the essence of a thing and are, therefore, only accidental properties. *Propria* are necessary accidental properties. Spinoza is well acquainted with this terminology. In the *Short Treatise* I.1 he says about 'propria': 'God is, indeed, not God without them, but he is not God through them, because they indicate nothing substantive, but are only like *Adjectives*, which require *Substantives* in order to be explained' (G I, 18; C I, 64; see also the almost identical passage in I.3 of the same work [G I, 35]).

[6] For a detailed account of these matters, see Viljanen's contribution to this volume.

in their affections, then since a substance is prior in nature to its affections (by p1), if the affections are put to one side and [the substance] is considered in itself, i.e. (by d3 and a6), considered truly, one cannot be conceived to be distinguished from another, i.e. (by P4), there cannot be many, but only one [of the same nature or attribute], Q.E.D. (1p5)

In this proof Spinoza makes implicit use of the *principle of the identity of indiscernibles*: numerically distinct entities by necessity have different properties; numerical distinctness has to be, as it were, latched onto a difference of properties.[7] I would argue that Spinoza reasons in the following way. We have two kinds of properties available in the *Ethics*: attributes and modes. The proof, therefore, runs as follows:

1. Numerically distinct substances must differ from one another either by their attributes or by their modes.
2. However, numerically distinct substances cannot differ from one another by their modes alone.
3. Thus numerically distinct substances must differ from one another by their attributes.

Why is 2 the case? Jonathan Bennett attributes the following modal argument to Spinoza: Modes are accidental properties. But no substance can be individuated by its accidental properties, because accidental properties are properties that can be lost by a substance. Therefore it could happen that two distinct substances became identical with respect to their properties and – by the Principle of the Identity of Indiscernibles – thus became numerically identical. This, however, would be absurd. Bennett regards this argument as invalid, because from the fact that two substances differ only in their accidental properties, it does not follow that they could become qualitatively identical: 'From the premiss that (Fx and possibly Fy) it does not follow that possibly (Fx and Fy). That move is an instance of the notorious modal fallacy of inferring from (P and possibly Q) that possibly (P and Q): to see the invalidity, take the case where Q is not-P'.[8] I think that Bennett is on the right track here: Spinoza's argument is based on the fact that modes are accidental properties and that no substance can be individuated by its accidental properties.

But this can be shown without having to rely on the argument that Bennett rejects. Suppose that it is an accidental property that individuates a substance. An accidental property being a property that an object does not possess in all possible worlds in which it exists, there is at

---

[7] In formal notation: $(\forall F)\,(Fx \leftrightarrow Fy) \rightarrow (x = y)$. See also Viljanen's contribution to this volume.

[8] Bennett 1984, 68.

least one possible world in which the object exists without possessing the property.[9] In the case under consideration, however, the property is supposed to be the property by virtue of which the object is the very individual that it is. But it seems absurd to say that there is *one and the same* object both in the actual world and in a possible world, in which, however, it is a *different* individual or no individual at all. Let us call, for example, the property that individuates Socrates 'being-identical-to-Socrates' (however this property may be spelled out in detail). It does not make sense to say that there is a possible world in which Socrates exists but in which he is not identical to Socrates (although there certainly are possible worlds in which he exists and is not called 'Socrates'). What individuates a substance must therefore be an essential property, and only attributes are essential properties in the ontological framework of Spinoza's *Ethics*.[10]

So there can be at most one substance per attribute and thus at most as many substances as there are attributes. No more, but perhaps fewer. And for Spinoza there are fewer indeed, because for him there is no substance besides God. So let us now turn to Spinoza's proof for the uniqueness of the divine substance:

Since God is an absolutely infinite being, of whom no attribute which expresses an essence of substance can be denied (by d6), and he necessarily exists (by p11), if there were any substance except God, it would have to be explained through some attribute of God, and so two substances of the same attribute would exist, which (by p5) is absurd. And so except God, no substance can be or, consequently, be conceived. For if it could be conceived, it would have to be conceived as existing. But this (by the first part of this demonstration) is absurd. Therefore, except for God no substance can be or be conceived, Q.E.D. (1p14d)

---

[9] Keeping Spinoza's necessitarianism in mind, we must say that possible worlds in this case are worlds that are compatible with the essential properties of God.

[10] The fact that only necessary properties individuate substances is to a large extent Aristotelian and scholastic common sense (see Carriero 1995, 251). What is new, however, is that Spinoza – just like Descartes, at least in some passages – identifies these essential properties of a substance with its *summum genus*. That is a crucial step, because for an Aristotelian there are of course different substances of the same *genus*. For an Aristotelian the essential properties of a substance are made up of its *species infima*: the *summum genus* at the top of the Porphyrian Tree – say, being a substance – is divided into 'material' and 'immaterial', 'material' is divided into 'living' and 'nonliving', 'living' into 'sentient' and 'nonsentient', 'sentient' into 'rational' and 'nonrational' (or 'brute'). Only here, on the lowest level, do we find the essence of things, as for example in the case of a human being the essential property of being a rational, sentient, living, material substance. Not so in Descartes and Spinoza, according to whom there is no hierarchy of essential properties that could be arranged in the form of a Porphyrian Tree. The *summum genus* is identical to the *species infima*: it defines the essence of a thing.

Let us suppose that God exists; then there is a substance that by def-inition has all attributes – according to 1d6: 'By God I understand a being absolutely infinite, i.e., a substance consisting of an infinity of attributes, of which each one expresses an eternal and infinite essence.' Because for Spinoza infinity implies totality,[11] this substance takes pos-session, as it were, of all the attributes, so that no remainder is left to individuate any further substance. It is worth pointing out that this is a 'top down' and not a 'bottom up' proof. That is, Spinoza does not proceed in such a way that he examines the attributes in order to track down something *in them* that points to the fact that they are all attributes of one and the same substance. Rather he proceeds from the definition of God. From that definition it follows that all the attributes are attributes of God. If we were to limit ourselves to the investigation of the attributes alone, without invoking the definition of God, we would never discover that the attributes are attributes of the same substance; we only learn this by grasping the definition of God – and by knowing that God exists. As I said before, if all attributes are attributes of the same substance, no attribute is left to individuate a substance distinct from it.[12]

But, so one might object, could it not be that God possesses all the attributes – say, the attributes $a$, $b$, and $c$ – and that there is another substance, distinct from God, that possesses only one attribute – say, attribute $a$? In this case, although God comprised all the attributes, there would be another substance that was essentially different from God,

---

[11] See for example 1p17s: 'But I think I have shown clearly enough (see p16) that from God's supreme power... infinitely many things in infinitely many modes, *i.e., all things*, have necessarily flowed, or always follow' (italics mine). Spinoza could argue: if the infinite does not contain everything, then there is something outside of the infinite, that is, there is more than the infinite, which is absurd, because the infinite by definition is that which cannot be part of something larger. See Bennett 1984, 76.

[12] The proof presupposes that God exists. But here arises a delicate problem: If God exists, we can grant that there can only be one substance. But if there are several substances, then God does not exist. It is therefore crucial for Spinoza to prove the existence of God. And he does so in 1p11. Unfortunately, this proof is based on the perfectly general proof that existence belongs to the essence of any substance, that is, that any substance necessarily exists (1p7). So the proof does not enable us decide whether God exists (and hence whether there is only one substance) or whether there are several substances (meaning that God does not exist). Spinoza seems to be well aware of this problem and tries to solve it by arguing that God has 'more power to exist' than any other substance with fewer attributes (see 1p11s). For this problem, see Kulstad 1996 and Della Rocca 2002. Kulstad tries to solve the problem by suggesting that God is a compound substance for Spinoza – a thesis that seems to me rather problematic, as will become apparent below. Della Rocca develops a quite elegant argument that is based on the Principle of Sufficient Reason and the idea of a 'conceptual barrier' between the attributes.

precisely in not having *all* the attributes but only *one*. The Principle of the Identity of Indiscernibles would thereby be satisfied.[13] The problem would not arise if Spinoza could use the premise that no substance, including God, had more than one attribute; but he clearly rejects this view.

The problem could be solved by inserting the premise that each attribute *completely* expresses the essence of its substance. But why should Spinoza accept this premise? He could easily derive it from the well-known scholastic doctrine of God's simplicity, as John Carriero has pointed out.[14] This doctrine, found, for example, in Augustine, Anselm, and Aquinas, says that God is devoid of any complexity or multiplicity of parts: neither does he have spatial or temporal parts, nor is he composed of essence and existence, form and matter, or act and potency, nor does the distinction of properties and the subject of properties apply to him.[15] If, however, the distinction of properties and the subject of properties does not apply to him, then God is not only (e.g.) omniscient, omnipotent, and perfectly good – he *is* omniscience, he *is* omnipotence, he *is* perfect goodness. And this is exactly the premise that Spinoza needs for 1p14 (and 1p5): God does not have a complex essence resulting from a conjunction of all attributes $(a + b + c)$, but his essence is, by virtue of his simplicity, *identical* to attribute $a$, *identical* to attribute $b$, *identical* to attribute $c$, so that the attributes $a$, $b$, and $c$ are *each* the essence of God.[16] In this way it is impossible for two substances to have an attribute in common and to be nonetheless distinct by virtue of their essences.

The simplicity doctrine could be pressed into service for understanding 1p5 and 1p14. But does Spinoza actually adopt the simplicity thesis? There are some clear indications that this is the case. First, he *explicitly*

---

[13] This problem is already relevant to the first step of the monism argument, 1p5. Could it not be that there are several substances that share the same attribute if they have one attribute in common but differ by some other attributes? This objection can already be found in Leibniz (1999, 1768). Different attempts to solve this problem are discussed in Garrett 1990 and in Viljanen's contribution to this volume.

[14] See Carriero 1994.

[15] According to Leftow (1990), the motive behind the simplicity thesis is the desire to preserve the idea that God is a totally independent being. If God is the creator of everything that is not identical to him and if God is not the creator of his essential properties then God's essential properties have to be identical to God.

[16] That follows, for example, from 2p1s, where Spinoza writes, '[s]o since we can conceive an infinite Being by *attending to thought alone*, Thought (by 1d4 and d6) is necessarily one of God's infinite attributes' (italics mine). For more textual support of the thesis that each attribute is sufficient to conceive the essence of the divine substance, see Della Rocca 2002, 19 ff., and Crane and Sandler 2005.

endorses the simplicity thesis in some early texts,[17] viz., in the *Metaphysical Thoughts*, published in 1663 (CM II.5, 'Of God's Simplicity'; G I, 257–8),[18] and in a letter to Hudde of 16 April 1666;[19] second, he argues in 1p12 and 1p13 that God is indivisible; third, he puts forward some claims in the *Ethics* that otherwise would be quite inexplicable, viz., the claims that substances and attributes are identical[20] and that essence and existence are one and the same in the case of God.[21]

But the simplicity thesis is not without difficulties. If God is simple, he is identical to his properties, which is already quite an odd consequence.[22] Moreover, if God is identical to his properties, his properties are identical to each other by virtue of the transitivity of identity. If God is not only omniscient, omnipotent, and perfectly good,

[17] Gueroult (1968, 233 ff., 446 ff.) alleges that Spinoza does not endorse the simplicity thesis in the *Ethics* any more, but I see no need to accept this view.

[18] 'Ostendendum itaque Deum non esse quid compositum, ex quo poterimus concludere ipsum esse ens simplicissimum' (G I, 258).

[19] 'Id [viz. ens necessarium] simplex, non verò ex partibus compositum esse' (G IV, 181).

[20] 'substantias, sive quod idem est [ . . . ] earum attributa' (1p4), 'Deus, sive omnia Dei attributa' (1p19). This identity of substance and attribute follows already from the definition of "substance": a substance is that which neither is in another nor is conceived through another. But a substance is conceived by its attribute. Thus the attribute is not anything distinct from the substance but identical to it.

[21] 'Dei existentia, ejusque essentia unum & idem sunt' (1p20). See also 'existentia attributorum ab eorum essentia non differat' (Ep10, to de Vries, G IV, 47). In the *Short Treatise* I.1 Spinoza uses this identification of essence and existence for a separate proof of the existence of God: 'The essences of things are from all eternity and will remain immutable to all eternity. God's existence is [his] essence. Therefore . . . " (G I, 15; C I, 61).

[22] For Plantinga (1980, 47) this is an absurd consequence of the simplicity thesis:

There are two difficulties, one substantial and the other truly monumental. In the first place if God is identical with each of his properties, then each of his properties is identical with each of his properties, so that God has but one property. This seems flatly incompatible with the obvious fact that God has several properties; he has both power and mercifulness, say, neither of which is identical with the other. In the second place, if God is identical with each of his properties, then, since each of his properties is a property, he is a property – a self-exemplifying property. Accordingly God has just one property: himself. This view is subject to a difficulty both obvious and overwhelming. No property could have created the world; no property could be omniscient, or, indeed, could know anything at all. If God is a property, then he isn't a person, but a mere abstract object; he has no knowledge, awareness, power, love or life. So taken, the simplicity doctrine seems an utter mistake.

The difficulty of God's being a property might be mitigated if properties are not conceived as abstract objects but as 'acts' in the Thomistic sense. God would then be 'pure act' without there being a substance, different from it, in which that act would inhere. This is suggested in Rogers 2000, 27 ff.

but identical to omniscience, omnipotence, and perfect goodness, then omniscience, omnipotence, and perfect goodness are identical. But omniscience, omnipotence, and perfect goodness do not *seem* to be the same. So how can the simplicity of God be preserved?

## 2. THE SIMPLICITY OF SUBSTANCE AND THE MULTIPLICITY OF ATTRIBUTES

Let us take a look at four attempts to show that the simplicity of God is compatible with the multiplicity of his attributes.

*First attempt*: It follows from the simplicity of God that all his properties are identical, which, however, seems wrong. But how do we know it is wrong? We know it – or think we know it – because we know that property instances in the case of finite creatures are not identical: Socrates's wisdom, at least, is not identical to his goodness. He could instantiate the one without instantiating the other. But perhaps, so the proposal goes, we are using these expressions equivocally: property A and property B could be different as regards finite creatures and *apparently* identical as regards God, because in the latter case 'A' and 'B' are nothing but different names for a third property C in God that is not instantiated in finite creatures. In this case it might be said that God has *only* property C (there is no multiplicity in him); this property C, however, is designated by a *plurality* of names that are transferred from the realm of finite creatures to God. In this way the essence of God is on the verge of becoming something unintelligible to us human beings. God's justice, for example, would be something completely different from human justice, for they would have nothing in common but their name.[23]

Could this be an attractive way to understand the relation between substance and attributes in Spinoza?[24] I do not think so, because for

---

[23] The idea that the multiplicity of divine attributes and the simplicity of God could be reconciled by rejecting univocity is to be found in, for example, Descartes: the perfections whose traces can be found in creatures do not univocally pertain to God, and so God remains ultimately unintelligible for finite minds (see *Resp.* II; AT VII 137–8). As to the problem of Descartes's attitude to univocity see esp. Goudriaan 1999, 213–19.

[24] As, for example, Hegel (1985 [1832], 101) thinks: '[The attributes] are for him [viz. Spinoza] not even moments [of the substance], because the substance is in itself the absolutely indeterminate, and the attributes, as well as the modes, are distinctions made by the external intellect', and 'As far as absolute indifference might seem the basic determination of the Spinozistic substance, it may be noted here that this is indeed the case in this respect that in both of them all determinations of being, as well as in general every further concrete difference of thinking and extension etc., are posited as vanished. If one stops at this abstraction, it is totally indifferent how

Spinoza the essence of God is intelligible to the highest possible degree. The attributes have a double function in the *Ethics*: they express the essence of God and are the determinables by means of which the modes – that is, the finite things – are conceived. The predicates that express the attributes are therefore used univocally in relation to God and in relation to the modes. When Spinoza writes that an attribute is 'what the intellect perceives of a substance, as constituting its essence' (1d4), this does not involve any subjectivization of attributes,[25] because 'what is contained objectively [that is, as representational content, AS] in the intellect must necessarily be in nature' (1p30d). So the essence perceived is nothing but the essence as it is in itself: '[B]y God's attributes are to be understood what (by d4) expresses an essence of the Divine substance, i.e., what pertains to substance' (1p19d). If, however, the predicates are used univocally in relation to God and in relation to finite beings, then our old problem remains unsolved: either the attributes are identical both in God and in the realm of finite beings – which seems wrong – or they are *not* identical both in God and in the realm of finite beings – which seems to violate divine simplicity. How can simplicity and univocity be made compatible?

*Second attempt*: Perhaps one could distinguish between (abstract) properties and (concrete) property instances. So it could be argued that in God the property instances are identical, whereas the (abstract) properties are different and can be separately instantiated by finite beings.[26] At least this view would have the consequence that God, although identical with a property, would not be an abstract object, but something concrete. But this attempt fails, too: First, because it is difficult to see why the property instances should be identical, if the properties are not. It seems that two property instances can only be identical if the properties are (at least) necessarily coextensive;[27] but the problem is that they are not coextensive in the case under consideration. And if we limit this account to the *divine* property instances and say that the *divine* properties are necessarily coextensive and their instances therefore identical, it is hard to see how the univocity with the properties pertaining to finite beings can be preserved; for in this case, strangely, 'God has divine F' would not entail 'God has F'. Second, the proposal fails because the ontological

---

this that has perished in this abyss looked like in his determinate being [*Dasein*]' (ibid., 380).

[25] *Contra* Wolfson 1934 I, 152.

[26] See Bennett 1969, 628–37. A similar position can be found in Mann 1982; for criticism, see Morris 1987.

[27] Necessary coextensivity is a necessary condition for property identity; it is not so clear whether it is also a sufficient condition, as Mann contends. See Davis 2001, 71–4.

separation of (abstract) properties and (concrete) property instances violates the principle of God's independence. For if the essential properties of God were abstract entities that existed independent of their instances and if God existed only *by virtue of* instantiating these properties, then God's existence would depend on something that was neither identical to God nor created by God. (God cannot be identical to these properties, because it is only due to this nonidentity that they could be excluded from God's simple being.) But the idea that God depends on something that is not identical to him is unacceptable both to a traditional theist, for whom God is perfectly self-sufficient, and to Spinoza, for whom God can only be and be conceived through himself and cannot, therefore, depend on anything else.[28]

*Third attempt*: Should one say instead that the different attributes are nothing but different aspects of what is actually one attribute and that the differences are only due to a conceptual distinction (*distinctio rationis*) created by the intellect?[29] In this case it only *seems* to us that, for example, thinking and extension are two different attributes that are separately instantiable; if we had a sufficient insight into the nature of things, we would clearly and distinctly see that the apparently distinct attributes are actually one and the same attribute, seen from two (incomplete and therefore inadequate) viewpoints. This was indeed Spinoza's position in his *Metaphysical Thoughts*: 'And from this we can now clearly conclude that all the distinctions we make between the attributes of God are only distinctions of reason [*distinctionis... rationis*] – the attributes are not really [*reverâ*] distinguished from one another' (CM II.5; G I, 259; C I, 324–5). In the *Ethics*, however, things are different: Here Spinoza says explicitly that different attributes 'must be conceived to be really distinct [*realiter distincta*] (i.e., one may be conceived without the aid of the other)' (1p10s).[30]

---

[28] Moreover, Spinoza rejects the existence of universals anyway (see 2p40s1).

[29] This is a view held, for example, by Crane and Sandler 2005, 197: 'a distinction between attributes is a mere *distinctio rationis* and therefore not sufficient for metaphysical individuation.'

[30] 'attributa realiter distincta concipiantur, hoc est, unum sine ope alterius' (1p10s). The view that in the *Ethics* the difference between the attributes is merely subjective is criticised in Gueroult 1968, Appendices 3 and 4, 428–68. Even for those who do not see any simplicity thesis at work in Spinoza's *Ethics*, 1p10s offers a problem concerning the compatibility between the unity of the divine substance and the plurality of its attributes, because according to the Cartesian view there is a *distinctio realis* if and only if two entities can exist separately from each other, and for Descartes that two entities can possibly exist separately from each other is sufficient for them to be two substances. So if the attributes are really distinct, there should be many substances – one per attribute. But for Spinoza there is only

*Fourth attempt*: An interesting proposal on how to solve the simplicity problem has been made by Gilles Deleuze. Deleuze suggests that
the *distinctio realis* between Spinoza's attributes should be understood
along the lines of the Scotist *distinctio formalis*.[31] In the following I
would like to take a closer look at this proposal. Duns Scotus, to whom
we owe this term, distinguishes between a *distinctio realis* and a *distinctio formalis* as follows: *x* is *really* distinct from *y* if *x* can exist
without *y*, or *y* without *x*, or both.[32] Moreover, there is a *formal* distinction between *x* and *y* if the definition of *x* does not include the notion of
*y* or the definition of *y* does not include the notion of *x* or both.[33] Duns
Scotus thinks it is possible that *x* and *y* are *really* identical (i.e., they cannot exist independently from each other) but *formally* distinct (i.e., their

one substance. Spinoza seems to be committed both to the singularity of substance and to the multiplicity of substances. What kind of tie could unify these
substances into a single substance? If God is composed of several substances, his
unity is only an accidental one and he is an aggregate conceived through its parts
and not a substance conceived through itself. If, however, he is a substance, the
attributes have to be essentially united in such a way that they are not capable of
existing separately – and so are not really distinct. Della Rocca (2002) argues that
many attributes can pertain to one and the same substance precisely *because* they
are really distinct: if each attribute is conceived through itself, no attribute can
*exclude* the other. But because each attribute expresses the complete essence of
the substance, the question remains of how one and the same thing can have many
essences.

[31] Deleuze 1997 [1968], 63–7. (But see Gueroult 1968, 238, n. 38: 'C'est pourquoi Dieu
n'est pas un être absolument simple où les attributs cesseraient de se distinguer.
Leur distinction n'y est pas simplement virtuelle, et actuelle seulement dans leurs
effets, – comme le professent les thomistes, – ni simplement formelle (par leur
définitions), – comme le veulent les scotistes, – car ils y demeurent des *réalités
diverses*, incommensurables, ne s'intégrant dans un être, indivisible et non pas
simple, que par l'identité de l'acte causal par lequel ils se donnent l'existence et
produisent leurs modes.') On the *distinctio formalis* in Duns Scotus, see Grajewski
1944. The relation between the simplicity of God and the multiplicity of divine
attributes in Duns Scotus is discussed in Cross 2005, 99–114.

[32] See Henninger 1989, 71.

[33] Henninger's (actually more complex) definition is based on the following passage
by Duns Scotus (1968, 766): 'To include something formally means to include
something in its essential *ratio*, so that, if a definition were assigned to the including item, the included item would be either its definition or a part of its definition.
Just as the definition of goodness in general does not include wisdom, infinite goodness does not include infinite wisdom. So there is a certain formal non-identity
of wisdom and goodness as far as their definition would be different if they were
definable.' ([I]ncludere formaliter est includere aliquid in ratione sua essentiali,
ita quòd si definitio includentis assignaretur, inclusum esset definitio, vel pars
definitionis. Sicut autem definitio bonitatis in communi non habet sapientiam in
se: ita nec infinita infinitam. Est igitur aliqua non identitas formalis sapientiae &
bonitatis, inquantùm earum essent distinctae definitiones, se essent definibiles.')

definitions can be conceived independent from each other – mutually or unilaterally). He applies this distinction of *distinctio realis* and *distinctio formalis* to the divine attributes and believes that in this way he can salvage divine simplicity from the threat that is posed to it by the multiplicity of divine attributes. He argues as follows: the divine attributes are formally distinct, that is, they can be defined independently from one another. To God, however, they only appertain to the mode of infinity and by virtue of this infinity are identical in God. Their *formal* distinction, however, remains uninvolved because 'infinity does not destroy the formal definition of that to which it is added.'[34]

Let us ask first, Why are the attributes, for Duns Scotus, identical by virtue of divine infinity? The reason for this lies in the fact that for Duns Scotus the simplicity of God is entailed by the infinity of God. The proof that Duns Scotus presents in the *Tractatus de primo principio* for that claim takes the form of a *reductio ad absurdum*. Assume that the infinite God is a whole constituted of parts. If so, the parts are either finite or infinite. They cannot be finite, however, because from something finite nothing infinite can be composed. They also cannot be infinite, because the part has to be smaller than the whole and an infinite is not smaller than another infinite.[35] Thus God is not a whole composed of parts, and hence must be simple [Q.E.D.].[36] If God is simple, there is no real multiplicity in him. Accordingly, the infinite divine attributes cannot be parts that constitute God. So if we transpose a property, for example wisdom, into the mode of infinity – that is, if we conceive it as appertaining to an infinite being – then no second property in God would fail to be really identical to the first. Thus the divine attributes are really

---

34 '[I]nfinitas enim non destruit formaliter rationem illius, cui additur' (ibid.).

35 See also 1p15s: 'If corporeal substance is infinite, they say, let us conceive it to be divided in two parts. Each part will be either finite or infinite. If the former, then an infinite is composed of two finite parts, which is absurd. If the latter [NS: that is, if each part is infinite], then there is one infinite twice as large as another, which is also absurd.' Spinoza's opponents want to show by the following argument that space cannot be an attribute of God: (a) space is divisible, (b) nothing that is divisible can be infinite, (c) God is infinite, (d) therefore space is not an attribute of God. Spinoza accepts (b) but denies (a). Therefore space can be an attribute of God.

36 '*Ex infinitate sequitur omnimoda simplicitas*. Prima [simplicitas] intrinseca in essentia – quia aut componeretur ex finitis in se aut ex infinitis in se; si primum, igitur finitum; si secundum, igitur pars [non] minor toto' (Duns Scotus 1982, 134–5). However, the premise that a part has to be smaller than the whole and that therefore nothing infinite can be a part of the infinite seems to be a highly problematic view, as Cantor has argued: the set of all even integers is a subset of the set of all integers – but both sets have the same cardinality because there is a bijection from one set to the other.

identical by virtue of God's infinity. But Duns Scotus emphasises that nevertheless they remain at the same time formally distinct:

I admit that the notion [*ratio*] of [divine] wisdom is infinite, and so is the notion of [divine] goodness, and that therefore this notion is identical to that, for an opposite is not compatible with the infinity of the other extreme. Nevertheless this notion is not formally that one. For it does not follow: "It is really identical to the other, therefore it is formally identical to it." There is, indeed, a true identity of A and B without A formally including the notion of B.[37]

The formal difference of divine attributes is, however, not to be mistaken for a conceptual difference, viz., with differences that exist only *in mente*; rather, the different predications have different 'truth makers' in the thing itself:

A definition does not only signify a notion produced by the intellect but a quiddity of the thing: There is, therefore, a formal nonidentity on the part of the thing. By this I mean that the intellect that composes 'Wisdom is not formally Goodness' does not create the truth of this composite by its act of composing, but it finds the extremes – whose composition brings forth the true composite – in its object.[38]

The crucial question is, How is it *possible* that the attributes are really identical and formally distinct? Duns Scotus's radical thesis seems to commit him to suspending the converse of the Principle of the Identity of Indiscernibles – the Principle of the Indiscernibility of Identicals[39] – so that it is possible that, although x and y are identical, x has different properties from y.[40] In this way it becomes possible that God is identical to his wisdom and identical to his goodness, and hence – by the transitivity of identity – that God's wisdom and God's goodness are really identical (that they are one and the same *res*, not numerically different constituents of God), but that nevertheless wisdom and goodness are

---

[37] '[C]oncedo, quòd ratio sapientiae est infinita, & ratio bonitatis, & ideò haec ratio est illa per identitatem; quia oppositum non stat cum infinitate alterius extremi: tamen haec ratio non est formaliter illa. Non enim sequitur, est verè idem alteri, ergo formaliter idem eidem. Est enim vera identitas A, & B, absque hoc quòd A includat formaliter rationem ipsius B' (Duns Scotus 1968, 770).

[38] '[D]efinitio non tantùm indicat rationem causatam ab intellectu, sed quidditatem rei: ergo non est [*read*: est non-] identitas formalis ex parte rei. Et intelligo sic, quòd intellectus componens istam, *sapientia non est bonitas formaliter*, non causat actu suo collatiuo veritatem istius compositionis: sed in obiecto inuenit extrema, ex quorum compositione fit actus verus' (Duns Scotus 1968, 766).

[39] In formal notation: $(x = y) \rightarrow (\forall F)(Fx \leftrightarrow Fy)$.

[40] This step also has some benefits for Scotus's Trinitarian theology; see Iribarren 2002.

formally distinct, because they have separate definitions. So from their real identity it does not follow that they are indistinguishable.[41]

I propose that we read Spinoza as endorsing such a conception of real identity and formal distinction.[42] Let us take a closer look at 1p10s, where Spinoza writes: '[A]lthough two attributes may be conceived to be really distinct (i.e., one may be conceived without the aid of the other), we still can not infer from that that they constitute two beings, *or two different substances*.' Within a Cartesian framework this statement would not make any sense. If two beings can be conceived separately they are really distinct; but to be really distinct means for Descartes to be able to exist separately, and this in turn is the criterion for there being numerically distinct substances.[43] But Spinoza's statement begins to make sense once we take 'real difference' to mean the same as the Scotist 'formal distinction': formal distinction in no way entails numerical difference among substances.

The upshot of all this is that the attributes of the substance, for example, extension and thought, are formally distinct, for each attribute is 'conceived through itself': its definition does not include the notion of the other. Therefore it *seems* as if they could exist independent of each other as is alleged in Cartesian substance dualism – as if they were really (that is, numerically) distinct. And we can indeed examine the attributes themselves as thoroughly as we like; nothing in them will reveal their identity. But if we know that they are attributes of God and that God is simple, we can conclude that the attributes are really identical – God *is* extension, God *is* thinking, etc. – without abolishing thereby their formal distinction.

But why then does Spinoza appeal to a 'real distinction' and not so much as mention a 'formal distinction' between attributes? Is our hypothesis not falsified at the outset by the wording of the text? I do not

---

[41] See Adams 1986, esp. 417.

[42] Perhaps it might be surmised that Spinoza in fact does not reject the Principle of Indiscernibility of Identicals but only abandons the transitivity of identity. Spinoza, however, accepts the latter explicitly – at least at the time he wrote the *Metaphysical Thoughts*: 'As to my saying that the Son of God is the Father himself, I think it follows clearly from this axiom, namely, that things which agree with a third thing agree with one another' (Ep12A; Spinoza 1995, 108). It is true, however, that if Spinoza rejects the Principle of Indiscernibility of Identicals, the transitivity of identity has to be limited to establish numerical identity; it must not encroach on cases of *formal* identity. It should be noted, by the way, that the Principle of Indiscernibility of Identicals should not be mistaken for its converse, the Principle of the Identity of Indiscernibles. As we have seen, Spinoza makes use of this principle in the first step of his argument for monism (1p5).

[43] See Descartes's *Meditation* 3 (AT VII, 78) and *Principles of Philosophy* 1.60 (AT VIII/1, 28; CSM I, 213).

think so. For a formal distinction *is* a real distinction in the wider sense, that is, a distinction that has its foundation in the things itself and that is not only imposed on them by us. As stated already, 'A definition does not only signify a notion produced by the intellect but a quiddity of the thing: There is, therefore, a formal nonidentity on the part of the thing.'[44] This is why some followers of Duns Scotus took the formal distinction as a species of the real distinction.[45]

## 3. SPINOZA'S IDENTITY THEORY OF MIND AND BODY

It may seem that the question of how to bring divine simplicity into agreement with the multiplicity of divine attributes is a rather remote theological conundrum that is of little philosophical interest. Even in contemporary theology the simplicity thesis cannot be said to enjoy excessive popularity. But as a committed substance monist, Spinoza is able to derive from the simplicity thesis a theory about the relation between body and mind in finite beings that is not without interest and that I would like to address briefly in this last section. An infinity of attributes pertain to the divine substance, of which, however, we only know two: thought and extension. How are human beings related to these attributes? Human beings obviously are not substances – there is only one, viz., the divine substance. Because there is nothing apart from substances and modes, human beings must be modes: modes of the divine substance. But which attributes are they modifications of? Human beings have both physical and mental properties, and so their physical properties are modifications of the attribute of divine extension, and their mental properties are modifications of the attribute of divine thinking – portions of divine thinking, as it were. Because thinking and extension are identical in God, the same is true for the modes of thought and extension that constitute human beings: each mental property is identical with a physical property (and vice versa). So the thesis of divine simplicity, together with substance monism, entails an identity theory of mind and body – a theory that enjoys great popularity in the contemporary philosophy of mind. So the question arises of whether Spinoza could make an interesting contribution to the debate.[46]

For identity theorists, mental phenomena, such as pain, are identical with neuronal states – say, with the firing of C-fibres. Thus, statements about pain refer to the same entity as statements about the firing of

---

[44] 'Definitio autem non tantùm indicat rationem causatam ab intellectu, sed quiditatem rei: ergo non est identitas formalis ex parte rei' (Duns Scotus 1968, 766).

[45] So for instance in William of Alnwick. See Noone 1999, 53–72.

[46] On Spinoza's identity theory of mind and body and its relation to contemporary discussions, see Pauen 2003.

C-fibres. Yet pain and the firing of C-fibres *seem* to be very different. This difference is explained by the identity theorists as a difference in the kind of access to one and the same thing. On the one hand, we have a direct, 'inner' access to the firing of our C-fibres that is not mediated by outer perceptions: this is the phenomenon of pain. On the other hand, we have access to the firing of our C-fibres via outer perception and scientific instruments – through an objectifying knowledge of our C-fibres. The identity theory has the advantage that it can solve the problem of mind–body interaction in a particularly simple and elegant way. If a mental state is identical to a physical state it is hardly surprising that it is able to cause another physical state. The dualist, in contrast, faces a serious problem here. The problem is not so much – as is often assumed – that mental and physical properties are so heterogeneous that their causal interaction becomes a mystery. That would only be a problem for someone who advocates a 'transmission' theory of causality according to which the causal agent literally passes on one of its properties to the object in which the effect appears – as, for instance, a billiard ball seems to communicate its movement to another billiard ball through hitting it. It is clear that the mind has no properties that the body could employ and vice versa. But there is no compelling reason to adhere to such a transmission theory of causality; even our paradigm dualist Descartes does not seem to have endorsed it. The real problem of mind–body interaction is due to the laws of conservation: if there is only a certain quantity of energy in the physical world, which remains constant, it seems impossible to add any energy from the outside by way of causal influence from the mind, or to discharge any energy to the outside by affecting the mind. For the identity theorist no such problem arises; but there are problems of a different kind to be dealt with. If we say that two representations that seemingly refer to different objects are in truth nothing but two different perspectives on one and the same object, it must be possible to explain how these different perspectives are brought about. If we say that the morning star and the evening star are in truth one and the same object, it must be possible to explain why the same astronomical object appears at one time as the brightest star in the morning sky, and at another time as the brightest star in the evening sky. In the case of the evening star and the morning star, astronomy provides us with the required explanation. But it is extremely difficult to offer a similar explanation of how pain and the firing of C-fibres are related. Because most contemporary identity theorists are physicalists, they would have to tell a physicalist story about why the firing of C-fibres, 'seen from the inside', *is pain*, that is, why pain feels like it does. That, however, seems a difficult task. Usually we proceed as follows when it comes to reductive explanations: if we want to say, for example, that water is identical to $H_2O$, we first determine the causal role that water has and then show that $H_2O$ can play exactly that role. But if we say that pain is identical to the firing of C-fibres, a similar procedure does not seem to be viable, because pain cannot be completely determined by its causal role. Pain seems to have an intrinsic, qualitative aspect that cannot be substituted by some nonmental causal surrogate.[47] As long as the identity theorist is unable to explain this qualitative aspect of mental properties by a physicalist story it seems that, after all, pain and the firing of C-fibres turn out to be two essentially different events or objects.

Spinoza's theory can be taken as an attempt to benefit from the advantages of an identity theory without accepting its pitfalls. Mental properties and physical properties are, on this view, really identical, so the problem of how mind and body could possibly interact does not arise. Yet at the same time they are formally distinct and neither can be reduced to the other, so Spinoza can do justice to the dualistic intuition. If one and the same thing seems to be a mental item from one perspective and a physical item from another perspective, then, as was said above, something should explain how one and the same thing can appear in these two ways. If, however, it is possible that one and the same thing can have two *natures*, a unifying explanation need not – indeed, cannot – be given. But even if it were conceded that it is possible that one and the same thing has two natures – that something can be really one and formally multiple – the question would still remain as to *why* one should plead for identity, given the different natures. Whoever does not accept the simplicity of God and the modal status of human beings may still argue that the identity thesis is the best way to explain the causal interaction between mind and body.

It may be objected that Spinoza denies any such interaction, for no mode pertaining to one attribute can be the cause of a mode pertaining to another attribute, as he makes clear in 3p2: 'The Body cannot determine the Mind to thinking, and the Mind cannot determine the Body to motion, to rest or to anything else (if there is anything else).' The reason is as follows. If A is the cause of B, B is conceived through A. But each attribute is conceived through itself and cannot contain any conceptual reference to another attribute. Causal closure pertains to each attribute. This has as a consequence that no modes of different attributes can causally interact with each other. What the identity theory can explain, however, is their *apparent* interaction in the case of mind and body. If it seems that a mode of thought A causes a mode of extension B, the mode

---

[47] Thus for example Swinburne 1997, 45–61. A useful overview of the topic is given in Pauen 2002, 188–216.

of thought A that apparently causes the mode of extension B is actually identical with the mode of extension A*.[48]

The idea of applying the Scotist theory of formal distinction to the mind–body relation can already be found in Johannes Caterus, who observes in his objections to Descartes's *Meditations* that for Duns Scotus separate conceivability does not entail the possibility of separate existence:

His [Descartes's] proof of the supposed distinction between the soul and the body appears to be based on the fact that the two can be distinctly conceived apart from each other. Here I refer the learned gentleman to Scotus, who says that for one object to be distinctly conceived apart from another, there need only be what he calls a *formal and objective* distinction between them (such a distinction is, he maintains, intermediate between a *real* distinction and a *conceptual* distinction). The distinction between God's justice and his mercy is of this kind. For, says Scotus, 'The formal concepts [*rationes formales*] of the two are distinct prior to any operation of the intellect, so that one is not the same as the other. Yet it does not follow that because justice and mercy can be conceived apart from one another they can therefore exist apart.' (*Meditations*, Obj. I; AT VII 100; CSM II, 72–3)

This passage does not tell us whether Caterus would like to embrace the thesis of real unity and formal distinctness of body and mind; at least he asserts it as a possibility in order to show that Descartes's argument for the real distinction of mind and body is not conclusive. Descartes answers that for him there is no formal distinction as a distinction *sui generis*.[49] Spinoza, however, whom we know to have been a diligent

---

[48] It could be argued that Spinoza should accept the possibility of causal interaction between body and mind if he endorses an identity theory, because in this case there is no good reason to consider this interaction as mere speciousness (see Delahunty 1985, 197). Della Rocca, however, objects that for Spinoza causal contexts are 'referentially opaque', so that coreferential expressions cannot be substituted. See Della Rocca 1996a, Ch. 7.

[49] In his answer to Caterus, Descartes identifies 'formal distinction' with 'modal distinction' (*Resp.* I; AT VII, 120–21; CSM II, 85–6), that is, with a distinction between two modes, in which each mode can be completely conceived without the other, but in which neither can be conceived without a third that in its turn is completely intelligible without the modes, viz., the substance whose modes they are (Descartes's example: *figura* and *motus* of a thing). Later on, he revises this account and identifies 'formal distinction' with 'conceptual distinction' (*distinctio rationis*), that is, with a distinction in which neither of the *distinguenda* can be completely conceived without the other (Descartes's new example: *substantia* and *duratio*). (See *Principles of Philosophy* 1.62; AT VIII, 30; CSM I, 214–15 and the *letter to* ***, 1645 or 1646; AT IV, 349.) Descartes's views are discussed in Justin Skirry 2004, 121–44.

reader of Descartes's work, may have taken up Caterus's hint and drawn his own conclusions from it. At least this passage shows that Scotist ideas were by no means unknown in Spinoza's time, so that Spinoza may very well have been acquainted with them without ever having read any of Duns Scotus's texts.[50,51]

[50] According to Ludger Honnefelder (2005, 132), the seventeenth century was '[t]he "golden age" of Scotism'.

[51] I would like to thank Valtteri Viljanen (and the 'Rationalist Circle' at Turku), Mike Stange, and Sasha Newton for help and advice.

# 5    Spinoza and the Stoics on Substance Monism

From his day to ours, commentators have been struck by the Stoic currents flowing through Spinoza's thought. Leibniz branded him a leader of a "sect of new Stoics" which held that "things act because of [the universe's] power and not due to a rational choice" (Leibniz 1989, 282). A few years later Bayle said in his *Dictionary*, "The doctrine of the world-soul, which was ... the principal part of the system of the Stoics, is at bottom the same as Spinoza's."[1] In our times, scholars such as Amélie Oksenberg Rorty and Susan James – hailing Spinoza as "the best of Stoics" – have written articles with titles such as "Spinoza the Stoic" in which they argue that he matched or even surpassed the Stoicism of the ancient Stoics in all respects: metaphysically/physically, methodologically/logically, and normatively/ethically.[2]

The similarities between Stoicism and Spinozism[3] are impressive, and they naturally lead to the thought that much would be learned about the two systems as well as larger philosophical issues if it could be determined how deep they run. In this essay, I contribute to that project, but with two important limitations. First, my exploration is purely philosophical; I will say nothing about Spinoza's knowledge of Stoicism. It is not that I don't have views on the issue or that I find it uninteresting; rather, it simply isn't possible for me to undertake both conceptual analysis and *Rezeptionsgeschichte* in the space available. Second, I will not provide a global comparison of the sort found in, say, James (1993) or Long (2003). Such work has its value, serving to

---

[1] Bayle (1740), article on Spinoza, entry A (my translation).
[2] See James 1993 and Rorty 1996. Others who have remarked on and discussed Spinoza's Stoicalness include Bidney 1940, Graeser 1991, Matheron 1994b, and Long 2003.
[3] In this paper, I will use 'Spinozism' (and its cognates) because it will often be the only unstrained pairing of Stoicism. It should be understood, however, that 'Spinozism' refers to Spinoza's own thought and its implications. In this respect, it differs crucially from the most common usage of 'Cartesian,' which is commonly taken to refer to Descartes's followers and general legacy, not necessarily the ideas of the man himself.

drawattention to the possibilities and excitement that lie in studying Spinoza *vis-à-vis* the Stoics. Yet it should be seen as propaedeutic: for our understanding of their relationship to mature, a different calibre of research is needed, one that offers a more fine-grained analysis. This essay belongs to that second wave of scholarship, as it aspires to examine systematically a specific tenet of Stoicism and Spinozism.

The tenet on which I will focus is the most distinguishing feature of the metaphysical system found in Spinoza's *Ethics*: namely, the claim that there is only one substance, out of which all else is somehow constituted. Spinoza argues for this early in the *Ethics*. Moreover, it figures crucially in issues such as the immortality of the soul that he addresses later in the book. For their part, although the Stoics' substance monism may not be as transparently important, it is nevertheless a pillar of their system. As we shall see, Spinoza's substance monism is similar to but not identical with that of the Stoics. By comparing his views on the one substance with those of the Stoics, we can better understand what is unique about Spinoza as well as what he shares with these philosophers, to whom he is so often related. In the first section of this chapter, I provide a broad overview of their respective monisms.[4] Once that is completed, my focus narrows to the argumentative bases for their theories. My goal throughout is to expound not on the concept of substance itself but rather on the idea that the whole world can be intelligibly and profitably conceived as a single being.

## I. STOIC AND SPINOZISTIC MONISMS

The aim of this section, then, is to frame out substance monism as conceived by Stoics and Spinoza. My approach will be dialectical, contrasting the two parties on specific issues, but because this conversation will flow more readily if I clarify roughly what I take the concept itself to mean, I shall start by making several points about substance monism *per se*.

As I shall understand it, substance monism is a philosophical thesis about the ultimate constituent of all being, holding that there is only one thing out of which everything else is derived. So discrete nameable members of the world, such as planets and desks and dogs and human beings, are not substances in the strict sense of that term; they are different ways in which substance has been configured or altered. Substance monism must be distinguished from a different kind of monism, propounded by the likes of William James, which holds that though there

---

[4] For brevity's sake, I will often speak of 'monism' instead of 'substance monism.' It should be understood that the monism in question is substance monism.

is only one type of stuff (say, matter), there are multiple tokens of this type, each of which counts as a substance.[5] In the next paragraph, I shall explain that monism does not have to agree that there is only one kind or type of stuff. Here I want to emphasise that monism denies that tokens of substance qualify as substances in their own right. It does not necessarily follow that those tokens – those discrete nameable members of the universe – are illusory or have no being. For this conclusion to follow, the additional premise that only substances are real or have being is needed. To be sure, monists may find themselves under considerable pressure to accept this premise, if only because they may have trouble explaining how things can be real without being substances in their own right. Yet there is no immediately obvious reason that a monist must be committed to the illusoriness of modifications of substance; and as we shall see at the end of this section, neither the Stoics nor Spinoza think of themselves as undertaking such a commitment.

Now, the single substance can be conceived in different ways. To the extent that there are substance monists nowadays, most of them would presumably think of it as broadly material, perhaps captured by the space-time continuum of theoretical physics.[6] It is also possible to take substance as broadly mental, so that thought or intensionality lies at the basis of all reality.[7] A third option takes substance to be *both* physical *and* mental; such a theory would therefore deny James's assumption that substance is a single kind of thing. How this might work is complicated; because it is how both Stoics and Spinoza understand substance, I shall say more about it in the pages that follow. For the moment, I will note that regardless of how substance is conceived, all substance monists agree that the ordinary phenomena of experience are not substances in the true sense; rather, they think that substance in the true sense is an abstract entity whose nature is discovered through philosophical reflection.[8]

---

[5] See James 1978. As I understand it, James' so-called "neutral monism" is actually slightly different from the theory alluded to in this sentence, in that it is neutral (hence the name) about the nature of the single kind of stuff out of which all individuals are derived.

[6] This seems to be the position that Theodore Sider (2001, 110) calls "substantivalism." Sider says that Quine toyed with it in the 1970s.

[7] If Plotinus's first Hypostasis or Principle, sometimes translated as 'the One,' is the only true substance in his metaphysical system, then he may provide an example of this kind of substance monism. See, for example, *Enneads* V.1 and Emilsson 1996, esp. n. 47.

[8] The three versions of substance monism just mentioned do not exhaust the possibilities. A pair of others are first, that substance is neither matter nor thought but some other knowable entity, and second, that the nature of substance is ineffable, neither matter nor thought nor anything else graspable by the human mind.

Coming to the Stoics, if that is approximately what substance monism is, then some doubt might immediately arise as to whether they really are substance monists. That is because Stoics made 'substance,' *stricto sensu*, one of their four basic ontological categories or genera, and so they thought many things were substances in this technical sense.[9] Such pluralism, licensed by their basic metaphysics, might seem flatly incompatible with monism. Without denying either of the premises, I do want to insist on the invalidity of the inference. The reason is simple: 'substance' can be used in many different ways; although it may be true that one sense of 'substance' implied or was compatible with pluralism, Stoics had another sense that was monistic. This is shown by such passages as "Zeno says that the whole world and heaven are the substance of god... "[10] and by images that depict "the whole cosmos as a living being [*zôion*], animate and rational."[11] In Stoicism, the cosmos or nature (*phusis*)[12] could be conceived as a single substance unified extensionally and intensionally by a single "breath" (*pneuma*) that was its "commanding faculty" (*hegemonikon*).[13] As we read in one text,

Zeno said that this substance itself is finite and that only this substance is common to all things which exist.... [S]ince it is as birthless as it is deathless because it neither comes into being from the non-existent nor turns into nothing, it does not lack an eternal spirit [*pneuma*] and liveliness which will move it in a rational manner.... And they call this [i.e., the cosmos] a happy animal and a god.[14]

Because Stoics think of "the world as a unitary system that contains all beings" (Long 2003, 10), they should be recognised as substance monists.

---

[9] See esp. Simplicius, *On Aristotle's Categories*, 222 (L-S 169). A word on translations: unless otherwise indicated, all Stoic translations will be from Long and Sedley 1987 or Inwood and Gerson 1997. When referring to them, I will employ the abbreviations "L-S" and "I-G," respectively. As for Spinoza, the *Letters* and TTP are from Spinoza 2002; all others are from C.

[10] Diogenes Laertius, *Lives of Eminent Philosophers*, VII.148 (L-S 266).

[11] Diogenes Laertius, *Lives of Eminent Philosophers*, VII. 139 (L-S 284).

[12] The distinction between cosmos and nature, important in some domains, does not enter here, because Stoics used both terms to refer to the same entity, which I am calling the single substance.

[13] See Galen, *On Bodily Mass* VII.525 (L-S 282). Note that here and throughout I am taking Chrysippus's theory to be canonical, so where there are deviations between his doctrine and those of others, I am silently following him. In the present case, for example, Cleanthes conceived of "vital heat" or "designing fire" and not breath as the unifying and sustaining power of the cosmos. See Cicero's report of Cleanthean physics in *De natura deorum*, II.23–30 (I-G 144–6).

[14] Chalcidius, *Commentary on Plato's* Timaeus, c. 292 (I-G 172). N.B.: The second two bracketed inserts are I-G's.

In the next section, I shall explore their argument for monism, so for now I want to expand on a few properties they attribute to the single substance. Foremost among these is corporeality. A simple argument led them to think that substance must be a body. Apparently accepting Plato's[15] idea that the ability to act or be acted upon is the hallmark of existence,[16] Stoics argued (not implausibly) that because only bodies have this ability,[17] it follows that only bodies exist.[18] Because it is plain that the single substance exists – after all, it is somehow constitutive of the whole universe – it must be the case that it is a body.[19]

The single corporeal substance is actually composed of two fundamentally different kinds of bodies, known as the "two principles" or *archai*.[20] Seneca explains what these are: "Matter lies inert, an entity ready for anything but destined to lie idle if no one moves it. Cause, on the other hand, being the same as reason, shapes matter and directs it wherever it wants, and from matter produces its manifold creations."[21] Both matter (the "passive principle") and cause (the "active" one) are bodies, so the distinction between cause and matter does not entail the introduction of an immaterial entity. What it does introduce is the notion of two kinds of bodies characterised qualitatively, as either intrinsically active or intrinsically passive. Because this notion is absent from the popular understanding of matter nowadays, scholars sometimes resist labelling Stoics "materialists." So A. A. Long (1986, 154) writes, "The Stoics are better described as vitalists. Their Nature... is a thing to which both thought and extension are attributable."

---

[15] See the *Sophist* 246a–b. For an excellent analysis of how the Stoics read this dialogue, see Brunschwig (1988).

[16] See, for example, Sextus Empiricus, *Against the Mathematicians*, VIII 263 (L-S 272).

[17] See, for example, Cicero, *Academica*, I.39 (L-S 272).

[18] See, for example, Alexander of Aphrodisias, *On Aristotle's Topics*, 301.23–5 (L-S 162).

[19] Even though Stoics vigorously argued that only bodies exist, they did not also assert that ontology is exhausted by bodies. It is possible that things could have being without having the peculiar kind of being known as 'existence.' In the Stoics' case, they posited "something" (*ti*) as the highest ontological category; immediately below "something" are "things which are incorporeal" and "things which are corporeal." This is the level at which existence enters into ontology, for it is here that bodies are encountered for the first time. They exist and incorporeal things do not. For a helpful introduction to Stoic ontology, see Long and Sedley 1987, 163f. For important criticism of Long and Sedley's commentary, see Brunschwig 1988.

[20] See, for example, Diogenes Laertius, *Lives of Eminent Philosophers*, VII.134 (L-S 268). Following all of the commentators cited in this essay, I am discounting the suggestion found in the *Suda* that the *archai* are incorporeal.

[21] *Ep.* 65.2.

On a related point, matter and cause are constantly conjoined with one another. Conceptually, they can and must be distinguished; by isolating them in our thought, we can identify their properties and understand the roles they play in the production of the universe and its constituents. Factually, however, they do not and never can appear apart from one another. There is no such thing as pure undifferentiated matter; it is always determined in some way or another by cause. Likewise, there is no such thing as pure undifferentiating cause; it is always determining matter in some way or another. As David Sedley (1999, 384–5) describes their relationship, "In any physical process a portion of matter [= passive principle], the essentially passive and formless locus of change, is altered by god [= active principle], the intelligent creative force which imbues it through and through and endows it with whatever properties it may have" (my brackets).

As a final preliminary point, Stoics are substance monists only at the level of fundamental physics: it is only when considering the ultimate object of physical inquiry that they defend monism. Because the single substance – that is, the world – as constituted by matter and reason can account only for purely general matters such as the possibility of change, it cannot explain localised phenomena. To obtain these explanations, Stoics accept pluralism. So, for example, Stoics subscribe to the traditional four-elements theory of fire, water, air, and earth. *Inter alia*, these elements are necessary for cosmological purposes, serving to explain how the world came to have earth at its centre and fire at the periphery.[22] Although the elements are reducible to the irreducibly basic substance described above, Stoics resisted the reduction when they were engaged in cosmology, climatology, and other matters.

I shall have more to say about Stoic monism in the pages below, so let me now turn to Spinoza. Starting with his acceptance of monism, it is traceable to his earliest writings. In the *Treatise on the Emendation of the Intellect*, for example, he frequently uses expressions suggestive of substance monism, such as when he speaks of the "wholeness," "order," and "unity" of "Nature."[23] In the *Short Treatise*, he explains that all "attributes which are in Nature are only one, single being... " and "Nature is a being of which all attributes are predicated" (KV 1.2.; G I, 23 and G I, 27, respectively). Like the Stoics, Spinoza does

---

[22] Cf. Stobaeus 1.129 (L-S 280) and Cicero, *De natura deorum* 2.23–5 (L-S 281).

[23] For 'wholeness,' see, for example, G II, 17 and G II, 28. For 'order,' see, for example, G II, 21 and G II, 25. For 'unity,' see, for example, G II, 36. For 'Nature' (with a magisterial N), see, for example, G II, 22 and G II, 35. It must be granted that in this work, Spinoza is not explicitly a substance monist, but the prevalence of words and concepts that are consonant with substance monism implies both a familiarity with and an acceptance of that thesis.

not consistently use the word 'substance' in his earlier writings when speaking of substance monism, favouring instead 'Nature' or 'God.' It is plain, however, that the view before him in those works is substance monism.[24] And it becomes utterly transparent in the key text from the *Ethics*, 1p14: "Except God, no substance can be or be conceived."

Because Spinoza is one of history's best exemplars of substance monism, there is no need to belabour the point. Instead, it is more interesting to consider whether any important differences between Spinoza and the Stoics are generated by the prominence of substance in Spinoza's thought. He states that there is only one substance; moreover, by devoting Part 1 of the *Ethics* to substance, he unambiguously signals that understanding it is a prerequisite to understanding the epistemological, psychological, and moral issues broached in Parts 2–5. By contrast, whereas the Stoics are substance monists, this is not completely obvious; nor is it obvious that they place substance at the basis of all philosophical investigation. Now, these differences may only be a matter of emphasis, not logic or content, but they deserve notice in this comparative essay. Whereas Spinozism is unmistakeably centred on substance, the same is not true of Stoicism.

And yet, if we are weighing emphasis here, we ought to add two more observations to the balance. From the Stoic side, they do make philosophical investigation begin with nature: we must first learn about it before we can advance to logic and ethics.[25] So, one might think, although they may not call it *substance*, they do have nature, and its conceptual and argumentative status seems similar to that of Spinoza's substance. Moreover, from Spinoza's side, he engages in a series of equations between God, substance, and nature. These equations at least partially validate the thought that Spinozistic philosophical investigation commences with an entity whose parameters are just as wide as the Stoics' nature. So, because Stoics have a concept that is equivalent in key respects to Spinoza's substance, and vice versa, the differences identified in the previous paragraph may appear not so great after all.

Because I want to return to first-order issues, I will let my readers decide what to make of that methodological conundrum.[26] Crucially

---

[24] So, for example, he argues in the *Short Treatise* that God is unitary and also that he is all-inclusive – in his words, "outside God there is nothing at all" (G I, 27). Given that there is only one God and given that he exhausts all existent being, it follows that there can only be one thing that exists. This is Spinoza's position in the *Short Treatise*; it is substance monism in all but name only.

[25] See, for example, Diogenes Laertius, *Lives of Eminent Philosophers*, VII. 39–41 (I-G 110–11). For discussion, see Annas 1993, Chapter Five, followed by Inwood 1995.

[26] I will also return to a question of method toward the end of this section.

among the remaining points I wish to make, Spinoza took the single substance to be composed of an "infinite" number of "attributes."[27] There
are problems surrounding the notion of infinity that we can ignore,[28] but
we must attend to the notion of attributes. In the official definition
of attribute Spinoza writes, "By attribute I understand that which the
intellect perceives of substance, as constituting its essence" (1d4). A key
exegetical problem spawned by this definition concerns the relationship
between substance and its attributes. There are, in the words of a recent
commentator, "two schools of thought" on this issue: first, there is the
view that "attributes really do constitute the essence of substance, and
do not merely appear to do so"; second, there is the view that attributes
do not really constitute substance's essence, but only appear to do so
from the perspective of the intellect (Lennon 2005, 19–20). If the former so-called "objective" interpretation is right, then because Spinoza
tells us that two attributes of substance are thought and extension,[29] it
follows that the essence of substance is *both* thought *and* extension.
By contrast, if the latter "subjective" interpretation is borne out, then
substance is essentially neither thought nor extension but something
else altogether. The minutiae of the debate between the opposing sides
are daunting.[30] Fortunately, we do not need to get into them to draw
useful connections between Spinoza's monism and that of the Stoics.

Recall how Stoics think that substance is, ultimately, wholly corporeal. Contrast this with Spinoza's substance. If it is taken 'objectively,'
then it is both thinking and extended, because those two attributes
really do capture two aspects of substance's being. On the other hand,
if it is taken 'subjectively,' it is neither thought nor extension, because
those two attributes are only two ways in which substance's being is
perceived. In either case, Spinoza's substance is not, ultimately, wholly
corporeal.[31] We have here, then, a basic metaphysical difference between
the Stoic conception of substance versus Spinoza's.

I do not think the difference can be denied but it may seem nuga-
tory from one perspective. Granted, Stoic substance is corporeal; yet
it is constituted by the twin principles of cause and matter. As noted
above, scholars of Stoicism take 'cause' and 'matter' to be equivalent
to 'thought' and 'extension,' respectively. So embedded in the Stoic

[27] See 1p11.
[28] For discussion of them, see Bennett 1984, 75–9.
[29] See 2p1 and 2p2.
[30] For a helpful summary, including a persuasive assessment of the merits of both
    sides, see Lennon 2005, 20–27.
[31] As he writes in 1p15s, "everyone who has to any extent contemplated the divine
    nature denies that God is corporeal" (G II, 57). See also his November or December
    1675 Letter (Ep73) to Oldenburg (G IV, 307).

substance are both thought and extension. Now consider Spinoza. The subjective interpretation does not read his 'substance' in these terms, because it denies that attributes are anything more than how substance appears to the intellect. So, if one favours the subjective interpretation, one will think that Spinoza's substance is greatly different from the Stoics': it is different both in that it is not wholly corporeal, and also in that it is not really mental and physical. However, things will look different from the perspective of the objective interpretation. Because it holds that substance's attributes really do reveal aspects of substance's being, and because substance has the attributes of thought and extension, it holds that substance is both thinking and extended. True, the objective interpretation does not find Spinoza's substance to be essentially corporeal in the way that the Stoics' substance is, for it sees Spinoza's substance as essentially thinking *and* extended. That disagreement notwithstanding, the objective interpretation gives us as good a reason to attribute intensionality and extensionality to Spinozistic substance as we have to attribute those same properties to the Stoic substance. So, from the perspective of the objective interpretation – which is the consensus view among scholars today[32] – Stoic and Spinozistic substance do not appear so different after all.[33]

The next issue I want to raise is tied to the foregoing; it concerns the way in which thought and extension are connected to one another. Two points in particular must be made about Spinoza's views on this matter. First, acknowledging that mental states plainly have something to do with physical states, he postulates a striking relationship between the mental and the physical, declaring that "The order and connection of ideas is the same as the order and connection of things" (2p7). In Spinoza's view, for any given mental state $x$ of substance, there is a state $x^*$ of substance that exactly corresponds to $x$, except that $x^*$ is physical. As he restates this doctrine of "parallelism" in 2p7s, "The thinking substance and the extended substance are one and the same substance, which is now comprehended under this attribute, now under that."[34] Because thought and extension are attributes of the same substance, and because this substance necessarily possesses those attributes (just as it necessarily possesses all attributes), it is impossible for them to exist apart from one another.

At the same time, because thought and extension are fundamentally different ways of being, it is also impossible for them to exist in a causal or logical relation to one another. And here we come to my second point

---

[32] Cf. Lennon 2005, 20.
[33] I will shortly address how Stoics and Spinoza conceived of thought and extension.
[34] See also 3p2s (at G II, 141.).

about Spinoza's views on the relationship of the mental to the physical. Mental states can give rise to other mental states; physical states can give rise to other physical states; but as Spinoza writes in 3p2, "The Body cannot determine the Mind to thinking, and the Mind cannot determine the Body to motion, to rest or to anything else. . . . " We can look at Spinoza's arguments for this barrier, but I find the suggestion that such dualism is part of the 'cast'[35] of his mind to be at least as edifying.

Even without plumbing the depths here,[36] an intriguing similarity and a striking difference with Stoicism's two principles are evident. Like Spinoza's attributes, the Stoic principles are inseparable. Although for the purposes of theory Stoics and Spinoza argued that the principles or attributes of substance must be distinguished from one another, they also argued that it is impossible for thought ever to occur apart from extension (and vice versa). So everything that exists – both substance and its products – will always be a combination of the mental and the physical. Both Stoics and Spinoza take this to be true.

On the other hand, they disagree on another matter: whereas Spinoza's attributes stand in no causal or logical relation to one another, the Stoic principles are defined by their causal relationship. The passive principle is matter *informed by cause*; the active principle is cause *in matter*. Put another way, "Matter needs [cause] in order to be a particular entity, and [cause] needs matter in order that there shall be some entity for [it] to characterize" (Long and Sedley 1987, 271). Although some of the differences discussed in this section may seem insignificant upon inspection, this one has implications that render it decidedly nontrivial. Let me explain.

Because of the independence of thought and extension, Spinoza cannot invoke words and ideas belonging to one attribute when explaining phenomena in terms of the other. Because all explanations must proceed solely in terms of one attribute, it follows that each attribute must possess sufficient conceptual resources to satisfy the explanatory demands being placed on it. So thought and extension, as formulated by Spinoza, are conceptually very rich. To cite but one instance, because all extended phenomena must ultimately be accounted for in terms of the attribute of extension, then because extended phenomena are active, it follows that extension itself is active. This is in sharp contrast with the Stoic concept of matter, which is simply defined as "what has 'threefold extension together with resistance'"[37] The broader point is

[35] See Bennett 1984, 47–50.
[36] For more, see Della Rocca 1996a, Ch. 7.
[37] Galen, *On incorporeal qualities*, 19.483 (L-S 272).

that, although both parties agree that substance is both thinking and extended, they disagree on the proper characterization of thought and extension. Stoics define thought and extension in terms of activity and passivity: all agency and whatever it takes to be an agent (reason, knowledge, the ability to formulate intentions, causal efficacy, etc.) belongs to thought, whereas extension amounts basically to occupying space. Just as he did Descartes,[38] so Spinoza would have found fault with what he would consider the Stoics' wrongheaded dualism of activity/passivity and their impoverished conceptions of thought and extension.

Moving on, my comparison has so far touched on four issues: the acceptance of substance monism; the status substance ought to have in philosophical investigation; whether substance is 'objectively' thought and extension; and how thought and extension are related. The next and final set of points I want to make concern the substance–mode ontology.

To understand the ontology, it helps to work through an example – say, one involving the attribute[39] of extension. Spinoza denies that individual extended objects such as bicycles and flowers "follow" immediately from that attribute.[40] This is because the attribute of extension is by definition always and everywhere the same, whereas individual extended objects are by definition temporally limited and nonuniform. The only modifications that the attribute of extension can have immediately are those features of the extended world that hold true constantly and universally. In a letter, Spinoza names one such mode: motion-and-rest.[41] It is always and everywhere true that extension will undergo motion-and-rest; therefore, the attribute of extension may be said to be modified by motion-and-rest. In Spinoza's parlance, motion-and-rest is an immediate "infinite modification" of the attribute of extension. Like the attributes, the immediate infinite modes are also modified; in their case, they are modified by what are sometimes called "mediate infinite

---

[38] In his last two letters, Spinoza criticises Descartes's nondynamic conception of extension. As he writes in one of them, "from Extension as conceived by Descartes, to wit, an inert mass, it is not only difficult, . . . but quite impossible to demonstrate the existence of bodies. . . . For this reason I have not hesitated . . . to affirm that Descartes' principles of natural things are of no service" (Ep81).

[39] To avoid confusion, let me say that when I speak of "attribute" here, I can be understood as speaking of "substance." By preferring "attribute" to "substance," I am following Spinoza's lead, for when he discusses the generation of the world out of God, he tends to speak of "attributes" and not "substance" or "God."

[40] As he writes in 1p21, "All the things which follow from the absolute nature of any of God's attributes have always had to exist and be infinite. . . . "

[41] See his 29 July, 1675 letter to Schuller (Ep64). In that same letter, he also names such a modification of the attribute of thought, saying it is "absolutely infinite intellect." For discussion and references, see Miller 2003a, n. 14.

modes."[42] And so ensues a series in which one mode is modified by another more limited mode, until finally we arrive at the most finite of modes, such as bicycles and flowers. In this way, a hierarchy of being can be seen to exist, all firmly rooted in God or substance, but all real in its own way.

This ontology is reflected in the method that Spinoza recommends for philosophical investigation. He writes in the *Theological-Political Treatise* (Ch.7; G III, 102),

> Now in examining natural phenomena we first of all try to discover those features that are most universal and common to the whole of Nature, to wit, motion-and-rest and the laws and rules governing them which Nature always observes and through which she constantly acts; and then we advance gradually from these to other less universal features.

Spinoza subscribes to a top-down model of philosophical and scientific investigation: he thinks we must start with the most abstract theoretical entities, learn their properties, and then deduce the ways in which they can be modified.[43] This process is repeated for each level in the scale of nature, until eventually we deduce the properties and activities of the most finite or particular of modes. Two features of Spinoza's prescription for philosophical investigation must be stressed. First, it is inherently nomological: the "laws and rules governing" natural phenomena structure all inferences we are to make about the phenomena under investigation. Second, it is deductive, not inductive: from the correct laws of nature plus the relevant particular facts we are always able to arrive at the right understanding of the phenomena before us. Justifying this view of philosophizing is Spinoza's belief that the world itself is as interconnected as the philosophical system he is creating. In the words of one commentator (Garrett 2003, 100–101), "Spinoza's *Ethics* is intended to exhibit the structure of nature," with the geometrical method "mirroring the immanent necessity of nature."

---

[42] The best (and perhaps only) example of a mediate infinite mode is the whole of the physical universe, taken as one individual. This is what Spinoza calls the "face of the whole universe" (Ep64). This follows directly upon the attribute of extension and the immediate infinite mode of motion-and-rest because it presupposes both of them – and nothing else.

[43] Thus his is a version of what Ian Hacking (1999, 197) calls "the method of hypothesis." As opposed to the bottom-up approach of the "method of induction," which proceeds from simple observations and modest generalizations based on those observations to grander generalizations and ultimately theories and laws of nature, the method of hypothesis enjoins us to "make guesses, deduce testable consequences, conduct experiments, throw out the bad guesses that are refuted by experiment, and proceed to new conjectures" (ibid.).

Comparing these ideas to Stoicism, it must be admitted that Stoics lack the formal apparatus – both the substance–mode ontology and the *mos geometricus* – so prominent in Spinoza. Yet there is no reason to think that they would object to either. God or substance is the eventual cause of everything, but lesser beings are held to be authentic causal agents. In both the hierarchy of beings it posits and its refusal to reduce finite beings to God, then, Stoic ontology resembles Spinoza's.

The assertion of such ontological similarity is strengthened by the similarity of their methods. Consider this passage from Cicero:

> I have been led on by the marvellous structure of the Stoic system and the miraculous sequence of its topics.... Nothing is more finished, more nicely ordered, than nature; but what has nature, what have the products of handicraft to show that is so well constructed, so firmly jointed and welded into one? Where do you find a conclusion inconsistent with its premise, or a discrepancy between an earlier and a later statement? Where is lacking such close interconnexion of the parts that, if you alter a single letter, you shake the whole structure?[44]

It is evident that Stoicism aspired to craft a system every bit as rigorous as Spinoza's.[45] Moreover, the rationale for this aspiration seems the same as we find in Spinoza: philosophy ought to be systematic, because that which it seeks to understand – nature and all it contains – are seamlessly linked by an unbroken and unbreakable series of causal links.[46]

For all these similarities, there is one possible and possibly significant difference. As noted above, Spinoza's method is thoroughly nomological. Now, the status of laws of nature in Stoicism is contested,[47] but on one of the two prevailing views, they neither conceptualised laws of nature in terms remotely similar to Spinoza nor applied the laws in a manner at all reminiscent to how Spinoza applied them. Whether or not one will be impressed by this difference depends on one's views about the importance of laws of nature. On one influential view, however, scientific explanation *just is* explanation by reference to laws of nature.[48] If

---

44 *De finibus* III.74 (Rackham trans.).
45 Speaking about the passage of *De Finibus* III just quoted, Long writes, "What is undeniable is the attempt to present a set of moral truths which are so related that the last is entirely consistent with the first.... The procedure, like some of the thought itself, reminds one of nothing so much as the *mos geometricus* of Spinoza. Spinoza is of course still more formal, but his practice of setting down one continuous chain of reasoning consisting of propositions, proofs and corollaries would have won the firm approval of Chrysippus" (Long 1986, 185).
46 See Alexander of Aphrodias, *De fato* 191 (L-S 337).
47 The debate is summarised in Miller 2003b, 117–20.
48 This view flourished especially in the middle two quarters of the twentieth century, when it was defended by the likes of Carnap and Hempel. As Carnap bluntly put it, "you cannot give an explanation without also giving a law" (Carnap 1998, 680).

that is true, then the absence of laws in Stoicism, and their presence in Spinozism, means that any explanations of natural phenomena offered by the former will not be scientific, whereas Spinoza's may be (whether they will in fact pass the bar depends on how Spinoza has employed his laws).

## 2. ARGUMENTS FOR SUBSTANCE MONISM

The broad comparison that I have been conducting could be extended by considering a number of other issues. Although that would be instructive, I want to change my approach for the remainder of this chapter. Narrowing my focus, I will probe each party's argument for monism.

As an opening point, let me observe that most scholars of Stoicism take a dim view of the prospects here. Some think that Stoics simply didn't have an argument for substance monism. So Long and Sedley (1987, 270) write, "Stoic physical theory starts from the presupposition that a single world-order exists."[49] Others are of the more charitable opinion that transmission is at least partially to blame for the paucity of argument. In this vein, David Furley (1999, 433) says,

Stoic cosmology is known to us mainly through doxographers, who as a rule were not interested in the reasoning with which the philosophers defended their doctrines, and through the works of opponents of the Stoics, who were generally not as concerned as they should have been to give a fair account of Stoic arguments. As a result, although we know the doctrines at least in outline, we know too little about the context within which they were framed.

The contrast with Spinozism on this issue – viz., the known rational basis for substance monism – could hardly be greater. Unlike the Stoics, Spinoza argues at length and with great care for his monism. Also unlike the Stoics, Spinoza's arguments for monism have been preserved. Lest one wonder about the import of these differences, I shall only say that arguments are the essence of philosophy; insofar as Stoicism as it is known to us lacks the arguments that we find in abundance in Spinozism, the latter's monism is going to be more philosophically satisfying. In any case, these differences must be mentioned in the comparison I am undertaking. It is significant that the known Stoic arguments for monism are so thin whereas Spinoza's are robust.

With that said, I return to the Stoics. Though I accept what the scholars mentioned above said about Stoic arguments, I still want to advance – if only for the purposes of discussion – a tentative guess as

---

[49] As Sedley (1999, 382) reiterated a decade later, "Unlike the case of Epicurean physics, for Stoic physics we do not have any text which *argues* for the theory from first principles."

to why they were monists. Stoics held that the world "does not lack any parts."[50] Because it does not lack any parts, there are no possible parts that would constitute additions to the world if they were actualised. Because the world cannot be added onto in any way, it must be though of as the whole.[51] Now, we can distinguish a range of ways in which something could be a whole, from a loose collective whose parts are unified only by physical or temporal proximity, to a fully integrated organism, all of whose individual members and actions are subordinated a set of impulses or ends emanating from a single controlling authority. As a text quoted in the previous section shows,[52] when Stoics describe the world as a whole, they have the latter model in mind. The world has this high degree of integration thanks to the existence of a "breath [pneuma] which pervades the whole" of it, so "unifying" and "sustaining" the world's parts that they are rendered "inseparable and mutually coherent with themselves."[53] Now, once the world has been shown to be a whole akin to a living organism, the possibility that there could be members of the world sufficiently independent of the world as a whole to qualify as substances in their own right is eliminated. So the only thing that could qualify as a substance in the present sense of the word is the world itself. To say that is to assert substance monism.

Turning now to Spinoza, because this is beyond the purview of my paper, I won't try to advance a novel interpretation of his argument for monism or even summarise all of the extant readings. Instead, I shall rely on a helpful synopsis recently given by John Carriero.[54]

There are, Carriero explains, two basic approaches to Spinoza's argument for monism.[55] One of these, which Carriero calls 'Individuation-Oriented Interpretations' (IOI), takes it to be based on the impossibility of any real differences occurring in nature. In 1p4, Spinoza states what he takes the requirements for individuation to be: "Two or more distinct things are distinguished from one another, either by a difference in the attributes of the substances or by a difference in their affections." There are two conceivable ways in which a pair of objects, $x$ and $y$, may be differentiated from one another: either by being different substances/having different natures, or by being in different states/having different properties. In 1p5d, Spinoza eliminates the latter possibility,

---

50  Calcidius 293 (L-S 269).
51  Sextus Empiricus, *Against the Mathematicians*, IX 332.
52  Diogenes Laertius, *Lives of Eminent Philosophers*, VII.139 (L-S 284).
53  Alexander of Aphrodisias, *On Mixture*, 223 (L-S 283). Cf. Stobaeus 1.166 (L-S 296).
54  See Carriero 2002.
55  Even if there are more than these two – and after criticizing both of them, Carriero tries to advance his own third reading – it is certainly true that *most* interpretations can be placed under one or the other.

arguing that because states/properties are derivative of natures, they ought to be "put to one side" in favour of directly considering the natures of x and y in themselves. Thus it turns out that the only way in which x and y can be distinguished is if they have different natures or are different substances. This reflection on individuation, supporters of IOI contend, quickly leads to the conclusion that two things are really distinct iff they are different substances. Now, because Spinoza elsewhere proves that finite things such as cups and cars do not qualify as substances, it follows they are not really distinct. It is true that IOI must allow the actual demonstration for monism, 1p14d, to carry some weight, because Spinoza's reflections on individuation only lead him to grant real distinction to substances. This is not embarrassing to IOI, however, because they never need be seen as elevating individuation to the exclusion of all else. Rather, all they maintain is that individuation is the linchpin of Spinoza's monism.

Opposed to IOI are what Carriero calls "Substance-Oriented Interpretations" (SOI), whose essential claim is that Spinoza "is led to monism through reflecting on the notion of substance" (Carriero 2002, 38). For example, one common SOI has Spinoza dissatisfied with Descartes's remarks on substance in the *Principles of Philosophy*, I 52 and 53. There Descartes defines a substance as that "which exists in such as way as to depend on no other thing for its existence." Because he realises that only God would satisfy this definition, he quickly advances a second, weaker one, which says that things are substances that "need only the concurrence of God in order to exist." According to the current SOI, Spinoza reacted with disgust to Descartes's relaxing of the conditions for substancehood: moving boldly where Descartes hesitated, he argued unequivocally for the monism implied by the strong conception of substance. A different SOI would also find Spinoza disgusted with Descartes, but it takes his disgust to be based on an antecedently developed conception of substance, not indebted to his study of the Frenchman. On this reading, Spinoza accepts some conception of substance, such as that "a substance is something that does not exist in another thing" (Carriero 2002, 43). Where he differs from others who embrace this same conception is that Spinoza (in the words of one commentator) "restricts its application by firmly insisting upon its rigid logical meaning."[56] If one reflects hard enough on the meaning of substance, one will ultimately find that only one thing can satisfy its conditions. According to this SOI, Spinoza is supposed to have reached this insight. And so he was led to monism.

---

[56] H. A. Wolfson, as quoted by Carriero 2002, 43.

Now, if Spinoza's case for monism is to be understood in either of the foregoing ways, how does it relate to the Stoics'? What lies at the basis of Stoic monism is the intuition that the world constitutes a genuine and well-integrated whole. By contrast, Spinoza's monism is usually held to be based on either individuation or the nature of substance.[57] Because I do not have the space to argue for this here, I will simply assert that the foundations of Stoic monism, so conceived, are not equivalent to the foundations of Spinozistic monism, so conceived. This underscores a point that, although familiar, bears repeating: substance monism is a substantive philosophical thesis; substantive philosophical theses can be proven by many different means; as a result, even parties who agree about the theses themselves will not necessarily agree about why they are so.

If the foundations for Stoic and Spinozistic monism are different, however, are they incompatible? Or would each side have welcomed the arguments of the other as further reinforcing a conclusion it was keen to establish? In particular, what would Spinoza say of the Stoics' line of reasoning? The rest of my essay will be devoted to this question.

Consider my reconstruction of the Stoic argument. As I have presented it, the universe can be conceived as a whole, according to Stoics, because of a ubiquitous physical force rendering all its parts inseparable and mutually coherent. Now, I previously left indeterminate the character of this force. To specify it only very partially, *pneuma* is both "not without sensation and reason" and "divine."[58] Even without expanding on them, these properties are important clues to the way in which *pneuma* organises the universe's parts into a coherent whole. There are two basic (and not necessarily mutually exclusive) explanations for how it is that complex entities qualify as true individuals and not mere collections of parts: teleological and nonteleological. The teleological explanation holds that a complex entity is an individual when and only when all of its parts are acting in concert for the attainment of some end(s). By contrast, the nonteleological account says that complex wholes are real individuals just in case their constituents attain and preserve a certain relation to one another. Given the anthropomorphic and theological properties that Stoics attribute to the universal breath responsible for turning the universe into a whole and therefore a substance, it is plain that they opt for the former. That is, Stoics regard the most complex of all possible entities – the universe and all it contains – as

---

[57] Even though he offers an interpretation that is neither individuation- nor substance-based, Carriero's take on Spinoza's monism also grants no part to the wholeness of the world, for he makes his monism "a response to revisions in the concept of matter wrought by Descartes's science" (Carriero 2002, 38).

[58] Cicero, *De natura deorum* II.29 (I-G 146).

a genuine individual partially[59] because they believe there to be a divine being that both establishes a set of ends and compels all members of the universe to serve those ends.

Turning to Spinoza, though there is scholarly dispute about his views on teleology,[60] there is no doubting his opposition to universal teleology of the sort ascribed by Stoics to nature. As he declares in one of the more famous passages of the *Ethics*, "All the prejudices I here undertake to expose depend on this one: that men commonly suppose that all natural things act, as men do, on account of an end; indeed, they maintain as certain that God himself directs all things to some certain end" (1app; G II, 78). Because the Stoic case for monism presupposes precisely this kind of teleology, Spinoza would have no truck with it.

Yet Spinoza did have a sophisticated and powerful theory regarding the nature of wholes or complex individuals,[61] which he deployed to areas as diverse as physics and the philosophy of mind.[62] Moreover, it is arguable that his views on wholeness influenced his views on other matters.[63] Given that he took wholeness so seriously, it is certainly possible that his monism was partially motivated by thinking of the world as a whole. If that were so, then whatever their differences over teleology, Stoics and Spinoza would both concede roughly the same pivotal role to wholeness in their acceptance of monism.

Now, to do full justice to this proposal, various refinements would need to be introduced.[64] However, because I believe there is one problem that would eventually torpedo it, regardless of all the qualifications and complications, I will cut to the chase. The problem is this: Spinoza's account of the wholeness of complex entities pertains to objects *within* nature. It is not at all obvious that he could or would apply it to nature taken as a whole – which is to say, to substance. The reason is that nature/substance does not have parts (1p12). Because nature/substance does not have parts, it does not have parts that need to retain their

---

[59] Let me stress that the Stoics' account of the universe's wholeness could also draw upon nonteleological factors. It only matters to my argument that teleology be a necessary and not a sufficient part of their case for wholeness.

[60] For an opinionated guide through the terrain, see Curley 1990.

[61] The theory is most fully developed in the digression into physics after 2p13s.

[62] See the material following 2p13s and 2p15, respectively.

[63] For example, it is plausible to think that he was able to conceive of the "whole of Nature" as one complex individual (2p13le7s) precisely because of his theory of wholeness.

[64] For example, because the discussion after 2p13s is of bodies, not ideas, changes will have to be made before we can apply that account of wholeness to intensional entities. But given his parallelism, we should suppose that such changes are possible: complex mental entities come to be and perdure when their parts (which would be individual ideas) attain a stable intensional relationship with one another.

relationship to one another in order for it to be and remain in existence. So there must be some entirely different explanation for the being and continued existence of nature as a whole.

What we learn from comparing Stoic versus Spinozistic arguments for monism, then, is that they are *both* different *and* incommensurable. Stoic arguments rely on views about the nature of wholeness; they are also deeply teleological. Spinozistic arguments draw on a theory of individuation or of substance *per se*; they are utterly devoid of teleology. I do not wish to be taken as suggesting that the clash over the rational basis for monism overrides all of the congruencies in the contents of the theories themselves discussed in the last section. But I do think they merit our attention as we consider Spinoza *par rapport aux Stoïques*.

# 6   Spinoza on Necessity

## INTRODUCTION

Many passages in the *Ethics* give the impression that Spinoza accepts necessitarianism.[1] This is the doctrine that everything that is the case is necessarily the case or, in Leibnizian terms, that the actual world is the only possible world.

Some of the passages that produce this impression are the following:

(1) ...there must necessarily follow from the necessity of the divine nature an infinity of things in infinite ways (that is, everything that can come within the scope of the infinite intellect). (1p16d)[2]

(2) Nothing in nature is contingent, but all things are from the necessity of the divine nature determined to exist and to act in a definite way. (1p29d)

(3) Things could not have been produced by God in any other way or in any other order than is the case. (1p33)

(4) ...I have here shown more clearly than the midday sun that in things there is absolutely nothing by virtue of which they can be said to be "contingent"...a thing is said to be "contingent" for no other reason than the deficiency of our knowledge.... (1p33s1)

(5) Whatever is within God's power must be so comprehended in his essence (1p34) that it follows necessarily from it, and thus necessarily exists. (1p35d)

(6) ...all things follow from God's eternal decree by the same necessity as it follows from the essence of a triangle that its three angles are equal to two right angles. (2p49s)

Curley (1969) and Curley and Walski (1999), however, regard this impression as illusory. On their view, Spinoza holds that finite modes really are contingent and, indeed, that the actual world composed of them is only one of many possible worlds.

[1] Don Garrett (1991) uses this term in "Spinoza's Necessitarianism." Curley and Walski call this "strict necessitarian" in opposition to their own interpretive view, which they dub "moderate necessitarianism" (Curley and Walski 1999, 241–2). The propriety of the term "moderate necessitarianism," in their view, is evidently based on Hume's talk of the "Doctrine of Necessity" (Curley and Walski 1999, 243 n. 6).

[2] Translations in these numbered quotations (1–6) are from Spinoza 2002.

Papers by Carriero (1991), Garrett (1991), Huenemann (1999), and Koistinen (2003) have forcefully argued, in contrast, that Spinoza accepts necessitarianism.[3]

In this paper, I propose to contribute to this debate. My main aim is fourfold:

i. to elucidate Spinoza's reasons for holding that what is caused is necessary,
ii. to help to elucidate the reasoning in 1p33d,
iii. to provide additional reasons for rejecting a Leibnizian interpretation of Spinoza's views on necessity, and
iv. to provide a preliminary comparison of Spinoza's views with a modern attempt to represent an ontological argument for God's necessary existence.

The first section of the paper is concerned primarily with the *Short Treatise* (I.6, "On Divine Predestination"), which is apparently a precursor of 1p33d. The second section considers 1p33d itself, while the third argues that Spinoza employs a unitary concept of necessity. The fourth section, finally, describes Gödel's ontological argument and provides at least an initial discussion of its relations to Spinoza's views.

## 1. *SHORT TREATISE* I.6

Necessitarianism entails the doctrine that whatever happens, necessarily happens, which we may call "universal event necessitarianism" or "event necessitarianism" for short. This should be distinguished from the doctrine of "universal causation," according to which every event has a sufficient (proximate) cause, even if there is a necessary connection between a sufficient cause and its effect.

The claim that if something has a sufficient proximate cause, then it must happen, and hence that the doctrine of universal causation entails event necessitarianism in the above sense, seems to rest on a simple mistake. For it is one thing to say that

1. if the cause is given, then the effect must occur

and it is another to say that

---

[3] Carriero's acceptance of necessitarianism is indicated on pp. 59–60 of Carriero 1991. On p. 75, however, he regards Spinoza as making a "distinction between the noncausal and causal senses of necessity" and he supposes that in Spinoza's view there are many "internally possible" worlds, but only one "absolutely possible world." However, Carriero's view and his point on p. 75 ff., I take it, is merely that there are many internally, formally, or logically consistent descriptions whose "correlates" would be different "possible worlds," but only one such "possible world," namely the actual one, is really possible, in Spinoza's view.

2. it must be that if the cause is given, then the effect will occur.

It may be that this difference, like that between "What goes up must come down" and "It must be that what goes up comes down," is not ordinarily stressed. But the difference can be represented clearly in an ordinary modal logic such as T, S4, or S5. Let "L" express "it is necessary that" and let "p" and "q" represent "event $c$ occurs" and "event $e$ occurs," respectively. Then

3. $(p \rightarrow Lq)$
and
4. $L(p \rightarrow q)$

exhibit the difference between the above sayings.

The question whether $e$ necessarily occurred is not settled by noting that there was a (proximate) sufficient cause of it. For all that follows from this, when causes are regarded as necessitating their effects, is that there is a necessary connection between cause and effect. Thus 4, but not 3, follows. In a standard modal system such as S5, one will not obtain the conclusion that $e$ necessarily occurred simply from this, nor from this in conjunction with the claim that $c$ in fact did occur. "$(p \& L(p \rightarrow q))$" does not entail "$Lq$."

"$(Lp \rightarrow Lq)$" does follow from 4, however, and it may thus seem that you must establish not merely that $c$ occurred, but that it necessarily occurred, to obtain the conclusion that $e$ necessarily occurred. (You must apparently establish not merely that p, but that Lp.) But to show that $c$ necessarily occurred, you must apparently show (for the same reason) that its cause necessarily occurred and so on, through a finite or infinite regress.

But if it is a mistake to think that $e$ necessarily occurred simply because it had a sufficient cause, it is also a mistake to think that it did not necessarily occur simply because it would not have occurred if its cause had not occurred. (This is to say, roughly, that "$L(-p \rightarrow -q)$" does not entail "$-Lq$.") To show that $e$ did not necessarily occur, one must apparently show, not merely that it would not have occurred, if its cause had not occurred, but in addition, that its cause did not necessarily occur. For "$L(-p \rightarrow -q) \& -Lp$" entails "$-Lq$." But to show that the cause of $e$ might not have occurred seems to require that we show *its* cause might not have occurred, and so on, through a finite or infinite regress of causes.

Thus the dispute concerning whether $e$ necessarily occurred seems irresolvable by this means, for each thesis about event $e$ can apparently be established only by establishing that thesis for a preceding event, and so on.

In several passages, Spinoza seems to equate or even confuse the question of whether something has a sufficient cause with the question of whether it had to happen. One of these is found in 1p33s1, where Spinoza indicates that one reason for calling a thing "necessary" is that its existence "necessarily follows...from...a given efficient cause" (Spinoza 2002, 236).

Another is found in Part I, Chapter 6 of what is perhaps his earliest extant work, the *Short Treatise*. There we find the following argument for the conclusion that there are no accidental things – that is, "things which may happen and may also not happen":

That which has no cause to exist cannot possibly exist; that which is accidental has no cause; therefore.... (Spinoza 2002, 54)

The first premise here seems to exhibit the apparent confusion that we just noted, for it fails to recognize that something may have a sufficient cause and yet not necessarily exist (because its cause did not necessarily exist). One who wishes to accept the doctrine of universal causation as a necessary truth, while denying that every event that does occur, necessarily occurs, will allege that the first premise should be, "It cannot be that that which has no cause exists," rather than "That which has no cause cannot exist." The former is equivalent to the assertion that necessarily everything that exists has a cause, while the latter is equivalent to the claim that everything that has no cause necessarily does not exist (or "Anything that has no cause cannot exist").

Spinoza's discussion does not stop here, however. The surface structure of the argument just quoted is evidently that of Barbara, and so acceptance of the conclusion seems avoidable only by calling into question the truth of the premises. Spinoza thus immediately proceeds, after giving this argument, as follows:

The first is beyond all dispute; the second we prove thus: If any thing that is accidental has a definite and certain cause why it should exist, then it must necessarily exist; but that it should be both accidental and necessary at the same time, is self-contradictory; Therefore...

Perhaps some one will say, that an *accidental* thing has indeed no definite and certain cause, but an accidental one. If this should be so, it must be either *in sensu diviso* or *in sensu composito*, that is to say, either the existence of the cause is accidental, and not its being a cause; or it is accidental that a certain thing (which indeed must necessarily exist in Nature) should be the cause of the occurrence of that accidental thing. However, both the one and the other are false. (Spinoza 2002, 54)

Here it is clear that Spinoza is considering the type of position that we have described above, that is, universal causation without event necessitarianism. Two positions are evidently possible. Although the thing in question has a (sufficient proximate) cause,

    i. it is not necessary that if the cause is given, then the effect is given, i.e., there is no necessary connection between cause and effect, or

    ii. there is a necessary connection here, but the effect is not necessary because the cause does not necessarily exist (or occur).

Let us consider each of these in turn.

Spinoza's rejection of the claim that there is no necessary connection between cause and effect is supported here by an argument that is not easy to follow. He writes,

> . . . if the cause were no more compelled to produce one thing rather than another, that is, if the cause were no more compelled to produce this something than not to produce it, then it would be impossible at once both that it should produce it and that it should not produce it, which is quite contradictory. (Spinoza 2002, 54)

There seem to be two errors here – one in the text and one in the argument. For it clearly *is* impossible at once that the cause both produce and not produce the effect, as it is generally the case that it is impossible that both p & −p. Much better sense would thus be made here if the passage asserted that if the cause were not compelled to produce the effect then it would be *possible*, rather than impossible, that it both produce and not produce the effect. For it is this that is "regt strydig" ("quite contradictory"). Both versions of the *Short Treatise* that we possess, however, have "onmogelijk"[4] rather than "mogelijk," and the error is not one of English translation.

The emended version of the argument seems to contain a clear mistake in reasoning, however. For from the claim that there is not a necessary connection between cause and effect, it will not follow that (it is possible that) the cause both produces and not produces the effect. It will follow that although the cause produced the effect it did not necessarily produce it. Hence it follows that it is possible that it produced it (since in fact it did so), and that it is possible that it did not produce it (since by hypothesis it did not necessarily produce it). But "It is possible that p and it is possible that −p" does not entail (in S5 or similar systems) "It is possible that both p and −p," and so nothing contradictory follows from the denial of a necessary connection. Thus it does not follow that

---

4 Codex A spells this "onmogelyk." See G I, 40 and Spinoza 1986, 178.

it is possible both that the cause produces the effect and that it does not produce the effect.

Although it may be argued that Spinoza's conclusion is correct – that there is a necessary connection between cause and effect – this is not a conclusion that can reached by the apparent strategy of this argument of the *Short Treatise*. It may be because of this that in the *Ethics*, this claim is set out as an axiom (1a3).

Regarding the idea that the effect of a cause does not necessarily exist because its cause does not, that is, (ii) above, Spinoza writes,

> ...if the accidental something is accidental because the existence of its cause is accidental, then that cause must be accidental because the cause which has produced it is also accidental, et sic in infinitum.

> And since it has already been proved, that all things depend on one single cause, this cause would therefore also have to be accidental: which is manifestly false. (Spinoza 2002, 54)

Thus we see that in the *Short Treatise*, as in the *Ethics*, Spinoza accepts an infinite regress of (finite) causes and rejects the view that since the cause of such a thing does not necessarily exist, the effect does not necessarily exit. He holds instead that no element in the infinite sequence is "accidental," because "all things depend on one single cause," namely God, who is not "accidental." He does not here explain, however, how it is that all things, and hence, presumably, each element of the infinite causal "chain," depend on one thing and yet each is caused by some finite element of the chain.

In the *Ethics* the connection between God and finite things is also problematic and Spinoza's acceptance of an infinite regress of finite causes forms the basis of Leibniz's criticism that the infinite chain never leads back to God. Concerning proposition 1p28, Leibniz writes:

> Rightly understood, this opinion leads to many absurdities. According to it, things would not truly follow from the nature of God. For the determining thing is in its turn determined by another thing, and so on to infinity; thus things are in no way determined by God. God merely contributes something absolute and general of his own. It would be more correct to say that one particular thing is not determined by another in an infinite progression, for in that case things would always remain indeterminate, no matter how far you carry the progression. All particular things are rather determined by God. (Leibniz 1969, 203)

## 2. *ETHICS* 1P33 AND ITS DEMONSTRATION

The difficulty in seeing how God causes a finite thing, given that there is an infinite regress of finite causes of it, appears to infect Spinoza's demonstration of 1p33 as much as the argument from the *Short Treatise*.[5] For the idea that a finite thing could have been different is there held to require that God could have been different. The proposition and its demonstration are as follows:

1p33. Things could have been produced by God in no other way, and in no other order, than they have been produced.

Dem. For all things have necessarily followed from God's given nature (by p16), and have been determined from the necessity of God's nature to exist and produce an effect in a given way (by p29). Therefore, if things could have been of another nature, or could have been determined to produce an effect in another way, so that the order of Nature was different, then God's nature could also have been other than it is now, and therefore (by p11) that [other nature] would also have had to exist, and consequently, there could have been two or more Gods, which is absurd (by p14c1). So things could have been produced in no other way and no other order, etc, Q.E.D. (C, 436)

The first part of Spinoza's argument here seems to be that if a thing had been different or if its effect had been different, then the order of nature would have been different and thus the nature of God would have been different. Hence, if some thing could have been different, then the nature of God could have been different.

Leibniz's objection to 1p28, however, seems applicable here as well. For when Spinoza asserts that God is the cause of a finite thing, or that such a thing follows from the necessity of God's nature, he seems to mean that God, insofar as he is modified by another finite thing, is the cause of it, and God's nature or essence is "constituted" not by modes, but by attributes.

Curley and Walski hold that the expression "order of nature" (*ordo naturae*) sometimes refers, in Spinoza's writings, to the laws of nature, not to a sequence of finite things. They may also appear, at first sight, to hold that it does so in 1p33d as well. In fact, however, they instead say that in this demonstration the change in the order of nature is "the result of a change in *the causal laws which necessitate the existence and effects* of finite modes...."[6] In this way they maintain that 1p33 and its demonstration are consistent with their view that, according to Spinoza, God could have produced an alternative series of finite modes.

---

[5] This difficulty also arises in Ep12 where Spinoza comments on an argument by Crescas for the existence of God. Spinoza maintains here that there is an actually infinite series of causes of a thing and that each thing that does not necessarily exist by its nature is determined to exist by something (God) that does necessarily exist by its nature. See Spinoza 2002, 791.

[6] Curley and Walski 1999, 256.

This, however, fails to note or account for the generality of Spinoza's first sentence. For Spinoza speaks in 1p33d of "all things" as having been "determined by the necessity of God's nature to exist and produce an effect in a given way," and he cites 1p16 and 1p29 to support this. That finite modes are intended to be included in the scope of "all things," however, is clear from Spinoza's citation of 1p28 in 1p29d.

Also important to note are the contents of the two scholia to 1p33. The first maintains that "there is absolutely nothing in things on account of which they can be called contingent." The second holds that things have been produced by God "with supreme perfection" and it even considers and rejects this claim:

... even if it were supposed that God had made another nature of things, or that from eternity he had decreed something else concerning nature and its order, no imperfection in God would follow from that.

An apparent ancestor of this scholium is *Short Treatise* I.4, "On God's Necessary Actions," which begins, "We deny that God could omit doing what he does.... " This is expressed as well in I.6, "On God's Predestination," of the same work. Because God's production of a finite mode is one of God's actions, it follows that God cannot omit to produce each finite mode that in fact he does produce.

The second part of Spinoza's argument in 1p33d maintains that if God's nature could have been different, then that nature would have to exist (by 1p11), and hence there would be two or more Gods.

Spinoza's whole argument, adapted to talk of "possible worlds," might be thought to proceed as follows. Assume that God could have produced another world (or could have lacked some feature that he in fact has); that is, assume that there could have been a being just like God except that it produced another world. Such a being, which according to Spinoza would be an absolutely infinite substance, is one that can be shown to exist (by "the ontological argument"), if it is possible. But to assume that there could have been such a being is to assume that such a being is (or was) possible. Hence such a being does, and must, exist. But there cannot be more than one God (or substance), and hence God could not have produced another world.

Indeed, it might be added, this is what seems to Spinoza to destroy Leibniz's general position: that a being just like God, except that it produces another world, would be a being (even according to Leibniz) which is, *if possible, then actual*. So of course if there could have been such a being, there would have been (and must have been) such a being.

The argument might also be expressed in this way (although its structure is not transparent):

1. Every substance that is possible is actual.
2. A substance that creates another world is possible.
   Therefore,
3. A substance that creates another world is actual.

But if there is a *necessarily unique* substance, we can conclude that this is the only possible world. Thus in 1p33d we have in effect a *reductio* in which Spinoza rejects 2, since there cannot be two or more substances.

The main trouble with this argument proceeds via the semantics of modal logic. A simple mistake will be said to have been made, because even if there is a necessarily existent and necessarily unique substance, it does not follow that it has all of the same properties "in all possible worlds." One can consistently say that there is a substance found in each possible world, that in each world there is only one, and even that it is the very same one in each world. Here we have it, as a gift, that identification "across" possible worlds has been accomplished, or that there is here "transworld identity." But, the objector will say, the substance that is in world $W_1$ may have a property in that world that the very same substance lacks in another world, $W_2$.

So it is not a contradiction in any standard modal system to say, "Necessarily there exists a unique substance, it is possible that some substance has property P, and it is possible that some substance does not have property P." That is, the following three claims are consistent with each other. Take "M" as "It is possible that," "Sx" as "x is a substance," and "Px" as "x has property P"):

4. $L(\exists x)(\forall y)(Sy \leftrightarrow y=x)$
5. $M(\exists x)(Sx \& Px)$
6. $M(\exists x)(Sx \& -Px)$.

Indeed, 5 and 6 are also consistent with a strengthened form of 4, namely,

4a. $L(\exists x)(\forall y)L(Sy \leftrightarrow y=x)$.

Spinoza's argument in 1p33d, however, is intuitively successful and it is in fact immune to the preceding critique. For he does not try to show merely that if God could have produced a different world, or could have had some property he does not have, then an ontological argument would apply to show that such a God would have to exist. He tries instead to show that if God's *nature* could have been different, then a God of that nature would have to exist (and thus there would be two or more Gods, which is absurd). This difference is crucial, for God's nature or essence is not a contingent property of God. It is a necessary one.

If everything (and every property of God) follows from the necessity of God's nature, then Spinoza is quite right to hold that God can omit to do nothing he in fact does and that he cannot do anything more than what he in fact does. This will be the only possible world and God will have no contingent properties. His challenge to Leibniz will then be to provide a satisfactory explanation of why God has property P, for any contingent property that God has.

The claim that there is only one possible world has apparent consequences for logical theory. For the leading heuristic idea concerning the semantics of modal logic has been the notion of a possible world. The idea has been, for example, that the truth-conditions for sentences such as "Lp" and "Mp" (which are intended to represent "It is necessary that p" and "It is possible that p," respectively) can be provided by saying, "In every possible world it is the case that p" and "In at least one possible world it is the case that p." (Of course you may want to talk about worlds that are possible "relative to" another, instead of "every possible world," but this complication is inessential here.)

Now if you suppose, with Spinoza, that there is "really" or "metaphysically" only one possible world, then "Lp" will be true if and only if "p" is true, and each will be true if and only if "Mp" is true. For if there is only one possible world, "p" will be true in at least one world if and only if it is true in all worlds.

But a logic that is complete is one in which, if $\psi$ is a consequence of $\phi$, then $\psi$ is derivable (by means of the inference rules) from $\phi$, for all sentences $\phi$ and $\psi$. If there is only one possible world, and this is built into the semantics, then "p," "Lp," and "Mp" will be consequences of each other and hence, if the logic is complete, there will be a derivation of "Lp" from "p," and a derivation of "p" from "Mp." We will then have a modal propositional logic that "collapses" into propositional logic in the sense that "(L$\phi$ $\leftrightarrow$ "$\phi$)" and "(M$\phi$ $\leftrightarrow$ "$\phi$)" will both be provable, for every sentence $\phi$.

This result is bound to be unacceptable to many, but this is not the place to provide rejoinders to the various objections that will no doubt be made. The general position that would be advocated maintains that there is just one kind of necessity, and that the distinctions drawn terminologically with the expressions "logically necessary," "logically possible," "physically necessary," and "physically possible," for example, are at bottom epistemological.

### 3. REAL CONTINGENCY

It is sometimes said, of course, that there is a nonepistemological distinction between absolute and relative (or hypothetical) necessity, and this type of position has been employed by Curley in elucidation of Spinoza's position as follows:

> ... we can most easily come to terms with Spinoza if we represent him as holding the following view. All propositions are either necessarily true or necessarily false.... But, restricting ourselves to truths, not all truths are necessary in the same sense. Some are absolutely necessary, in the Leibnizian sense that their denial is explicitly or implicitly self-contradictory: their truth follows from the essence or definition of the subject. But others are only relatively necessary. Their denial does not involve a contradiction, either explicitly or implicitly.... (Curley 1969, 89)

> Relative necessity is like Leibniz' hypothetical necessity. It has the form: given $p$, $q$ is necessary.... The proposition (or set of propositions) relative to which $q$ is necessary provides an explanation in terms of efficient causation. (Curley 1969, 90)

> Consider the case of true propositions of the form "$x$ exists" where the values of the variable $x$ are singular referring expressions for example, "God," "Spinoza," "this table," etc. It is clear that, like Leibniz, Spinoza would say that only one such proposition is absolutely necessary, namely, "God exists." Otherwise he would not say that "The essence of things produced by God does not involve existence" (*E* IP24). (Curley 1969, 90)

Explication of the notion of relative necessity as something that has the form "given p, q is necessary" is of course insufficient. For is "p" given or not? If it is, then "q is necessary" will be true, and the distinction between "absolute" and "relative" necessity will collapse. It will collapse, that is, unless there is some further difference in the kind of necessity (or sense of "necessarily") that is expressed by saying that God necessarily exists and by saying Spinoza necessarily exists in 1670 (or that "God exists" and "Spinoza exists in 1670" are necessarily true.)

As set out above, this further difference appears to be that between something that is logically true and something that is not logically, but is necessarily true, or between something whose negation yields a contradiction (presumably in a finite number of steps) and something whose negation does not. An alternative explication of the former would be to say, "necessarily, if p then q," in which event "it is necessary that q" (or "q is necessary") will *not* follow, apparently, unless it can be established that it is necessary that p. Here you might say that the kind of necessity involved is the same as "absolute" necessity, but that because of the infinite regress (of finite causes) it will never be the case that, for example, it is necessary that Spinoza exists in 1670.

This interpretation of Spinoza thus maintains, and seems to require, that there be two notions of necessity, or two readings of "necessarily," which we may dub "metaphysical" and "causal," and that "singular things necessarily exist" will on the former reading be false, but on the latter, true. Hence there will be a sense of "can" or "contingent" or a notion of possibility on which "God can exist without singular things" is true, namely, when it means that it is metaphysically possible that God exist and no singular thing exists.

But while a distinction like that indicated above is no doubt suggested by 1p33s1, the distinction itself is not, I think, to be found there. For Spinoza maintains in 1p33s1, not that there are two notions or kinds of necessity, or that "necessary" has two meanings, but that there are two reasons ("rationes") for which things are said to be necessary. What he says is

A thing is called necessary either by reason of its essence, or by reason of its cause. For a thing's existence follows necessarily follows either from its essence and definition, or from a given efficient cause.

Although the use of "ratio" (reason) in the text may itself suggest two concepts or meanings of "necessary," such a reading cannot evidently be sustained. For in the same scholium Spinoza states that it is also for two reasons, or causes, that a thing is said to be impossible, and that there is one reason ("causa"), namely lack of knowledge, for saying that a thing is contingent. (Cf. 4d3 and 4d4, however.)

Now while the distinction between saying that there are two notions of necessity and saying that there are two reasons for saying that a thing is necessary may be thought somewhat too "refined" (especially in light of Spinoza's later distinction, marked with different words and definitions, between what is possible and what is contingent), it is not, I think, one that can be ignored here. For if we ask Spinoza with what "kind" of necessity God produced singular things, and with what "kind" of necessity God himself exists, the answer in each case is the same. It is, although there may be a better term, with "geometrical" necessity, as we learn from 1p17s:

... I think that I have shown clearly enough (see Prop. 16) that from the supreme power or infinite nature of God, infinite things in infinite ways, that is, all things, have necessarily flowed, or have always followed by the same necessity, in the same way [semper eâdem necessitate sequi, eodem modo] as it follows from the nature of a triangle, from eternity and to eternity, that its three angles are equal to two right angles. (My translation)

Again, in 2p3s:

... in Proposition 16 of Part I we have shown that God acts with the same necessity [eâdem necessitate agere] by which he understands himself, that is, just as it follows from the necessity of the divine nature (as all maintain with one mouth) that God understands himself, it also follows with the same necessity [eâdem etiam necessitate sequitur] that God does infinite things in infinite ways. Next we have shown in Proposition 34 of Part I that the power of God is nothing besides his actual essence [actuosam essentiam]; and so it is as impossible to conceive that God does not act as that God does not exist [adeóque tam nobis impossibile est concipere, Deum non agere, quàm Deum non esse]. (My translation)

Spinoza's position thus seems clear: God acts with the same necessity as that by which he exists. His action, however, is his production of things. Thus, since everything follows from God with the same necessity as that by which he exists, they exist with the same necessity as that by which he exists. The further suggestion that even if their necessary existence accrues to them for a different reason, the *sense* in which God produces things is different from that in which he produces himself, is also explicitly rejected by Spinoza in the scholium to 1p25:

... it follows that from the given divine nature both the essence and the existence of things must necessarily be concluded, and, in a word, in the sense (eo sensu) in which God is said to be the cause of himself he should also be said to be the cause of all things. (My translation; both Shirley and Curley correctly, and perhaps preferably, use "in the same sense" for eo sensu)

Finally, to quote the translation of an earlier work, we find the following in the Dutch version of the *Metaphysical Thoughts*:

But we also say that the necessity of really existing is not distinct from the necessity of essence (II, ix). That is, when we say that God has decided that the triangle shall exist, we are saying nothing but that God has so arranged the order of nature and of causes that the triangle shall necessarily exist at such a time. So if we understood the order of causes as it has been established by God, we should find that the triangle must really exist at such a time, with the same necessity as we now find, when we attend to its nature, that its three angles are equal to two right angles. (CM I.3; G I, 243; C, 309)

The intended reading of Spinoza must furthermore maintain that there *is* a sense in which God did not necessarily produce the things that he did produce, but in the relevant discussions of this (in 1p33d and 1p33s2 for example), there is no hint that this is the case. In addition, 1p33s1 itself maintains, as previously noted, that "there is absolutely nothing in things on account of which they can be called contingent." Again, 1p33s2 argues that even if, contrary to Spinoza's own position, God's will pertains to his essence, things could not have been produced in any other way or order than they have been produced. This is a thesis that Spinoza does *not* regard as ambiguous.

Spinoza's position seems to have been expressed as clearly as it could have been: there is only one kind of necessity, but it is ascribed to things for different reasons. He seems, then, to have held that there is no sense, contrary to Leibniz, in which singular things could have been different.

A further argument for the Leibnizian interpretation of Spinoza may be drawn from 2a1, which is used in 2p10d to reject as *absurd* the claim that man, or a man, necessarily exists. The axiom itself asserts, "The essence of man does not involve necessary existence, that is, from the order of nature, it can as much happen that this or that man exists, as that he does not exist." This is used as follows in the demonstration of 2p10:

Therefore, if the being of substance pertained to the essence of man, then substance being given, man would necessarily be given (by d2), and consequently man would exist necessarily, which (by a1) is absurd, Q.E.D. (C, 565)

This may seem to provide conclusive support for the Leibnizian interpretation, but it does not. The claim in 2a1 that it can as much happen that a man exist as that he does not exist can be seen to be true solely by noting that it *does* happen from the order of nature that the man exists (at one time) and that he does not exist (at another time). Thus for this reason it is possible that he exist at one time and possible that he not exist at another. Similarly, the claim in 2p11d that is based on this – that it is absurd for man (or a man) to exist necessarily – should consequently be taken to mean that it is false that he necessarily exists at all *times*.

What is perhaps more problematic about 2a1 and its use in 2p10d is that if we judge solely from his use of the axiom there, Spinoza could just as well have asserted merely that the essence of man does not involve existence. The argument in 2p10d could then simply note that since the essence of substance does involve existence, by 1p7, no man is a substance or, more strongly, that the essence of man is not the essence of substance.

What is then problematic for the non-Leibnizian interpretation is the suggestion made by Curley and others that "existence does not pertain to the essence of x" means "x does not necessarily exist." In earlier papers, in fact, I put such a construction on this myself. It seems clear from the passages cited above, however, that Spinoza holds that everything is necessary in the same way or sense, although not for the same reason. "The essence of x involves existence" should not then be regarded as equivalent to the claim that x necessarily exists. The former entails but is not entailed by the latter.

Thus several difficulties, as well as the perhaps natural thought that there is not one kind of necessity, make a dual reading of Spinoza's position on necessity an attractive one. So it is not without reason that several recent discussions of Spinoza have attempted to introduce a second ("causal" or "nonlogical") notion of necessity in defense and exposition of his position.

That there are different kinds of necessity does not, as we have seen, appear to be Spinoza's own position. In addition, it is not incidental to note that the introduction of a second notion of necessity, aside from requiring Spinoza to concede the correctness of Leibniz's general position (that in one sense God could have produced a different world), is also available to Spinoza's opponents in 2p10cs. So if there is a "causal" sense in which God can exist, and hence be conceived, without singular things, then Spinoza's redefinition of "what pertains to the essence of a thing" is unnecessary. For if there is a notion of "causal" necessity, distinct from "metaphysical" or "geometrical" necessity, one may reply to Spinoza's objection by saying that what pertains to the essence of a thing is that without which the thing can, in a noncausal sense, neither be nor be conceived. God will not, therefore, pertain to the essence of a created thing because, although such a thing can neither be nor be conceived without God, this is so only in a causal sense. The availability of this response to Spinoza's objection may indeed be a further indication that Spinoza had a unitary notion of necessity. For the problem that Spinoza sees in the traditional definition seems to arise only if no distinction has been drawn between a "causal" and a "metaphysical" notion of necessity.

Now a few brief remarks on Spinoza's notion of "what pertains to the essence of a thing" may usefully be made here before proceeding to Section 4. We often enough suppose that what is "contained in" the essence of a thing is any "essential property" of it, that is, any property that the object necessarily has. It is thus natural to think that if, according to Spinoza, an individual object necessarily exists, then it should be true (and he should assert) that existence *is* contained in, or pertains to, the essence of that individual. He does not assert this, however, and this fact might be taken as evidence for the view that individual finite objects, according to Spinoza, do not necessarily exist, or do not necessarily exist in the same way or sense in which God does.

The argument here is defective, however, because Spinoza's conception of what pertains to the essence of a thing is simply not the same as our (allegedly muddled) notion of a "de re" necessary property. That this is so should be clear from the claim in 2p27 that things (properties) that are common to everything constitute the essence of no singular thing. Thus, for example, extension (which constitutes the essence of God) is essential to every body, but it does not constitute the essence of any finite body. What constitutes the essence of a finite object is thus not just any property that the object necessarily has. It is rather something unique to the individual – something which, when given, the thing is given, and something from which every property of the object (*when considered alone*) can be concluded.

The claim that existence is not contained in the essence of a created thing does not then mean or entail that the object does not necessarily exist. It instead entails and, I think, means that its existence cannot be concluded solely from the statement of what the object or its essence is (although it can be concluded from this in conjunction with a statement that something else, its cause, "necessitated" its existence).

Spinoza's notion of what constitutes the essence of an individual is thus the notion of an individual essence and is very like Leibniz's notion of a complete concept of an individual substance – in that necessarily, if the concept or essence is instantiated, then that unique object, with all of the properties that it has when considered without relation to others, is given. It is an individual "whatness" that, with only one exception, does not (when considered alone) guarantee existence.

### 4. ON GÖDEL, GOD, AND SPINOZA

In the following section I provide a brief description of Gödel's ontological argument, note that Spinoza appears to have accepted some of the central premises of this argument, and give brief replies to two objections recently made to it.

### Gödel's Argument

Gödel's ontological argument is set out in a second-order quantified modal logic.[7] Its basic strategy can be described as trying to establish, solely by appeal to necessary truths, that (i) if there is a God, then necessarily there is one. Hence if it is possible then it is necessary that there be a God.[8] That a God necessarily exists is then proven by showing that (ii) it is possible for a God to exist.

---

[7] See Sobel 1987. A transcription of Gödel's argument is contained in Appendix 2 and of Dana Scott's notes on this in Appendix 3. The article itself provides a fine discussion of the arguments and a formal reconstruction of them. A revised and expanded version of this is found in Chapter IV of Sobel 2004. Anderson 1990 also provides a useful exposition and discussion of Gödel's argument. See also Perzanowski 1991.

[8] Take "L" as "It is necessary that," "M" as "It is possible that," and "p" as "God exists." If "$(p \rightarrow Lp)$" is established on the basis of S5-necessary truths, then we can conclude "$L(p \rightarrow Lp)$," from which "$(Mp \rightarrow MLp)$" follows. But since "$(MLp \rightarrow Lp)$" is a theorem of S5, "$Mp \rightarrow Lp$" follows. Sobel also gives a derivation of "p" itself in the Brower system B, where "$(MLp \rightarrow p)$" is used instead of "$(MLp \rightarrow Lp)$." See Sobel 2004, 150–52.

The proof of (ii) is itself interesting, in part because it relies solely on a notion of positive properties, in terms of which God is defined. Of more concern here, however, is the argument for (i). Gödel defines a God as a being with all positive properties, he takes the essence of a thing to be a property of it that "entails" or "necessitates" all of its properties, and he supposes a necessary existent to be a thing any essence of which entails that it, or rather a thing of that type, necessarily exists.[9]

With these definitions in place, Gödel's argument for (i) proceeds by showing that any being that is a God has an essence, namely being a God,[10] and that necessary existence is a property of it. (For necessary existence is a positive property.) Hence if there is a God, there necessarily is one.[11]

Although Gödel's handwritten notes do not explicitly deal with the question of God's uniqueness, Dana Scott's do. They maintain that any essence of an individual is necessarily a property of that individual, from which it follows that there is at most one God.[12] It is also evident that if there were two or more Gods, each would have all positive properties (by the definition of a God). Each would also have only positive properties, as Sobel makes clear.[13] Indeed, since every God would necessarily have all and only positive properties, one might well wonder in what their difference could consist.

## Spinoza

Spinoza's writings contain interestingly similar doctrines. In 1d6, God is defined as "an absolutely infinite being, that is, substance consisting of infinite attributes, each of which expresses eternal and infinite

---

[9] Gödel's formal representation of these (and Sobel's) can be restated with no substantive change as "Gx ↔ (∀φ)(Pφ→ φx)," "φ Ess x ↔ (φx & (∀ψ)(ψx → L(∀y)(φy → ψy)))," and "NEx" ↔ (φ Ess x → L(∃x)φx)," respectively. (Lexicon: Gx: x is a God; Pφ: φ is a positive property; φ Ess x: φ is an essence of x; L: it is necessary that.)

[10] This argument is set out in Dana Scott's notes and is sketched in greater formal detail by Soble. It assumes that not being φ is a positive property iff being φ is not a positive property and that if being φ is positive, it necessarily is, that is, (P(−φ) ↔ −P(φ)) and (Pφ → LPφ). See Sobel 1987, 244.

[11] See Sobel 1987, 247 for a detailed formal reconstruction of the proof.

[12] That the essence of x is necessarily a property only of x is expressible as follows: φ Ess x → L(∀y) (φy → y=x). Since (Gx → G Ess x), it follows that (Gx & Gy) → x=y. Sobel 1987 considers the issue on p. 245 and in n. 6, p. 259.

A contrast with Spinoza is implicit, for Spinoza maintains that extension constitutes the essence of God and he also hold that there are modifications of God that are themselves extended.

[13] Sobel 1987, 244. Ax. 1, P(−φ) ↔ −P(φ), along with the definition of "Gx," entails that (Gx & φx) → P(φ).

essence."[14] In the *explicatio* to this we also learn that, "if something is absolutely infinite, whatever expresses essence and involves no negation pertains to its essence." Since attributes express essence and involve no negation, this is strikingly close to a definition of God as being that consists of all attributes, that is, as being, or a being, that has everything that is purely positive.

Gödel's thesis that all of the properties of a thing are entailed by its essence is perhaps suggested, but it is not asserted, in 1p16d.[15] In contrast, the *Treatise on the Emendation of the Intellect* explicitly maintains that all properties of a thing follow from its definition.[16] His formal definition of essence in 2d2 is clearly different from Gödel's, however.

Definitions 1d1, 1d7, and 1d8 are all relevant to Gödel's definition of necessary existence.[17] But of these, only definition i is employed in Spinoza's ontological argument, that is, in the first demonstration of 1p11.[18]

Despite such verbal similarities, important divergences also exist both in their arguments and in their conceptions of God. As Sobel emphasizes, Gödel employs a very broad notion of a positive property (including, for example, self-identity), whereas Spinoza maintains that the known attributes are restricted to thought and extension. At least some moral and aesthetic properties are evidently regarded as positive, and attributed to God by Gödel, but certainly not by Spinoza. In addition, Spinoza's argument, in contrast to Gödel's, makes explicit use of notions of substance and of causality, and it makes no explicit appeal

[14] Spinoza 2002, 217.

[15] Spinoza there maintains that from the definition of a thing, a number (plures) of properties can be inferred, which really follow from the thing's essence, and the more essence a thing has, the more properties follow from it. (This is used to argue that "infinite things in infinite ways, that is, everything that can fall under an infinite intellect" follow from the essence of God. On the face of it, then, every property of God follows from God's essence.)

[16] For the definition of a created thing, "We require a concept, *or* definition, of the thing such that when it is considered alone, without any others conjoined, all the thing's properties can be deduced from it ... " (TdIE, § 96). For the definition of an uncreated thing, "Finally (though it is not very necessary to note this) it is required that all its properties be inferred from its definition" (TdIE, § 97). (Note in addition that on Spinoza's account the definition of a thing "will have to explain the inmost essence of the thing... " [TdIE, § 95].)

[17] The latter defines eternity as "existence itself, insofar as it is conceived to follow necessarily from the definition alone of the eternal thing." In 1d7 a thing is defined as free when it "exists from the necessity of its nature alone and is determined to act by itself alone" and 1d1 defines "cause of itself" as "that whose essence involves existence.... "

[18] Definition 1d1 is explicitly cited in 1p7d, which itself is cited in 1p11d.

to modal reduction theorems such as the S5 thesis that if it is possibly necessary that p then it is necessary that p, that is, (MLp → Lp).

## Two Objections

Further consideration of the above similarities and differences between Gödel and Spinoza would perhaps be fruitful, but my aim here is instead to consider at least briefly two major objections raised by Sobel to Gödel's theory. These objections are that Gödel's God is not properly called "God" (Sobel 1987, 250) and that his God, or perhaps rather the whole theory, is "*logically* embarrassing" (Sobel 1987, 250 and Sobel 2004, 132).

"God" is held to be a misnomer, for the God in question would lack properties necessary for it to be sensibly worshipped. Gödel's God "would *not* be omniscient, omnipotent, just, or benevolent, and would indeed lack every 'attribute of God' that might recommend it as an object of worship... " (Sobel 1987, 250).[19]

Although little is said of what worship is, and why God is to be worshipped, that may not matter. The objection is interesting in part because the moral characteristics that Gödel's God lacks, according to Sobel, are ones that Spinoza's God could not have. Indeed, the objection is reminiscent of charges of atheism brought against Spinoza. God does not act purposively or intentionally, according to Spinoza, and this is enough in some eyes to discredit his use of the term "God" ("Deus").

Omnipotence, omniscience, and indeed consciousness are another matter. The ordinary view is that there could have been only mindless beings, that in fact some beings are mindless, and that some are also inanimate. If the ontological argument is successful, and if some of Spinoza's other arguments are too, then these ordinary views are false. Sobel speaks here of the burden of the argument,[20] but surely more must be done to this resolve the issue. The burden of the argument might rest, as Sobel claims, on those who would reject our ordinary views. But if so, a determination that that burden has or has not been met requires an examination of the proofs they have offered. In the case of Spinoza, at least, an adequate formal representation of these proofs has yet to be given.[21]

---

[19] This objection is reiterated and discussed at more length in Sobel 2004, 128–32.

[20] Sobel 1987, 250 and Sobel 2004, 131.

[21] My own attempt, set out most fully in Jarrett 1978, is at best a start, and use of some of the ideas, as well as the logic, of Gödel's notes might well help to provide a more adequate representation. Also see Friedman 1978.

Sobel's second objection mentions a logical embarrassment, for in Gödel's system, "whatever is true is so necessarily and...whatever exists does so necessarily" (Sobel 1987, 251 and Sobel 2004, 133–4). As Sobel shows, this is provable in Gödel's system, at least when supplemented with a thesis about property abstraction.[22]

Here again what Sobel finds objectionable, Spinoza takes as a desideratum. It is true that there is a very large interpretive issue here, as well as a (nearly indistinguishable) issue about the representation of Spinoza's views. But why, exactly, is the unconditional necessity of all things a logical embarrassment?

It could be maintained, of course, that by definition a proposition or statement is logically necessary solely in virtue of its logical structure and that any necessity other than this is simply a different kind of necessity. "All cats are cats" would then be logically necessary, whereas "The cat is on the mat," or "Nothing travels faster than light," would not be, in the absence of special definitions. But one could also maintain, as far as I can see, that there is just one kind of necessity, which in some cases, but not all, can be seen to be present by the elucidation of logical structure. To hold this would be to regard the structural difference between "All cats are cats" and "The cat is on the mat" as primarily epistemological. Logic, supplemented by a finite analysis of terms, simply reveals the necessity of some claims (taken in abstraction from others), while it does not reveal the necessity of others.

There is no doubt that a doctrine of the complete necessitation of all things will encounter objections from areas as diverse as morality (free will) and physics (quantum indeterminacies). But these present no logical problem, granting that one would neither begin nor wish to begin an exposition of modal logic or ontology with the thesis that what is so is necessarily so. What logical problem, if any, does the doctrine of necessity raise for Gödel or Spinoza?

It might be thought, concerning Gödel's theory, that because every property of God is a necessary one, no distinction can be drawn between

---

[22] The thesis is: "Properties $\delta[\phi](\alpha) \leftrightarrow \phi'$ where $\delta$ is an individual variable, $\alpha$ is a term, $\phi$ is a formula, and $\phi'$ is a formula that comes from $\phi$ by proper substitution of $\alpha$ for $\delta$" (Sobel 1987, 251). Thus, for example, $(\exists y)(y \neq a \leftrightarrow â[(\exists y)(y \neq a)]a$, that is, "Something is distinct from a just in case a has the property of there being something distinct from it." From this it follows, for example, that if it is the case that Q, then any object you select has the property of being such that Q. Anything that is so can then be construed as a property of a God (or of anything else). But every property of God is necessitated by God's essence and hence is necessarily instantiated by God. Thus it is necessarily the case that Q. (Sobel gives a short and elegant exposition of this argument on p. 253.) See also Sobel 2004, 133–4.

any property of God and God's essence. (This would be a difficulty, insofar as Gödel appears to hold that there is more than one positive property of God.) No distinction of this sort could be drawn if "$\varphi$ is an essence of x" were defined as "x has $\phi$ and x's having $\phi$ strictly implies that x has $\psi$, for every property $\psi$ that x has."[23] Indeed, if this were so, every property of any object would "constitute" its essence. It is instead defined as "x has $\phi$ and being $\phi$ strictly implies being $\psi$, for every property $\psi$ that x has,"[24] however, which is not, so far as I can see, derivable from "x has $\phi$ and is (a) God."[25]

The difficulty regarding Spinoza's theory, or formal representations of it, seems more severe.[26] For Spinoza maintains that the essence of substance involves existence (or necessary existence), whereas the essences of modes do not. One attempt to represent the claim that the essence of x involves necessary existence would be as follows:

iii. If $\phi$ is the essence of x, then x's being $\phi$ strictly implies that x exists.[27]

The trouble is then that if modal distinctions collapse, it can be established that everything that exists, not just substance, satisfies (iii), and so the essence of each mode will involve necessary existence.[28]

An alternative to iii would represent "the essence of x involves existence" as Gödel defines "x has necessary existence":

iv. x has Necessary Existence if and only if for every property $\phi$, if $\phi$ is an essence of x then necessarily there exists a $\phi$.[29]

But this is no better. For as Sobel has shown, "Everything has Necessary Existence" ("$(\forall x)NEx$") is provable in Gödel's system when supplemented with apparently innocuous principles.[30] It remains to be seen whether some variation of a formulation such as iii or iv can be employed to provide an adequate representation of Spinoza.

[23] This is to define "being $\phi$ is an essence of x," that is, "$\phi$ Ess x" as "$\varphi x$ & $(\forall\psi)$ $(\psi x \to L(\varphi x \to \psi x)$."
[24] That is, "$\phi$ Ess x" is defined as "$\phi x$ & $(\forall\psi)$ $(\psi x \to L(\forall y)$ $(\Phi y \to \psi y))$."
[25] This is, simply, "$(\phi x$ & $Gx)$."
[26] It can be shown, on the other hand, that if Gx & Fx and if nothing other than x has F, then F Ess x.
[27] Take "$\phi$ Ess x" as "$\phi$ is the essence of x" (or even "$\phi$ is an essence of x") and regard "$(\exists y)(y = x)$" as "x exists." Then iii is "$\phi$ Ess x & $L(\phi x \to (\exists y)(y = x))$."
[28] The argument for this is short, for if $(\exists y)(y = x)$, then (since modal distinctions collapse) $L(\exists y)(y = x)$, and thus $L(\phi x \to (\exists y)(y=x))$.
[29] This is "$NEx \leftrightarrow (\forall\varphi)(\varphi$ Ess x $\to L(\exists x)\varphi x)$."
[30] Sobel 1987, 252; Sobel 2004, 133–4. See Anderson 1990, 296–7 for emendations of Gödel's axioms where "on at least one reasonable way of formalizing the proof," there is no modal collapse.

### 5. CONCLUSION

It is noteworthy that whether intended by Gödel or not, the premises of his *Ontologicisher Beweiss* plausibly yield, as Sobel has shown, the conclusion that whatever is so is necessarily so. For the same or a very similar doctrine constitutes a central part of Spinoza's metaphysics, despite the fact that the technical apparatus employed by Gödel was unavailable to Spinoza. Whether Gödel's formulation of the argument can help advance our representation of Spinoza's thought is an open question.

Descartes tried to combine the ontological argument with the thesis that God could will just about anything, and that what is good depends on His will. Leibniz tried to combine it with the thesis that God could have produced a different world, but because of His wisdom and benevolence, He would certainly will to produce, and hence actually would produce, the best possible world. What is best is then something independent of God's will (like a target at which he aims), and somehow what God will certainly do He is not necessitated to do.[31]

Spinoza, in contrast, combined the ontological argument with the thesis that there could be real contingency neither in God nor, consequently, in the world. For Spinoza's concept of God is the concept of completely unlimited being, containing nothing negative, and therefore, on the face of it, admitting of no real distinction between the potential and the actual. If the world is dependent on such a purely actual God, either as an effect on its cause, or a property on its subject, no other conclusion appears possible.

---

[31] These views are targets of attack in the last paragraph of 1p33s2.

# 7    Knowledge in Spinoza's *Ethics*

In this chapter I discuss how Spinoza deals in the *Ethics* with some basic issues in the theory of knowledge, including perception and intellectual knowledge, belief, error, justification, and skepticism. I begin in Section 1 with his explanation of the nature of the mind within the context of his broader metaphysics, because this explanation is fundamental to his treatment of these epistemological topics. I then consider his theory of perception, the distinction between adequate and inadequate ideas, and his threefold classification of knowledge into imagination, reason, and intuitive knowledge. In Section 2 I take up his theory of justification and his response to skepticism; and in Section 3 I deal with his theories of belief and error. I conclude Section 3 with some observations regarding the implications of his theory of belief for his views on knowledge.

## I. MIND AND COGNITION

### *The Human Mind as a Mode of the One Substance*

Part 2 of the *Ethics* opens with a number of propositions that generally continue the account of the relation between God or substance and finite things that begins with 1p15. Thought and extension are attributes of the one substance (2p1, 2p2). Because every attribute is conceptually independent of every other (1p10), and because a causal relation implies a conceptual relation (1a4), it follows that there is no causal interaction between modes of different attributes; that is, within each attribute the chain of causality is closed (2p5, 2p6). But although there is no causal interaction between bodies or modes of extension and ideas or modes of thought, there is a complete parallelism between the modifications of each of the attributes.[1] The well-known parallelism

---

[1] I ignore whatever complications arise for the parallelism doctrine if one takes Spinoza to hold that there are more attributes besides extension and thought. This is primarily a metaphysical issue, not an epistemological one.

140

doctrine is expressed in 2p7, that "The order and connection of ideas is the same as the order and connection of things," which is a consequence of 1a4, that "The knowledge of an effect depends on, and involves, the knowledge of the cause," and also (unnoticed by Spinoza) 2p3, that "In God there is necessarily an idea, both of his essence, and of everything that necessarily follows from his essence." A deeper explanation of the parallelism asserted by 2p7 is given in the scholium to 2p7c:

[T]he thinking substance, and extended substance are one and the same substance, which is now comprehended under this attribute, now under that. So also a mode of extension and the idea of that mode are one and the same thing, but expressed in two ways.

... Therefore, whether we conceive nature under the attribute of Extension, or under the attribute of Thought, or under any other attribute, we find one and the same order, or one and the same connection of causes, i.e., that the same things follow one another.[2]

Thus, the parallelism between ideas and their objects is a consequence of their identity. The passages continues with Spinoza offering a kind of cautionary note to the effect that, despite the identity of ideas and their objects, the conceptual independence of modes of different attributes precludes causal relations between them, and therefore

so long as things are considered as modes of thinking, we must explain the order of the whole of nature, or the connection of causes, through the attribute of Thought alone ... I understand the same concerning the other attributes.

The human mind is the idea (in God) whose object is the human body (2p11, 2p13). Thus, the "union of mind and body" for Spinoza is an instance of the general identity of objects and ideas described in 2p7cs (above; see also 2p21s), and all individuals, like human beings, are animate, "in different degrees" (2p13cs). But although understanding the basic ontology of the mind is a matter of seeing how, in general, ideas relate to their objects, as Spinoza points out,

[I]deas differ among themselves, as the objects themselves do, and ... one is more excellent than the other, and contains more reality, just as the object of the one idea is more excellent than the object of another and contains more reality.

It follows that the specific cognitive functions and capacities of the human mind must be understood in terms of the mind's object, the body. Continuing the above passage, he writes,

[I]n proportion as a Body is more capable than others of doing more things at once, or being acted on in many ways at once, so its Mind is more capable

[2] All quotations from the *Ethics* are from C.

of perceiving many things at once. And in proportion as the actions of a body depend more on itself alone, and as other bodies concur with it less in acting, so its mind is more capable of understanding distinctly. And from these [truths] we know the excellence of one mind over the others, and also see the cause why we have only a completely confused knowledge of our Body.... (2p13cs)

Spinoza's intent thus appears to be to explain all the mind's cognitive functions in terms of psychic mechanisms that parallel events and processes in the body.

### The Imaginative Faculties: Perception, Imagining, Memory, and Introspection

Spinoza's account of sensory perception (perception of external objects) rests on three basic propositions. The first is 2p12:

SP1: Whatever happens in the object of the idea constituting the human mind must be perceived by the human mind, or there will necessarily be an idea of that thing in the mind; that is, if the object of the idea constituting a human mind is a body, nothing can happen in that body which is not perceived by the mind.

This proposition is essentially a consequence of the parallelism doctrine, taken in conjunction with the definition of the mind as the idea of an actually existing body: because the order and connection of ideas is the same as the order and connection of things, given that the mind is the idea of the human body, the ideas of things that happen in the human body must be in the human mind.[3] The importance of this proposition is that it provides the basis for explaining how the mind has cognitive access to the physical realm, even though there can be no causal links between the mind and the physical realm (2p5).

The second basic proposition in the account of sense perception is 2a1 (following lemma 3):

SP2: All modes by which a body is affected by another body follow from the nature of the body affected and at the same time from the nature of the affecting body[.]

This axiom is an expression of Spinoza's concept of causality according to which a cause necessarily determines its effect, and a thing can have no properties except what it derives from its cause.

[3] Spinoza offers a more detailed proof of 2p12 (which I discuss below), but remarks in the scholium that the proposition is "evident, and more clearly understood" from 2p7.

The third proposition is 1a4:

SP3: The knowledge of an effect depends on, and involves, the knowledge of its cause.

The mind has ideas of, or perceives, all that happens in the body (SP1, above). But what happens in the body – the modifications or affections of the body – is the effect of some external body acting on the human body, and therefore (by SP2 and SP3, above), the idea of such an affection of the body must involve the nature of the human body, together with the nature of the external body. Thus, the mind perceives external bodies and the human body itself through its ideas of the affections of the body (2p16c1, 2p19). Spinoza notes, however, that these ideas "indicate the constitution of our own body, more than the nature of external bodies" (2p16c2).

The same three principles that underlie the account of perception also explain our ability to imagine things that are not present (and why we can suffer hallucinations): if the body is affected in a way that "involves the nature of an external body, the human mind will regard the same external body as actually existing, or as present to it" irrespective of whether or not the external body does actually exist or is present (2p17, 2p17c). Memory is explained as an association of ideas that involve the nature of external bodies, which parallels a physiological link, established by conditioning, between bodily states (2p18, 2p18s).

By 2p3, God has an idea of the mind, and by 2p7 and its scholium, this idea of the mind is united to its object, the mind, just as the mind is united to its object, the body (2p20, 2p21, and their demonstrations). In other words, just as mind and body "are one and the same individual, which is conceived now under the attribute of thought, now under the attribute of extension," so "the idea of the mind and the mind itself are one and the same thing, conceived under one and the same attribute, namely, thought" (2p21s). Our ability to introspect the contents of our own mind – to have ideas of our ideas – is thus explained by Spinoza as follows: (1) the ideas of the ideas of the affections of our body are in God's idea of the human mind (2p22d); (2) God's idea of the human mind is identical with the mind (2p21s). Therefore, our mind contains ideas of our ideas.

## A Problem for Spinoza's Theory of Perception

One difficulty for Spinoza's theory lies in the implausibility of the claim of 2p12 (SP1, above) that the human mind *perceives* everything that happens in the body. A solution to this might seem to lie in a proper interpretation of the two usages of "idea of" to which Spinoza himself draws attention in 2p17cs:

[W]e clearly understand what is the difference between the *idea of*, say, Peter, which constitutes the essence of Peter's mind, and the *idea of* Peter which is in another man, say, Paul. For the former directly explains the essence of Peter's body, and does not involve existence, except as long as Peter exists; but the latter indicates the condition of Paul's body more than Peter's nature.... (My emphasis)

According to one usage "idea of" involves the relation between an idea or mode of thinking and the mode of extension with which it is identical (its correlate); according to the other it involves the relation between an idea and the external cause of the bodily modification with which the idea is identical. One important point of discussion among commentators has been whether the relation between an idea and its correlate is representational in a mental or psychological sense (representation by a mind, to itself), as opposed to the sense of mere correlation (as distance on a map may represent actual distance between geographic locations, or rings on a tree trunk may represent the age of the tree).[4] For our purposes here this is important because, if Spinoza held that the relation between ideas and their correlates is mere correspondence or correlation, then the problem mentioned above – the implausibility of the claim that we perceive everything that happens in the body – does not arise. On such an interpretation, his theory of perception (properly stated) would be that we perceive external objects through having ideas that correspond with (but do not represent, in the mental sense) modifications of the body caused by external objects, not that we perceive external bodies through *perceiving* the modifications of our body. Spinoza would be subject to the minor criticism that he should not have (carelessly) asserted in 2p12 that the human mind perceives everything that happens in the body, but his theory of perception is seen as not involving or resting on this claim.

Although at least one commentator has offered an interpretation along these lines, this does not seem to have been Spinoza's view.[5] That ideas, at least insofar as they are in God, represent their extended correlates in the mental sense is indicated by Spinoza's citation in the demonstration of 2p7, of 1a4, that "The knowledge [*cognitio*] of an effect

---

[4] The notion of mental representationality here in question corresponds with what Searle (1992, 78–82) has called the "intrinsic intentionality" of thought.

[5] Radner (1971, 346–51) argues that Spinoza intentionally explains the mind's ability to have ideas that represent external objects in terms of the nonrepresentational relation of correlation that holds between its ideas and states of the body (that are caused by external objects). As she points out (339–40), her view contrasts with those of earlier commentators who took Spinoza to have confused the two relations denoted by "idea of."

depends on, and involves, the knowledge of its cause," and also by those subsequent passages in which he equates God's having the idea of a thing (the idea which is identical with the thing) and his having knowledge of it. One such passage occurs in the demonstration of 2p9c:

Whatever happens in the singular object of any idea, there is knowledge of it in God, only insofar as he has the idea of the same object.

Dem. *Whatever happens in the object of any idea*, there is an idea of it in God... but the order and connection of ideas (by p7) is the same as the order and connections of things; therefore, *knowledge of what happens in a singular object* will be in God only insofar as he has the idea of the same object.... (My emphasis)

Significantly, 2p9c is explicitly invoked by Spinoza to prove 2p12 (SP1, above), that the human mind must perceive everything that happens in its object (the body). There he reasons that because, by 2p9c, God has knowledge of what happens in an object insofar as he has the idea of the object or constitutes its mind, he will have knowledge of whatever happens in the object of the human mind, which is to say, "the mind will perceive it." Thus, for Spinoza, that the human mind *perceives* all that happens in the human body is an instance of, and follows as a consequence from, the mentalistic representational nature of the relation between every idea and the modification of extension with which it is identical.

Another possible way to deal with the apparent implausibility of the claim that we perceive everything that happens in our bodies is suggested by Michael Della Rocca's interpretation of what it means for our ideas which represent both their bodily correlates and an external object to be "confused."[6] According to Della Rocca these ideas should not be understood as having two contents, one of which (directly) represents the bodily modification and one of which (indirectly) represents its external cause; rather they should be taken as having a single content that is a confused amalgamation of the properties of both. If Della Rocca's interpretation is correct, then such ideas can be understood as mental representations of their bodily correlates, which are not sufficiently clear to be perceived as such.[7] (We perceive everything that happens in

---

[6] Spinoza explicitly characterizes all the ideas by which we perceive things through the ideas of the affections of our body as confused in 2p28, 2p29c, and 2p29cs. See the discussion of adequate and inadequate ideas below.

[7] Della Rocca 1996a, 57–64. So far as I can see, Della Rocca does not point out this further advantage of his interpretation of what it means for these ideas to be confused.

Della Rocca's account of what it means for ideas to be confused is preceded by a discussion of the issues involved in the debate over Spinoza's two usages of "idea

the body in the nonopaque sense of "perceive," or the sense in which I can perceive the mayor crossing the street without perceiving that it is the mayor who is crossing the street.)

But even if we can allow that the human mind perceives everything that happens in the body by taking such perceptions to be so confused that one of their objects is unrecognized, there is another closely related problem that is not so easily solved. It is that the general nature of the argument for 2p12 seems to make it equally applicable to every "mind." As Spinoza remarks in 2p13s, all things are animate; that is, there is an idea in God of each thing, which is related to that thing as the human mind is related to the human body. Thus, the reasoning Spinoza uses to prove 2p12 appears equally to prove that the "mind" or idea of a rock or the solar system must perceive whatever happens in its body, a consequence that many find at least implausible if "perceive" is taken to entail any sort (even confused) of consciousness. But because this seems to be a problem for Spinoza's philosophy of mind more than for his epistemology, I shall not pursue it here.[8]

## Epistemic Value: Adequate versus Inadequate Ideas

In the *Ethics* Spinoza holds a correspondence theory of truth: "A true idea must agree with its object" (1a6).[9] A main aim of *Ethics* Part 2 is to

of," which includes useful accounts of the views of several previous commentators. Della Rocca's own view is that whereas "idea of" may refer to different relations between an idea and its representational object (depending on whether the object is taken to be the bodily modification with which it is identical or the external cause of the modification), there is a single sense in which it represents both objects, and thus it has a single content. Della Rocca is particularly concerned to differentiate his view from that of Jonathan Bennett, who, in stressing the differences between what he calls the "directly of" and the "indirectly of" relations, appears to hold that ideas represent their two objects in different senses, and have two separate (direct and indirect) contents (Bennett 1984, 153–9).

[8] Margaret Wilson (1999) argued that the generality of Spinoza's conception of the mind as God's idea of the body prevented him from being able to distinguish conscious entities from nonconscious ones, and conscious states within a mind from nonconscious ones. As a point of criticism, this seems somewhat mitigated by the fact that no one has yet solved the "hard problem" of consciousness (unless one counts substance dualism as a solution).

[9] By contrast, a coherentist conception of truth at least seems to feature prominently in the *Treatise on the Emendation of the Intellect* (see especially §§ 69–72; G II, 26–27). Curley (1994) traces the development of Spinoza's treatment of truth from his earlier works through the *Ethics*.

*Ethics* 1a6 says only that agreement between an idea and its object is a necessary condition of truth, but in 2p32d, Spinoza explicitly takes it to assert agreement as a sufficient condition, so it seems right to say that for Spinoza truth consists in the agreement between an idea and its object.

demonstrate that the human mind has at least some true ideas, and to explain what differentiates them from false ones. Spinoza proceeds by (1) introducing the notion of an adequate idea (2d4, below); (2) showing which of our ideas are adequate, and which are inadequate (2p24–p31, 2p38–p40, 2p46–p47); and (3) arguing that all of our adequate ideas are true (2p34):

An adequate idea is one which considered in itself, without relation to an object, has all the properties, *or* intrinsic denominations of a true idea.

Spinoza adds in explanation that

I say intrinsic to exclude what is extrinsic, viz. the agreement of the idea with its object. (2d4)

Although this formulation suggests that there are certain features of adequate ideas directly accessible to a knower, whose presence is a guarantee of the truth of her idea (analogous to clearness and distinctness in Descartes), in the *Ethics* Spinoza does not take an epistemic approach to adequacy, and he does not spell out precisely what he means by the "intrinsic denominations" of a true idea.[10] Rather, he approaches the topic metaphysically, explaining adequacy and inadequacy, and proving which ideas are adequate or inadequate, in terms of the relation between our mind and God's infinite intellect.[11] The key passage occurs in 2p11c:

[T]he human Mind is a part of the infinite intellect of God. Therefore, when we say that the human Mind perceives this or that, we are saying nothing but that God, not insofar as he is infinite, but insofar as he is explained through the nature of the human Mind, *or* insofar as he constitutes the essence of the human Mind, has this or that idea; and when we say that God has this or that idea, not only insofar as he constitutes the nature of the human Mind, but insofar as he also has the idea of another thing together with the human Mind, then we say that the human Mind perceives the thing only partially, *or* inadequately.

Spinoza's characterization here of an inadequate idea (in the human mind) as one which God has "not only insofar as he constitutes the

---

[10] Spinoza does use "clear and distinct" in such a way as to make it fairly evident that he takes all clear and distinct ideas to be adequate, and vice versa; and similarly he uses "confused" and/or "mutilated" as at least extensionally equivalent to "inadequate" (see for example 2p35, 2p36). "Clear and distinct" may well be the "intrinsic denominations" he has in mind in 2d4, but he does not offer any explanation of this notion.

[11] In contrast, the discussion of the topic in letters 59 and 60 (between Tschirnhaus and Spinoza) proceeds from the point of view of the knower (Spinoza 1995, 287–91; G IV, 268–71). See note 14 below.

nature of the human Mind, but insofar as he also has the idea of another thing together with the human mind" is ambiguous. It could mean either that

> 3a. an idea is inadequate in the human mind if its object is not wholly represented by (in) God insofar as he constitutes the (nature of the) mind (and otherwise adequate)

or that

> 3b. an idea is inadequate in the human mind if God insofar as he constitutes the (nature of the) mind is not the sufficient cause of the idea (and otherwise it is adequate).

If Spinoza's intended meaning were captured by a, then because God's idea of a thing contains a complete representation of whatever is or occurs in the thing (by 2p7 and 2p9c), Spinoza should conclude that the ideas of the parts of the human body and of its affections are adequate in the human mind.[12] In fact, he concludes that both are inadequate (2p24 and 2p28); and his general line of reasoning in the demonstrations of these propositions, as well as in those of 2p25, 2p26c, 2p27, 2p29, 2p30, and 2p31, suggests that it is b that accurately expresses what he means by an inadequate idea. In other words, an idea is inadequate in a mind if its sufficient cause (in Spinozistic terms, adequate cause) lies partly outside that mind; and adequate if its sufficient or adequate cause

---

[12] Bennett appears to think Spinoza's meaning in 2p11c is captured by a, because he says that 2p11c "seems to imply that you perceive x inadequately if x is a physical item some of which lies outside your body" (1984, 177). Bennett goes on to say that Spinoza changes the condition of inadequacy in 2p24 (and subsequent propositions): "What we find in p24d is that an idea of mine is inadequate if it is *caused from* outside my mind . . . " (ibid.). This seems ungenerous because the original passage (2p11c) surely admits of the b interpretation. Radner's discussion of the meaning of adequacy and inadequacy (applied to ideas) does not make explicit mention of 2p11c, but she maintains that "We have an adequate idea of X if the idea which represents X to us is the idea which represents X to God – that is, if the idea by which God knows X is in God in so far as he forms the nature of the human mind (E, II, 34 D)" (1971, 352–3). The passage she cites as support here seems inconclusive with respect to the question of the condition of adequacy. She admits the consequence of the interpretation, that the human mind's ideas of the affections of the body are adequate, not inadequate, as Spinoza claims, maintaining that "Spinoza's claim that we do not have adequate ideas of our bodily affections is based upon a confusion between 'adequate' as applied to ideas and 'adequate' as applied to causes" (ibid., 356). The further consequence of her interpretation, that Spinoza's entire theory of the passions turns out to be based on a mistake, seems sufficient to render it unacceptable.

lies wholly within it.[13] Because the causal order of ideas replicates the causal order of things, the sufficient cause of the idea of $x$ is the idea of the sufficient cause of $x$. Hence, an idea of a thing $x$ is adequate in a mind if that mind has, in addition to its idea of $x$, the idea of the sufficient or adequate cause of $x$.[14] Put in slightly different terms, to have an adequate idea of a thing is to have a complete explanation of it.

In God all ideas are adequate, because God has the ideas of all things, and "the order and connection of ideas is the same as the order and connection of things" (2p3, 2p7, 2p32, 2p36d). The human mind, however, has only inadequate ideas of the affections of the body (2p28), the parts of the body (2p24), the body itself (2p27), external bodies (2p25), the mind itself (2p29), its own ideas (2p28), the duration of the body (2p30), and the duration of external bodies (2p31). This is because each of these items is an existing finite mode, and, as such, the result of an infinite chain of finite causes (1p28). The ideas of the causes of these things – complete explanations of them – are thus beyond the reach of the human mind.[15]

Insofar as the mind has the idea of any finite mode, it also has the idea of the attribute through which that mode is conceived (extension or thought). And because an attribute has no cause beyond itself, its idea is necessarily adequate in the human mind. That is, God has the idea of an attribute insofar as he has the idea of any modification of

---

[13] Interpretation b is also supported by the demonstration that ideas that follow in the mind from adequate ideas must also be adequate (2p40), which reads:

For when we say that an idea in the human Mind follows from ideas that are adequate in it, we are saying nothing but that (by p11c) in the Divine intellect there is an idea of which *God is the cause*, not insofar as he is infinite, nor insofar he is affected with the ideas of a great many singular things, but *insofar as he constitutes only the essence of the human Mind*.... (Emphasis mine)

[14] This is consistent with Spinoza's response (Ep60) to Tschirnhaus's inquiry (Ep59) regarding true and adequate ideas, in which Spinoza appears to agree with Tschirnhaus's tentative characterization of an adequate idea as one that expresses or involves the complete and ultimate cause of the thing (Spinoza 1995, 287–91; G IV, 268–71).

[15] According to Bennett, the notion of adequate ideas that Spinoza is employing in 2p24–p31 "must involve only their whole *proximate* causes lying inside the person's mind; it could not be the whole infinite causal chain leading to the idea" (1984, 178). But this would imply that ideas of some bodily affections would be adequate, namely, those whose proximate causes lie entirely within the body, and Spinoza does not seem to allow for our having adequate ideas of any of our bodily affections. Further, Spinoza is quite explicit that insofar as things depend on an infinite regression of causes we cannot have adequate knowledge of them. (See 2p30, 2p31, and their demonstrations.)

that attribute; hence all the mind's ideas of the affections of the body involve an adequate idea of extension.[16] In addition, because an adequate idea is one that is caused by God insofar as he constitutes the human mind, it follows that the ideas of those things that immediately or mediately follow from (are caused by) an attribute – its infinite and eternal modes – are adequate (2p40 and 2p40d). The ideas of the attributes and what follows from them make up what Spinoza refers to as the "common notions" (2p38c, 2p40s, 5p12d, 5p28d). Spinoza also proves that we have adequate knowledge of God's essence (2p45–p47); but because the attributes constitute God's essence, this knowledge does not appear to involve anything beyond what is contained in the most basic of the common notions. What is added by 2p45–p47 is that the most basic knowledge of what is common to all finite things is also knowledge of the divine essence. (This is a consequence of God's immanent causality.)[17]

## Spinoza's Three Kinds of Knowledge

In God all ideas represent the modes of extension with which they are identical; hence "All ideas, insofar as they are related to God are true," that is, agree with their objects (2p32, by 2p7, 1p6). Because an adequate idea in the human mind is one that God has "insofar as he constitutes the essence of the human mind," it follows that all ideas that are adequate in the human mind are true (2p34, by 2p11c). But insofar as the human mind has inadequate ideas, or ones that are "mutilated and confused," it is subject to falsity and error (2p35).[18]

All thinking that involves susceptibility to falsity or error falls under the heading of what Spinoza calls "knowledge of the first kind" or "opinion" or "imagination" (2p40s2, 2p41). It includes what is derived both from sense experience and "from signs" – from hearing or reading about a thing.[19] Because all such imaginative cognition is ultimately derived from the mind's regarding things through its ideas of the affections of the

[16] See 2p38d, discussed below.
[17] See 1p18.
[18] See pp. below for discussion of Spinoza's treatment of falsity and error.
[19] The exact characterization of the experiential component of the first kind of knowledge (the component not based on signs) is that it is what is derived "from singular things which have been represented to us through the senses *in a way that is mutilated, confused, and without order for the intellect* (see 2p29c); for that reason I have been accustomed to call such perceptions *knowledge from random experience*" (2p40s2; emphasis mine). This seems to leave open the possibility that structured observation and experiment might play some role in the higher kinds of knowledge (discussed below), although Spinoza does no more than hint at such a possibility in the *Ethics*. E. M. Curley draws on the *Treatise on the Emendation*

body, it is necessarily subjective, or indicative of the state of the body rather than the nature of any external object, and illusory insofar as it is taken to be representative of the nature of things beyond the state of the body. One important class of illusory imaginative ideas is composed of value concepts: "good," "evil," "order," "confusion," "beauty," and "ugliness," like "warm" and "cold," are properties of our own responses to things which we project onto the things themselves (1app).[20]

Ordinary universal notions in terms of which we think about the world – man, horse, dog – and those denoted by such highly general "transcendental" terms as "being," "thing," and "something" form another broad category of ideas that are illusory insofar as we take them to represent the real natures of things (2p40s1). These ideas owe their origin to the inability of the body to form more than a certain limited number of images at once. When that number is exceeded, the images in the body become run together to a greater or lesser degree, and their corresponding ideas exhibit more or less confusion.[21] Like the imaginative ideas of individual bodies, these imaginative universals indicate the constitution of our own body more than the nature of external bodies (2p16c2); and, as Spinoza points out, they vary from one person to another, "in accordance with what the body has been more often affected by, and what the mind imagines or recollects more easily" (2p40s1). In both of these respects they are unlike the common notions, which are

*of the Intellect* to argue that for Spinoza intuitive knowledge and possibly also reason require the use of experiment (Curley 1973a, esp. 56–9).

   With respect to his classifying knowledge derived from signs as knowledge of the first kind, it is important to keep in mind that Spinoza explains language and language use as a function of imaginative thinking, that is, in terms of an association between ideas of words or utterances and ideas of things, which parallels a linkage between images of words (or utterances) and images of things in the body. See 2p18s.

20   Regarding "order" Spinoza writes

   [W]hen things are so disposed that, when they are presented to us through the senses, we can easily imagine them, and so can easily remember them, we say that they are well-ordered; but if the opposite is true, we say that they are badly ordered, or confused. (1app)

21   Transcendental terms "signify ideas that are confused in the highest degree," whereas universal terms denote ideas that represent distinctly some common feature of how the body is affected by a certain "kind" of external object. For example, the universal notion "man" is generated when

   so many images ... are formed at one time in the human Body that they surpass the power of imagining – not entirely, of course, but still to the point where the mind can imagine neither slight differences of the singular [men] (such as the color and size of each one, etc.) nor their determinate number, and imagines distinctly only what they all agree in, insofar as they affect the body. (2p40s1)

adequate and true representations of their objects, common to all minds (2p38c).

The common notions form the basis of what Spinoza calls "reason" or "the second kind of knowledge" (2p40s2). Because these notions are of what is "equally in the part and in the whole" and "does not constitute the essence of any singular thing" (2p37), this knowledge is general or universal, comprising the basic and derived laws of physics for extension, and their analogues in psychology for thought.[22]

Because reason perceives things truly, or as they are in themselves, it perceives them as necessary or determined in every respect, and not contingent (2p44 and 2p44d). Things are viewed by us as contingent, or able to be otherwise than as they are (or will be or have been), only insofar as we think of them imaginatively.[23] This happens because in the course of experience the images of things become linked with images of other things in more than one way. For example, on some mornings I wake up and it is sunny, on others it is rainy or cloudy. Thus, the idea of morning becomes linked with both fair weather and foul; and when I think, say, of tomorrow morning I vacillate between one association and the other. Thus, from the point of view of imagination, it is uncertain and hence contingent what tomorrow's weather will be (2p44s).

Spinoza's assertion that "It is of the nature of Reason to perceive things under a certain species of eternity" (2p44c2) raises the question of whether he means to treat time (temporal passage), like contingency, as a kind of illusion arising from the imaginative perception of things. In the demonstration of 2p44c2 he offers two lines of thought, neither of which supports such an interpretation. The first implicitly refers back to the definition of "eternity" at 1d8 as "existence itself, insofar as it is conceived to follow necessarily from the definition alone of the

---

[22] The exact formulation that Spinoza gives for the second kind of knowledge is that it is what derives from our having "common notions *and adequate ideas of the properties of things* (see 2p38c, 2p39, 2p39c, and 2p40)." 2p39 and p39c raise the possibility that there are general properties shared by the human body and other bodies which it interacts with, which are "equally in the part and in the whole" of both, which (unlike the laws of physics which govern all bodies) are not common to every body, but which are adequately known. What these might be is a mystery, because Spinoza gives no examples, and it is not obvious how they could be adequately known. His remarks in 2p44c2d, 5p12d, and to a lesser extent, 5p28d, however, support that he took what is known by reason to be only the common notions and what is derived from them.

Curley (1969) first articulated the interpretation of the attributes and eternal modes as the basic and derived laws of extended and thinking nature.

[23] See 1p33s1: "A thing is called contingent only because of a defect in our knowledge. . . . " See also 2p31c. It is important to note, however, that Spinoza also uses "contingent" to refer to the real property of every mode of being determined to exist by something beyond its own essence. See 4d3.

eternal thing." In it Spinoza reasons that the necessity with which reason regards things (2p44) "is the very necessity of God's eternal nature," and "Therefore it is of the nature of Reason to regard things under this species of eternity" (2p44c2d). Thus, to regard things "under a species of eternity" is, first of all, simply to regard them as necessitated through God.

Spinoza's second line of reasoning in the demonstration of 2p44c2 is as follows:

Add to this that the foundations of Reason are notions (by p38) which explain those things that are common to all, and which (by p37) do not explain the essence of any singular thing. On that account, they must be conceived without any relation to time, but under a certain species of eternity.... (2p44c2d)

The premise that the common notions are of things that are "common to all" and "do not explain the essence of any singular thing" by itself supports only the inference that the common notions must be conceived without relation to a *particular* time. It leaves open the interpretative possibility that by "conceived... under a certain species of eternity" Spinoza means nothing more than conceived as (necessitated by God and) true at all times, or omnitemporally true.

As reflected in his remark in 2p44c1s, that "no one doubts but what we imagine time, viz., from the fact that we imagine some bodies to move more slowly, or more quickly, or with the same speed," Spinoza does view time in the sense of a measure of the duration of a thing (a year, an hour) as an arbitrary abstraction of imagination, a construction of the human mind that has no basis in the nature of things.[24] But time in this sense (a measure of duration) is not the same as time in the sense of temporal passage – past, present, and future. Further, Spinoza's remarks to the effect that reason is affected equally by the idea of a past, present, or future thing (4p62 and 4p62d, 4p62s), and that reason counsels us to want a greater future good in preference to a lesser present one (4p66), taken literally, imply that reason itself views things as past, present, and future (even while viewing them as governed by omnitemporally true laws of nature), and thus that these temporal attributes are real.[25]

[24] As Donagan (1988, 110–11) points out, however, this does not mean it is false to say that something has existed or endured for a year.

[25] Although it seems to me that Spinoza's conception and characterization of reason or the second kind of knowledge (and also the third kind of knowledge) do not require that "conceived under a certain species of eternity" mean anything more than "conceived as being necessitated by God and as omnitemporally true," I do not mean to deny that there may be features of Spinoza's metaphysics that can be best understood if Spinoza is assumed to deny the reality of temporal passage. But I leave this question for the expositors of Spinoza's metaphysics. For two very interesting and opposed interpretations, see Donagan 1988, which takes temporal

Spinoza characterizes what he calls the third kind of knowledge (or intuitive knowledge) as knowledge that "proceeds from an adequate idea of the formal essence of certain attributes of God to the adequate knowledge of the essence of things" (2p40s2; 5p25d). This description, taken in conjunction with the mathematical illustration that follows, implies that it is a kind of immediate grasping of the essence of a thing through the nature of an attribute (2p40s2). Commentators have generally taken the "things" that are known in this way at least to include particulars, and some have taken intuitive knowledge to be restricted to particulars.[26] Parkinson (1964, 86) challenges both the interpretation of intuitive knowledge as immediate and as being of particulars, holding that it is "ordinary deductive knowledge," but that "it does not make conscious reference to general rules," and that it "pursues its deductions in greater detail than reason does."[27]

One serious problem that Spinoza's characterization of the third kind of knowledge presents for nearly all interpretations is that because particular things (and, for that matter, specific natural kinds of things) do not follow either immediately or mediately from an attribute, it is puzzling how knowledge of the essence of particulars (or kinds) can "proceed" from knowledge of the formal essence of an attribute.[28] Writers who have suggested that, in one way or another, the third kind of knowledge depends on experience seem to be on the right track, but I believe they are mistaken insofar as they continue to take Spinoza's "proceeds" (*procedit*) as signifying either immediate or mediate (deductive) inference. What Spinoza seems to be trying to capture with his characterization of the third kind of knowledge is the notion of reduction, not deduction or immediate inference. Spinoza held that all the modes of an attribute possess certain common fundamental properties, which are expressed in the common notions, and that the conception of any modification of an attribute must involve these properties. It seems that he must also have held the stronger, reductionist, view that the essence of every individual mode (e.g., every body) could be completely

passage to characterize both the existence of God and finite things; and Parchment 2000, which construes it entirely as an illusion of finite minds.

[26] Bennett (1984, 364–9) and Curley (1973a, 56–8) are among the latter. Carr (1978) takes the objects known by intuition to include finite modes and the attributes themselves.

[27] Parkinson bases his position particularly on Spinoza's remark in 2p47 that "we can deduce from this knowledge [of God's essence] a great many things which we can know adequately, and so can form that third kind of knowledge ... "; and on Spinoza's apparent claim in 5p36cs, that the understanding of what the mind is and how it depends on God that is provided in Parts 2 and 5, is an example of the third kind of knowledge.

[28] This applies to Parkinson, as well as other commentators, because he accepts Spinoza's example of the human mind in 5p36.

expressed or conceived in terms of the common notions of its particular attribute (e.g., in terms of extension and motion and rest). The common properties themselves, of course, do not constitute the essence of any particular thing (2p37), but rather a specification of them does, for example, the specification of the relation of motion and rest among the parts of a complex body (2p13le3d2). When we are able to make such a reduction for some particular or natural kind of particular, we have intuitive knowledge of it. Commentators are right that we need experience to make the reduction, at least to the extent that we need it to identify or pick out the kind or particular, the concept of which is to be reduced.

At the end of 5p36cs, Spinoza uses the example of our knowledge of the human mind to illustrate "how much knowledge of the third kind can accomplish, . . . and how much more powerful it is than the universal knowledge I have called of the second kind." We know based on reason (the second kind of knowledge) that the human mind depends on God if we know by reason the general truth (expressed at 1p15) that all things depend on God. By contrast, we know based on intuition that the human mind depends on God when we infer this from "the very essence of" the mind – from our conception of the mind as the idea (in God) whose object is an actually existing human body. This concept of the mind is reductive in that it expresses the essence of the mind in terms of the properties which are common and fundamental to every mode of thinking, namely, being an idea with a certain content or object, and it is therefore an instance of intuitive knowledge. Spinoza does not elaborate on what is accomplished by this particular instance of intuitive knowledge, but even a very brief reflection on its role in generating his theory of knowledge, psychology, and ethics testifies overwhelmingly to its power.

## 2. JUSTIFICATION IN THE *ETHICS*

Spinoza addresses the issue of justification or, as he puts it, "how a man can know that he has an idea that agrees with its object," in 2p43. Essentially his view is that our adequate ideas are justified because we have adequate knowledge of them. It is, as I shall show, a coherentist or non-linear notion of justification.[29] The proposition and its demonstration and (relevant parts of) the scholium are as follows:

---

[29] In the earlier *Treatise on the Emendation of the Intellect*, there is evidence that Spinoza initially held a foundationalist view of the justification of knowledge. For a discussion of the passages in the *Treatise* that support this interpretation (§§ 33–6; G II, 14–15), and why he ultimately rejected a foundationalist view, see Steinberg 1998.

2p43. He who has a true idea at the same time knows that he has a true idea, and cannot doubt the truth of the thing.

Dem. An idea true in us is that which is adequate in God insofar as he is explained through the nature of the human Mind (by p11c). Let us posit, therefore, that there is in God, insofar as he is explained through the nature of the human Mind, an adequate idea, A. Of this idea there must necessarily also be in God an idea which is related to God in the same way as idea A (by p20, whose demonstration is universal).... But idea A is supposed to be related to God insofar as he is explained through the nature of the human Mind; therefore the idea of idea A must also be related to God in the same way, i.e. (by the same p11c), this adequate idea of idea A will be in the Mind itself which has the adequate idea A. And so he who has an adequate idea, or (by p34) who knows a thing truly, must at the same time have an adequate idea or true knowledge, of his own knowledge. I.e., (as is manifest through itself), he must at the same time be certain, Q.E.D.

Schol. In p21s I have explained what an idea of an idea is. But it should be noted that the preceding proposition is sufficiently manifest through itself. For no one who has a true idea is unaware that a true idea involves the highest certainty. For to have a true idea means nothing other than knowing a thing perfectly, or in the best way. And of course no one can doubt this unless he thinks that an idea is something mute, like a picture on a tablet, and not a mode of thinking, viz. the very [act of] understanding. And I ask, who can know that he understands some thing unless he first understands it? I.e., who can know that he is certain about some thing unless he is first certain about it? What can there be which is clearer and more certain than a true idea, to serve as a standard of truth? As the light makes both itself and the darkness plain, so truth is the standard both of itself and of the false.

. . .

Finally, as to . . . how a man can know that he has an idea that agrees with its object? I have just shown, more than sufficiently, that this arises solely from his having an idea that does agree with its object – or that truth is its own standard. Add to this that our Mind, insofar as it perceives things truly, is part of the infinite intellect of God (by p11c), hence it is as necessary that the mind's clear and distinct ideas are true as that God's ideas are.

The argument given in the demonstration above is as follows:

1. For the human mind to have a true (adequate) idea is for there to be an idea which is adequate in God insofar as he constitutes the human mind. (2p11c.)
2. Ideas of ideas follow in God in the same way (the same order and connection) as the ideas themselves. (2p20, which itself derives from 2p7.)
3. The human mind has true (adequate) ideas of its true (adequate) ideas. (From 1 and 2.)

4. Certainty is having a true (adequate) knowledge of one's knowledge. (Definition.)
5. A person who has a true (adequate) idea will be certain of her knowledge. (From 3 and 4.)[30]

The notion of certainty as *reflective* knowledge of one's knowledge is a justificational concept, not mere psychological certainty.[31] One who has it is not merely in a state of unwavering belief, but rather has an absolute guarantee that her idea is true. Further, as examination of what is involved in having adequate knowledge of one's knowledge will show, such certainty or justification turns out to be a holistic notion; that is, it does not attach to any ideas in isolation from all others. Thus, for Spinoza, the justificational structure of knowledge is not foundational. That is, there are no ideas or bits of knowledge that are certain or justified independent of, and prior to, the justification of others, and from which the certainty or justification of all the others is derived.

There are two ways in which the certainty (justification) of any idea is linked to the certainty of others. The first is that by 2p43, a person who knows that $p$ is thereby certain that $p$ (has adequate knowledge of her knowledge that $p$) and also certain that she is certain, and certain that she is certain that she is certain, and so on *ad infinitum*. But that the certainty of an idea is linked to certainty regarding the idea of the idea in this way does not show that Spinoza's concept of justification is holistic, rather only that it is linearly infinitely regressive.[32]

[30] It should be noted that in the argument Spinoza uses "true" and "adequate" as interchangeable, although he has not proved that they are extensionally equivalent. He cites 2p34 as justification, apparently forgetting that this proposition established only that all adequate ideas are true, and not the converse. If the converse is not granted, then the argument can only establish that a person who has true ideas *that are adequate* knows that she has true ideas and cannot doubt them. In other words, the only true ideas we are justified in believing are those that are adequate.

[31] It can, in fact, occur in the absence of psychological certainty, as I shall show below.

[32] A standard objection to any epistemological doctrine such as that expressed by 2p43, which requires or implies that an infinite number of knowledge or justification claims must be satisfied if one is to be true, is that they place an impossible requirement on knowledge or justification. (See for example Steup 1989, 193.) As an objection against Spinoza this seems to miss the point of 2p43, which is to explain how, as well as prove that, we can be certain of our knowledge. Spinoza's doctrine of the idea of an idea entails that for any $n$th level iteration of the "idea of" relationship, if the idea of $x$ is in the mind, then the $n$th level iteration of the idea is also in the mind, and "in the same way" as the idea itself. Spinoza could use mathematical induction to argue that all the infinite iterations of an idea are in the mind. Thus, on Spinoza's metaphysics, the requirement that an infinite number of knowledge claims must be satisfied if one is to be true is not impossible to satisfy.

The second way in which the certainty of an idea is linked to that of other ideas emerges from an examination of what is involved in being certain or having an adequate idea of an adequate idea. We have an adequate idea or knowledge of a thing when we understand it as following from its ultimate cause, or when we have a complete explanation of why it exists and has the properties it has.[33] Thus, adequate knowledge of an adequate idea $A$ will involve the cause of $A$ and will explain why $A$ adequately represents its object. But the explanation of why an idea $A$ is adequate in some mind (or in the human mind in general) will necessarily involve the nature of the mind and its relation to the rest of reality, or in other words, the conception of the mind as God's idea of an actually existing body.[34] Spinoza provides an example of adequate knowledge of an adequate idea in 2p38, whose demonstration proves that and explains why the common notions are adequately conceived by the mind. This explanation is that because the "objects" of the common notions are equally in the part and in the whole of all bodies, their ideas will be adequate in God insofar as God has any idea, including that of the human body, and because the mind simply is God's idea of the human body, these ideas will be adequate in the mind.[35] Adequate knowledge of an adequate idea therefore involves virtually the entire basic metaphysical system of the *Ethics*. For this reason certainty (the adequate idea or knowledge of an adequate idea) is necessarily a holistic property, one that emerges at the level of reflective knowledge only insofar as a person grasps the entire basic metaphysical system. Thus, in the order of justification, no adequate ideas are prior to any others. Rather, the certainty of any idea or knowledge consists in a person's having at the same time the system of knowledge within which that idea itself and its adequacy can be completely explained.[36]

[33] See above.

[34] It is significant that Spinoza answers the question posed in 2p43s, "how a man can know that he has an idea that agrees with its object," partly by stating that "our Mind, insofar as it perceives things truly, is part of the infinite intellect of God[.]" Clearly it is *knowing* this relation between the human mind and the mind of God, and not merely the fact that the relation exists, that enables someone to know that his true (adequate) idea is true (or alternatively, enables him to have an adequate idea of his adequate idea).

[35] 2p47 also provides an example of adequate knowledge of adequate knowledge, but its proof ultimately depends of 2p38. See 2p45–p47 and their demonstrations.

[36] Spinoza does hold, of course, that knowledge must reflect the causal order of nature – that things must be known through their causes (144), and the first cause must be known prior to everything else. For this reason, all our adequate knowledge terminates in (is caused by) the idea of God, or one of God's infinite attributes. But this causal foundationalism does not commit Spinoza to a foundationalist view of the justificational structure of knowledge.

Although some commentators have taken Spinoza's remarks in the scholium to 2p43 that true ideas involve the "highest certainty" and that truth is "its own standard," to indicate that he took at least some true ideas to be self-evident, hence justified independently of their relation to any others,[37] I believe that these remarks must be interpreted in light of 2p43 and its notion of certainty as involving reflective knowledge. True ideas involve the highest certainty because if there is a true idea in the mind then necessarily there is also a true idea of that idea in the mind. And for truth to be "the standard of itself and the false" means simply that it is by means of true ideas of our ideas – and not by means of a divine guarantee – that we know our true ideas are true.[38] For truth to be its own standard in this sense is not for a true idea considered apart from our reflective idea of it to be self-evident or certain.

Understanding that certainty is reflective knowledge that is possible only when a person has the entire basic metaphysical scheme solves a problem that arises at least partly from the geometric form of presentation of the *Ethics*. This is that the basic definitions and axioms do not appear to be self-evident, and without some justification of the starting points, the entire system is insecure.[39] Taking the definitions (and axioms) as stipulative is no solution, because then the entire *Ethics* becomes no more than an exercise. The answer is that the definitions and axioms are true, but a reader cannot be certain or know they are true until she has assimilated the metaphysical system.

Spinoza does not explicitly take up skepticism or challenges to the possibility of knowledge in the *Ethics*. In his earlier *Treatise on the Emendation of the Intellect* he does spend some time answering the type of skeptical argument that is based on the assumption that in order to know a thing, one must know that she knows it. Such arguments proceed by purporting to show that in order to satisfy a single knowledge claim, an infinite number must be satisfied, which is taken to be impossible. In the *Treatise* Spinoza responds by denying the assumption: in order to know a thing it is not necessary to know that one knows

---

[37] Bolton 1985; Matheron 1994a.

[38] Nor is there anything else external to our ideas by which we can know they are true – that is, we can't get outside our ideas and compare them to their objects.

[39] A number of writers have pointed out that Spinoza's definitions and axioms are not self-evident, including Hampshire (1962, 30), Kennington (1980, 297–8), Bennett (1984, 16–25), Curley (1986, 152–8), and Walker (1989, 50). Hampshire also views the definitions and axioms as being justified on grounds of coherence. Bennett thinks that the *Ethics* is best viewed "as a hypothetico-deductive system" that as a whole is confirmed by empirical and philosophical data. But this would make at least some things that are known by the first kind of knowledge (imagination) justificationally prior to what is known by reason, and that seems objectionable as an interpretation of Spinoza's view.

it.[40] In the *Ethics*, however, he explicitly holds that if someone knows something then she knows that she knows it (2p43), and draws on his metaphysical doctrine to show how this is possible.[41]

If a skeptic were to argue, based on the general deceptiveness of the senses, that we can never be certain of anything, Spinoza would respond by agreeing that knowledge based on sense perception is always liable to error, but that once we understand the nature of the mind and its relation to the body and the rest of reality, and how the senses work, we will be able to distinguish the adequate ideas of the intellect from inadequate ones based on sense perception (imagination). And if the skeptic were to base his argument on the possibility of an omnipotent deceiver, Spinoza would respond similarly: once we know the nature of things – God, the mind, and the mind's relation to God and the rest of reality – we know there is no omnipotent deceiver, because we know that our adequate ideas must be true.[42]

From the perspective of the Cartesian method such a response to skeptical doubts from within Spinoza's metaphysical system seems unsatisfying. According to Descartes, the way to answer the skeptic is to begin by doubting everything that can be doubted, and then build the metaphysical system from the foundation of self-evident, hence self-justifying, simple truths that even the skeptic cannot doubt. If what I have said about Spinoza's view regarding the justificational structure of knowledge – how we can know that our true ideas are true – is correct, that is not Spinoza's way. We know that our true ideas are true because we have adequate knowledge of them; and adequate knowledge of an adequate idea involves (adequate) knowledge of the entire basic metaphysical system. No single adequate idea is justificationally prior to any other, and there is no way into the system from self-justifying simple truths. For Spinoza, the skeptic is refuted at the end, not the beginning, of the knowledge enterprise.

### 3. BELIEF AND ERROR

Spinoza denied Descartes' analysis of judgment (occurrent belief) as involving the two separate faculties of intellect, by which we perceive ideas, and will, by which we freely affirm or deny their truth. According to him every act of the mind is determined (2p48), and no separation can be made between volitional and cognitive acts of mind – "singular

---

[40] TdIE, §§ 33–4; G II, 14–15.

[41] See the explication above of the proof of 2p43, and n. 31.

[42] As I show below, however, there is a sense in which one can "know" these truths about God and the mind's relation to God, yet remain in a state of doubt.

ideas and volitions are one and the same" (2p49cd; see also 2p49, 2p49c). Thus, Spinoza appears to reject not merely Cartesian voluntarism about belief, but, more radically, that there is a distinction to be made between judging or believing that $p$ and merely representing to oneself that $p$. Spinoza acknowledged the obvious objection that "experience seems to teach nothing more clearly than that we can suspend our judgment so as not to assent to things we perceive" (2p49cs).[43] In response, he offered his own analysis of suspension of judgment as a certain kind of complex perception or idea:

[W]hen we say that someone suspends judgment, we are saying nothing but that he sees that he does not perceive the thing adequately. Suspension of judgment, therefore, is really a perception, not [an act of] free will.

Spinoza goes on to explain his analysis of suspension of judgment by contrasting it with a simpler state of mind in which a person merely perceives a thing:

[L]et us conceive a child imagining a winged horse, and not perceiving anything else. Since this imagination involves the existence of the horse (by p17c), and the child does not perceive anything else that excludes the existence of the horse, he will necessarily regard the horse as present. Nor will he be able to doubt its existence, though he will not be certain of it.

. . .

[I]f the Mind perceived nothing else except the winged horse, it would regard it as present to itself, and would not have any cause of doubting its existence, or any faculty of dissenting, unless either the imagination of the winged horse were joined to an idea which excluded the existence of the same horse, or the Mind perceived that its idea of a winged horse was inadequate. And then either it will necessarily deny the horse's existence, or it will necessarily doubt it. (2p49cs)

This passage appears to show that Spinoza holds a kind of default theory of belief: if $A$ has an idea that $p$, then she will believe that $p$ unless she has some other idea that excludes $p$ or she perceives that her idea that $p$ is inadequate. His answer to the objection based on our apparent ability to represent things to ourselves without judging them to be true or false is that an idea is a belief unless it occurs in a certain context of other ideas that prevents its being a belief.

Closer attention to Spinoza's analyses of suspension of judgment and denial reveals that neither is adequate. Suspension of judgment is characterized as the perception that one's perception of a thing is inadequate.

[43] A similar point can be made nonintrospectively if we grant that an idea or representation can have a truth-functionally complex structure such that affirming a complex representation does not involve affirming its component representations, such as "if $p$ then $q$." See Geach 1965.

By his own account, however, we can have only inadequate knowledge of the physical objects in our immediate vicinity, although when we become aware of this, we do not thereby cease to believe in their existence, or that they have more or less the properties we perceive them as having. In general, the perception that our perception that $p$ is inadequate is compatible with belief that $p$; hence his analysis of suspension of judgment is not successful, at least if we take "suspension of judgment" in its ordinary sense, according to which it is incompatible with belief.[44]

The account of denial in terms of exclusion fares no better, although for different reasons. Spinoza says that if the mind joins the idea of the winged horse to an idea that excludes the existence of the same horse, then the mind will necessarily deny the horse's existence. In virtually all of the passages where Spinoza speaks of an idea's excluding something, exclusion appears to be a logical relation consisting in incompatibility between the contents of, or states of affairs expressed by, ideas.[45] An idea excludes some state of affairs $p$, if and only if the state of affairs it expresses, $q$, cannot coexist with $p$, or $q$ implies $\sim p$. But if exclusion is so understood, then a problem arises, because logical incompatibility is a symmetrical relation. That is, if $q$ implies $\sim p$, then $p$ implies $\sim q$. And if this is so, then a person who has the idea of a winged horse and an idea that excludes the existence of the winged horse simply has ideas that exclude each other's objects, and there is no reason that such a state of mind should constitute either the belief that the winged horse does not exist, or the belief that it does exist (that the state of affairs which excludes the winged horse does not exist). In other words, representation of a state of affairs $q$, along with another state of affairs $p$ that is excluded by (and hence excludes) $q$, cannot in itself constitute either the belief that $q$ and $\sim p$ or that $p$ and $\sim q$. This is because the logical relations that obtain among a person's ideas are alone insufficient to determine what s/he believes. Spinoza's attempt, in 2p49cs, to differentiate belief from denial in terms of exclusion also fails.

Setting the Cartesian analysis aside, we can think of belief as an idea of whose truth we are convinced, one that has a certain hold on us or that exerts a certain degree of force in our mental life. To judge that $p$ is to experience the force of the idea that $p$. Spinoza deals with the dynamics of our mental life in Part 3–Part 5p20, where his main focus

---

[44] Margaret Wilson makes this point (1978, 146).

[45] See 2p34, 3p10, 3p13, 3p13d, 3p18s1, 3p19d, 3p20d, 3p25d, 3p26s, 3p36d, 3p42d, 3p47s, definitions of the affects 13 explanation, 4p1s, 4p9d, 4p10d, 4p13d, 5p7d. For a fuller discussion of the notion of "exclusion" see Steinberg 2005, 157, n. 6.

is the passions, not knowledge. The passions, however, no less than knowledge, consist in ideas:

An Affect that is called a Passion of the mind is a confused idea, by which the Mind affirms of its Body, or of some part of it, a greater or lesser force of existing than before, which, when it is given, determines the Mind to think of this rather than that. ("General Definition of the Affects")

Spinoza's account of the strength of the passions rests on a conception of ideas in general as dynamic entities. As an idea, a passion is an individual mode of thought or singular thing that strives to persevere in its own being, or has a force of existing of its own (3p6, 4p5, 4p6). Because its object (a modification of the body) is caused by something external to that object, its own force of existing partially derives from and depends on the idea of that external thing (4p5). Because it is an idea of a bodily modification, its strength is proportionate to that of the bodily modification, and it will persist as long as the bodily modification persists. Finally, it can be restrained or removed only by an idea that excludes the given bodily modification, and whether it is restrained or removed depends on the strength of the excluding idea (4p7 and 4p7d).

The intrinsic force by which every idea strives to continue in existence is strengthened or restrained by other ideas that posit or exclude the existence of its object. Thus, an affect toward a thing that we imagine as actually present is stronger than one that we imagine as not present but in the past or future because "an imagination (by 2p17) is more intense so long as we imagine nothing that excludes the present existence of the external thing" (4p9d; see also 4p9c). Similarly, we are affected more intensely by things that we imagine as in the immediate future or recent past than by those that we imagine as temporally more distant because insofar as we imagine the former "we thereby imagine something that excludes the presence of the thing less" than when we imagine the latter (4p10d).

Using the notion of the strength or force of an idea, we can explicitly formulate the concept of belief that seems to be at work in the *Ethics* as follows: to say that $A$ believes that $p$ is to say (1) $A$ has the idea that $p$ and (2) $A$'s idea that $p$ is stronger than every idea $q$, which $A$ has, that excludes $p$. The notion of the strength of an idea can be understood in terms of its effects – its ability to generate (alone or with other ideas) new ideas and to influence the content or direction of our thought.

To return to Spinoza's example of the winged horse: if someone has the idea of a winged horse and another idea that excludes the existence of a winged horse, then *if the idea that excludes the existence of the winged horse is stronger*, his state of mind should be thought of as denial that a winged horse exists. We noted above that perceiving that one's idea that $p$ is inadequate is not in general incompatible with belief that $p$. The notion of suspension of judgment that Spinoza is trying to account for in 2p49cs, in which a person represents a state of affairs to himself without believing that it obtains, however, is able to be captured by the notion of vacillation, to which Spinoza refers in 3p17s.[46] A person who vacillates between two ideas of roughly equal strength, one of which posits the existence of a winged horse, and one of which excludes its existence, can be understood as doubting or suspending judgment with respect to the winged horse, in a sense that does imply nonbelief.

Because Spinoza rejects the Cartesian analysis of belief, he must also reject Descartes's explanation of error as resulting from the mind's (freely) affirming (or denying) something it does not clearly and distinctly perceive.[47] According to Spinoza, error consists in a lack or privation of knowledge (2p17cs, 2p35s). Thus, when the mind imagines external bodies that are not present, it "does not err from the fact that it imagines, but only insofar as it is considered to lack an idea that excludes the existence of those things that it imagines to be present to it" (2p17cs). A slightly more complicated kind of case is discussed in 2p35s:

[W]hen we look at the sun, we imagine it as about 200 feet away from us, an error that does not consist simply in this imagining, but in the fact that while we imagine it in this way, we are ignorant of its true distance and of the cause of this imagining. For even if we later come to know that it is more than 600 diameters of the earth away from us, we nevertheless imagine it as near. For we imagine the sun so near not because we do not know its true distance, but because an affection of our body involves the essence of the sun insofar as our body is affected by the sun.

What is missing from both of these passages is any reference to the strength of the ideas involved. In the first Spinoza should say that the mind does not err in imagining a nonexistent external body except insofar as it lacks a *stronger* idea that excludes the existence of the external body; and in the second he should say that the perceptual error is due to the lack of sufficiently *strong* ideas (knowledge) of the sun's true distance and of the causes of the imaginative idea of the sun as 200 feet

---

[46] In this passage Spinoza refers back to 2p44s.
[47] CSM II, 40; AT VII, 58.

away.[48] In other words, having a false idea – one that misrepresents its object – is not error unless that idea is a belief.[49]

Understanding that for Spinoza belief is a function of the relative force of an idea within a mind explains why there is no contradiction in his maintaining that everyone has certain adequate ideas, although at the same time recognizing that many people have beliefs that are inconsistent with such ideas.[50] He asserts, for example, that everyone has adequate ideas of the common properties of bodies (2p38c), and of God's "eternal and infinite essence" (2p47). But he also acknowledges that many people have erroneous beliefs about the nature of extension, such as that it is divisible and composed of parts, that it is finite, and that it is created by a transcendent God (1p15s); and that many have anthropomorphic beliefs about God (1p15s; 2p3s). Given the conception of belief as an idea that is stronger than any of its competitors, this can be explained by saying that such persons' adequate ideas concerning the nature of bodies and God's nature are weaker than their imaginative ones.

Similarly, Spinoza can draw on the distinction between the dynamic qualities of an idea and its logicosemantic ones to explain why the fact that some (many) people doubt or deny their true or adequate ideas[51] (e.g., of God and extension) does not contradict 2p43's assertion that we cannot doubt our true ideas. What 2p43 claims is only that if a person has true ideas, then she must have (what may be called) *logical* certainty, true ideas of her ideas (knowledge of her knowledge). It does not claim that these ideas must be strong enough to defeat their rivals, or that a person with true ideas cannot be in a state of *psychological* doubt with respect to those ideas. Logical certainty and doubt consist in having an adequate idea of one's knowledge and perceiving

---

[48] Following another discussion of the sun example in 4p1s, Spinoza does, however, remark that

> [I]maginations do not disappear through the presence of the true insofar as it is true, but because there occur others, *stronger than them*, which exclude the presence of the things we imagine, as we showed in 2p17.

This, and another reference to 2p17 in Spinoza's account of the strength of the passions (occurring in 4p9d), indicate that the notion of the strength of an idea is implicit in his basic conception of an idea.

[49] In 2p33d, and 2p35d, Spinoza appears to take "error" and "falsity" as interchangeable. His intention is these passages should be understood to be to equate not error and misrepresentation, but rather error and false belief.

[50] Curley (1973a, 54) and Delahunty (1985, 76) both draw attention to this problem.

[51] Or, if they considered their true or adequate ideas of God and extension, would doubt or deny them.

that one's idea of a thing is not adequate, respectively. Psychological certainty is having a belief which is unwavering, whereas psychological doubt is vacillation. We can be logically certain of our true ideas at the same time that we psychologically doubt them, and, vice versa, we can be psychologically certain of what we only inadequately perceive.[52]

As Spinoza makes clear in his treatment of the passions, true ideas have no special compelling force in virtue of their being true (4p1, 4p14). The advantage which true ideas possess over their rivals consists chiefly in two things: (1) the objects of the most fundamental true ideas – the common notions and what can be deduced from them – are involved in every idea (everything posits them);[53] and (2) true ideas are linked by logical and explanatory relations by which they posit each other. Thus, a system of ideas such as the *Ethics* lends significant additional force to the individual ideas it contains. Still, it is possible that a person might master the *Ethics* and remain in (psychological) doubt regarding its truth. Perhaps she was taught another system of belief at an early age by beloved parents or teachers – cognitive states are not isolated from the influence of emotion; or perhaps, for some unknown reason, she remains in the grip of some pervasive systematic error, such as skepticism. In any case, the realization of a system of true ideas in a mind is finite, and there is no guarantee that it will ever prevail. "There is no singular thing in nature than which there is not another more powerful and stronger. What ever one is given, there is another more powerful by which the first can be destroyed" (4a1).

---

[52] Insofar as Spinoza is willing to call the state of mind in which a person has logical certainty that *p* (a true idea of her true idea that *p*), but fails even weakly to believe that *p*, knowledge, he is committed to the nonstandard view that one can have knowledge without belief.

[53] See 5p7d.

# 8    Spinoza on Action

## I. INTRODUCTION

When philosophers write about action, what they mostly have in mind is events in which something mental becomes realised by the body through the agent's will. The work of the will is to translate the mental antecedent, which may be a desire, or an intention, or more generally some kind of pro-attitude, to the bodily realm. The mental antecedent of action gives the aim, the agent has beliefs as to how to reach it, and the will (or acts of will) has the role of executor. There are versions of causal theories of action where the role of the will is redundant. What happens in an action is just that the pro-attitudes cause the relevant bodily movements in the right way. In any case, it seems that this view of what could be called overt actions is rather natural. In overt actions, the body is governed by the mind.

However, there are also actions that could be labelled as acts of the understanding or doxastic actions. Forming a belief on the basis of evidence seems to require an act of the understanding. Inferring from premises to a conclusion seems to be an active process – not something that just happens to the person. For these kinds of actions it is difficult, or perhaps impossible, to give a purely causal account in terms of beliefs causing other beliefs. It is the agent who draws the conclusion and has to take care of the inference going right or of the belief being formed correctly by the evidence at hand. What is distinctive to these kinds of actions is that there is a sense in which the agent involved in them does not aim at good, or does not try to get rid of some uneasiness, but aims at truth. These kinds of acts may be called acts of the understanding.

Spinoza meditated very profoundly both about overt actions and about acts of the understanding. He was, however, very sceptical about the possibility of overt human actions and advocated an error theory with respect to them. There are no overt human actions, Spinoza seems to hold, and instead the locus of real agency lies in the understanding. Spinoza even saw in the use of the understanding the only thing that is really good, and thought that only those things that prevent human beings from understanding are bad.

In this paper, I will first explicate Spinoza's conception of the human being. The focus here will be on his view of the mind–body union and on his view that mind and body are the same thing but conceived differently. After that preliminary section, my aim is to consider Spinoza's notion of the will and its identification with the intellect as it is presented in the concluding propositions of the second part of the *Ethics*. After that I will consider Spinoza's error theory of human action as it is presented in 3p2s. In the last section, Spinoza's notion of real agency is given a close look.

## 2. SPINOZA ON MIND–BODY UNION AND IDEAS

In Spinoza's account of the world, there is room for exactly one substance, which he calls God. Thought is an infinite attribute of God, and because Spinoza adheres to what is called, after A. O. Lovejoy (1936), the principle of plenitude, everything that expresses this thought, that is, everything that can possibly be thought, is thought by God. This means that all possible ideas are realised in God. However, God is not only a thinking thing but also a thing that has infinite extension and, in fact, has all kinds of other attributes that are not expressed by our existence and that we are unable even to think about. However, what is important is that ideas do not have their own objects but acquire their objects from other attributes. So if *H* is God's idea about an extended item *E*, then God's thought is directly about *E*. Without that extended item, its idea could not exist in God. The object of that idea exists because the extended realm also obeys the principle of plenitude. Because that principle holds, extension takes all possible forms, or is modified in all possible ways that express extension. Thus, there cannot be an extended item without an idea that has that item as its object, nor can there be an idea of an extended object in God without that extended item existing. If one sees the infinite extension as God's body, then this could be expressed by saying that all ideas of God that are about extended objects have as their direct objects modifications of God's body.

The view that God's idea of an extended item requires the being of that item faces a natural objection: According to Spinoza, all attributes are conceived through themselves (1p10). Thus, the attribute of thought is conceptually independent from the attribute of extension, and so any mode of thought should be conceivable without any extended item. But what has been said means that no idea can be conceived without its object. Thus, this way of treating the issue breaks the conceptual barrier between different attributes.

However, there is also a rather straightforward way to meet this objection. Ideas are conceptually tied to their objects. For example, the idea of a triangle seems to acquire its identity through its having a triangle as its object. Consider what makes it different from the idea of a square: it seems that it is the very fact that the former is about a triangle and the latter about a square. What may be felt as a problem is that in my interpretation ideas require the existence of their objects, whereas in more traditional interpretations ideas are seen representations of their existing objects; the representations themselves are ontologically independent of their objects. However, this does not speak in favour of the representationalists, because this kind of ontological independence of ideas from their objects is nowhere required by Spinoza.

So what does Spinoza mean by saying that attributes, and thus also the attribute of thought, are conceived through themselves? I believe that the key to this lies in the special nature of the attribute of thought. Thinking is an activity that takes objects. It is the activity of thinking that is conceptually different from the other attributes. For example, in extending himself in infinitely many ways God does not, thereby, take any objects. The ability to think about something is conceptually distinct from all the other ways God is.

A human being, for Spinoza, is generated through God's taking a special thing as the object of his thought:

The first thing that constitutes the actual being of a human Mind is nothing but the idea of a singular thing which actually exists. (2p11)

The thing of which the idea is has to be such that changes in it are reflected in the idea, which means that in the human mind there have to be perceptions of whatever happens in the object. But the only thing that satisfies this is, for a subject, the body that is called the human body. To that body we are tied in a very specific way: we can feel that it is affected in many ways. I can feel what happens to my feet when I step into a puddle, but I cannot feel what happens to my shoes.

Spinoza's fascinating account of the mind–body union entails that my mind is a part of God's mind. Moreover, it should be kept in mind that it is not merely I who feel or perceive what is happening in my body, but God, insofar as he constitutes my mind. This points in the direction that *I* am identical with God insofar as he constitutes my mind, which is not the same as to say that I am identical with my mind. Understanding subjectivity is quite difficult in Spinoza's monism. It is very tempting to conclude from what he says about the relation between mind and body that I am just the complex idea whose object is a certain body. But this seems to me too hasty a conclusion. What I would like to claim is that we, as subjects of thought, are more tightly connected to God than just being ideas that he has. The step from someone's having an idea of something to that idea, *eo ipso*, becoming a conscious subject seems unbridgeable to me. The way I read Spinoza is that for him any subject is embedded in a larger subject, so that they all together constitute God.

In 2p11c, Spinoza gives a definition of what he means by saying that the mind perceives this or that. This means that God insofar as he constitutes the human mind perceives this or that. So I will also speak of the mind having such and such ideas, but by this I mean that the subject who constitutes the mind has such and such ideas.

The ideas the mind has Spinoza divides into adequate and inadequate ideas. What is constitutive to the ideas the mind has is that they involve affirmation. The ideas are not, as Spinoza (2p43c) puts it, mute pictures on a tablet but involve an activity that could be called judging; and they should also be distinguished from images, which are like pictures without taking any stand on how the world is. What is distinctive to adequate ideas is that they have truth as an intrinsic property. This makes it possible to characterise truth without taking into account the object of the idea. The adequate ideas are special actions of the mind that reveal their own truth. This may be clarified a bit by an appeal to Leibniz's conception of truth. According to Leibniz, all truths are basically analytical truths.[1] This means that in an affirmative judgement, *a* is *P*, the predicate *P* can be extracted from the subject *a*. However, this kind of analysis is possible for finite minds only in connection with so-called truths of reason. The point is that there is a criterion of truth for judgements that is object-independent: a judgement is true if and only if the predicate is involved in the subject. There is no need to compare the object of the judgement to the judgement, or to the idea expressed by the judgement. It may be that similar considerations motivated Spinoza: an adequate idea can be said to be true by virtue of its form, or formal being, alone. For Spinoza, inadequate ideas are the source of falsity. The typical examples of inadequate ideas are those based on perception. What is typical in perception is that the ideas received in perception point to their causes and they mislead the mind to attribute the properties of its direct object, which is a modification of the body of the perceiver, to its cause. In this way such ideas do not necessarily agree with their object when the object is taken as the cause of the modification of the body. In fact, this answers a question Leibniz (1969, 197) was wondering about: how can there be, in Spinoza, room for ideas that do not agree with their objects once the idea directly refers to the object?

---

[1]  See, for example, Leibniz 1989, 45.

### 3. BELIEF AND IDEAS

The affirmation involved in ideas based on inadequate perception is felt by the agent as somehow spontaneous. I look at my desk and in seeing a green book I affirm the greenness of the book. Could I have withheld from making that judgement or affirmation? Or to put the point slightly differently: is believing voluntary? This is a very important issue, which has much bearing on epistemology and especially on doxastic agency. It is well known that for Descartes believing is in some sense a voluntary action. The understanding presents ideas to the will and it is up to the will whether to accept them. At least this is the case with ideas that are not clear and distinct. With respect to them it is always possible for the will not to act. However, it seems that once the understanding presents to the will something that is clear and distinct the will somehow has to give assent to it. But this is not, according to Descartes, inconsistent with the will freely accepting it. Any belief for Descartes involves, then, two faculties: the understanding and the will.[2]

For Spinoza, Descartes's view is unacceptable. There is no such thing as will seen as a faculty of making choices. The will already lies in the intellect. When seen from God's viewpoint, even the intellect is not a faculty but something that belongs to the *natura naturata*, which follows from God's essence, more specifically from the attribute of thought, by eternal necessity. From this perspective the intellect is in particular ideas, and in criticizing Descartes, without mentioning him, Spinoza should show that nothing should be done to ideas to acquire beliefs.

It should first be noted that in Spinoza's necessitarianism freedom of belief is, of course, impossible. Even if the formation of belief required an act of the will, this act of the will would occur by necessity. Thus, irrespective of the considerations whether ideas are voluntary, there is no room for freedom of belief. Because for Spinoza willing is connected to believing, this can also be expressed by saying that according to Spinoza there is no freedom of the will. Will is, then, something that is connected to doxastic agency:

[I]t should be noted here that by will I understand a faculty of affirming and denying, and not desire. I say that I understand the faculty by which the Mind affirms or denies something true or something false, and not the desire by which the Mind wants a thing or avoids it. (2p48s)

In presenting his theory of will, Spinoza first argues rather quickly that will and intellect are not separate *faculties*. He argues, by relying on

---

[2] Descartes presents his theory of belief formation in *Meditation* 4 (CSM II, 37–43; AT VII, 53–62).

his determinism, that we possess no freedom with respect to the acts of the intellect and this should be sufficient for proving that we possess neither the faculty of willing nor that of understanding. There are nothing but particular volitions and ideas that exist in an infinite causal series of finite items. So what we mean by will or intellect has to be a common feature shared by all particular volitions and by all particular ideas. If this feature is the same for ideas and for volitions, will and intellect are identical. Thus, the relation of particular volitions to the will in general and the relation of particular ideas to intellect in general are analogous to the relation that particular stones bear to stoneness:

From this it follows that these and similar faculties are either complete fictions or nothing but Metaphysical beings, or universals, which we are used to forming from particulars. So intellect and will are to this or that idea, or to this or that volition as "stoneness" is to this or that stone, or man to Peter or Paul. (2p48s)

Thus, in order to understand the essence of will and intellect, one has to investigate the particular volitions and particular ideas with the aim of identifying the common essential feature shared by all ideas and the common essential feature shared by all volitions.

Spinoza finds the common feature shared by all ideas in the notion of affirmation and negation. In every idea we either affirm or negate a predicate of a subject. This is rather natural because ideas as representations of something consist of two elements, a subject and a predicate, an idea being an action where the predicate is either attributed to the subject or negated of it.[3] Spinoza emphasises that ideas are inherently action-like already in the definition of idea:

By idea I understand a concept of the Mind that the Mind forms because it is a thinking thing.

Exp.: I say concept [conceptum] rather than perception, because the word perception seems to indicate that the Mind is acted on by the object. But concept seems to express an action of the Mind. (2d3 and its explication)

To use Spinoza's own example: to have an idea of a winged horse is nothing but to affirm wings of a horse. It is the act of affirmation that is common to all ideas, and thus the question of the identity between intellect and (epistemic) will is the question of whether for believing an idea (or what it represents) something more is needed than the

---

[3] In what follows, I will only consider affirmation. But, *mutatis mutandis*, everything that is said about affirmation can be said about negation, too.

affirmation involved in the idea itself. Spinoza argues for their identity as follows:

In the Mind (by p48) there is no absolute faculty of willing and not willing, but only singular volitions, viz. this and that affirmation, and this and that negation. Let us conceive, therefore, some singular volition, say a mode of thinking by which the Mind affirms that the three angles of a triangle are equal to two right angles.

This affirmation involves the concept, or idea, of the triangle, i.e., it cannot be conceived without the idea of the triangle. For to say that A must involve the concept of B is the same as to say that A cannot be conceived without B. Further, this affirmation (by a3) also cannot be without the idea of the triangle. Therefore, this affirmation can neither be nor be conceived without the idea of the triangle.

Next, this idea of the triangle must involve this same affirmation, viz. that its three angles equal two right angles. So conversely, this idea of the triangle also can neither be nor be conceived without this affirmation.

So (by d2) this affirmation pertains to the essence of the idea of the triangle, and is nothing beyond it. And what we have said concerning this volition (since we have selected it at random), must also be said concerning any volition, viz. that it is nothing apart from the idea, Q.E.D. (2p49d)

In this demonstration, Spinoza proceeds as follows. He first gives an arbitrary example of a volition (i.e., a belief), which is the mode of thinking by which the mind affirms that the three angles of a triangle are equal to two right angles. But it is evident that this volition cannot be conceived without the idea of a triangle. However, in addition to this, it also has to be shown that the idea of the triangle must involve the affirmation that its three angles are equal to two right angles. Surprisingly, Spinoza, without giving any argument, is satisfied with just claiming that this is the case. But why cannot one think of a triangle, that is, have an idea of it, without any thought about the sum of its angles? That the sum of the angles of a triangle is equal to two right angles is not included in the definition of a triangle and, for that reason, a triangle should be conceivable without that fact. Moreover, as Edwin Curley (1974, 169) has pointed out, Spinoza's example seems not completely arbitrary. Had Spinoza used as his example some empirical truth, such as that Charles Dickens walks, he should have argued that we cannot conceive Charles Dickens without walking, which seems altogether false. Let us consider the second part of the demonstration more fully.

First, one should bear in mind that what Spinoza is trying to prove in 2p49d is that believing in an idea is not distinct from the act involved in the idea itself. He is not trying to argue that if *a* is *P* any idea of *a* involves the idea of *P*. Moreover, Spinoza's argument presupposes that ideas are affirmations and also the nominalistic thought that particular ideas are all the ideas there are. This kind of nominalism implies that there is no such entity as the idea of the triangle apart from the particular affirmations and, moreover, neither is there room for such an entity as the idea of Charles Dickens apart from the particular affirmations concerning Charles Dickens. Once these remarks are kept in mind, the second part of the proof is easy to understand. It just says that if one affirms $P$ of $a$, then one has a singular idea of $a$ under $P$. This idea of $a$, of course, cannot be conceived without this particular affirmation because it is just this affirmation that distinguishes this idea from other particular ideas of $a$. Thus, an idea of a thing necessarily requires (i.e., cannot be conceived without) an affirmation, and an affirmation about a thing necessarily requires (i.e., cannot be conceived without) an idea of that thing. And so affirmations (volitions) are identical to ideas.[4]

Ideas, for Spinoza, are the most fundamental elements in our minds. All other modes of thought, such as desires, presuppose ideas. One cannot desire anything without having an idea of what one desires (2a3). Thus, the fundamental power of mind is the power of affirming (and denying).

## 4. SPINOZA'S APPARENT DENIAL OF FINITE AGENCY

### 4.1. Ordinary Conception of Human Action

What we have seen Spinoza to have shown is that there is no such thing as doxastic contracausal freedom. The inhabitants of the mind are particular ideas that involve affirmation, and the activity of affirming is ultimately God's activity.[5] However, what Spinoza must also argue for is that there is no freedom in our overt actions in which the mind seems to govern the body. The picture of human action that is somehow plausible and could be called the *ordinary conception of human action* (OCHA) involves, at least, the following two principles:

1. *Principle of freedom.* In acting completely freely, I am not caused to act by anything that is external to me. In a sense, I am

---

[4] It may be of some interest to note that the criterion of identity Spinoza uses here is the same as the one used by Descartes (CSM II, 95; AT VII, 132) in his argument for the real distinction between mind and body.

[5] Even though all ideas involve affirmation, this does not force Spinoza to accept the absurdity that all ideas are beliefs. It may happen that an idea is in conflict with other ideas and is thereby prevented from being a belief. This happens, for example, in optical illusions. One could put the point so that an idea is a belief, if nothing prevents it from being a belief. See also Diane Steinberg's chapter in this volume.

the original cause of my free actions by freely deciding to perform them. According to this principle, agency requires self-
determination.

2. *Principle of content-sensitive mind–body interaction.* In acting,
beliefs and desires are causally efficacious. They partake in moving the body. If I raise my hand because I desire to vote and believe
that by raising my hand I vote, then this desire and belief contribute causally to my hand's rising. In short, it is constitutive of
action that mental items are causally efficacious. However, desires
and beliefs need not be determining causes. In acting, desires and
beliefs are translated into the physical realm.

Spinoza wants to argue that these principles are false, and thus he can
be said to endorse an error theory of human action.

In 1app, Spinoza criticises the principle of freedom involved in the
common conception of human action. That this criticism finds its place
in 1app is understandable, because the necessitarianism and determinism of the first part seem to make the principle of freedom false. According to Spinoza, the belief in freedom derives from two theses: (i) human
beings seek their own advantage and they are conscious of this; (ii)
human beings are born ignorant of the causes of their actions. These two
theses generate a model that emphasises final causes. It is the advantage of a course of action that makes a human being pursue for it. For
example, somebody may be said to exercise because of health. Here
health is seen as the final cause, that is, that for the sake of which, and
exercising would be its "effect." Because the agent chooses to exercise
without being aware of the determining effective cause of her choice,
she believes that she chooses it freely. This line of thought is present at
3p2s:

[E]xperience itself, no less clearly than reason, teaches that men believe themselves free because they are conscious of their own actions, and ignorant of the
causes by which they are determined. . . .

So Spinoza seems to believe that in some sense the common conception
of action, with the emphasis on final causes, does not involve causal
determination. Were the agent to conceive the final causes or ends as
determining his actions, he would not have the mistaken belief in indeterministic freedom. I am inclined to interpret this as meaning that
according to the common conception of action, what aim to pursue is
freely chosen by the agents. I have now set as my aim the writing of
this chapter, but I could have chosen to pursue for another goal, for
example, washing the dishes. In human action final causes, then, have
a close resemblance to what is now called reasons for action. Thus, the

common conception of action says that agents have reasons for several alternative actions and from those reasons they freely choose the one that they believe is the most advantageous – agents freely act for the sake of reasons.

The common conception of human action is intuitively appealing. The task Spinoza takes, in the Appendix to the first part of the *Ethics* as well as in 3p2s, is to argue against it from premises that have an empirical nature, as it were. Spinoza believes that he has proved from the principles of reason both determinism and the self-sufficiency of the extended and thinking realms, but this common conception of action quite directly challenges these "truths of reason", because both self-determination and reasons' having relevance to how our bodies move are in conflict with the view that bodies exist in a closed physical universe where any bodily event is a link in an infinite causal series consisting solely of physical events. The difficulty Spinoza faces here seems to be common in early modern rationalism. In the *Meditations*, it was Descartes's purpose to lead the mind away from the senses to justify the worldview of the new science. To reach that aim, Descartes felt the need to construct sceptical scenarios that would somehow draw a wedge between us and the world outside and finally to show the naturalness of the worldview adopted by the new science. Thus, Descartes aims to show that what we experience is not inconsistent with the worldview of the new science. In 1app and especially in 3p2s Spinoza is doing something similar; that is, he is trying to show that the conception of ordinary agency predicted by the new science does not contradict experience. Thus, it should be emphasised that, in the passage just cited, Spinoza claims that "experience, itself, no less clearly than reason, teaches . . . ".

In arguing that the belief in indeterministic freedom is illusory, Spinoza tries to show how this belief is false without appealing to his own metaphysics. What he tries to do is to show that once we correctly analyse experience, belief in indeterministic self-determination fades away. Let us, then, see how Spinoza does this.

First, Spinoza reminds us that according to the common conception of action not all our actions are free. When we seek something with a strong affect, we do not believe we are acting freely:

That is why most men believe that we do freely only those things we have a weak inclination toward (because the appetite for these things can easily be reduced by the memory of another thing which we frequently recollect), but that we do not at all do freely those things we seek by a strong affect, which cannot be calmed by the memory of another thing. But if they had not found by experience that we do many things we afterwards repent, and that often we see the better and follow the worse (viz. when we are torn by contrary affects), nothing would prevent them from believing that we do all things freely. (3p2s)

Here the idea is that explaining the lack of freedom with respect to those actions that are done from a strong affect is not to point out that they somehow overcome the agent's power of willing as such. Rather, the explanation is that because they are done from a strong affect, those affects are not extinguished by other affects so easily. An affect can be destroyed only by a stronger affect. Now, situations in which we do not follow our best judgements teach us about this. There is an affect that the best judgement involves, but its strength is often surpassed by that of other affects, and such cases teach us, according to Spinoza, that we are not always free. If I am eating food towards the taste of which I am somewhat neutral and happen to remember that such food is harmful to my health, and there is alternative food available, stopping eating the unhealthy food creates no problem for me. It is the idea of the food's being harmful that, according to Spinoza, destroys the desire to eat it. But if the food is incredibly delicious, it may happen that the thought of the food's being unhealthy has no effect and I go on eating, realizing that I am a slave to its wonderful taste. So there is a kind of struggle between affects that are contrary to each other. Because these kinds of weak affects are easily beaten by other affects, there arises the illusion that acting in conformity with such weak affects is somehow in our power. But, if the affect is strong, as a drug addict's affect could conceivably be, it is not easily defeated by other affects and, thus, it feels somehow compelling. Knowledge of the harmful effects of drug abuse often does not correct the addict's behaviour.

However, what Spinoza seems to suggest is that experience confirms, or at least is in accordance with, a complete denial of freedom in the sense of contracausal self-determination, and it is the phenomenon of excusing oneself that should convince us of this. Excusing oneself is an excellent example for Spinoza's purposes. As we recall, what he is trying to show here is that the belief in contracausal freedom is baseless. However, if one operates with a Cartesian theory of mind, where our mind is seen as transparent, our inability to find any causes for those actions we think are free should give excellent confirmation for there being no (determining) causes for such actions or, maybe better, for decisions to perform them. However, when agents do what they later repent, they may at the time of the action have the belief that they are acting completely freely, but repentance quite often becomes connected with excusing oneself:

So the drunk believes it is from a free decision of the Mind that he speaks the things he later, when sober, wishes he had not said. So the madman, the chatterbox, the child, and a great many people of this kind believe they speak from a free decision of the Mind, when really they cannot contain their impulse to speak. (3p2s)

Let us concentrate on the drunk. When the drunk acts, he may be perfectly happy with what he is saying. No determining causes are visible to his inner eye. However, while sober, he sees in his former behaviour something that is completely strange to him and this needs an explanation in which mere brute causes, which do not constitute reasons, are cited.[6] What this example shows is that we do not always completely know what is happening in us – the inner sense may be deceiving – and we should not move from ignorance of causes to their denial. So it seems that what Spinoza is doing here is to create scepticism with regard to the inner sense in the same way as Descartes makes questionable the outer senses. For Descartes (CSM II, 12; AT VII, 18), it is not wise to trust in something that has once deceived us, and what Spinoza purports to do with his argument is convince us that our inner sense sometimes deceives us. One might, I assume, try to save the inner sense as giving correct information by insisting that the drunk is drunk and that this unhappy condition prevents his inner sense from functioning correctly. This means that we should identify some kind of normal conditions under which the inner sense works correctly, but it seems that this is an impossible task, and, in any case, it seems that Spinoza succeeds in showing here what he wants to show; that is, that we treat it as perfectly natural to see causes effecting our actions even when we are unaware of such causes.[7]

Weak-willed actions show that our actions are not always sensitive to the reasons we think to be the best. However, it is also natural to hold that a weak-willed agent acts for a reason. Somebody having a smoke may well do that in order to relax while simultaneously knowing smoking to be bad. So the arguments from akrasia and repentance may show that in these cases the agent is caused to act by something he is not aware of, but these arguments do not show that reasons in general do not contribute to acting. Thus, the denial of the principle of freedom

---

[6] What is typical in cases of repentance as well as in akratic actions is that in trying to understand his behaviour, the agent is no longer looking for reasons, or final causes, of his actions but instead efficient causes, that is, answers to the question, 'What made me do it?' Understanding one's own irrational behaviour cannot, of course, be a matter of explaining it in terms of one's own (conscious) aims. See also Davidson (1982, 42).

[7] On this, see also KV 2.17.

in OCHA does not entail the denial that when we act our reasons contribute causally to the bodily events, that is, the denial of the principle of content-sensitive mind–body interaction.

### 4.2. Powerlessness of Reason: Against the Principle of Content-Sensitive Mind–Body Interaction

It might be claimed that acting for a reason is nothing but being caused to act by that reason. For example, the akratic smoker smokes because she finds it relaxing. In short, that we do not act freely from reasons does not entail that we do not act from reasons, and one of Spinoza's concerns seems to be that we do not act from reasons because that would mean that the mind can determine the body, which, according to him, is false.

In 3p2s, Spinoza attempts to show that our decisions and reasons for these decisions bear the same relation to our bodily behaviour while we are awake as they do while we are asleep:

[W]hen we dream that we speak, we believe that we speak from a free decision of the Mind – and yet we do not speak, or, if we do, it is from a spontaneous motion of the Body. And we dream that we conceal certain things from men, and this by the same decision of the Mind by which, while we wake, we are silent about the things we know. We dream, finally, that, from a decision of the Mind, we do certain things we do not dare to do while we wake.

When we are asleep our body does not track our decisions. If that happens it is, according to Spinoza, a coincidence. It also seems that this is something that "everybody" accepts and is confirmed by experience. But if we are inclined to say that dream decisions differ from decisions while we are awake, we should give the relevant difference.

As commonly accepted, the body is not responsive to these dream decisions. Moreover, these decisions are not, a point also commonly accepted, thought of as free even though for the dreamer they appear to possess that feature. So the decisions of the mind should be divided into free and unfree decisions, but because there is no phenomenal difference between these decisions, it is best to reject the notion of an independent free decision completely:

So I should very much like to know whether there are in the Mind two kinds of decisions – those belonging to our fantasies and those that are free? And if we do not want to go that far in our madness, it must be granted that this decision of the Mind which is believed to be free is not distinguished by the imagination itself, or the memory, nor is it anything beyond that affirmation which the idea, insofar as it is an idea, necessarily involves (see 2p49). And so these decisions of the Mind arise by the same necessity as the ideas of things that actually exist.

Those, therefore, who believe that they either speak or are silent, or do anything from a free decision of the Mind, dream with open eyes. (3p2s)

In addition to rejecting the notion of a free decision,[8] Spinoza gives here his substitute for it. Spinoza claims (i) that free decision is, in fact, not distinct from imagination or memory, and (ii) that free decision is not distinct from the affirmation that is essential to an idea. Let us consider these suggestions in some detail.

The point in referring to imagination is that imagination is based on how our body is affected by external things and imagination has its own order that varies from person to person depending on their experiences. In any case, the order of imagination is not free and does not involve any kind of activity on the part of the subject. Moreover, imagination is essentially tied to bodily images. Without such images there cannot be ideas of imagination, which ideas, however, have to be kept strictly distinct from those images. So the order of imagination is dictated by the body and with respect to it we are as unfree as we are when we perceive external things. In saying that the free decision is nothing but the affirmation involved in the idea, what Spinoza attempts to do is to identify the idea that is commonly thought to be the free decision. This kind of idea just represents something that goes on in the body. It is an interesting matter for investigation what kind of ideas Spinoza would identify with particular desires or decisions. I believe Spinoza sees a particular desire as an idea in which the agent represents herself as doing something and the idea gives pleasure to her. Thus, I desire to eat ice cream only if the thought of eating ice cream is something that I find pleasant.

It is not quite clear to me why Spinoza, while giving his substitute for the free decision, brings memory into the picture. Maybe the point is, at least partly, about the means to carry out our decisions. It might be claimed that even if our decisions to do something are akin to perceptions, we still choose the means. For example, I desire to give a call to a friend of mine. Once I remember the phone number, I desire to dial it. I realise that by dialling that number I will reach my friend and thus the thought of dialling the number is pleasant to me. Choosing the means does not, then, involve any free decision because for Spinoza the way memory works is completely dictated by the body.

---

[8] It should be noted that these dream decisions are in an interesting sense separated from real life decisions. It does not seem true to say that somebody who in her dreams decides to do something, without her body responding in any way, tries to move it. This case differs from the one where somebody tries to move her body just to realise it is paralysed.

There also is a letter (Ep58; Spinoza 1995, 284) where Spinoza seems to endorse the error theory of action. He writes,

conceive, if you please, that while continuing in motion the stone thinks, and knows that it is endeavouring, as far as in it lies, to continue in motion. Now this stone, since it is conscious only of its endeavour and is not at all indifferent, will surely think it is completely free, and that it continues in motion for no other reason than that it so wishes. This, then, is that human freedom which all men boast of possessing, and which consists solely in this, that men are conscious of their desire and unaware of the causes by which they are determined.[9]

We may become aware of where our body is taking us, but that kind of awareness or consciousness has no causal relevance to our actions – if we were not conscious of those ends, the body would do what it does. Desires when we are awake are no more causally effective than when we are dreaming. Thus, we are just passengers in a ship but so united to the ship that we take its aims, that is, to where it is directed to by external causes, as our own aims. So Spinoza really seems to believe that our thoughts about what is useful really have no causal relevance.

## 5. SPINOZA'S REVISIONARY THEORY OF AGENCY

Spinoza's view of human agency seems rather desperate. The picture that emerges is indeed not that of being the captain of the ship I call my body, but rather like a passenger in a ship pushed by God. Contrary to what one might expect on the basis of the first and second parts of the *Ethics*, Spinoza does not completely abandon freedom. Human beings are capable of freedom, not of freedom of choice but of freedom of origination as one might call it. In 1d7 Spinoza explains what he means by a thing that is free:

That thing is called free which exists from the necessity of its nature alone, and is determined to act by itself alone. But a thing is called necessary, or rather compelled, which is determined by another to exist and to produce an effect in a certain and determinate manner.

Thus a free thing is something that enjoys both freedom of existence and freedom of action. Spinoza believes that we enjoy the kind of freedom of action characterised at 1d7; that is, we can determine our actions from ourselves. Before understanding how this is possible, we must investigate what could be called Spinoza's new theory of agency.

After having criticised the faulty, probably what he took to be the Cartesian, picture of doxastic and overt agency, Spinoza begins in the

---

[9] John Carriero (2005) gives a meticulous analysis of this letter and especially of this passage.

third part of the *Ethics* to build a new picture of human agency. As we have seen, the human mind is, for Spinoza, a complex idea that has the human body as its object. Human beings do not have faculties of will or decision, and the complex idea of mind that has the human body as its object is formed by God. However, as in anything that exists also in human beings, there is something that seems to make a dramatic change to the somewhat helpless picture of human beings. Spinoza claims in 3p6 that anything that exists strives to exist, and this striving he calls *conatus*.[10]

*Conatus* or striving has much work to do in Spinoza's philosophical system. It can be seen to give an answer to Descartes's question of why individual things persist or move from one moment of time to another. But most importantly, Spinoza uses it to give a plausible account of the nature of the thinking subject once freely operating mental faculties are removed from it as fictions.

The human mind is, as we already know, an idea that has the human body as its object. The existence of an idea is conceptually dependent on the existence of its object. The body is constantly affected by external things that may make it stronger or give it more reality; the external bodies may also make it weaker or cause a decrease in the body's level of reality. Because the idea is directly related to the object, the changes in the object are, of course, changes in the idea. After a change in the object of the idea has occurred, the idea becomes the idea of the object so changed. Moreover, according to the *conatus* thesis, the body strives to exist, and so it seems that the mind's striving to exist is derivative from the body's striving to exist. The mind strives to exist through its object's (i.e., the body's) striving to exist. So it seems that the mind has no *conatus* of its own, and, in fact, Spinoza's thought experiment of the thinking stone presented earlier gives a picture that resembles this. But we will soon see that there is room for an independent *conatus* of the mind or intellect.

At 3p9s, Spinoza gives the following three-faced characterisation of the *conatus* of the mind:

When this striving is related only to the Mind, it is called Will; but when it is related to the Mind and Body together, it is called Appetite. This Appetite, therefore, is nothing but the very essence of man, from whose nature there necessarily follow those things that promote his preservation. And so man is determined to do those things. Between appetite and desire there is no difference, except that desire is generally related to men insofar as they are conscious of their appetite. So desire can be defined as appetite together with consciousness of the appetite.

[10] For a detailed analysis of *conatus*, see Viljanen 2008a.

Let us consider this with the help of an example. Hunger is an appetite. It is something that is related both to my mind and body, because in hunger I feel an uneasiness in my stomach. This feeling is unpleasant, so I strive to get rid of it. Now, because of this emotional component, one might be inclined to say that this appetite is a desire: while having this unpleasant feeling I am necessarily conscious of it. However, this kind of consciousness is not what Spinoza means here. The appetite does not become a desire before I realise that food removes it. Thus, appetite does not become a desire before one understands what removes or satisfies it, that is, before one is conscious of the object that satisfies it. However, it is rather natural to hold that the nonconceptualised hunger and desire for food are identical to each other.

Of the trio appetite, desire, and will, the last is maybe the most problematic. As has been stated above, there is no faculty of willing for Spinoza, but only particular volitions that are judgements (or propositions in contemporary terminology). Whereas appetite and desire can be seen as moving forces, will seems to have a function of reporting. How can will, then, be held to be the striving of the mind to exist? The explanation for this is dependent on Spinoza's view of the mind as a complex idea of the body. The mind cannot exist without an object whose existence it affirms through its judgements; as long as I judge something my mind exists. For the mind the striving to exist is striving to affirm, and the striving to affirm is what Spinoza here means by will.

Our appetites and our desires as conceptualisations of those appetites are based on the body. They depend on our being able to feel or sense the body's affections, as the example of hunger shows. However, with will, the situation is different. We are caused to perform the volitions, that is, to take a new state of the body as the object of the affirmation through a prior affirmation. So it is not the body's state that makes us make an affirmation about it but prior affirmations; thus the will is conatus as it is related only to the mind.

The picture the conatus doctrine gives of our motivation is heavily body-guided. However, Spinoza gives the mind a rather strong role in the fifth part of the *Ethics*, where he claims that the mind has some power over the affects. The mind, then, has its own motivational force. The point is that because the mind is the idea of the body, if the mind is able to determine itself, it thereby determines the body, too.

In order to begin to understand the independent motivational role of the mind, Spinoza's theory of formal essences should be considered in some detail. For Spinoza, there is in God an idea of the formal essence of any possible individual thing even before the thing is actual. These ideas of formal essences, as well as the formal essences themselves, are eternal. It is not at all clear why Spinoza has to postulate them, but I believe that the following serves at least as a partial explanation. That some particular thing becomes the object of a particular idea may seem unproblematic. However, Spinoza thought that an explanation should be provided for the substance's capability to take just some particular thing as the object of its thought. The idea of an object is not caused by the object and so one begins to wonder how the object relationship is formed; that is, *how does God find a particular thing* as an object of his thought? The oddity of this question disappears when one considers the power of thinking and the power of extending as two distinct powers. Why shouldn't the power of thinking just have a life of its own with no connection to the life of the power of extending? How is it possible that they match?

Spinoza's answer to the question just posed is, I believe, this. The attribute of thought contains the formal essences of all individual things and thus there is in God an eternal idea of my formal essence (2p3 and 2p8). When my body becomes actual it is the idea of this formal essence that becomes actual, too. One might think of these ideas of formal essences as ideas of geometrical forms that acquire a physical realisation in the attribute of extension. The ideas of formal essences are then a priori requirements, as one might want to put it, for there being ideas that have actual things as their objects.[11]

When the formal essence becomes realised, the thing becomes actual and has actual essence, and according to the *conatus* principle, this kind of thing strives to exist; that is, it strives to keep its formal essence actual. This is the striving of the mind irrespective of what really happens in its object, that is, in the body. Nothing that happens in the empirical body can annihilate this striving. Thus, there is room in Spinoza for a battle between the intellect and the body. The characteristic action of the body-independent part of the mind is thinking through adequate ideas, which could be described as adequate thinking. It is this kind of thinking that makes geometry, for example, possible as a science. Here it seems that Spinoza is influenced by Descartes's suggestion about the possibility of geometrical constructions or geometrical imagination. Geometry requires, Descartes suggests, a body towards which the mind can turn.[12] For Spinoza such a "body" is the formal essence of the human body.

The conception of the human being Spinoza has in mind is the following. It is clear that for him a human being has a body that is united

---

[11] On Spinoza's theory of formal essences, see Don Garrett's contribution to this volume.
[12] See CSM II, 51.

to a mind. What it means to say that a human mind belongs to some-body is, however, a question that is worth pondering. The key to this is that the existence of any mind–body union is due to an act of God. Simultaneously with my body's coming into existence, that is, when the formal essence of my body becomes actual, God forms an idea of it. But if we think that God in all his might forms my mind, then the being that has my mind is God – not me, because I am not identical to God. So in this picture my subjecthood seems to disappear: where is the self whose mind is formed through God's thinking of a body? The solution to this problem lies, I believe, in a passage that has already been cited (2p11c):

[W]hen we say that the human Mind perceives this or that, we are saying nothing but that God, not insofar as he is infinite, but insofar as he is explained through the nature of the human Mind, or insofar as he constitutes the essence of the human Mind, has this or that idea. . . .

What this suggests is that any subject is, in a sense, identical to God. God's mental striving is infinite and my mental striving is a part of God's infinite striving. When I think something, this means, for Spinoza, that it is God qua a certain force thinking this something. Thus, *I* am identical with *God acting qua a certain force*. So, it is I who, in my generation, affirm the existence of a certain body, which via this object-taking becomes my body. Thus, one should make a distinction between the self and its mind. It is possible for the self to exist without any body and for that reason without any actual mind. The eternal activity of the self consists, at least partly, in thinking about a formal essence. When a body realises the formal essence, the self begins to think of that realised formal essence, that is, its actual body, and strives to do so.

What the above considerations tell us is that any self is endowed with an intelligence. A self has its own power of thinking, which is a part of God's infinite power of thinking. Thus, a self has the capacity to act. When the self acts, it forms adequate ideas through its own power, and this kind of agency is real, because in it the forming of ideas is explainable by referring only to the nature or essence of the self. So the adequate ideas formed by the intelligence fulfil Spinoza's definition of agency:

I say that we act when something happens, in us or outside us, of which we are the adequate cause, i.e. (by d1), when something in us or outside us fol-lows from our nature, which can be clearly and distinctly understood through it alone. On the other hand, I say that we are acted on when something hap-pens in us, or something follows from our nature, of which we are only a partial cause. (3d2)

That our full activity consists in the formation of adequate ideas is indicated by 3p1:

Our Mind does certain things [acts] and undergoes other things, viz. insofar as it has adequate ideas, it necessarily does certain things, and insofar as it has inadequate ideas, it necessarily undergoes other things.

The possibility of acting is very important in Spinoza's system. Without such an activity we would be helpless bystanders in a life dictated by the body. The capability of acting has a twofold function. First and foremost, it is understanding, which is not related to the body. For instance, geometrical knowledge is related to this kind of understanding. For Spinoza, the possibility of this kind of understanding is of the highest importance, because in his highly intellectualistic ethics, the only thing that is intrinsically good is understanding and the only reason for calling a thing bad is that it prevents us from understanding.

Because understanding is such a jewel, the body should be shaped in such a way that it is not affected in ways that hinder us from understanding. The possibility for this lies in the active intellect, which is able to reflect on the contents of the mind and thus is able to understand itself. Thus, in addition to contemplating the eternal essences, the intellect is also able to reflect the bodily-based ideas it has, and this kind of reflection is the second function of the intellect. This reflection, for example, makes concept formation possible by empowering the intellect to compare and combine the bodily-based ideas. Now, if the intellect understood the bodily-based ideas adequately, or clearly and distinctly, no room would be left for passions, whose passivity is due to their inadequacy. The reason for this is that there is no real distinction between the object of an idea and the idea itself (5p3 and 5p3d). When an adequate idea has an idea as its object, this object has to be an adequate idea. However, turning inadequate ideas into adequate ideas is not possible for us – at least not always – but it is possible for us to form some adequate ideas from any ideas we happen to have. Spinoza explains the possibility of this as follows. All bodies agree in certain features, and because of this universal agreement these features can only be conceived adequately. Thus, the intellect, when it reflects on these common features, forms adequate ideas, and in so doing it acts. This kind of activity goes against the negative passive pull of the inadequate idea involved in the passion and thus the intellect is able to make a change in the body and is not completely at its mercy.

## 6. CONCLUSION

What has been said in this essay must seem controversial to many who have been thinking about Spinoza on action and freedom. For example,

Spinoza at 3p2 powerfully claims that the mind cannot determine the body to motion or rest, and what has been claimed in this paper is that there is a striving of the intellect that has much to do with what is happening in the body. To me the point seems to be that in denying mind's power over the body, Spinoza is just denying that we have any absolute power of making our body move: we do not have such kind of "freedom which all men boast they possess." When I raise my hand in order to vote, the motion of my hand is completely determined by prior motion and rest.

But we are able to think. We are able to think through common notions and through the adequate knowledge we have about God. Whatever gives one the opportunity for this kind of adequate thinking does not determine the train of thought similarly to how a soccer ball's movements are determined in a soccer match. This kind of thinking activity has its own intellectual order, where new ideas are *inferred* from the previous ones in a way that is sensitive to their content. But even if this were granted, one might wonder what such adequate thinking has to do with the body. The adequate ideas cannot have affections of the body as their objects because our knowledge of these is inadequate.

I believe that the answer to the problem just presented is the following. For Spinoza, the mind does not consist of two separate parts of which one consists of bodily-related inadequate ideas and the other of adequate ideas that are not related to the body. The point Spinoza a bit unclearly makes is that all thinking is launched by our bodies being affected by external things. Without this kind of affection we could not have knowledge of the common notions nor of the infinite essence of God, which is the starting point of the third kind of knowledge, that is, of intuitive knowledge. Thus the route to these adequate ideas is bodily-based. Reason has as its object something that is involved in the body and thus its activity is necessarily body-related. It unfolds, connects, and compares those features that are in the body and thus the body has to be affected by that activity. Intuitive knowledge, on the other hand, does not need the body because it starts from the above, from the attributes of God. So it seems that in this kind of knowledge the object of knowledge is not the actually existing human body and, thus, this knowledge does not provide a counterforce in the fight against passions.[13]

[13] I would like to thank John Carriero, Tapio Korte, Hemmo Laiho, Juhani Pietarinen, Arto Repo, and Valtteri Viljanen for their useful comments. Discussions with Alan Nelson, Noa Shein, and Andrew Youpa have shaped the way I understand Spinoza's philosophy of mind. Special thanks go to Valtteri Viljanen for having so generously helped me in editing the whole volume.

# 9    The Anatomy of the Passions

In the near future, artificial hearts may be quite different from natural hearts. The pulse and variable speed of the human heart are difficult to reproduce in reliable machines, and they might also be inessential to the heart's main function, moving blood. So these devices will not reproduce them. Instead, they will provide a constant flow of blood. There is no need to be sentimental about this. We know that what is essential to being who we are resides no more in the heart than it does in the liver or any other mythological seat of the self. Still, what would it be like to have such a heart and be really *angry*? Anger clearly is a conscious state, of course, but a change in blood pressure and a pounding heart seem to be important parts of it. Is there any sense in which a person with a heart that provides a constant flow of blood could experience what we do when we are angry? Spinoza's account of the passions is one of the most immediately engaging parts of his account of the human being because it captures the intimacy of the physical and the psychological in passion. So many of our passions are, like anger, clearly psychophysical that something like Spinoza's identification of mental and physical states, a position often seen in other contexts as a liability of the *Ethics*, seems practically required of a good account of the passions.

This essay describes Spinoza's theory of the passions in the *Ethics* and focuses on the details of Spinoza's accounts of the mental and physical aspects of passion and on the ways in which those accounts correspond to each other. The first section here, which includes some background material from Spinoza's accounts of imagination and human striving, will explain how, in Spinoza's view, each passion is unique to the causal circumstances in which it arises. Differences among individuals, states of a single individual, and the external objects that interact with us all contribute, in the account of the *Ethics*, to differences among passions.

Although Spinoza holds that passions are unique to causal circumstances, he devotes a number of scholia and an appendix to Part 3 of the *Ethics* to descriptions of passions of particular kinds. The second section here will be an account of Spinoza's catalog of the affects, which includes, principally, this detailed account of the passions. I shall try, besides describing the catalog, to address some of the problems that the catalog introduces. The principal aim of this essay is to draw upon the details of Spinoza's account of the mechanisms that produce passion in order to address, or at least to clarify, the problems facing his catalog. The problems do not, I think, diminish the appeal of Spinoza's account of the passions, but they do reveal some of the difficulties facing a philosopher who attempts to capture the richness of human emotional life within the constraints of commitments to determinism and naturalism.

## I. PASSIONS AS UNIQUE TO CAUSAL CIRCUMSTANCES

There is a strong textual basis for taking Spinoza to hold that a passion, strictly speaking, is unique to the causal circumstances in which it arises. He writes at 3p56 that there are as many species of passions as there are species of objects that interact with us:

> As many species of joy, sadness, and desire, and consequently of each affect composed of these, such as vacillation of mind, or derived from them, like love, hate, hope, fear, etc. are produced, as there are species of objects by which we are affected.

One might think, reading this proposition in isolation, that the number of species of passions might be limited by the number of species of objects. Other passages, 3p51 and 3p57, suggest, however, that 3p56 should be taken instead as the claim that there are at least as many species of passions as there are species of objects. At 3p51, Spinoza writes, "Different men can be affected differently by one and the same object; and one and the same man can be affected at different times in different ways by one and the same object." Spinoza's examples following 3p51 suggest that being "affected differently" just means experiencing different passions: one person can fear an object that another does not fear; one and the same person can be bold in one interaction with an object but timid the next. At 3p57, Spinoza grounds this difference in the difference between the essences of different individuals (or, presumably, one individual at different times): "Each affect of any individual differs from the affect of any other as much as the essence of the one differs from the essence of the other." Insofar as human essences vary across individuals, and Spinoza suggests that they do at 3p57s, so will human passions vary.[1]

---

[1] The same scholium also suggests that species differ and that members of the same species may have similar affects: Spinoza writes that horses are driven by equine lust whereas human beings are driven by human lust. So there is evidence here both that Spinoza takes there to be something in essence in virtue of which all

It is not, then, different species of object alone that help us to distinguish among passions but the whole collection of causal circumstances in which passions arise. All of those states of the external world and all of those states of the human being interacting with that world that contribute to the production of a passion also differentiate that passion from other instances of passion. If all contributing causes can be similar in two different events, then there is some sense, on the basis of this evidence, in saying that there can be different instances of one and same passion. Otherwise, 3p51, 3p56, and 3p57 suggest that each passion is unique. This position, the claim that passions are unique to causal circumstances, is the subject of this section. I shall be particularly concerned to find a basis for the view in Spinoza's accounts of ideas of imagination and of the human striving for perseverance in being. The former is the source, in Part 2 of the *Ethics*, of Spinoza's account of how external objects interact with human beings; the latter is Spinoza's account of individual human activity, which is found in the early propositions of Part 3.[2] The account of passion that will emerge from the discussion requires both bodies of background information, for a passion, as Spinoza defines it in his "General Definition of the Affects" (G II, 203), is an idea of imagination that involves a change in the power with which one strives to persevere.

### Ideas of Imagination

The most attractive feature of Spinoza's account of the passions, the extent to which it captures both the psychological and the physical roots of passion, arises from his claims that the human mind is the idea of the human body (2p13) and that the correspondence runs deep: as a great number of bodies compose the human body so a corresponding number of correlate ideas compose the human mind (2p15).[3] At least many of our ideas, then, are ideas of some parts of our own bodies.

members of a species are alike and also that he takes individual essences to vary across members of the same species. I think, furthermore, that 3p51 suggests that a single person's essence can change. I present some evidence for this view in the discussion of individual essences and striving below.

[2] I only discuss the aspects of these parts of the *Ethics* that are immediately relevant to Spinoza's account of passion. Other chapters in this volume (see Koistinen and Youpa) discuss them in greater depth.

[3] I do not mean to claim definitively that all of the ideas that compose the mind are ideas of body, only that each body has a correlate in mind. 2p22 suggests that mind also contains ideas of ideas. A complete account of Spinoza's theory of minds must wrestle with the problem of whether these ideas should be identified with ideas of body, taken to be a part of those ideas, or perhaps taken to be separate ideas. 2p15 might be read to require one of the first two interpretations.

Spinoza explains the sensory perception of external objects and, as I shall emphasize below, passion within this general conception of the mind–body relation. Whenever an affection (or mode) of the body is the effect of an interaction of the body with an external body, the idea in the mind corresponding to that affection of the body will be an idea by which the mind regards the external body as present (2p17). For example, if I grasp a doorknob, the doorknob together with the properties of my hand produces a change in my body, perhaps a new configuration of my hand and the relevant parts of my sensory systems. The idea in my mind corresponding to the new state of my body will be, in Spinoza's terms, an idea of my body through which I represent the doorknob as present. Spinoza writes that the mind "imagines" when it has an idea of this kind, and he calls the affections of body to which ideas of imagination correspond "the images of things" (rerum imagines):

The affections of the human body, the ideas of which represent external bodies as present to us, we shall call the images of things, even if they do not reproduce the figures of things. And when the mind regards bodies in this way, we shall say that it imagines. (2p17cs; G II, 106)

Spinoza provides a somewhat different characterization of imagination later in Part 2. In introducing the three kinds of cognition at 2p40s2, he describes two different ways, sensation and report, by which we acquire knowledge by means of interaction with the external world. Then he writes, "In what follows I shall call both of these ways of attending to things cognition of the first kind, opinion or imagination." Because Spinoza seems to be describing the same kinds of ideas in both places, however, and because he refers to 2p17 in his discussion of imagination in the first scholium to 2p40, I take this second characterization to refer to the same group of ideas as the first: all instances of cognition that involve sensation and report are also ideas of modes of the body that are produced by external objects as partial causes and that represent those objects as present. What 2p40s2's characterization of ideas of imagination as cognition of the first kind adds to the characterizations earlier in Part 2, which will be of importance to the discussion of passion, is a further fact about the effects of such ideas: cognition of the first kind is the only cause of falsity (2p41). Passion, then, because it will turn out to be a variety of cognition of the first kind, will be an idea of the kind that is involved in error.

### Mental Striving

Spinoza introduces his account of individual human essence, the striving to persevere in being, in the early propositions of Part 3. At 3d2, he defines activity: we act whenever we are the adequate, or, to use a more familiar term, total cause of some effect, but we do not act, or are passive, whenever we are an inadequate or partial cause.[4] Spinoza formally defines the terms "affect" (*affectus*), "action" (*actio*), and "passion" (*passio*) at 3d3: an affect is any change to the body's power of acting, or the idea of such a change. An action is any such change of which we are an adequate cause and a passion is any other such change. So human affects are related to the general accounts of activity and passivity in that they are activity, or passivity, that involves a change to the body's power of acting, or the idea of such a change. From 3p1 to 3p9 Spinoza characterizes, first, the ways in which human minds cause effects and, next, the effects themselves of human action.

What is most important about Spinoza's discussion of causation in human minds is the relationship he finds between ideas in the human mind and human affects. At 3p1c he associates the degree of a mind's activity with the degree of possession of adequate ideas, and the degree of susceptibility to passion with the degree of possession of inadequate ideas: "From this it follows that the mind is subject to more passions the more it has inadequate ideas, and conversely, is more active the more it has adequate ideas." Then, at 3p3, he defends the related claim that minds act, in the restrictive sense of 3d3, only insofar as they have adequate ideas, and they are passive only insofar as they have inadequate ideas: "The actions of the mind arise from adequate ideas alone; the passions on the other hand depend on inadequate ideas alone." Spinoza holds, then, that the mind will act only from its adequate ideas and will be more active to the extent that it has more adequate ideas. The position concerning passion is slightly more complex. As with adequate ideas and action, Spinoza does hold that the mind is passive, that is, does something as a partial cause, only from inadequate ideas. However, he does not hold, as one might expect of the parallel case, that the mind is more passive to the extent that it has more inadequate ideas. He only holds, as 3p1c shows, that the mind is more subject to passion. I think that this is a strength of his position: because inadequate or partial causation involves causes other than the mind, particular external circumstances will determine when a mind that is subject to passion will suffer it. On the other hand, where the mind is a total cause of its actions, external causes will be irrelevant to action. So Spinoza should

---

[4] Spinoza does not use the phrase "total cause" to my knowledge, and he perhaps means something more by the phrase "adequate cause." In particular, he may use "adequate cause" to associate such causation with adequate ideas, a position I describe below. He does, however, use "inadequate cause" and "partial cause" interchangeably (3d1); this is what I think warrants my substitution of "total cause" for "adequate cause."

not be able to claim that the extent to which a mind is passionate depends on its ideas alone, but he should be able to make such a claim about activity.

Spinoza characterizes the effects of human action in the propositions beginning with 3p4, the doctrine that only external causes can destroy a thing. At 3p6 he argues from 3p4, perfectly generally, that each thing strives, to the extent that it can, to persevere in its own being.[5] The characteristic effect of my action (in the narrow sense of action established at 3d3), then, will be my perseverance in being. At 3p7 he argues that anything's striving is its essence, a claim that will become important, below, in my account of Spinoza's position on corporeal activity. At 3p9, he describes more specifically how the mind strives to persevere in its being: it strives both insofar as it has adequate ideas and also insofar as it has inadequate ideas. Because adequate ideas are associated with adequate causation, the first part of this claim suggests that insofar as I have adequate ideas I will be an adequate cause and so persevere in being. The ramifications of 3p9 for human passion, however, are somewhat mysterious. Because passions are inadequate ideas, 3p9 guarantees that the mind does strive to persevere insofar as it has passions. Spinoza, though, has characterized the effects of striving for a thing only insofar as it is an adequate cause, and, insofar as it acts from any inadequate ideas, the mind is only a partial or inadequate cause of its effects. So 3p9 amounts, for passions and other inadequate ideas, to the unsatisfying claim that the mind, insofar as it acts from inadequate ideas, acts in such a way that, if it were acting from adequate ideas, it would persevere in being.[6]

### Physical Striving

Although Spinoza focuses on human minds in the early propositions of Part 3, it will help to gain an understanding of his catalog of the passions, and, in particular, his accounts of desire and passive joy, to discuss striving in physical terms also. Spinoza does refer to the human body

---

[5] The importance of 3p6 to Spinoza's ethical theory, its apparent lack of substantial connection to earlier parts of the *Ethics*, and its prima facie implausibility have generated a great deal of interest among commentators. Recent discussions of interest include Della Rocca 1996b, Garrett 2002, and Lin 2004.

[6] I offer a detailed interpretation of 3p9 (LeBuffe 2004) in which I argue that the conscious anticipation of joy or the avoidance of sadness in any of our desires amounts, after a fashion, to a striving to persevere. On this interpretation, a person may, from a passion, consciously desire something besides perseverance, such as, for example, money. Such a desire nonetheless represents a striving for perseverance in the sense that this person will anticipate joy in the attainment of money, and joy, though the person may not know it, just is an increase in one's power of striving to persevere.

in the propositions immediately following 3p9, which he also uses to introduce the particular passions. Notably, he writes in the demonstration of 3p10 that the mind strives, principally, to affirm the existence of the body. To understand human striving as a physical striving, and to understand what this proposition and the other propositions concerning striving that precede it entail for the human body, however, will require a discussion of Spinoza's general theory of body.

He defines an individual body in the physical discursus following 2p13 (G II, 99–100):

When some number of bodies, of the same or different size, are so constrained by other bodies that they lean against one another, or if they move, either with the same or different degrees of speed, so that they communicate their motions to each other in a certain fixed ratio, we shall say that those bodies are united with one another and that they all together compose one body or individual, which is distinguished from others by this union of bodies. (2p13le3a2d)

What makes an individual body an individual, then, is either the way in which the parts that compose it are constrained by other bodies or the fixed system within which the bodies that compose it communicate their motions to one another. There is direct evidence that Spinoza takes at least the latter to characterize the human body.[7] At 4p39, in arguing about the human good, Spinoza refers back to the discursus and writes, "what constitutes the form of the human body consists in this, that its parts communicate their motions to each other in a certain fixed ratio."

The precise relation between striving and this fixed ratio is unclear, however, and it may be problematic. I will describe the apparent problem here because I think that the issues it introduces carry over into the interpretation of Spinoza's theories of desire and joy. I do not think that it is simply clear that Spinoza bungles the account. Spinoza qualifies some of the terms involved, especially "essence" and "power," in different ways in the *Ethics*, and a more detailed investigation of those terms would be required either to justify that charge or to explain why the apparent problem is not serious.

---

[7] There may be some reason to think that Spinoza takes both the constraint of other bodies and also the fixed system in which a body's parts communicate motion to characterize a human body. The fact, as I shall emphasize below, that inadequate ideas as well as adequate ideas contribute to the striving of the mind suggests that the mind's essence is in part a function of its interaction with external things. If the mind's striving is just the same as the body's, though, then the body's essence also will have to be in part a function of its interaction with external things. One natural way of conceiving of this interaction is in terms of constraint. One might also argue, however, that external objects help a body to maintain the characteristic proportion of motion among its parts, for example, by means of nourishment.

The problem is that some of Spinoza's claims in the *Ethics* suggest that the human body's striving just is the fixed ratio of motion among its parts; others suggest that striving is the body's power of acting; still others suggest, though, that the body's power of acting cannot be the fixed ratio of motion among its parts. A series of equivalencies in the *Ethics* can illustrate the problem. Here is 3p7: "The striving by which each thing strives to persevere in its own being is nothing but the thing's actual essence." From 3p7 it seems that Spinoza commits himself to

1. A man's striving is his essence.

A thing's essence, however, just is, arguably, its form. Spinoza uses the terms interchangeably in several places.[8] The Preface to Part 4 (G II, 208), which will become important again below, is one of them:

... when I say that something passes from a lesser to a greater perfection, and the opposite, I do not mean that it changes from one essence or [*seu*] form to another. A horse, for example, is as much destroyed if it is changed into a man as into an insect. Rather we conceive its power of acting, insofar as it is understood through his nature, to be increased or decreased.

This passage seems to suggest another equivalency involving essence:

2. A man's essence is his form.

So, if these identicals may be substituted in these contexts, 1 and 2 imply that

3. A man's striving is his form.

Spinoza offers an independent account of form at 4p39, however, which I have already quoted and which suggests

4. A man's body's form is the fixed ratio of motion among his body's parts.

Again, if substitution is permissible, 3 and 4 plausibly may be taken to imply that striving, regarded corporeally, is the fixed ratio:

5. A man's striving is the fixed ratio of motion among his body's parts.

This, then, is one account of corporeal striving that might be attributed to Spinoza.

A second account has a more direct derivation, which may, because often the context of Spinoza's use opens questions about the appropriateness of the substitution of one term for another, be a virtue for an

---

[8] Although I shall emphasize 4pref, 2p10 is also a notable instance.

interpretation of the *Ethics*. This is 4d8: "By 'virtue' and 'power' I understand the same thing, that is, (by 3p7) virtue, insofar as it is referred to
a man, is just human essence, or nature, insofar as he has the power of
effecting certain things that can be understood through the laws of his
nature alone." Spinoza qualifies the identification of power and essence
here. Arguably, though, 4d8 implies that

6. Power is a man's essence.

Substituting identicals again, 1 and 6 imply what Spinoza explicitly
affirms in the demonstration to 3p57:

7. Striving is a man's power.

Faced with 5 and 7, it seems natural to ask whether Spinoza presents
a man's power and the fixed ratio of motion among his body's parts as,
in some sense, the same, a position that 5 and 7 imply:

8. A man's power is the fixed ratio of motion among his body's parts.

Unfortunately, 8 is problematic, as Spinoza's discussions of destruction show. The passage I have quoted from 4pref suggests that Spinoza
thinks that a change in form does, but a change in power does not,
destroy a man. Spinoza's definition of the affects as such changes (3d3)
suggests this point about changes in power as well:

9. A change in power does not destroy a man.

By substitution again, 8 and 9 imply a similar claim about the fixed
ratio:

10. A change in the fixed ratio of motion among a man's body's parts
does not destroy him.

But 4pref, if we take form there to be identical with a fixed ratio of
motion, suggests that 10 is false. The point is more explicit at 4p39:
"Things that cause the human body's parts to have a different ratio of
motion and rest also cause (by the same Definition [from G II, 99–100,
quoted above]) the human Body to assume another form, i.e. . . . to be
destroyed." These passages suggest, to the contrary, that

11. A change in the fixed ratio of motion among a man's body's parts
does destroy him.

So 8, although it does derive from well-established positions in the
*Ethics*, generates contradictory conclusions.

4pref and 4p39 show that Spinoza rejects both 8 and 10. The textual
basis for both 5 and 7 is strong, however. Striving is sometimes regarded
as a person's power and sometimes as the fixed ratio of motion among

the body's parts. The account of striving in the *Ethics*, then, involves Spinoza's account of body in an important but, on the face of it, ambiguous way.

Spinoza typically writes about what striving aims at without describing increases or decreases in it. At 3p6, for example, Spinoza describes striving with respect to what it aims at, perseverance, rather than with respect to the degree to which it aims at something. If the notorious phrase "*quantum in se est*" in that proposition refers to something variable, then it is worth emphasizing that how one strives can change without striving itself changing.[9] Moreover, where Spinoza does write about increases or decreases, he typically writes about changes in power or perfection rather than striving. For example, he argues at 3p12, not that the mind strives to imagine things that increase the body's striving, but that the mind strives to imagine things that increase the body's power of acting. These general points suggest that, in most of the *Ethics*, Spinoza emphasizes the conception of striving captured by 5 and conceives of power, on the other hand, as what increases or decreases when a person strives more or less effectively.[10] However, the case for 7 also has, undeniably, a solid textual basis in the passages I have cited, especially the demonstration of 3p57. There Spinoza clearly takes striving itself to be capable of increasing or decreasing.

### Striving and Passion

Although striving for mind concerns the possession of adequate ideas and striving for body concerns the ratio of motion among the body's parts, mental and physical striving, in the *Ethics*, are supposed to be, in some way, the same thing. Spinoza's claim in the demonstration of 3p10 that mind's striving is, primarily, a tendency to affirm the existence of the body, together with his conception of the mind as the idea of the

---

9  Curley's translation of the phrase, "insofar as it can by its own power," suggests a distinction between the power with which a thing strives and striving itself. I think it relies therefore on an understanding of striving as the characteristic motion that a body maintains by means of its power and not as the power itself with which a body maintains its motion. This is, as I have argued, a plausible reading of striving. The translation's departure from the more vague Latin, however, may incorporate the reading too strongly into the text. At any rate, it is a very difficult phrase.

10 Spinoza's claims at 1p24 and its corollary are also strong evidence for the view that human striving should be identified with the body's form rather than with power. There Spinoza argues that the essence of things produced by God does not involve existence but that their existence and perseverance is something over and above their essence. This suggests a reading of 3p6 on which striving, as a person's essence, reflects what that person is, but the power of striving, the extent to which one is able to persevere is something different from the striving itself.

body, suggests that mental and physical striving are the same thing and that changes in the power of the mind will, in a sense, just be changes in the power of the body. The proposition immediately preceding the introduction of the passions, 3p11, offers evidence for this view: "For anything that increases or decreases, aids or restrains, our body's power of acting, the idea of that same thing increases or decreases, aids or restrains our mind's power of thinking." When a thing angers me, the physical characteristics of anger – higher blood pressure and a pounding heart, in the account I have given – are, on this account, a change in my body's power of acting, and the mental characteristics of anger – the perception of these things and perhaps something more – are a corresponding change in my mind's power of acting.

## General Accounts of Passion

Together, Spinoza's accounts of ideas of imagination and human striving help to clarify his account of passion. He offers a general definition of passion as part of his "General Definition of the Affects" at the end of Part 3 (G II, 203):

An affect that is called a passion of the mind is a confused idea, by which the mind affirms of its body, or some part of its body, a greater or lesser force of existing than before, and by which, when it is given, the mind is determined to think of one thing rather than another.

His first claim is that a passion of the mind is a confused idea. This statement is important because it implies that passions are ideas of imagination. Spinoza suggests at 2p40s2, in his introduction of the first kind of thought, and reaffirms at 2p41 his view that all confused ideas are cognition of the first kind. He labels all thought of the first kind "imagination" at 2p40s2. So everything that Spinoza writes in Part 2 concerning ideas of imagination, confused ideas, and error applies to the passions. This point can be seen vividly in an argument following the "General Definition of the Affects." Spinoza there makes use of the claim, from 2p16c2, that ideas of imagination generally indicate the condition of our bodies more than that of their external partial causes in order to argue that this point must be true of passions specifically; because passions are ideas of imagination, just as my perception of a doorknob as cold indicates, really, more about me (the condition of my sensory apparatus, say) than about the doorknob, so my fear of an airplane indicates more about me (my vertigo, perhaps, or my past experiences) than it does about the airplane.

Passions, however, are a specific kind of idea of imagination. Generally, as we have seen, ideas of imagination are ideas of those affections of the body that are themselves partial effects of external objects.

Passions are, specifically, those ideas of imagination "by which the mind affirms of its body, or some part of its body, a greater or lesser force of existing than before" (3gendefaffs). The phrase "affirms of its body" is familiar from 3p10 and suggests, what 3p11 confirms, that passions are mental correlates to changes in the body's power to persevere and are themselves changes to the mind's power. Where my body, or part of my body, is made more or less able to maintain the characteristic proportion of motion among its parts by an external object, the idea corresponding to this change, which represents that external object as present, is a passion.

Spinoza's accounts of ideas of imagination and the human striving for perseverance help to make sense of the textual basis, which I presented at the beginning of this section, for the view that passions are unique to causal circumstances. In the demonstration to the text I cited, 3p56, he relies upon his discussions of imagination at 2p40s2 and 2p17, in order to claim that each passion, as an idea of imagination, involves both the nature of an external body and the nature of our body. We know from his account of ideas of imagination at 2p17 and its informal material, both of which reemerge in the demonstration to 3p56, something about how passions involve external bodies: they must be ideas that represent external bodies as present. Because the representation of an external body is a part of any passion, passions will vary as objects vary. Spinoza writes (3p56d),

The joy that arises from an object, for example, A, involves the nature of that same object, A; and the joy that arises from object B involves the nature of that same object, B, and so the two affects of joy are different by nature, because they arise from causes of different natures.

If Spinoza had referred passions to the mind only, as, arguably, Descartes did, the fact that passions have different external objects as causes might not be enough to support the claim that different causes produce different passions. For, as two different causes can produce exactly the same motion in an object, so, at least conceivably, two different objects could give rise to the same state of body and so to the same state of the mind. Descartes makes use of reasoning similar to this in *Passions of the Soul*, Article 25:

The perceptions that one refers only to the soul are those whose effects seem to be in the soul itself, and for which one does not ordinarily know any proximate cause to which one can relate them. Such are the feelings of joy, anger, and others like them, which are excited in us sometimes by the objects that stimulate our nerves and sometimes also by other causes.

On Spinoza's view, however, passions always represent their external causes as present. So passions that arise from causes of different natures will on his account be different because their representational content will be different, even if they produce otherwise similar states in the human mind.[11]

Passions will vary as well to the extent that human essence, or striving to persevere in being, varies. The claim that striving varies across different people might not be convincing when we examine total causation. The best case that could be made for such a view would emphasize the different effects that you and I have in striving successfully: my striving as a total cause might seem to be different from yours in that I will succeed in persevering in *my* being and you will succeed in persevering in *yours*. Depending upon how one understands the perseverance of minds, however, this kind of reasoning may not be very moving for Spinoza.[12] It is, rather, the crucial, mysterious claim of 3p9 that we strive also insofar as we have confused ideas that guarantees that passions will vary as a result of variety in human nature. This claim suggests that the different ways in which individual human beings are situated in the world amount to essential, not merely accidental, differences among them. When we act as total causes, you and I both persevere, and one might argue that Spinoza is best understood as taking perseverance to be a single common thing. When we act from confused ideas as inadequate or partial causes, however, although we both, again, express our essence, as 3p9, invoking 3p7, guarantees, clearly Spinoza's view is that we produce very different effects. Suppose that my character, insofar as I am afflicted by passion, varies from yours because you are afflicted in a different way. For example, suppose that I am unduly tempted by

---

[11] Descartes's position is very complex and I do not mean to attribute to him, definitively, the position that passions do not represent. Article 17 of *Passions of the Soul*, for example, suggests that all passions, for him, including passions of the soul, represent the things from which the soul receives them: "one may generally call 'passions' all the various kinds of perceptions or cognitions that are found in us, because often it is not our soul that makes them such as they are, and because it always receives them from the things that are represented by them." This position is much closer to the one I attribute to Spinoza.

[12] Spinoza tends to identify successful perseverance across individuals. See 4p35 for this view in the *Ethics*. So, unlike a figure such as Hobbes, for whom one person's successful striving, in many cases, means another's failure, Spinoza holds that my successful persevering in my being at least never directly conflicts with your successful persevering in yours: the difference in our projects is not stark. Moreover, even if one favors a Hobbesian reading of Spinoza on which perseverance is something very close to biological survival, distinctions of the sort in question do not necessarily pick out a relevant dissimilarity across individuals even if they do pick out different projects. Even if my perseverance is something different from yours, you and I, insofar as we are both striving to persevere, are engaging in activities of a similar kind, and in such a way that one might meaningfully say, even though we are engaged in a conflict, that our states are similar. See Andrew Youpa's essay, in this volume, for a comparison of Hobbes and Spinoza.

money and you by fame. If I come across a suitcase full of cash, I may want to keep it; if you do, you may want to bring it to a television station. The claim of 3p9 that we strive insofar as we have inadequate ideas amounts to a claim that our different situations in the world may contribute to this difference in the character of our passions and so in our behavior. Differences in the passions that arise in us may result, on Spinoza's account, from differences among the particular inadequate ideas that we possess, then, as well as from differences among the objects we encounter.

A similar argument can be made about a single individual in different circumstances. The inadequate ideas that I have will vary depending upon what external objects affect my body at different times. Because I strive insofar as I have inadequate ideas and because my striving is my essence, I myself may vary across time also. The passions that arise in me, then, will change if my situation in the world changes. This position might be difficult to reconcile with an interpretation of striving on which it is, like the ratio of motion among the body's parts, fixed. However, it seems quite compatible with the interpretation of striving as something that itself admits of change, and both interpretations have some textual basis.

## 2. THE CATALOG OF PASSIONS

Spinoza's argument that any passion will be unique to its causal circumstances does not prevent him from offering an extensive catalog of the varieties of passion. At 3p11s, after arguing that the idea of a thing that increases or decreases the power of the body always itself increases or decreases the power of the mind, Spinoza goes on to call such increases or decreases in the power of the mind passions, and he labels all increases in the mind's power "joy" (*laetitia*) and all decreases "sadness" (*tristitia*). This scholium introduces the most basic terms of Spinoza's catalog:

We see, then, that the mind can undergo great changes, and can pass now to greater, now to a lesser perfection, passions that certainly explain to us the affects of joy and sadness. By "joy," therefore, I shall understand in what follows a passion by which the mind passes to a greater perfection. By "sadness," however, a passion by which it passes to a lesser perfection. From this point, I shall call the affect of joy, when it is related to mind and body at once, "pleasure" or "cheerfulness"; that of sadness, however, "pain" or "melancholy." But, it should be noted, pleasure and pain are ascribed to a man when one part of him is affected more than the others, but cheerfulness and melancholy when all parts are equally affected. Next, I have explained what desire is in 3p9s, and, other than these three, I acknowledge no other primary affect: for I shall show in what follows that the rest arise from these three.

Spinoza's views about the different kinds of passion emerge from this passage. In the scholium, Spinoza substitutes the terms "greater perfection" and "lesser perfection" for terms that occur in 3p11 itself, "increase of power" and "decrease of power."[13] So his perfectionist terminology is consistent with the conception of passion that I have presented in the first part of this essay: all passions are changes the mind, or part of the mind, undergoes by which it either increases in power, in which case the passion is a form of joy, or decreases in power, in which case the passion is a form of sadness.[14]

In this section, I shall present Spinoza's catalog of the affects that derive from these three primary affects. I shall turn, then, to a discussion of two central problems that Spinoza's account faces: 1. Desire seems to be presented, incoherently, both as striving itself and also as a change in striving; 2. It is difficult to understand how any passion could contribute to the mind's activity, which is what forms of passive joy do. I hope to use the details of Spinoza's general, mechanistic account of passion from Section 1 to resolve, or at least sharpen, these problems. I also hope that the discussion of these problems will produce useful suggestions about how Spinoza's catalog of the passions, in general, is to be understood.

## The Catalog of Affects

Spinoza dedicates a great deal of the material of Part 3 of the *Ethics*, including a long appendix, to the discussion of particular affects. Table 1 lists them in English and provides some further information about the relation of each affect to others. This table, or any table like it, will simplify or deemphasize elements of Spinoza's very rich presentation. My main purpose here is to capture the various categories that Spinoza introduces at 3p11s and to place the particular affects within them.[15] I

---

[13] Spinoza, as I have noted above, has already defined the passions as changes in power, at 3d3, which also warrants this substitution. Moreover, the end of 4pref, which I have quoted above, contains an explicit definition of change in perfection as a change in power of acting.

[14] The end of da3 (G II, 192) makes this equivalence explicit with respect to sadness.

[15] A number of different tables, with different formats, may be found. Two especially useful tables, with different purposes, are provided by Voss (1981, 171–4) and Delahunty (1985, 232). Voss's table is an excellent resource for students interested either in Spinoza's account of the passions in the *Short Treatise* or in the relation of Spinoza's accounts to Descartes's *Passions of the Soul*. Delahunty's table, like this one, is an attempt to place affects within general categories, but he makes different compromises; in particular, he leaves out the distinction between active and passive affects, with interesting results. Bennett (1984, 263) provides a simpler table that contains the opposed pairs of affects only. Such an emphasis is well placed, as I shall argue in the Conclusion.

have also provided a Latin version in Table 2. Students of Spinoza in English should be aware that scholars vary quite dramatically in their translations of Spinoza's terms for the affects, especially his terms for the primary affects *laetitia* and *tristitia*, translated here as joy and sadness. Although translations elsewhere in this essay are my own, I have adopted Curley's translations of particular affects, both in this table and throughout this essay, so that students may refer to them in context in a single source.

READING THE TABLE

> *Horizontal rows*: Affects in the same horizontal row are those Spinoza associates, usually as contraries, in the *Ethics*. For example love and hate are on the same horizontal row because love is "joy with the concomitant idea of an external cause" and hate is "sadness with the concomitant idea of an external cause" (3p13s). Spinoza offers a more detailed presentation of passions than he does of active affects, and, although there are some clear similarities across the categories, such as similarities between nobility and passive love and between active self-esteem and passive self-esteem, it may be controversial to group any active affects with passions; thus there are no horizontal rows grouping a variety of one with a variety of the other.
>
> *Vertical rows*: Affects in vertical rows are similar in kind. Font style changes and, when necessary, indentations mark increasingly general categories. For example, sense of shame is always a variety of timidity, which is always a variety of fear, which is always a variety of sadness, which is always a passive affect. Some passions are, in some cases but not others, a variety of others. Such relationships are too complex for the table to capture and are not indicated on it.
>
> *Affect entries*: Each affect is listed together with the most prominent passage, or occasionally passages, where it appears. The passages listed are found in Part 3 unless otherwise specified. The mark "ad" refers to the "Definitions of the Affects" following Part 3.

## Desire

Spinoza includes forms of desire among both the active affects and the passions, and he consistently describes desire as an affect. The problem of desire is that, by the definitions Spinoza supplies of "desire" (*cupiditas*) and "affect"(*affectus*), it seems difficult to understand how desire

TABLE 1. Affects in the *Ethics* (English)

| Active Affects d3 | | Passive Affects d3 | | |
| --- | --- | --- | --- | --- |
| Active Joy p58, 5p10s | Active Desire p59 | Passive Joy p11s | Passive Desire p11s | Sadness p11s |
| | | Pleasure p11s | | Pain p11s |
| | | Cheerfulness p11s | | Melancholy p11s |
| | | **Love p13s** | | **Hate p13s** |
| | | *Favor p22s* | | *Indignation p22s* |
| | | Compassion ad24 | | **Envy p24s** |
| | | *Thankfulness or Gratitude p41s* | [These affects are also desires] | *Jealousy p35s* |
| | | *Immoderate loves p56s* | Immoderate loves p56s | **Cruelty p41cs** |
| | | *Devotion ad10* | | |
| | | Inclination ad8 | | *Disgust, Weariness p59s* |
| | | Mockery ad11 | | Aversion ad9 |
| | | Hope p18s2 | Timidity ad39 | Fear p18s2 |
| | | | | *Timidity p39s* |
| | | | | *Sense of Shame p39s* |
| | | | | *Consternation p39s* |
| | Tenacity p59s | Confidence p18s2 | Emulation p27s and Benevolence p27c3s | Despair p18s2 |
| | *Moderation p59s* | Gladness p18s2 | | Remorse p18s2 |
| | Sobriety p59s | [correlate to Pity] p22s | | Pity p22s |
| | *Presence of Mind p59s* | | | Despondency ad29 |
| Active Self Esteem p53, p58, 4p52 | Nobility p59s | Pride p26s | Ambition p29s | |
| Love of God 5p15, 5p15, 5p36s | Courtesy p59s | Overestimation p26s | Human Kindness p29s | |
| | Mercy p59s | Scorn p26s | | |
| | *Morality 4p37s1* | Praise p29s | Longing ad32 | Blame p29s |
| | *Being Honorable 4p37s1* | Love of Esteem p30s | Anger p40s | Shame p30s |
| | | (Passive) Self Esteem p30s | Vengeance p40s | Repentance p30s and |
| | | | Daring ad40 | Humility p55s |
| | | | | Longing p36s |

TABLE 2. Affects in the *Ethics* (Latin)

| | Actio d3 | | Passio d3 | | |
|---|---|---|---|---|---|
| [Active] Laetitia p58, 5p10s | [Active] Cupiditas p59 | [Passive] Laetitia p11s | [Passive] Cupiditas p11s | Tristitia p11s |
| [Active] Acquiescentia in se ipso p53, p58, 4p52 | **Animositas p59s** | Titillatio p11s | | Dolor p11s |
| | Temperantia p59s | Hilaritas p11s | | Melancholia p11s |
| Amor Dei 5p15, 5p36s | Sobrietas p59s | | | |
| | Animi praesentia p59s | Amor p13s | | **Odium p13s** |
| | Generositas p59s | Favor p22s | | Indignatio p22s |
| | Modestia p59s | Misericordia ad24 | | Invidia p24s |
| | Clementia p59s | | | |
| | Pietas 4p37s1 | Gratia or Gratitudo p41s | [These are also desires] | Zelotypia p35s |
| | Honestas 4p37s1 | Amores Immoderati p56s | Amores Immoderati p56s | Crudelitas p41cs |
| | | Devotio ad10 | | |
| | | | | Fastidium, Taedium p59s |
| | | Propensio ad8 | | Aversio ad9 |
| | | Irrisio ad1 | | |
| | | Spes p18s2 | Timor ad39 | Metus p18s2 |
| | | | | Timor p39s |
| | | | | Pudor p39s |
| | | | | Consternatio p39s |
| | | Securitas p18s2 | | Desperatio p18s2 |
| | | Gaudium p18s2 | Aemulatio p27s and | Conscientia Morsus p18s2 |
| | | [correlate to Commiseratio] p22s | Benevolentia p27c3s | Commiseratio p22s |
| | | Superbia p26s | | |
| | | Existimatio p26s | | Abjectio ad29 |
| | | Despectus p26s | | |
| | | | Ambitio p29s | |
| | | | Humanitas p29s | |
| | | Laus p29s | | Vituperium p29s |
| | | Gloria p30s | | Pudor p30s |
| | | (passive] Acquiescen-tia in se ipso p30s | Desiderium ad32 | Poenitentia p30s and Humilitas p55s |
| | | | Ira p40s | Desiderium p36s |
| | | | Vindicta p40s | |
| | | | Audacia ad40 | |

could be an affect. He introduces desire, at 3p9s, as human appetite, that is, striving itself, together with consciousness of appetite. Later, he uses the term more loosely to refer to striving in any of its senses: "Here, therefore, by the word 'desire' I understand any of a man's strivings, impulses, appetites, and volitions, which vary as the constitution of man varies" (Definition of the Affects, 1). Spinoza, though, also lists desire among the primary affects at 3p11s, and he defines 'affects' (3d3) as those "affections of the body by which the body's power of acting is increased or decreased, aided or restrained, and, at the same time, the ideas of these affections." So desire must be both striving, and especially the consciousness of striving, and also a change in a person's power of acting.

I have argued above that 'striving' is ambiguous in Spinoza: it might be identified either with a person's power or with the form of a person's body. The problem of desire is clearer and so more difficult when striving is taken to be identical with a person's power. If striving just is power, then the problem of desire is that Spinoza takes desire to be a change in power and also power itself. He does seem to do this in the demonstration to 3p57:

Joy and sadness are passions by which each individual's power, or striving to persevere in his own being is increased or decreased, aided or restrained (by 3p11 and 3p11s). But by the striving to persevere in one's being insofar as it related to mind and body at the same time, we mean appetite and desire (see 3p9s). Therefore, joy and sadness are desire, or appetite, insofar as it is increased or decreased, aided or restrained by external causes.

The first sentence here restates Spinoza's view that joy and sadness are changes to a person's power and identifies power and striving. The second sentence identifies striving and desire. That would seem to be a good reason to conclude that joy and sadness are related to desire, as changes in it, but not that they are desire itself. Spinoza's conclusion is different, though. He claims that joy and sadness just are desire "insofar as it is increased or decreased, aided or restrained by external causes." How, though, can a change in striving be the same thing as striving?

One might attempt to save Spinoza from the problem by emphasizing the close relation between desire and passion. The best strategy for doing so, I think, would be to show that, like a car that never proceeds without either accelerating or braking, a human being never strives at all unless, at the same time, his or her striving is also increasing or decreasing. There is textual support for such a view. At 3p18, Spinoza argues that the image of a past or future thing affects a mind with joy or sadness in the same way, although (because the mind vacillates with respect to its imagination of objects remote in time) not with the same constancy, that the image of a present thing does. The argument of 3p28 that we always desire what we anticipate will help us attain joy or avoid sadness and the fact that Spinoza does not describe any desires, except perhaps emulation, that are not desires of this kind suggest together that desire always aims at some such imagined benefit.[16] It would follow then that any particular desire, as one instance of the imagination of a future joy or sadness, would itself occur with either joy or sadness as a part of it.

Although I think that it is right that for Spinoza, a person never desires without, at the same time, being affected by either joy or sadness, I have several reservations about this strategy. The first is based on the principle of charity in interpretation: even if desire and changes in desire are intimately involved in this way, the initial charge – that it simply does not make sense to identify a thing with a change to itself – remains unanswered on this interpretation. It may be true, for some drivers, that their cars never proceed without either accelerating or braking. This finding, however interesting, would still not make proceeding just the same thing as acceleration or braking. Similarly, even if we are convinced by the argument that Spinoza conceives of the human being as, in desiring, always undergoing some sort of change in power, that point alone does not absolve him of the charge that, on the interpretation of striving as power, he conflates power itself with a change in power.

My other reservations are based upon other textual evidence of Spinoza's position. One problem is that this particular solution does not show why Spinoza gives a separate place to desire among the primary affects. If desires are themselves affects only because desire is, in some way, identical to joy or sadness, then there ought to be only two, not three, primary affects; all desires ought to be classified as forms of either joy or sadness. In his accounts of particular desires, though, Spinoza never calls a desire an instance of joy or sadness. On the contrary, Spinoza consistently provides accounts of desires that are separate from his accounts of joy or sadness. He accounts for desires, as a class of affects, separately, both in introducing the primary affects at 3p11s and also at the beginning of the "Definitions of the Affects." He also treats particular kinds of desire as something different from particular kinds of joy or sadness. This is clearest in the "Definitions of the Affects," where he writes, after da31, "I have completed what I proposed to explain about the affects of joy and sadness. I proceed, therefore, to those that I relate to desire." This trend is also evident where Spinoza introduces forms of desire within the formal apparatus of Part 3. Although, there, he often introduces a sort of desire as related closely to some form of joy or

---

[16] I have argued this point in detail elsewhere (LeBuffe 2004, 135–40), on the basis of 3p28.

sadness, he never identifies a particular form of desire with a particular form of joy or sadness. Even where, as with thankfulness at 3p41s, Spinoza supplies a single term for both a variety of joy and a variety of desire, he distinguishes between the joy and the desire that the term designates: "This reciprocal love, and consequent (3p39) striving to benefit the one who loves us and who (3p39) strives to benefit us, is called thankfulness, or gratitude." Spinoza might mean here that "thankfulness" is the name appropriately applied either to this kind of love or to this kind of striving, or he might mean that "thankfulness," used properly, applies to the love and the striving at once. On either reading, though, he distinguishes between the love and the desire consequent to it. This is typical of Spinoza's presentation of desires in the *Ethics*: they arise from joy or sadness.[17] If desires were, on his view, affects just because desire is identical to joy or sadness, it seems implausible that Spinoza would consistently treat them independent of the forms of joy and sadness that he describes.

Another problem with the view that desire is power is that, where he does attribute a degree to desire, Spinoza notably does not, as one might expect he would if he took desire to be identical to power, make the change in the degree of desire equivalent to the relevant change in power. When I am saddened, one might expect that, if desire were just power itself, as Spinoza insists at 3p57, my desire, like my power, would decrease. Spinoza writes at 3p37, however, that the greater my sadness is, the stronger will be my desire to be rid of it. This suggests, first, that he understands desire, not as something identical to sadness, but as something, as he writes explicitly at 3p37, that arises from sadness, and, second, that the intensity of a person's desire is something different from the degree of that person's power. The intensity of desire, 3p37 suggests, is something like urgency, or perhaps the degree to which I devote myself to attaining a desired end; the degree of power I have, however, is my ability to persevere. So Spinoza's description of the intensity of desire also seems to betray an understanding of desire different from the one that might be drawn from 3p57.

Desire is also difficult to explain on the view of striving as the characteristic ratio of motion among a body's parts: on this view, the claim that desire is an affect amounts to the claim that the characteristic ratio just is, in some sense, a variety of change in the person's power. Although

---

[17] For examples of claims in the *Ethics* in which Spinoza takes desire to arise from some other affect, see 3p41s and 3p37, which I discuss in this section, and also definition 36 in the "Definitions of the Affects," 4p15, 4p18, 4p44, 4p58s, 4p59s, 4p60, 4app30, and 5p4s.

this view is odd, and my explication of it will be mostly conjectural, I think that it is more promising than the alternative. It is not so clearly problematic as the view that power just is a change in power, and it may fill an important need in Spinoza's psychology.

Striving, in a way, always is the same thing. On the account of the early propositions of Part 3, a person always strives for perseverance. Desire, as consciousness of striving, then, ought to be always the same also. It clearly seems not to be always the same, though. I desire a wide variety of things from a wide variety of motives, and my desires vary with my mood and environment. Spinoza needs, then, to account for the variety of conscious desires without abandoning the view that they are all, in an important way, the same.

By identifying striving with the fixed ratio of motion among a body's parts and desire with striving and consciousness of it, Spinoza can maintain both his commitments. Desire is always the same, on this reading, in that it is always the consciousness of the fixed ratio, which remains the same as long as the body survives. Spinoza defines desire, however, as striving together with the consciousness of striving, and how a person is conscious in desiring may vary even while the characteristic ratio of motion among the parts of that person's body does not. To say that a desire that arises from an affect, sadness, for example, just is sadness is, on this view, too strong. That desire, like all other desires, is the fixed ratio itself together with consciousness of it. However, to the extent that this desire differs from other instances of desire, its difference is a function of the affect that gives rise to it. Suppose, for example, that I fear a large dog. That fear may explain why my conscious desire is now different from what it has been. I desire to flee the dog. Although the desire can be explained, as all desires can on Spinoza's view, as a desire rooted in the striving to persevere in being, it can be differentiated from other desires by reference to features it has in virtue of its relation to this passion: I want to flee because I want to remove any objects that sadden me, and I want to flee the dog because that is the object in question.

It seems to me that, when Spinoza writes that affects give rise to desires, he holds that something like this happens. As I encounter or otherwise imagine an object that saddens me, two things happen. First, my power decreases; second, the way in which I perceive my striving, that is, the way in which I consciously desire, changes. In terms of power, sadness is a transition: so long as I am sad, I am losing power. The effects on desire may be, by contrast, constant: so long as I am sad, I consciously desire to remove the cause of my sadness. Spinoza associates an instance of desire like this one, although it is, like any other, a consciousness of striving, with sadness because the differences that it has from other kinds of desires are a function of the affect that gives rise to it.

I have already mentioned Spinoza's General Definition of the Affects above. That is a rare passage in which Spinoza includes a general account of desire together with general accounts of joy and sadness. In this context, the important phrase is the last one, "[An affect is a change in power] by which, when it is given, the mind is determined to think of one thing rather than another." Spinoza describes joy and sadness as the relevant kinds of changes of power, and then, at the end of his discussion of the definition, he writes:

> Finally, I added, "by which, when it is given, the mind is determined to think of one thing rather than another," in order to express, besides the nature of joy and sadness, which the first part of the definition explains, the nature, also, of desire.

This phrase, which one might hope would be clearer, provides some support for the conjectural account of desire I have offered here. Besides changing power, joy and sadness cause the mind to think of one object rather than another. This account may express the nature of desire in the sense that it explains why a particular instance of desire is called one thing rather than another: it is called longing or timidity or ambition because it, although it is in any case striving, is also a certain kind of consciousness of an external object. What kind of consciousness desire is depends upon the type of joy or sadness that gives rise to it. That is why, on this account, desire also may be called an affect.

An advantage of this account is that it suggests a plausible explanation for the presence of a catalog of the passions in the *Ethics*. The terms in the catalog that represent desires do not necessarily pick out items that are essentially different. A single psychological state may be characterized equally well, for example, as an instance of sadness, or of attempted perseverance, or of aversion. To call that state either an instance of desire or an instance of passion, then, is merely to emphasize features of interest to some particular context rather than to mark that state as different in kind from others. The catalog of passions, under this conception of it, is a collection of terms that are of pragmatic rather than metaphysical significance. So it does not somehow offer an alternative to the view that passions are unique to causal circumstances. Instead it offers a way to talk about different aspects of passion, aspects that otherwise different instances of passion may share, that are of ethical or psychological interest. In the case of desire, the catalog provides the terminology to describe the conscious motivational attitudes that we have toward external objects while we experience different instances of sadness and joy.

*Passive Joy*

Whereas Spinoza's definitions of some of the most basic terms of his catalog create the problem of desire, the problem of passive joy emerges from a tension between the catalog and the general accounts of passion and action that underlie it. I do not think that this tension amounts to a flat inconsistency in the *Ethics*. There are no positions in the book that rule out the possibility of a kind of passion that makes the mind more powerful. The problem is rather that, given Spinoza's association of activity with adequate ideas at 3p1c and elsewhere, there does not seem to be any explanation from him of how some passions, all of which are inadequate ideas, might be thought to increase power. Paul Hoffman describes the problem well:

It is very hard to see how something acting on our mind, and thus causing inadequate ideas could thereby increase our power of acting. Spinoza identifies our power of acting with our power of understanding, that is our power of having adequate ideas (3p59). How could our being caused to have certain inadequate ideas increase our power of having adequate ideas, since adequate ideas follow only from other adequate ideas?[18]

Although the problem of passive joy cannot be resolved completely, I think that Spinoza's accounts of ideas of imagination, striving, and the affects do help to mitigate it. I can offer two suggestions, based upon those accounts. The first will show that most of what Spinoza calls passive joy he does not consider to be an increase in our power of acting. The second will show that, even if some of what Spinoza writes about activity, at 3p1c, 3p59, and elsewhere, seems to imply that power is a function of our adequate ideas, his accounts of imagination suggests that our power is really a function of two different factors.

The first suggestion is that passive joy in the *Ethics*, regarded as a change in the body, is an increase in the activity of the body or of one of the body's parts. Passive joy need not, therefore, be an increase in the whole body's activity or, by parallelism, the mind's. This suggestion arises out of Spinoza's account of striving for bodies. Recall that Spinoza defines an individual (G II, 99–100) and the human body (4p39) as a number of bodies that communicate their motions to one another in a certain fixed ratio (G II, 99–100). I argued in my discussion of corporeal striving that striving may be identified with this ratio.

This conception of striving figures prominently in Spinoza's "Definitions of the Affects" and in his catalog. Affects are increases or decreases in the power of acting. For a body, as a whole, we might well understand

---

[18] Hoffman 1991, 177. Other prominent discussions of the problem include Wartof-sky (1973, 348–9); Neu (1978, 97–8); and Delahunty (1985, 233).

this change in the following way: an increase in the power of acting, or in activity, is an increase in the body's ability to maintain the fixed ratio of motion among its parts. One might reasonably conclude from this point, on the basis of some of what Spinoza writes about changes in perfection at 3p11s or, more directly, from what he writes about changes in power at 3d3, that passive joy, regarded as a change in the body, would be an increase in the body's power to preserve the fixed ratio of motion among its parts that is partially caused by an external object. A corporeal version of the problem of passive joy then would be this: an increase in the body's power to preserve the characteristic ratio of motion among its parts cannot have an external cause.

Spinoza's General Definition of the Affects, though, offers an importantly different characterization of passion, which makes many form of passive joy something other than a change in the body's power (I have added italics here): "An affect that is called a passion of the mind is a confused idea, by which the mind affirms of its body, *or some part of its body*, a greater or lesser force of existing than before...." On this definition of passion, a passion of the mind is an idea corresponding to a change in power to body *or to some part of it*. Although Spinoza omits this caveat in his definition of the affects at 3d3 and again in his introduction of passive joy at 3p11s, there is strong evidence that he takes it to be implicit in the latter. Shortly after introducing joy, there, he introduces pleasure (*titillatio*) and defines it as a form of joy in which one part of the body is affected more than the others. Arguably, Spinoza typically conceives of passive joy as pleasure, rather than a kind of joy that affects the whole body at once. At 4p44s, Spinoza writes that the affects that buffet us daily are generally related to some part of the body that is affected more than the rest.

A passion that, regarded corporeally, is a change in the activity of a part of the body, rather than of the whole body, will be, regarded ideationally, a change in the activity of one of the mind's ideas, rather than of the whole mind. Spinoza writes in the demonstration to 2p15 that the idea of the human body, that is, the mind, is composed of ideas of the parts of the body, so a change in one of the bodies that compose the body will, for Spinoza, require a parallel change in one of the ideas that compose the mind. Just as in the case of the body, though, an increase in the power of a part of the mind need not amount to a general increase in the power of the mind. So passive joy, conceived as an increase in the power, not of the whole person, but of a part of the person, need not be an increase in the person's power at all.

On the first suggestion, then, the problem of passive joy is not as troubling as it might at first appear. Spinoza's discussion of passive joy at 3p11s might at first appear to be a characterization of all forms of passive joy as inadequate ideas that increase a person's power of action. Spinoza's characterization of the mind's activity at 3p1 and its corollary do not explain such increases, so the initial impression 3p11s presents is that one of Spinoza's primary affects, insofar as it is a passion, is unrelated to his other characterizations of activity and unexplained by anything else in the *Ethics*. On the first suggestion, we should notice that only one class of passive joy, that is, cheerfulness, or the class of passions that increase the activity of the person as a whole, is unexplained by his characterizations elsewhere. Other forms of passive joy, those that are increases in the power of activity of one of the person's parts, are well grounded in Spinoza's accounts of body and are not changes of the sort that we would expect 3p1 or its corollary to describe.

The second suggestion is that there is a source in the *Ethics*, namely, Spinoza's account of ideas of imagination, for a view on which passions may increase the activity of a person as a whole. Because 3p1 and its corollary are not explicitly exclusive accounts of activity, this account may be taken to supplement the account of activity that those arguments provide: the mind is more active to the extent that it possesses adequate ideas and it is also less active to the extent that it is afflicted by passion. A passion cannot contribute to a mind's activity by giving it another adequate idea: passions are never adequate ideas. A passion can, however, restrain another passion that afflicts the mind. So passion can contribute to the activity of the mind in the second way, by restraining passions that afflict it.

This suggestion arises out of Spinoza's account of ideas of imagination, which, I have argued above, include all passions, and Spinoza's account in Part 2 of the *Ethics* of error and how it may be avoided. On his account, which is founded on the argument of 2p17, error is avoided when the body is affected in such a way that it excludes another affect that, unimpeded, would cause error. The scholium to 2p35 introduces an example familiar from Aristotle, Cicero, and Descartes, which helps to clarify this dynamic.[19] Spinoza argues there that our sensory idea of the sun, on which it seems very near to us, does not change even after we come to know the sun's true distance. The proposition that ideas of imagination are the only cause of falsity, 2p41, suggests that if an idea does not change in the presence of another, then, for Spinoza, its tendency to give rise to falsity does not change either. So my sensory idea of the sun as near continues to have the causal characteristic of giving

[19] See Descartes's *Meditation* 3 (AT V2, 39) and the Preface to the French edition of the *Principles* (AT IXB, 6); Cicero's *Academica* 2 xxvi, to which Descartes refers in the *Principles* passage; and Aristotle's *De Anima* 428b. Stephen Menn (1998, 274–5) drew my attention to the *Principles* and Cicero.

rise to the false judgment that it is near even after I have knowledge of the sun's true distance. If I judge correctly, then, it is only because the causal power of my idea of its true distance is stronger than and restrains the other idea.[20]

Because passions are ideas of imagination, the example in 2p35s should apply to passions as well as to sensory ideas. The scholium to 4p1, which revisits the sun example, provides evidence that Spinoza does take the 2p35s account to apply to passions. After reciting the example there, Spinoza writes:

> ...and so it is with other imaginations by which the mind is led into error, whether they indicate the natural constitution of the body, or that its power of acting is increased or decreased, they are not contrary to the true, nor do they disappear in its presence.

He explicitly refers in this passage to those ideas of imagination that indicate that the body's power of acting is increased or decreased, which, as we have seen already, are passions. So Spinoza clearly holds that passions may be restrained in the same way that sensory ideas may be restrained because he takes his claims about ideas of imagination in general to apply to the particular case of passion. A passion that afflicts the mind may be restrained in the same way that a misleading sensory idea of the sun may be restrained.

One might infer from the sun example, in which knowledge conflicts with an idea of imagination, that conflicts of the type Spinoza describes are limited to cases in which adequate ideas conflict with inadequate ideas. In his normative ethics, especially at 5p10s, Spinoza does indeed emphasize the usefulness of active affects, or those affects that arise from understanding, for the restraint of passions. At 4p1s, however, Spinoza explicitly argues that other inadequate ideas may also restrain inadequate ideas:

> It certainly happens, when we wrongly fear some evil, that the fear disappears when we hear the truth; but the opposite also happens, when we fear an evil that is certain to come, our fear disappears on hearing false news. So imaginations do not disappear in the presence of the true insofar as it is true but because others stronger than them occur, which exclude the present existence of the things we imagine, as we showed at 2p17.

This passage suggests that the sort of conflict described at 2p17 and 2p35s may be a conflict of one inadequate idea with another or of one passion with another. The second suggestion makes use of this point:

---

[20] Michael Della Rocca has recently published a very interesting article on Spinoza's account of the power of ideas. It includes a detailed interpretation of a dynamic similar to the one I discuss here (Della Rocca 2003, 209).

the mind's power can, in effect, increase when one, less harmful, passion restrains another passion that had decreased its power.

Spinoza claims at 4p7 that one affect can restrain another. That proposition, therefore, is the most explicit textual evidence for the suggestion that passions can make the mind more powerful by restraining the influence of other passions that makes the mind less powerful: "An affect cannot be restrained or cancelled except by an affect opposed to and stronger than the affect to be restrained." As I have mentioned, where Spinoza gives advice for the restraint of passion based on 4p7 at 5p10s, he most strongly recommends cultivation of active affects, nobility and tenacity. The corollary after 3p1 suggests why: nobility and tenacity will give a mind the benefits of canceling sadness without the additional risk of a new, inadequate idea. However, because many people in many situations cannot cultivate these active affects, Spinoza also explicitly argues that some passions may be good, when they restrain other, more harmful passions. These passions include pain (4p43), hope and fear (4p47, 4p54s), and humility and repentance (4p54s), all of which Spinoza calls either good or advantageous in the right circumstances. The demonstration to 4p8 shows the relevance of this label, "good," to joy:

> We call good, or evil, that which is helpful to, or harmful to, preserving our being (4d1 and 4d2), that is (3p7), that which increases, or decreases, aids, or restrains, our power of acting. Insofar, therefore, (by the definitions of joy and sadness in 3p11s), as we perceive a thing to affect us with joy, or sadness, we call it good, or evil.

Pain, then, for example, although it is itself a form of sadness (*tristitia*), may make the mind more active, and so be good for the mind, by restraining another passion, pleasure, whenever it is excessive (4p43): "So we can conceive [pain] to be such that it can restrain pleasure, so that its condition is not excessive, and, to that extent, bring it about that the body is not made less capable, and so, to that extent, it will be good." "Not made less capable" is the key phrase here. When a passion restrains another that, until that point, had made the body less capable, it arguably makes the body as whole more capable. In other words, the passion will make the mind more active.

On this second suggestion, the interpretation of 3p1c as an exhaustive characterization of the mind's activity is not quite right. The mind's activity is a function of two things, not just one: it is indeed made more active by new adequate ideas, as 3p1c suggests, but it is also made less active by many passions. Anything that can remove those harmful passions, and some other passions can, will also make the mind more active. The second suggestion does not capture what Spinoza usually means when he calls something a form of passive joy. Most of the instances of one passion restraining another than I have mentioned here involve what he would label forms of sadness. The second suggestion does show, however, that Spinoza's theory of ideas of imagination includes an account of how a passion can increase the power of the whole mind: it does so whenever one passion restrains another in the appropriate way.

Both suggestions offer valuable responses to the problem of passive joy that are well grounded in the arguments of the *Ethics*. On the first, which derives from Spinoza's account of the physics of bodies, Spinoza's view that mind is made more active by adequate ideas is made consistent with most of his remarks about passive joy. The various passions that Spinoza labels passive joy may be either increases to the mind's power as a whole, or increases to the power of some part of the mind. Those forms of passive joy that refer to changes in the power of some part of the mind are perfectly consistent with the conception of the mind's power as a function solely of its adequate ideas. On the second suggestion, which derives from the account in Part 2 of the epistemology of sense perception, Spinoza does have the resources to explain how a passion may, although it is an inadequate idea, nonetheless increase the mind's activity. In the right circumstances, a passion may restrain another passion that is decreasing the mind's activity and thereby, indirectly, increase the mind's activity.

Neither suggestion, however, makes sense of everything that Spinoza writes about passive joy. The first suggestion, which I think best captures the conception of passive joy that the *Ethics* offers, still cannot explain those forms of passive joy that increase the activity of the mind as a whole. The scholium to 3p11, however, explicitly defines one of the forms of passive joy, cheerfulness, as a passion that we ascribe to a man insofar as all of his parts are equally affected. The second suggestion cannot explain those forms of passive joy that increase the mind's activity as a whole and that do so regardless of particular circumstances. On the account of passive joy the second suggestion provides, a passion only increases the mind's activity in particular circumstances, namely circumstances in which the mind is made less active by an opposed passion. Spinoza, however, does suggest that one form of passion makes the mind more active regardless of circumstances. He argues at 4p42 that cheerfulness is always good. So the second suggestion cannot explain cheerfulness either.[21]

It is not coincidental that both suggestions fail to explain cheerfulness: Spinoza takes circumstances in which one passion may restrain another to the profit of the whole person to arise only when the passions

[21] Delahunty (1985, 233) notes that cheerfulness is especially troubling.

in question involve a change that affects one part of the body more than others. This point is suggested by the fact that all of the circumstances Spinoza describes (at 4p43 and the propositions that refer back to it, 4p44 and 4p47) in which a passion makes the whole person more active are circumstances in which both the offending passion and the remedy are changes to a part of the body rather than the whole. The general idea, which is best captured by 4p43's demonstration, is that one affect (pleasure, at 4p43) acts on one part of the body in such a way that it outstrips (*superet*) the others, thereby harming the whole. The opposed passion (pain, at 4p43) functions as a corrective to that part, and brings it back into the service of the whole body's striving. Spinoza seems also to rely on the view that circumstantial value arises only for passions that affect one part of the body more than others in the demonstration to 4p42. There Spinoza takes the fact that cheerfulness affects all of the body's parts at once to be a reason for concluding that its value does not change with circumstances at all:

Cheerfulness (see its definition at 3p11s) is joy, which, insofar as it is related to the body, consists in this, that all parts of the body are affected equally, that is (by 3p11), the power of acting of the body is increased or aided, so that all of its parts persist in the same ratio of motion and rest to one another. So (by 4p39) cheerfulness is always good and it cannot be excessive.

He makes a similar argument with respect to melancholy, sadness affecting the whole body equally, in the same demonstration. So the one unexplained view is the source of the other: Spinoza's view, on which there are some forms of passive joy that affect the body as a whole, implies, given his views about how passions restrain one another, that there are also some forms of passive joy that help the whole person regardless of circumstance.

I think that the real problem for Spinoza's account of the affects, then, is a problem of cheerfulness, not joy. It is not especially problematic for the arguments of the *Ethics* either that there are forms of passive joy or that the body can become more active as a result of passion. There are good grounds in Spinoza's physics for the first claim, and in his epistemology of sense perception for the second, and neither is inconsistent with his central claims about activity. The claim, though, that there is a kind of passive joy that makes the body as a whole more active and that does so regardless of circumstances does not arise from Spinoza's physics, his account of imagination, or his central claims about activity. It remains in need of explanation.

Some evidence that it is cheerfulness and not passive joy that is the real problem in Spinoza's account of the passions is that Spinoza himself, although he does not seem to acknowledge, in the *Ethics*, any problem with passive joy generally, does notice that cheerfulness is mysterious. This is 4p44s:

> Cheerfulness, which I have said is good, is conceived more easily than it is observed. For the affects, by which we are daily buffeted, are generally related to some part of the body that is affected more than the rest. Consequently, the affects are nearly always excessive, and hold the mind in the contemplation of only one object so that it cannot think of others.

The first suggestion emphasizes what Spinoza here takes to be generally the case with passion: passions typically relate to some part of the body rather than the body as a whole. When he turns to the exceptional case of cheerfulness, Spinoza seems to admit that it is an almost functionless category in the theory of the affects.

So there is a genuine problem for Spinoza. There is no explanation in the *Ethics* of how a passion could increase the power of the mind as a whole and regardless of circumstance, and 4p42 shows that Spinoza himself has trouble thinking about cheerfulness in concrete terms. But although cheerfulness is a real problem for Spinoza, it is not nearly as serious a problem as the problem of passive joy might have seemed to be. The problem of passive joy, unrevised, leaves one of Spinoza's primary affects, and therefore a great deal of Spinoza's moral psychology and his moral theory also, ungrounded and unexplained. Cheerfulness, though, plays only a small role in the *Ethics*; in fact, I have discussed three of the four passages in which Spinoza mentions cheerfulness: 3p11s, 4p42, and 4p44s. The fourth, a note explaining why he omits its definition in his "Definitions of the Affects" collected at the end of Part 3, only emphasizes the unimportance of cheerfulness to his main argument.

### 3. THE PLACE OF SPINOZA'S CATALOG OF THE PASSIONS WITHIN THE *ETHICS*

Many of Spinoza's claims about specific passions are best understood as responses to other philosophers' accounts or attempts to emphasize the differences between his views and received doctrine.[22] I have discussed

---

[22] As 3pref makes clear, Descartes's account of the passions is the most important single influence on Spinoza's. See Voss (1981, 1993) for a detailed account of the relation. Some of what Spinoza writes about the passions can only be understood as a response to Descartes. His discussion of wonder in the fourth of his "Definitions of the Affects" is a good example: "I do not number wonder among the affects, nor do I see why I should do this. . . . I acknowledge only three primitive, or primary, affects (as I indicated in 3p11s): namely, joy, sadness, and desire. I mention wonder only because it has become customary to indicate by other names certain affects, which are derived from these three when they are related to objects that evoke our wonder." He discusses wonder only because others, principally Descartes, who

his catalog in the context of his general account of passion in order to show that those claims, although they produce some tensions with Spinoza's account of passions as unique to causal circumstances, also play a significant role in the argument of the *Ethics*. Two points that have emerged in the discussions of desire and passive joy deserve emphasis.

First, in the discussion of desire, I have suggested that Spinoza's choice to produce labels for some kinds of passions rather than others is largely pragmatic. That is, Spinoza defines passions and makes points about them where it suits the purposes of his ethical argument to follow. Each object of a different nature and each perceiver of a different nature, in their interaction, produce a passion that is unique, so Spinoza's terms for the passions pick out groups of passions that are similar in some respect but not necessarily identical. "Fear," for example, picks out all of those passions that involve a decrease in power and also the representation of a thing that is doubtful (3p18s2). The claim that Spinoza's choice and use of this label is largely pragmatic amounts to the suggestion that Spinoza refers to one set of passions, rather than a different set, because some of his propositions concerning the influence or control of passions later in the *Ethics* involve just this set rather than another. To take one example, the case of fear, I think that because some desires that arise from passion can motivate the same sorts of actions that virtue can, Spinoza uses the label, "fear," to distinguish those actions from similar actions that follow from rational motives. The association of fear with what is doubtful, that is, not well known, then plays an important role in several ethical arguments in Part 4 (notably, 4p63 and 4app31).

An alternative interpretation of the catalog of the passions in the *Ethics* would be one under which the catalog is a kind of taxonomy, describing all the passions by describing sets of them that are somehow cordoned off from other sets by nature.[23] Spinoza does indicate some

makes it the first among his definitions of the passions, do. For Descartes's account of wonder, see *Passions of the Soul*, Article 53. Wolfson (1934 II, 180–220) remains a good source for the historical roots of Spinoza's accounts of the passions, both in Descartes and elsewhere. The second claim I make here, that some of Spinoza's claims are best understood as attempts to emphasize the differences between his views and received doctrine, refers to a number of passages where he refers to ordinary use (principally the note following the twentieth of his "Definitions of the Affects") and also to his critical discussions of traditional virtues at 4p50–p54.

23 Jonathan Bennett tends to present the catalog in this way. Here is his criticism of Spinoza's incorporation of desire among the affects: "The three kinds of affect have, then, some unity at the moral output end of the theory; but that does not give them an intrinsic similarity, unifying them at the input end, and Spinoza does not face that fact. It is as though, needing the concept *weed* in our gardening, we assumed that it belongs in our botanical theory" (Bennett 1984, 258–259). I agree with Bennett that desire is importantly unlike the other primary affects. The point

ambition to give a taxonomy of the passions. Even where he does so, however, at the end of his definitions of the affects in the formal argument of Part 3 (3p56s), Spinoza emphasizes the point that his catalog is not exhaustive, and writes that his purpose is to establish only what he needs to establish about the affects in order to give an account of their influence and of our ability to control them:

> I cannot describe the remaining species of affects here (because there are as many as there are species of objects), nor if I could, is it necessary. For it is enough, for what we aim at, namely to determine the strength of the affects and the power of the mind over them, to have a general definition of each affect.[24]

It is difficult to see what kind of natural cordoning Spinoza's terms might capture. Some of Spinoza's labels emphasize similarities among passions that share a particular kind of external object; others emphasize similar effects that various passions have on striving; others emphasize the similarities among experiencing persons; finally, others (fear, again, is a good example) emphasize more than one of these kinds of similarities. As a result, two terms at the same level of analysis may include some of the same passions. For example, "pleasure" refers to the effects on striving that occur with some types of joy but not others: where an external object increases the characteristic proportion of motion and rest of part of the human body, rather than the whole, Spinoza calls this passion a form of pleasure (3p11s). "Love," however, refers to any kind of joy that accompanies the idea of an external cause (3p13s). Although pleasure and love are both varieties of joy, the result of these definitions, as Spinoza notes in the demonstration to 4p44s, is that some forms of pleasure are forms of love and others are not. If Spinoza's catalog were a taxonomy, this would be similar to a taxonomy of animals under which, among marsupials, some kangaroos are koalas but some are not, and some koalas are kangaroos but some are not. The catalog is instead analogous to an account of useful facts to know about animals that draws upon knowledge of various sorts of things about them: some of those animals that may be domesticated do not, finally, make good pets because they are among those kinds of animals that are not affectionate. Spinoza writes at 4p44s, similarly, that in some of those instances in

---

that Spinoza's project is pragmatic, though, is the point that Spinoza is not trying to produce a theory of the passions in his catalog. All of its concepts are, like *weed*, concepts we use in practical contexts.

[24] Other important evidence that Spinoza is guided by pragmatic concerns in his account of the various passions includes the scholium to 3p59, at the end of the formal discussion of Part 3, and his note following definition 48, the last of his definition of particular affects in the "Definitions of the Affects."

which we feel joy with the accompanying idea of an external cause, the passion we feel is not necessarily a variety of cheerfulness (and so not necessarily good) because those instances are among the kinds of passion that are forms of pleasure.

The second point that emerged in the discussion of passive joy is that, among the various relations that Spinoza draws among varieties of passion, the most important is that of opposition, marked by horizontal rows on my tables. Spinoza typically conceives of the passions, both forms of joy and forms of sadness, as bad for people just because they create a kind of imbalance: one part of the body, and therefore also the mind, in a manner outstrips the rest. The opposed forms of passion, then, unless they are the problematic passions, cheerfulness and melancholy, hold the promise of restraining one another. They fit neatly into the accounts of body and of imagination in Part 2 of the *Ethics*, and they define the sorts of situations in which the imperfect remedy of restraining one passion by another is most likely to be helpful. In Parts 4 and 5, then, it is Spinoza's classification of opposites, pain as opposed to pleasure, for example, that will be most directly helpful.

Passive joy, desire, and sadness, and the varieties and subvarieties that fall under them, bear a less direct relevance to Spinoza's ethical argument. One might be tempted, either from one's own intuitions or from Spinoza's own claims at passages such as 3p39s, to identify all forms of joy with the good and all forms of sadness with the evil. An examination of Spinoza's claims about pleasure and pain in Part 4 here has shown, however, that this straightforward relationship between the passions and the ethical argument is hard to establish. Spinoza's catalog reveals a less tidy, richer relationship, in which we can attain the good, or avoid evil, by attending to various features of our joy and our sadness: their objects, the circumstances in which they arise, or the types of changes to the body that they represent.

An important lesson for readers of the *Ethics* to take from this characterization of Spinoza's catalog is that the various propositions he offers about the passions in Part 3 should be understood as arguments aimed also at Spinoza's stated purpose: determining the strength of the passions and the power of the mind over them. Propositions in Part 3 about the mind's passions alone (p12–p14, p37, and p44, p53–p55, p57) or about the mind's passions in relation to objects (p15–p36, p38–p43, p45–p56), and also Spinoza's propositions concerning active affects (p58–p59), are, like his catalog of passions, an attempt to establish facts about the affects relevant to the accounts of bondage and freedom that follow rather than an exhaustive treatment of the various sorts of interactions that minds and objects have in the affects we experience. They should therefore be interpreted in the light of Parts 4 and 5 of the *Ethics* rather than as an account of the affects that is supposed to be exhaustive and independent. That account is to be found in Spinoza's propositions concerning ideas of imagination, striving, and action and passion in general in Part 2 and the early propositions of Part 3.[25]

[25] Thanks to Olli Koistinen and Andrew Youpa for their helpful comments on drafts of this chapter. A version of the section on passive joy here was presented at the Midwest Seminar in the History of Early Modern Philosophy at the University of Chicago. Thanks to Karolina Hubner, Yitzhak Melamed, and Steven Nadler for their comments at the Seminar.

# 10 Freedom, Slavery, and the Passions

## I. SPINOZA'S PLATONISM

In the *Ethics* Spinoza offers us a model of the good life that we can use as a measure of human perfection; living well consists in conducting our lives as far as possible on the basis of a correct grasp of the abilities and weaknesses of human beings, together with a true understanding of the world they inhabit. A person who achieves this form of existence becomes what Spinoza calls a free man, who lives 'according to the dictate of reason alone' (4pref). Although this ideal consists in the possession of reason or understanding, it is also characterised by the absence of something that Spinoza regards as an imperfection, namely the dominance of affects or passions, whether negative ones such as envy and hatred or their positive counterparts such as love and joy. The passions are therefore viewed as obstacles to freedom, and as long as we are unable to control and transcend them there is a sense in which we are enslaved. 'Man's lack of power to moderate and restrain the affects I call Bondage [*servitus*]. For the man who is subject to affects is under the control, not of himself, but of fortune, in whose power he so greatly is that often, though he sees the better for himself, he is still forced to follow the worse' (4pref). Correspondingly, only insofar as we counteract our passions can we be said to be free.

In defending this alignment of reason with liberty and passion with slavery Spinoza is reiterating an outlook at least as old as Plato, for whom the mind is like a chariot pulled by two horses, one biddable and the other unruly (Plato 1997, 530–33, 253c–7). The biddable horse obeys the charioteer's commands, but the unruly horse, which represents the passions, goes its own way. The charioteer struggles to control it, but when he is unsuccessful the unruly horse gets the upper hand and determines what happens to the chariot and its driver. Just as the charioteer is unable to govern the horse, so we are often unable to govern our passions and the actions that flow from them. They are things that happen to us rather than things that we do; or, to put the point in Spinoza's terms, they enslave us by preventing us from acting virtuously in accordance with reason.

Against this view, Aristotle had protested that some passions, such as fear of shame or righteous anger, are not in the least enslaving but are integral to a good life. The key to virtue is to be able to discriminate between morally appropriate and inappropriate passions, and to act as the former dictate. Aristotle's influential claim was accepted by many of Spinoza's contemporaries, and he himself recognises its force. He allows that a man whose passions are based on inductively well-grounded judgments about the things he encounters is better off than someone whose judgments are fantastical; he recognises that the passions play a vital role in the process of becoming free; and he agrees that a free life has a vital affective dimension. The passions are therefore by no means an unmitigated moral disaster. Nevertheless, he is adamant that an Aristotelian conception of virtue falls short in its failure to recognise that even the most constructive passions are manifestations of a lack of self-control and are thus obstructions to the kind of freedom he is advocating. As long as we remain subject to them we are not fully in charge of what we feel and do; and to the extent that we lack this form of control we remain slaves.

As its opponents have pointed out ever since antiquity, this position is a perplexing one. To be sure, the view that our passions sweep us about, as Spinoza puts it, like waves driven by contrary winds makes some psychological sense (3p59s). For example, when mired in depression or extremely angry we do indeed sometimes feel that we have been taken over by something that we cannot control, and in the face of which we are passive. However, not all our affects answer to this description. We cheerfully identify with many of our everyday loves, hatreds, and desires, and whether or not we regard them as morally virtuous, they have a more active feel about them. Given this phenomenological diversity, is it not perverse to insist that whenever we experience a passion we are being controlled, either in the manner that the winds control the waves or as a master controls a slave? A second line of objection stems from the moral significance we ordinarily attach to passions of different kinds. If, as Spinoza believes, the life of the free man is a life of virtue, will it not include passions such as the ones that Aristotle identifies? Surely the free man will, for example, fear shame, hate injustice, and love his friends? But if we then stigmatise these aspects of his character by classifying them as a form of slavery, do we not ride roughshod over a significant ethical distinction between virtuous and vicious affects, and condemn ourselves to an impoverished ideal of the good life?

In his *Ethics*, Spinoza confronts and answers these objections. With characteristic thoroughness, he offers us a way to understand the claim that the passions enslave, and sketches an ideal kind of freedom in which their power to determine our lives is overcome. In a sense, then, we are left with nothing to worry about. But despite the elegance and consistency with which Spinoza integrates his conception of slavery into his philosophical system, the system itself fuels a nagging doubt. As the *Ethics* explains, humans are essentially embodied, and their passions are their experience of the way that their bodies are acted on by external things (3p3). Moreover, because their survival depends on numerous interactions, for instance, with kinds of foods or with other people, passions cannot be avoided. 'Man is necessarily always subject to passions' (4p4c). To some extent, then, slavery is an inevitable part of human existence. The freedom that Spinoza recommends is not fully attainable, and the model of the good life that he holds out to us will always be offset by *servitus*.

At this point, Spinoza's readers may feel torn between competing responses. On the one hand, the conviction that perfect liberty is incompatible with human corporeality has a long history and a deep appeal. Perhaps this is the tradition of thought to which Spinoza is contributing, and nothing more need be said. On the other hand, there is something mildly paradoxical and even sadistic about an image of the good life that will in practice always be at least in part a life of slavery. What drives a philosopher, one might wonder, so to define his terms that he is inexorably brought to this conclusion? Why must one accept slavery as the other face of freedom? The *Ethics* is of course designed to rule out and discredit such questions by presenting its conclusions as the fruit of incontrovertible inferences grounded on self-evident axioms and definitions. To feel the need to ask why the argument is set up in a particular way is to have failed to follow it. However, in spite of this internal discouragement, a reader may still be curious to know where Spinoza acquired the components of his philosophical armour, and what prompted him to assemble them as he did. The thinking that resulted in his extraordinary and path-finding system was, after all, partly about existing philosophical positions and the problems they created, and a grasp of these antecedents may enable us not only to reconstruct the intellectual milieu with which he was engaging, but also to enrich our understanding of his claims.

In this essay I propose that we can gain a fuller appreciation of Spinoza's reasons for conceiving freedom and slavery as he does by considering the definitions of these terms that drive the argument of the *Ethics* in the light of an early modern conception of *political* liberty. Spinoza holds that a true knowledge of the principles of ethics and politics can be deduced from knowledge of God (TTP 4.10–12; G III, 59–60), and this is indeed the direction of argument he follows in his *magnum opus*. However, we do not have to assume that this order of exposition is the only one capable of revealing how his system hangs together, and we may find it equally fruitful to argue in the other direction, from the political to the ethical and metaphysical. By starting with the political, I aim to show, we can gain a fuller appreciation of what it is about the passions that enslaves and what it takes to escape from slavery. In addition, we can gain a better understanding of why Spinoza needs to address this conception of slavery at all. The *Ethics*, I shall argue, brings together a view of political slavery that played a major part in seventeenth-century Dutch political debate with a broader conception of the passions as impediments to freedom. One of Spinoza's projects is to show how these two views can be integrated into a single, overarching conception of slavery and its positive counterpart, freedom.

## 2. A POLITICAL CONCEPTION OF SLAVERY AND FREEDOM

In the European republics of the seventeenth century, the notion of slavery had strong political connotations. As the Dutch had had occasion to argue during the period of their subjection to Spain, conquest could turn a free nation into a nation of slaves.[1] Moreover, it was widely assumed, individual subjects could be enslaved by their own government when it ruled for its own good rather than for that of the people. Sustaining both these claims was an enduring conception of slavery that had been influentially articulated in the *Digest* of the Roman law.[2] According to this account, a slave is someone who is subject to the power of another and is thus unable to act in accordance with his own will or *arbitrium*. By contrast, a free man is not subject to the power of anyone else and can therefore act as he wills. In the case of an individual slave who is subject to a master, one way for the master to exercise his power is to coerce the slave into doing his bidding. However, the *Digest* assumes, the presence of coercion is not what makes the slave unfree. Rather, his status as a slave rests on the fact that he is at his master's mercy, a situation that continues to obtain even if the master does not choose to exercise his power. A happy slave, for example, may never have to act against his own interests; but his ability to do what he wants nevertheless remains conditional on his master's will and pleasure, and this is what reduces him to slavery.

In the works of the Roman moralists and historians, this conception of servitude was applied to the relationship between subjects and rulers.

[1]  See Van Gelderen 1992, 117.
[2]  *Digest of Justinian* i., 1. 3. 2, in Mommsen and Krueger (eds.) 1985.

When rulers possess enough power to make and enforce laws as they please, their subjects are at their mercy in just the way that the individual slave is at the mercy of his master. A ruler may or may not choose to oppress his subjects; but in either case, the ability of subjects to pursue their interests depends on his discretion. They therefore satisfy the conditions of slavery, and are in fact enslaved. Among Roman writers, this contention gave rise to a debate about the kind of state that can best uphold the free status of subjects, and due to the ready availability of the works of authors such as Livy, Sallust, Seneca, and Tacitus, the issue remained central to political discussion in early modern Europe. Moreover, the controversy surrounding it received a new lease of life from the writings of Machiavelli, who used the Roman view in his *Discorsi* on Livy's history to rework and reiterate the claim that it is only possible to be a free man as opposed to a slave if one lives in a free state (Machiavelli 1996, 129–30).

What exactly is a free state? Although there was no agreement, in the Netherlands or anywhere else, about the precise form of constitution that answered to this description, the tradition of thought originating in Roman moral and legal theory bequeathed an account of the essential features of a polity made up of free men. As we have seen, the main predicament to be avoided was one in which a ruler could enslave a community of subjects by virtue of possessing the power to govern without regard to their interests. Most authors who took this requirement seriously were of the view that freedom is incompatible with government by an absolute monarch, or by a monarch who holds prerogative and hence discretionary powers. This antimonarchical position was in turn taken up in Holland during the latter part of the seventeenth century and used against pro-Orangist defenders of mixed constitutions, notably by the De la Court brothers, with whose writings Spinoza was familiar (De la Court 1972).[3]

Even after monarchy had been put aside, however, there remained a question as to what sort of constitutional checks and balances could ensure that sovereigns ruled in accordance with their subjects' interests. If we again consider the individual slave and remember that his servitude consists in his subjection to a power that is not constrained to take account of his interests, we can see that becoming free is for him a matter of becoming subject to his own power as opposed to that of his master, whether through manumission, escape, or revolt. So what we are looking for in the case of political freedom is a form of state in which individual subjects retain the power to act in accordance with their own wills, while at the same time living under the law. The

---

[3]  See also Scott 2002; Prokhovnik 2004.

traditional solution to this problem proposes that one can remain a free man within the state as long as one plays a part in making the law, thus ensuring that it takes account of one's interest. When the law is to this extent made in accordance with one's will, one can willingly obey it. The constraints it imposes on one's actions are consequently not imposed by a ruler, or indeed by anyone else, and therefore do not reduce one to servitude.

How can this kind of freedom be achieved? According to its defenders, political liberty can exist only where there is some form of popular sovereignty. Although there is still plenty of room to argue about the pros and cons of different types of constitution, the two essential requirements for any kind of free state are that the law alone should rule (and hence that there should be no discretionary powers) and that all subjects should in some sense participate in making the law. Only where these conditions are met can they properly be described as free men rather than slaves.

### 3. SPINOZA ON POLITICAL SLAVERY AND POLITICAL FREEDOM

In the *Theological-Political Treatise*, Spinoza argues that freedom is the paramount value of political life. The ultimate purpose of the *res publica*, he writes,

> is not to act as a despot, to restrain men by fear, and to make them subject to someone else's control, but on the contrary to free every person from fear so that he may live securely as far as possible.... It is not, I say, to change men from rational beings into beasts or automata, but rather that their mind and body should perform all their functions securely, that they should use their reason freely, that they should not contend with one another with hatred, anger or deception, or deal unfairly with one another. So the end of the state is really freedom. (TTP 20.5; G III, 241)[4]

Furthermore, political freedom can be achieved only when individuals are governed by a sovereign power that is constrained to take account of their interests. When a person is subject to the command of another, Spinoza explains, 'and the end of the action is not the advantage of the agent himself, but that of the person commanding, then the agent is a slave and useless to himself' (TTP 16.33; G III, 194). However, 'in a republic, a state where the supreme law is the well-being of the

---

[4] Throughout this essay I have used Edwin Curley's draft translation of the TTP, forthcoming in *The Collected Works of Spinoza*, Vol. 2 (Princeton University Press). I am grateful to Professor Curley for permission to use his translation.

whole people, not that of the ruler, one who obeys the supreme power in everything should not be called a slave, useless to himself, but a subject' (TTP 16.34; G III, 194–5).

Political freedom, as Spinoza presents it here, depends on two separable conditions, one of them necessary and the other highly desirable. First, in order to be free, one must live in a state where the law upholds the common good; or, as the *Theological-Political Treatise* puts it, where the supreme law is the well-being of the people (TTP 16.34; G III, 194). Within the tradition we have been examining, many authors argue that this requirement is satisfied only when the subjects of a free state *make* the law, because this is the sole means of ensuring that the law takes account of their interests. Spinoza, however, does not share this opinion. The important thing, in his view, is that the law should avoid arbitrariness by upholding the good of the people as opposed to that of the ruler, and the good of all the people as opposed to that of a particular faction. A free state will therefore need institutions capable of guaranteeing that this requirement is satisfied. Giving subjects the responsibility of making the law is certainly one mechanism for achieving freedom, and there is evidence that Spinoza regards it as optimal. 'Obedience has no place in a social order where sovereignty is in the hands of everyone and laws are enacted by common consent' (TTP 5.25; G III, 74). But because other institutional mechanisms may do the same job, no single type of constitution is essential to the existence of political liberty.[5]

The subjects of a state therefore cannot be free unless the law upholds their common good; but the quality of freedom that this alone yields is comparatively thin. Inserting a second condition, Spinoza adds that, in order to make their liberty more resilient, subjects must grasp the opportunity that this kind of law presents by obeying it willingly. Here again, his approach is cautious. It is perfectly possible, he concedes, to be a free subject whilst being made to obey the law against one's will, as long as the law does in fact protect the interests that one shares with other subjects. 'Action according to a command – that is obedience – does in some manner take away freedom; but it is not that aspect which makes the slave' (TTP 16.33; G III, 206). However, even though a subject who obeys the law unwillingly (for example, because he fears punishment) is not actually enslaved, his unwillingness is nevertheless an obstacle to the development of a stronger type of liberty. First, his grudging obedience may endanger or undermine the institutions essential to the freedom of the state. If his attitudes or behaviour make it difficult or impossible

---

[5] For example, in the TTP (17.26–40; G III, 205–6), Spinoza allows that the Jewish theocracy lifted the Jews out of slavery.

to enforce the common good, the law itself may become the creature of the sovereign or of a faction, in which case subjecthood will degenerate into slavery. Second, a subject who obeys out of fear is *like* a slave. As Spinoza puts it, 'he who acts from fear of evil is compelled by evil, acts like a slave, and lives under the command of another' (TTP 4.38; G III, 66).

This latter claim draws on a further traditional argument to the effect that living as a slave has predictable psychological consequences, so that slaves tend to be slavish. An individual who is under the command of a master and subject to his will is in a position of dependence, and lacks the power effectively to protect his own interests. At the limit, a master may have the legal right to kill him on a whim. In circumstances of such insecurity, slaves will as a rule fear their masters and do their best to placate them by any available means. Cringing, flattery, and deception consequently become their stock in trade, and form the elements of a character type that had been exhaustively explored by Roman moralists and playwrights, as well as by their early modern followers. Echoing this discussion in both the Preface to the *Theological-Political Treatise* and the *Ethics*,[6] Spinoza, too, condemns the superstition and hypocrisy that arise from fear and threaten the liberty of the state. Acting from fear of evil does indeed make us slavish. So although a man who is forced to obey a law that upholds his interests may possess a degree of liberty, his character is liable to reflect the fact that he does not yet have the fuller form of freedom attained by those who obey the law willingly.

Why, though, is willing the law thought to have such a transformative effect? The answer rests on the assumption that, in order to consistently and voluntarily obey the law, one must understand why it is in one's interest to do so. Even if particular laws are not to one's liking, life under a law that upholds the common good is the best of the available options because it is the only effective protection against slavery. A subject who recognises this fact will therefore see that it is in his interest to obey, and his understanding of his situation will move him to obey willingly.

Becoming free by coming to appreciate the benefits of conforming to the law's demands also brings about further attitudes and affects that are characteristic of free men. Where the law guarantees subjects the independence and security that slaves lack, they are not subject to arbitrary powers over which they have no control, and consequently have no need to resort to flattery or hypocrisy in their dealings with one another. As long as they respect legal limits, they can act as they wish and speak their own minds. Thus sustained, they can live well. They

---

[6] Flattery also gives rise to harmony, but by the foul crime of bondage, or by treachery (4app21).

can be just and honourable and can play a constructive part in maintaining the free state with which their individual liberty is inextricably bound up.

When these two conditions of political liberty are met, subjects are independent both in the sense that they are not subject to arbitrary power, and in the sense that obeying the law does not limit their individual freedom to act as they think best. This last point is important. A subject who so internalises the reasons for obeying the law that he would act as it dictates even if he were not commanded to do so is held to bring about a fundamental change in his situation. Instead of submitting to a command, and thus to the will of the sovereign as represented by the law, he acts in accordance with his own will. Instead of allowing the law to determine his action, he determines the course of events for himself. So although the legal command is still in place, there is a sense in which it has become powerless, because it no longer determines his actions. And because being a free man is, by definition, not being under the will of another, the subject is a free man with respect to the law.

If we now return to the earlier case of the man who obeys the law out of fear of punishment, we can see that the quality of his liberty does not approach that of the free man. From an institutional point of view he is free as long as the law upholds his interests, but from an individual point of view his course of action is determined by the force of the law. In this respect, then, he remains subject to the power of another, and is to this extent like a slave.

This argument implies, as Machiavelli had insisted in his *Discourses on Livy* (II.ii), that it is possible to be fully free only in a free state in which the law upholds the common good. Human beings are, in Spinoza's view, incapable of desiring states of affairs that they regard as fundamentally detrimental to their advantage. So a law that fails to protect the shared interests of those subjects who are bound by it cannot win their wholehearted, collective consent. Whether a sovereign forces them to act against their interests, or merely has the power to do so, their obedience will be accompanied by dissatisfaction or anxiety. In these circumstances they cannot release themselves from subjection to the law by obeying it out of a justified confidence that it can be relied on to uphold their interests, and thus cannot live as free men.

### 4. POLITICAL LIBERTY AS A MODEL FOR A COMPREHENSIVE THEORY OF FREEDOM

If the two claims set out in the previous section capture the crucial elements of what it is to be a slave and what it is to become a free man, we can go on to ask whether this model has a wider application.

This is one of the questions Spinoza implicitly sets out to answer in the *Ethics*. Taking up the analysis of political liberty that he and many other supporters of Dutch republican government had advocated, he aims to show that, as well as illuminating the relationship between a subject and the law, it can cast light on what it means to stand in a free relationship to all external things. The account of political liberty on which we have so far been concentrating thus becomes a single application of a more comprehensive theory of human freedom, which spells out the general principles underlying the political case.

This project is guided by a sensitivity to the peculiar blend of dependence and independence that characterises political liberty. Because it is only possible to be free when one lives in a free state, the freedom of individual subjects is inevitably dependent on a feature of their external circumstances: the existence of legal institutions of a certain type. These institutions create a form of independence that is sufficient to defeat the threat of slavery by ensuring that subjects are not at the mercy of the arbitrary exercise of sovereign power. In addition, they contribute to the conditions for achieving a further type of independence, which comes from obeying the law because one understands that one has good reason to do so. In order to extend the model to cover not just our relationship with the law, but also our relationship with the whole of our environment, Spinoza therefore needs to identify some analogue of these forms of dependence and independence.

Initially, it seems extremely unlikely that such an account will be forthcoming. Throughout much of the *Ethics*, Spinoza emphasises the numerous ways in which human beings are dependent on (or as he puts it, acted on by) external things in ways that are beyond their control. We are surrounded by things that are much more powerful than ourselves and are often unable 'to adapt things outside us to our use' (4app32). It is true that we can to some extent modify our natural environment in order to diminish the threats it poses; but we can never completely overcome its capacity to act on us in ways that may or may not be to our advantage, and whose effect on us is in this sense arbitrary. It is because our ability to live securely and healthily lies outside our control and is always to some degree precarious that the goods of health and security are referred to gifts of fortune (TTP 3.13; G III, 47). So although we are at least potentially capable of creating legal systems that enable us to live freely by guaranteeing the social and political interests that we share with others, we cannot eradicate our vulnerability to death, disease, and other natural threats. To this extent, we are bound to be dependent on the power of nature, and insofar as its effects may or may not serve our interests, they are arbitrary (4p2, 4p4).

Furthermore, this form of dependence is in Spinoza's view constitutive of our passions. When an external body acts on the body of an individual human being, it has an effect on their body that is determined partly by the nature of the external body and partly by the nature of the human body (2p16). The nature or essence' of each body is to be conceived in Spinoza's view as its *conatus* or striving to persevere in its being (3p7). As one body acts on the other, each strives to maintain the pattern of motion and rest by which it is constituted, and in this process the human body's capacity to maintain itself may be increased or reduced. For example, an encounter with a cluster of bacteria may diminish the body's power by causing a bad sore throat, whereas digesting a food that is rich in vitamins may enhance its ability to ward off infection (3p01).

Such changes are always experienced by one's mind, which has an idea of everything that happens to one's body, including the ways it is empowered or disempowered by interactions with external things. Like the body, the mind strives to persevere in its being, and its ability to do so is shaped by its ideas of the body's interactions with other things. When the body is affected in a debilitating way, as in the case of the sore throat, the mind experiences a parallel reduction of its power to persevere in its being and feels this as some kind of sadness. By contrast, when an interaction with an external thing empowers the body, the mind is also empowered and experiences some kind of joy. Its attempts to relate to its ideas of external things in ways that are empowering therefore manifest themselves as passions or affects, organised around the fundamental categories of desire, sadness, and joy (3p11, 3p12).

In registering the way our bodies are affected, the passions chart a form of dependence. We experience affects, Spinoza insists, when we are acted on by external things. However, the mere fact of dependence is not enough to enslave us to our passions. As we have seen, political slavery is not constituted by the mere fact that we are subject to the law; rather, it comes into being when the law is arbitrary, in the sense that it is created and enforced by a sovereign who may or may not take account of our interests. In Spinoza's analysis of the passions as manifestations of our dependence on external things, we find that arbitrariness is once again a central theme. As human beings, we strive to put ourselves in situations that empower us and make us joyful and to avoid situations that disempower us and make us sad. However, insofar as we are unable to control the way we are acted on by external things, we are also unable to control either our own power or the passions in which it is manifested. As Spinoza puts it, 'the man who is subject to affects is under the control, not of himself, but of fortune' (4pref). Things may or may not go well for him; but whatever course they take he is at the mercy of external events, and this is what makes him a slave.

Here, then, we have an initial explication of the claim that our passions enslave us, and an initial answer to the question of why Spinoza should say such a thing. But our appreciation of this phenomenon is not yet complete because, as well as *charting* our enslavement to external things, the passions contribute to it. In the *Ethics*, Spinoza takes pains to show how the psychological laws to which our passions conform introduce an element of arbitrariness into our affective responses., First of all, our disposition to form associations between ideas enables a passion to be transferred from one object to another. Suppose, for instance, that as a result of a recent encounter I both hate and fear A, and then come across B, whom I already hate. Because the two encounters have something in common (I hate both A and B), the second will reactivate the passions involved in the first. And because my hatred of A was accompanied by fear, my new experience of hatred will also make me afraid. I shall fear as well as hate B, whether or not I have any independent grounds for doing so (3p14). In addition, we form associations on the basis of resemblance. For example, if I love A and A reminds me of B, I shall also love B, regardless of her other qualities (3p16). This pattern of feeling determines some of our responses to individuals; but it also governs our feelings about social groups. As Spinoza explains, if a member of class A loves or hates a member of class B, she will feel the same passion for all members of the latter class (3p46). Laws of association thus shape our passions on the slenderest of pretexts. Moreover, they are not the only mechanisms to have this kind of impact, and are joined by a different, imitative process. When we encounter people for whom we do not yet have any particular feeling, we are liable to imitate their affects (3p22). If they are sad, we shall become sad, and if they desire some object, we shall come to want it (3p27 and 3p27s).

As these cases indicate, and as Spinoza explicitly observes, the laws governing our nature ensure that 'any thing can be the accidental cause of joy, sadness or desire,' and 'anything whatever can be the accidental cause of hope or fear' (3p15, 3p50). Our passions are often grounded on accidental associations and resemblances, and arise from processes of which we may not be aware (3p2). In these respects they contribute to the arbitrariness of the way that external things affect us, and thus to our slavery.

The kind of bondage that Spinoza has now identified presents a formidable challenge to the project of showing how human beings can become free. What we were looking for was a way of defeating the arbitrary control that external objects exercise over us. But what we have come to appreciate is just how dependent we are on external things.

By virtue of the laws of our own psychology, we co-operate in ensuring that they have arbitrary effects on us, so that our subjection to them can fairly be described as internally as well as externally caused.

It is not easy to see how we could escape this kind of slavery while remaining human. Worse still, its depth and pervasiveness cast doubt on our ability to achieve the kind of liberty from which our discussion began. Political liberty depends, as we have seen, on two sorts of independence: independence from subjection to arbitrary civil laws; and, in its fullest form, independence from the coercive force of even nonarbitrary laws. But if the individuals posited in the political model are subject to the more general form of arbitrariness manifested in the passions, it is not obvious that they will be able to sustain a free way of life. Among the feelings that will be generated by the combination of their own psychological dispositions and their encounters with external things, among which are hatred, envy, and fear; but these very passions are liable to undermine their capacity to maintain a system of nonarbitrary laws. It is difficult to be fair to people whom we hate, and fear is, in Spinoza's view, incompatible with completely willing obedience (TTP 17.8; G III, 202). Legislators will therefore tend to make arbitrary laws, the judiciary will tend to arbitrary enforcement, and subjects will view the law with suspicion or downright contempt (TTP 17.3; G III, 201). A form of slavery that is an aspect of our very situation as human beings will, it seems, undermine our attempts to create free states and condemn us to a double form of servitude.

### 5. DEFEATING THE ARBITRARY POWER OF EXTERNAL THINGS

Spinoza is not prepared to accept the conclusion we have arrived at, and sets out to show what other resources we can use to attain not only political freedom, but also a more comprehensive form of liberty. As the *Theological-Political Treatise* explains, he intends to show that the happiness that comes with a free way of life depends on our internal virtue rather than on the course of external events (TTP 4.46; G III, 68). Once again, moreover, his discussion mirrors the structure of his model of political liberty.

To see how he now proceeds, it will be helpful to focus on a feature of his model for which we have so far identified no analogue in his more general analysis of the relations between human beings and the rest of nature. As we have already seen, a political subject becomes fully free by obeying the law willingly, and in doing so defeats the law's capacity to determine what he does. Rather than being determined to act by a legal apparatus that is external to him, he takes control. Spinoza is careful to point out that the language of will and volition in which this description is couched is liable to be misleading. We need to appreciate that the ideas we describe as volitions are themselves caused by antecedent ideas, and are not 'free' in the sense of being undetermined (TTP 4.3–4; G III, 58; 1app, 3p2s[ii]). But this in turn gives rise to a problem. If all our ideas are determined, as Spinoza believes they are, we need some way to explicate the sense in which a man who willingly obeys the law can be said to control what he does. If his action, just like that of the man who obeys unwillingly, is determined by antecedent conditions, in what sense does he act freely? As we have noted, Spinoza takes over a longstanding view that the free man is able to obey willingly because he understands that it is in his interests to do so. For example, when a new law increases his taxes and unsettles his finances, he may feel anxious and tempted to cheat; but on rational reflection he will conclude that the benefits of upholding the legal system on which his liberty depends are greater than the financial gains of cheating, and will pay his bill in full. Nevertheless, we still need to ask how his understanding gives him a capacity to control what he does, and thus to sidestep the determining power of the law. To put the point in Spinoza's terms, it is still not clear why we are said to act when we obey the law because we understand the reasons for doing so, but are said to be acted on when we obey because we are afraid of being punished.

The *Ethics* resolves this puzzle by distinguishing the causal processes that are at work in each type of case, and its discussion of this point is grounded on the claim that ideas can be sorted into two categories: some are adequate or true, whereas the rest are inadequate or confused. As we have seen, some of the ideas in the human mind are ideas of the way the body is acted on by external things. These affects are inadequate and do not provide us with true or accurate ideas either of the human body or of the body acting on it. At the same time, however, the mind contains some adequate ideas. According to Spinoza, we possess, for example, an adequate idea of bodily extension. Because the extendedness of the human body does not depend on its interactions with external bodies, there is an idea of the body's extension in the mind that does not depend on the mind's ideas of external bodies. Here he introduces a crucial sense in which our adequate ideas are not the register of, and do not depend on, our bodily interactions with other things. They are not determined by these interactions, as our inadequate ideas are, and this gives them a kind of independence (3d1, 3d2, 2d4, 2p1, 2p2, 2p13).

Adequate and inadequate ideas provide the material for two kinds of thinking: imagining, and reasoning or understanding. The first of these deals in the inadequate ideas that we gain via our interactions with external things; but the kind of thinking that Spinoza describes as reasoning or understanding is a matter of clearly and distinctly perceiving how adequate ideas presuppose and follow from one another. Reasoning therefore relies on an ability to distinguish the various ways in which ideas are interrelated or, as Spinoza prefers to put it, the various types of causal relations between them. In particular, a competent reasoner must be alive to the difference between cases where one idea is the adequate or complete cause of another, and cases where the first idea is only the inadequate or partial cause of the second. For example, the inadequate idea that constitutes a passion is caused both by an idea of the human body and by an idea of an external body, and because each of these ideas is only a partial or inadequate cause of the passion, the passion cannot be conceived through (or understood as an effect of) the idea of the body alone (4p2). At least two ideas must be in play. The situation is different, however, when we clearly and distinctly perceive how one adequate idea follows from another. In this type of case, the first adequate idea is the complete or adequate cause of the second. Moreover, the capacity to reason from one adequate idea to another is, in Spinoza's view, a power of the mind that does not essentially depend on its causal relations with anything outside it. Reasoning is a manifestation of the mind's own power and is something that the mind does (3d2).

Both in his analysis of adequate ideas, and in his account of what it is to reason with them, Spinoza makes space for a conception of reasoning as an independent activity of the mind. At first sight, this is an odd position to hold, because our capacities to acquire adequate ideas and reason with them depend at least in part on the way we interact with external things, and thus on the inadequate ideas that constitute our affects. For example, our ability to extend our understanding will be determined by our education, our desires, and our physical circumstances, and to this extent will not depend solely on the mind. Spinoza agrees that this is the case. The power to reason is a manifestation of an individual's *conatus*, and will therefore vary with the constitution of his or her body and the particular conditions under which he or she lives. Equally, reasoning has to be learned. We are all born ignorant, 'and before men can know the true principle of living . . . much of their life has passed, even if they have been well brought up' (TTP 16.7; G III, 190). However, these features of the capacity to reason can be separated from reasoning itself. When we clearly and distinctly perceive the relations between one adequate idea and another, the mind exercises its own power and acts (5p3). Equally, to act from reason 'is nothing but doing those things which follow from the necessity of our own nature, considered in itself alone' (4p59).

It is not immediately obvious why Spinoza should be concerned to separate what he regards as the active aspect of reasoning from the external conditions on which it always depends; but if we look back to his model of political freedom we can see what is at stake. To gain the fullest form of political liberty, one must occupy a position where one is not dependent on the arbitrary power of the law, but can act independent of it in accordance with one's own desires. The way to achieve this, so the political model claims, is to obey the law because one understands that it is in one's interests to do so. When Spinoza seeks to vindicate his conception of freedom by spelling out the framework of adequate ideas and causes that distinguish reasoning from imagining, one of the features he needs to capture and explain is the association between reasoning, independence, and liberty around which the model is organised. A satisfactory account of reasoning or understanding must elucidate the sense in which it unleashes us from our dependence on the coercive force of the law and allows us to think and act for ourselves. The political model therefore embodies a number of requirements to which Spinoza is responding when he characterises reasoning as a power to act that depends on the mind alone. Part of his project is to assimilate the model of political freedom that is so central to the *Theological-Political Treatise* into a broader conception of a life in which the ability to live freely under the law is just one of a wide range of liberties that understanding makes possible.

Understanding or reasoning empowers us, as Spinoza sees the matter, in two intermingled ways. It allows us to see how we are situated by providing us with true ideas of ourselves and the things around us, and it gives us reasons for acting on our knowledge of how things stand. In some cases, it enables us to act in a manner that is also dictated by some external thing. For example, just as the free man willingly does what the law also commands, you may find that you can defeat the effect of a bout of flu that is acting on you, and giving you a passionate desire to go to bed, by way of understanding that in such circumstances going to bed is the best thing to do. Your action takes account of features of the situation that you do not control, such as the feeling of having a high temperature. But it is nevertheless said to be caused by your rational appreciation of your situation rather than by your passionate desire to lie down, so that you act rather than being acted on. In other cases, however, this type of concord between internal and external determinations does not obtain. An external thing may produce passions that prompt you to do one thing, while your understanding moves you to do something different. It is then an open question whether your understanding or power to act will be great enough to overcome the power of the external things that are acting on you, and thus whether you will be able to act freely (4p59).

So far, we have been considering the role of reason in releasing us from the power of external things. There is, however, a further way in which reasoning can liberate us, this time by altering the power of our own psychological impulses. 'The more an affect is known to us, then, the more it is in our power, and the less the mind is acted on by it' (5p3c). As we gain a more adequate understanding of ourselves, we come to recognise how the psychological laws governing our passions contribute to their arbitrariness, and thus to our enslavement. In addition, once we come to see this as a disempowering state of affairs, we shall strive to resist it; and one of the resources to which we shall appeal in order to do so is our capacity for reasoning. The more we understand the operations of the *conatus* that manifest themselves in our passions, the better placed we shall be to use this understanding to free ourselves from the bondage that the affects impose. Moreover, in the process, we shall increase our power to act.

To some extent, then, reasoning or understanding provides a means to resist the arbitrary power that external things exercise over us, as well as the psychological laws that contribute to our dependence. But how far can this process go? In the political case, liberty depends on external and internal conditions; on the existence of a certain type of law, and on the capacity of subjects to act in accordance with it. Although the first condition lies within human reach (it is possible, though difficult, to devise laws that successfully protect the common good), the second will in practice only be partially realised. Because the relevant kind of understanding is hard to achieve, at least a proportion of subjects will not attain it. They will obey the law out of some passion such as fear of punishment, and will thus fail to become fully free men. Turning now to Spinoza's broader conception of liberty, the situation appears to be still more bleak. On one side, at least some external things continue to exercise arbitrary power over us and thus continue to enslave us. Because we are not sufficiently powerful to create an environment in which we are totally protected from arbitrary interference, it seems that Fortune cannot be altogether vanquished, and we cannot hope to be entirely released from this aspect of our bondage. On the other side, our power to act is only as strong as our capacity to understand, and in practice this capacity is limited. Many people in many circumstances will therefore remain enslaved to the way that things act on them, and thus to the passions that these interactions engender.

Spinoza does not deny that the kind of freedom he envisages is largely unattainable. 'All things excellent', he remarks in another context, 'are as difficult as they are rare' (5p42s). But he is confident that, just as a group of subjects can enhance their political freedom by devising the right kind of law, freedom in the broader sense can be nurtured by a particular kind of community, which he describes as one of free men (4p71–p73). Like a constitution that protects subjects from the incursions of arbitrary political power, a community of free men devotes itself to the pursuit of the understanding through which the arbitrary power of nature can be defeated. By sustaining and encouraging its members' efforts to extend their active control over themselves and the natural world, it reduces both external dependence on the arbitrary power of nature, and, still more importantly, internal dependence on the way that things affect us. It thus generates a level of collective freedom far greater than anything an individual can attain alone, and concomitantly diminishes slavery.

The success of this enterprise depends, in Spinoza's view, on distinctive features of reasoning or understanding. Insofar as people grasp the world by means of the passionate kind of thinking known as imagining, they are bound to experience disempowering affects such as hatred and envy; and these in turn are liable to disrupt and degrade the quality of social life. In particular, passionate people are prone to compete for things they regard as empowering, such as love or money. In the marketplace, for example, the success of one merchant will excite the envy of another, and businesses that go badly will come to be held in general contempt. Furthermore, any or all of these outcomes can split a community, thus reinforcing the passionate struggle for power (4p32). By contrast, the understanding that free men strive to acquire is proof against envy and other forms of sadness. Unlike the objects of our passions, it is not a scarce good, and the fact that one person understands the causes of a phenomenon does not prevent others from understanding it as well (4p36). On the contrary, the more the members of a community pool their rational insights, the more powerful each of them becomes. People who are guided by these insights can consequently be depended on not to undermine each other's efforts to extend understanding and the form of independence that it brings. The more they understand, the more they are able to resist the arbitrariness that the passions manifest and intensify, and the more free they become. Once again, then, freedom can only be realised under certain conditions. A community of free men provides a bulwark against the arbitrary incursions of the passions, and in doing so minimises our vulnerability to the arbitrary incursion of nature. It provides an environment in which freedom can grow.

## 6. CONCLUSION

Throughout the *Ethics* Spinoza builds up an increasingly ambitious conception of liberty, which eventually transcends even the limits imposed by human embodiment. This edifice is partly founded on his conviction that, although the passions enslave us, we can to some extent throw off our servitude and become free. In working out this view, I have suggested, he produces a theory that mirrors the central features of a more limited conception of political liberty, to which he was also committed. In doing so, he unites a political conception of independence with a broader account of the passions, by showing that each is underpinned by a single interpretation of freedom and slavery. In both cases, slavery consists in subjection to an arbitrary power, and only if we appreciate this fact can we understand what it is about the passions that makes them inimical to freedom. Spinoza is not the only seventeenth-century author to link political liberty with its more general counterpart. Other defenders of republican government, such as Pieter De la Court's correspondent James Harrington, also point to the interconnections between political servitude and the slavery that the passions impose (Harrington 1992, 10). However, this evidence of a general interest in the relationship between the two allows us to speculate that one of Spinoza's many aims in writing the *Ethics* may have been to produce a rigorous analysis of the ideas on which the political conception depends, and to show that its ideal of political liberty can only be fully realised by a community dedicated to the more general pursuit of understanding, and thus to a more wide-ranging type of freedom. To put the point in terms of the debates in which Spinoza was involved, a republican style of government can only be reliably sustained where the pursuit of philosophical understanding is encouraged and protected. Although Spinoza defends this conclusion in the *Theological-Political Treatise*, it is in the *Ethics* that he provides his readers with a comprehensive account of his reasons for holding it, and fully explicates the extent of the arbitrariness or slavery against which human beings struggle. Political freedom then emerges as a special case of a more general kind of freedom, through which we can to some extent release ourselves from bondage.[7]

[7] I am grateful to Olli Koistinen and Quentin Skinner for their helpful comments on an earlier draft of this paper.

# 11    Spinoza's Theory of the Good

## I. INTRODUCTION

Following the preface, Part 4 of the *Ethics* opens with eight definitions and an axiom. It begins with these:

4d1. By good [*bonum*] I shall understand what we certainly know to be useful to us.[1]

4d2. By evil [*malum*], however, I shall understand what we certainly know prevents us from being masters of some good.

Goodness, according to 4d1, is the property of being useful, or advantageous. 4d2 says in effect that evil is a matter of having disutility, or being disadvantageous. The value of something is determined by how it well it serves someone. A thing's disvalue is determined by the severity of its disservice to someone.

Thus 4d1 makes clear that, for Spinoza, goodness, or value, is about being useful. Things are considerably less clear when it comes to Spinoza's theory of the good, his account of our ultimate end or *summum bonum*. Granted that something is good in case it is useful, the question is, useful for what? What, if anything, is the ultimate end or purpose by which to measure the utility of things?

Commentators are divided over the correct answer to this question. Wolfson (1934 II, 236–8), Curley (1973b, 369–71), and Bennett (1984, 297–8) take the answer to be self-preservation. Delahunty (1985, 227) suggests activity. Hampshire (1983, 51) singles out freedom. Garrett (1996, 290–91) regards the good as both self-preservation and understanding. Nadler (2002a, 136; 2006, 229) emphasizes understanding. And Bidney (1940, 338, 340, 344, 347–8) covers the bases: self-preservation, virtue, understanding, and joy. Despite this diversity, there is no dispute that any interpretation of Spinoza's theory of the good needs to pass through the *conatus* doctrine, 3p6, and its offshoot, 3p7:

---

[1] The translations of Spinoza's writings in this paper are from C. For the Latin I have consulted Spinoza 1914.

3p6. Each thing, as far as it can by its own power, strives [*conatur*] to persevere in its being.

3p7. The striving [*conatus*] by which each thing strives [*conatur*] to persevere in its being is nothing but the actual essence of the thing.

Things, according to 3p6, strive to persevere in being. Proposition 3p7 adds that a thing just is a striving to persevere in being. Striving to persevere in being is what makes a thing the very thing it is.

The *conatus* doctrine seems to lead straightaway to the view that self-preservation is our ultimate end. Because a thing is something that strives to persevere, the object of any other desire a person may happen to have derives its value from its conduciveness to the object of his or her essential interest; disvalue derives from a thing's incompatibility with the object of a person's essential interest. The *conatus* doctrine in conjunction with 4d1 and 4d2 implies that whatever is good is good in case it serves as a means to, or as a constituent of, perseverance in being. Bad things are bad in case they diminish or obstruct perseverance.

A naturalistic theory of value combined with psychological egoism adds up to a form of ethical egoism, the Hobbesian character of which is unmistakable. Hobbes no doubt influenced Spinoza, but how deep did this influence go? Specifically, is perseverance in being – where this is understood in the ordinary sense of prolonging the duration of an individual's own psychophysical existence – constitutive of, or an ingredient in, the good? I shall try to show that the text best supports a negative answer to this question: that the good, for Spinoza, does not consist in self-preservation in the ordinary sense. Central to the interpretation I defend is a distinction Spinoza draws between durational existence and eternal existence. That which constitutes the actual essence of each thing is, I shall argue, the striving for eternal existence, not mere durational existence.[2] Before doing so, I examine the merits of alternative views. In Section 2, I assess the strengths and weaknesses of a Hobbesian interpretation. In Section 3, I address the suggestion made by some commentators that at the heart of Spinoza's ethical theory is a paradox. In Section 4, I examine a functionalist interpretation of the *conatus* doctrine, and in Section 5, I defend the view that, for Spinoza, eternity is the good.

[2] Yovel 1999 advocates an interpretation that is close to the one I defend in this paper. In agreement with Yovel, I seek to show that the *conatus* to persevere in being is a desire for eternity. Contrary to Yovel, I do not maintain that, for Spinoza, the *conatus* to persevere in being is also a desire for survival in the ordinary sense of prolonging duration. On the reading I defend, the *conatus* to persevere is a desire only for eternity, whereas on Yovel's reading it is a desire for survival as well as for eternity. Also see Strauss 1965, 217–18 and Garrett 1996, 290–91.

## 2. PERSEVERANCE AND INTELLECTUAL PERFECTION

*Perseverance in being*, in a Hobbesian interpretation, is understood in the ordinary sense of prolonging the duration of an individual's psychophysical existence. Thus whatever character traits are good are good for the sake of prolonging the duration of our lives. Likewise with whatever reason prescribes. Reason does not prescribe anything, morally or otherwise, that does not contribute to the continuation of one's existence through time. An individual can be rationally required to do only what optimizes survival.

This approach might appear to have strong textual support. For example, Spinoza says, "No one can desire to be blessed, to act well and to live well, unless at the same time he desires to be, to act, and to live, i.e., to actually exist" (4p21). The good life, he seems to suggest, presupposes desiring to live. Unless an individual looks after his or her own survival first and foremost, he or she cannot have a happy life. He goes on to say, "The striving to preserve oneself is the first and only foundation of virtue" (4p22c). This might be taken to be evidence for the view that the foundation of Spinoza's ethical theory is the same as that of Hobbes's. Whatever rational authority the requirements of virtue have derives from their being instrumental to mundane survival. The path to virtue and happiness, it seems, is self-preservation.[3]

Nevertheless, contrary to Hobbes, Spinoza seeks to demonstrate that there is a *summum bonum* for man.[4] This alone casts some suspicion on any facile attempt to assimilate Spinoza's ethical theory to Hobbes's. All the more so does the *summum bonum* Spinoza proposes: "Knowledge of God is the mind's greatest good [*summum mentis bonum*]; its greatest virtue is to know God" (4p28). Supposing self-preservation involves nothing but prolonging the duration of an individual's psychophysical existence, it is implausible that knowledge of God can help, let alone help to the utmost degree.

This worry is allayed to some extent by Spinoza's unorthodox conception of God. Edwin Curley (1988, 125), a proponent of a Hobbesian reading, remarks,

To prevent misunderstanding, I should stress that when Spinoza speaks of the knowledge of God as the *summum bonum*, I take him to be understanding that phrase very broadly, not as limited to the kind of knowledge which would more conventionally be thought of as knowledge of God. Any kind of scientific

---

[3] Other passages that appear to support this Hobbesian interpretation include 4p8d, 4p18s, 4p20s, 4p25, 4p39, and 4app8.

[4] Hobbes 1994, 57.

understanding of any subject matter will count as knowledge of God (VPP24, 30). So for example, Freudian psychology, if it genuinely provided a scientific understanding of man, would be knowledge of God.

That scientific knowledge is the single most important thing for self-preservation is less implausible than that knowledge of God is the single most important thing. But though broadening the concept of knowledge of God makes the *summum bonum* less implausible, it remains dubious. No doubt scientific knowledge is important for the continued existence of human beings. Its importance for the survival of the minds in possession of it is doubtful, however. Independent of its application to technology and medicine, scientific knowledge is not sufficient for prolonging the duration of a philosopher's existence.

Still, the only relevant question is whether the text best supports a Hobbesian reading. Problematic for this reading are passages that stress the supreme importance of intellectual perfection.[5] Spinoza's view is not that knowledge, or understanding, is desired as a means to self-preservation, but that understanding is desired for its own sake. He says,

Next, since this striving of the Mind, by which the Mind, insofar as it reasons, strives to preserve its being, is nothing but understanding (by the first part of this demonstration), this striving for understanding [*intelligendi conatus*] (by p22c) is the first and only foundation of virtue, *nor do we strive to understand things for the sake of some end* (by p25). *On the contrary, the Mind, insofar as it reasons, cannot conceive anything to be good for itself except what leads to understanding* (by d1), Q.E.D. (4p26d, emphasis added)

Understanding is the object of a mind's *conatus*. A mind does not strive to understand as a means to anything else, not even self-preservation. A mind strives to understand for its own sake. He adds, "We know nothing to be certainly good or evil, except what really leads to understanding or what can prevent us from understanding" (4p27). Because whatever is good is good for the sake of understanding, it appears that understanding is the good. There is nothing apart from understanding for which it is good as a means. Spinoza concludes, "In life, therefore, it is especially useful to perfect, as far as we can, our intellect, *or* reason. In this one thing consists man's highest happiness, *or* blessedness. Indeed, blessedness is nothing but that satisfaction of mind which stems from the intuitive knowledge of God" (4app4). Intellectual perfection alone

---

[5] Passages problematic for a Hobbesian reading include, but are not limited to, the following: 4p26, 4p26d, 4p27, 4p72s, 4app4, 4app5, 4app32, 5p25, 5p26, 5p27, 5p32c, 5p34, 5p38, 5p39, 5p40c.

brings us blessedness, our highest happiness. There is therefore more to a striving-to-persevere-in-being than merely striving to prolong the duration of its own psychophysical existence. An individual at least also strives to understand.

## 3. UNDERSTANDING, ACTIVITY, AND PERSEVERANCE

No plausible interpretation of Spinoza's ethical theory can neglect its emphasis on intellectual perfection. A one-dimensional Hobbesian reading, therefore, will not do. A more plausible line of interpretation neither neglects the perfectionism nor abandons perseverance in the sense of prolonging the duration of psychophysical existence. Despite acknowledging these seemingly divergent strands of thought, some commentators maintain that there is no coherent theory underlying and unifying them. A paradox is said to afflict the heart of the *Ethics*. According to Henry Allison (1987, 148–9), "Given Spinoza's emphasis on the primacy of self-preservation, this identification of the true good with understanding is indeed paradoxical. In fact, it seems to contradict the claim that there is nothing for the sake of which we strive to preserve our being."[6] Spinoza's remarks concerning self-preservation and understanding are puzzling. It has been suggested that his doctrine of the *summum bonum* is among the most "mystifying and frustrating" in the whole of the *Ethics*, which, considering the competition, is no trifle.[7] Nonetheless, there is, I believe, a reasonably straightforward solution to the apparent paradox.

Note that what seems paradoxical is that more than one thing is said to be desired for its own sake and not for the sake of anything else: perseverance in being (4p25), on the one hand, and understanding (4p26d), on the other. Independent of the context of Spinoza's system, these claims are clearly incompatible. Yet 4p25 – "No one strives to preserve his being for the sake of anything else" – is cited in the argument for the view that no one strives to understand for the sake of anything else (4p26d). No one strives to understand for the sake of anything else, in Spinoza's view, *because* no one strives to preserve his being for the sake of anything else. Far from seeming paradoxical, the latter, as Spinoza sees it, entails the former. This strongly suggests that understanding constitutes

---

[6] In a similar spirit, Bidney (1940, 317) remarks, "Spinoza's Stoic rationalism with its acknowledgement of absolute moral standards is incompatible with his biological naturalism which teaches the complete relativity of all good and evil, virtue and vice, to the requirements of self-preservation."

[7] LeBuffe 2005, 243.

perseverance in being, or constitutes a type of perseverance.[8] To know is to be. That this is indeed Spinoza's view is underscored in the following passage: "No life, then, is rational without understanding, and things are good only insofar as they aid man to enjoy the life of the mind, which is defined by understanding. On the other hand, those which prevent man from being able to perfect his reason and enjoy the rational life, those only we say are evil" (4app5). This bears a resemblance to Aristotle's endorsement of the contemplative life in Book X of the *Nicomachean Ethics*. In light of the *conatus* doctrine, however, the resemblance disappears. It is not, as Aristotle and others have held, that the life of the mind – the life of reason – is the best among all available alternatives. For Spinoza, the life of the mind is life. Understanding constitutes the mind's existence.[9] A total absence of understanding is not ignorance, but nonexistence. Thus the life of the mind has no alternative. It can only be lived well or poorly.

The life of reason has no alternative, not because an active life of the body is not an ingredient in the good, but because it is inaccurate to think of a life of the body – physical activity and physical pleasure – as an alternative to the life of reason. Given Spinoza's identity thesis (2p7s), a life of the body is the counterpart of the life of reason.[10] The two

---

[8] Bidney 1940, 346; Garrett 1996, 290; Miller 2005, 163–4. For an alternative solution to the perseverance–understanding paradox to the one I am defending here, see LeBuffe 2005, 243–66. LeBuffe's solution involves a distinction between the object of metaphysical striving, on the one hand, and the object of conscious striving, on the other. Perseverance is the object of striving at the metaphysical level whereas understanding is the enlightened person's conscious object of striving. Although it reconciles Spinoza's seemingly incompatible views, a difficulty for this interpretation is that, in the demonstration of 4p26, the mind's striving to persevere is not treated as something distinct from the mind's striving to understand. On the contrary, Spinoza's view is that the mind's striving to persevere in being *is* the mind's striving to understand.

[9] Cook 1986, 198–207 contains an illuminating discussion of the sort of understanding Spinoza believes constitutes perseverance.

[10] There is a debate among commentators about whether Spinoza really believes that the body has a *summum bonum*, because he never actually describes anything as such. This issue acquires additional urgency from the puzzling turn in Part 5 to "those things which pertain to the mind's duration without relation to the body" (5p20s). The absence of any explicit reference to the body's *summum bonum* and his turn exclusively to the mind in the latter half of Part 5 might seem to be evidence that there are significant asymmetries between thought and extension and, as a consequence, that the parallelism doctrine (2p7) ultimately breaks down. Though an adequate discussion of this issue is beyond the scope of this essay, I believe that parallelism is at work in Spinoza's theory of the good. It is undeniable that the good of the body receives less attention in the *Ethics* than the good of the mind. But this is not conclusive evidence that the attribute of extension in

are inseparable aspects of the good. Indeed, 2p7s implies that a life of the body and the life of reason are one and the same life, conceived under different attributes. Activity is the bodily counterpart of the mind's power of reason (3p11, 3p12, 4p38, 4p39, 5p39; cf. 2p13s).[11] And although Part 4 of the *Ethics* focuses mainly on the good conceived under the attribute of thought, this should not be taken to mean that Spinoza endorses an ascetic existence. On the contrary, he leaves no question about his view of what David Hume later disparages as the "monkish" virtues:[12]

Nothing forbids our pleasure except a savage and sad superstition. . . . It is the part of the wise man, I say, to refresh and restore himself in moderation with pleasant food and drink, with scents, with the beauty of green plants, with decoration, music, sports, the theater, and other things of this kind, which anyone can use without injury to another. For the human Body is composed of a great many parts of different natures, which constantly require new and varied nourishment, so that the whole Body may be equally capable of all the things which can follow from its nature, and hence, so that the Mind also may be equally capable of understanding many things. (4p45c2s)

Just as reason constitutes the mind's existence, activity constitutes the body's. The good life encompasses both. In fact, it is impossible to flourish under one attribute without flourishing under the other (2p7). However, to avoid a potential misunderstanding, it is important not to construe the life of the mind (i.e., reason) and the life of the body (i.e., activity) too narrowly. For instance, Spinoza is not committed to the ridiculous idea that it is impossible to be a Nobel-prize-winning scientist without being a gold-medal-winning athlete. Rather, his view is that mental health, broadly construed as rationality, is the counterpart of physical health, where this includes the characteristic operations and

---

Spinoza's view turns out to be less essential than the attribute of thought. More important, the discussion in 4p38, 4p38d, 4p39, and 4p39d attempts to provide a rough outline of the good of the body, and 5p39 highlights the specific form of parallelism in question: "He who has a Body capable of a great many things has a Mind whose greatest part is eternal." For further discussion, see Bidney 1940, 343–7; Bennett 1984, 357–9; Delahunty 1985, 268–71; Miller 2005, 153–7 and 29n.

[11] This is not to say that the mind's power of reason is not activity in Spinoza's technical 3d2 sense. By 3d2, a mind is active to the extent that it exercises reason and intuition (e.g., 3p1, 3p1c, 4p23, 4p23d). But Spinoza also uses the word "act" in a sense that applies exclusively to the body, as when he says, "The idea of any thing that increases or diminishes, aids or restrains, our body's *power of acting*, increases or diminishes, aids or restrains, our mind's *power of thinking*" (3p11, emphasis added). Thus in Spinoza's view a mind is 3d2-active insofar as it exercises reason and intuition whereas a body is 3d2-active insofar as it acts or is capable of acting (cf., 4p38, 4p39, 5p39).

[12] Hume 1998, 146.

activities of the well-functioning biological organism (5p39s). Knowledge, in other words, is the counterpart of health. Absolutely perfect knowledge is the counterpart of absolutely perfect health.

This dual-aspect theory of the good has its source in Spinoza's dual-aspect theory of substance and its modes. Thought and extension are basic properties of substance and all that depends on substance. As such, thought and extension are causally and conceptually self-contained (1p10). No mode of thought brings about or explains any mode of extension, and nothing in extension brings about or explains anything in thought. Though self-contained, they are simply different aspects of one and the same thing: one and the same substance, and one and the same mode or series of modes (2p7s). The dual-aspect theory of substance and modes ultimately leads to the dual-aspect theory of the good. In the attribute of thought, striving to persevere in being is manifested as striving to understand. In the attribute of extension, it is manifested as striving to bodily activity. Understanding and activity are different aspects of one and the same perseverance and, as a result, of one and the same good.

### 4. DURATION AND PERSEVERANCE

For Spinoza, then, mental good functioning, bodily good functioning, and perseverance in being are not three different ways of being. Mental good functioning is perseverance under the attribute of thought; bodily good functioning is perseverance under the attribute of extension. Each expresses one and the same power to persevere. Nonetheless, critical for understanding Spinoza's theory of the good is the solution to a question concerning the type of perseverance that understanding and activity constitute. For instance, granted that understanding constitutes perseverance in being, is this *perseverance* in the ordinary sense of prolonging the duration of an individual's psychophysical existence? Or is it perseverance in some other sense, say, *eternal* perseverance? Or both?

The possibility that understanding constitutes durational perseverance was not foreclosed by our earlier objection to a Hobbesian treatment of the good. Recall that such a treatment is implausible because it fails to cohere with Spinoza's emphasis on intellectual perfection. The source of the problem is that in a Hobbesian reading understanding and perseverance are treated as distinct items. But, as we have seen, the evidence suggests otherwise. Yet it may still be the case that the type of perseverance in question is durational. If, for example, Spinoza conceives of an individual functionally, an individual will then persevere in being as long as it continues performing its function. The moment it ceases to perform its function, it no longer exists. Alan Donagan (1988,

151), a proponent of the functionalist reading, maintains, "Just as to be is to function, to persevere in one's being is to continue to function." On this view, what makes something an individual thing is that it is a functional unity, like the union the parts of a mechanical clock form in keeping time.

An advantage of this functionalist interpretation is that it can make clear sense of the intimate relation Spinoza finds between understanding and activity, on the one hand, and perseverance, on the other. Supposing that understanding and activity are an individual's essential functions, conceived under thought and extension, respectively, it follows that the duration of an individual's existence turns on how long it understands and operates. Regarding an individual's physical operation, Spinoza says,

Those things are good which bring about the preservation of the proportion of motion and rest the human Body's parts have to one another; on the other hand, those things are evil which bring it about that the parts of the human Body have a different proportion of motion and rest to one another. (4p39)

Talk of proportion of motion and rest is well suited to a functionalist gloss. What is more, it is difficult to imagine that anything but *prolonging duration* is meant by *preservation* of a body's proportion of motion and rest.

As difficult as it may be, durational perseverance does not appear to be what is intended. Someone is said to be perfect in Spinoza's view to the extent that he or she realizes the good, the ideal model of human nature (4pref). And Spinoza denies that a longer duration of existence makes a thing more perfect than something with a shorter lifespan:

Finally, by perfection in general I shall, as I have said, understand reality, that is, the essence of each thing insofar as it exists and produces an effect, *having no regard to its duration. For no singular thing can be called more perfect for having persevered in existing for a longer time.* (4pref, emphasis added)

At 2d6 Spinoza explained that "reality" and "perfection" mean the same thing. In 4pref, two clarifications are made in his account of reality–perfection. First, reality–perfection is, he suggests, a function of an individual's approximation to the model, or exemplar, of human nature.[13] Thus the more an individual resembles the model, the more real–perfect he is. Less resemblance means less reality–perfection. The second clarification is that reality–perfection does not depend on duration of existence. An individual's level of reality–perfection is not a

---

[13] Bennett (1984, 296) suggests that Spinoza's mature position does not contain a model of human nature, but I shall presuppose the standard reading according to which Spinoza never abandoned the idea of a model of human nature and that the model in question is the free man (4p66cs–p72).

function of the length of time the individual exists. As one commentator puts it, "It is to be noted that perfection as conceived has no reference to time or duration. The perfection of a thing refers to the quantity or power of being, to the kinds of functions it can perform, and not to the process or duration in which it performs them. A man is a more perfect being than a horse even though the horse may live longer."[14] If duration were part of perfection, not only would a horse be more perfect than a human in cases where the former outlived the latter, but also, and even more bizarre, an individual's teeth would be more perfect than their owner in cases where the former outlast the latter.[15]

It is not possible, then, to read off a thing's amount of reality–perfection from the quantity of time it has existed. Length of duration in existence indicates neither intellectual perfection nor intellectual imperfection. A longer lifespan does not make a person better. A foreshortened existence does not make a person worse. Nevertheless, perseverance in being is constitutive of the good (4p25). In the attribute of thought, perseverance is understanding. Thus the type of perseverance understanding supplies is not durational.

This does not mean that a functionalist reading ought to be abandoned in its entirety, however. The functionalist makes two claims: that, for Spinoza, (1) to be is to function, and that (2) to persevere in one's being is to continue to function. Given that perseverance in being (in some sense) is the good and that, by the remarks on perfection in 4pref, duration of existence does not contribute to the good, (2) therefore does not represent Spinoza's position. (1), nevertheless, may and, in fact, does correspond with his view of the individuation of finite composite bodies (2p13le3cd). A finite individual body is a finite individual body in virtue of being a functional unity. But a finite individual does not persevere in being as long as it continues to function. Rather, a finite individual perseveres in being, I argue in the following section, insofar as it functions, that is, insofar as it produces properties.

## 5. ETERNITY AND PERSEVERANCE

"By eternity," Spinoza tells us, "I understand existence itself [*ipsam existentiam*], insofar as it is conceived to follow from the definition alone of the eternal thing" (1d8). This is supplemented with an explication that says that such existence "cannot be explained by duration or time, even if the duration is conceived to be without beginning or end." Existing throughout all times does not make something eternal.

[14] Bidney 1940, 263–4.
[15] I wish to thank Olli Koistinen for this point.

Eternity, for Spinoza, is not the same as sempiternity. Rather, eternity – existence itself – is timeless, logically necessary existence.[16]

Only substance, or God, exists from the necessity of its own nature (1p14). Therefore, substance, or God, exists eternally, that is, has existence itself (1p19). A finite thing strives to persevere in its being because it expresses, in a limited way, God's power (1p25c, 1p36d, 3p6d). What a finite thing, as an expression of God's power, strives to obtain then is not existence throughout all times but, rather, eternity. It strives for existence itself. So, for example, when Spinoza says, "No one can desire to be blessed, to act well and to live well, unless at the same time he desires to be, to act, and to live, that is, to actually exist" (4p21), Hobbes is no help in apprehending the point being made. This is because, unlike Hobbes, Spinoza distinguishes between an individual's durational existence and its eternal, actual existence. In addition to the emphatic *ipsam existentiam* in his definition of eternity, the distinction is emphasized again in the following passage:

> By existence here I do not understand duration, that is, existence insofar as it is conceived abstractly, and as a certain species of quantity. For I am speaking of the very nature of existence, which is attributed to singular things because infinitely many things follow from the eternal necessity of God's nature in infinitely many modes (see 1p16). I am speaking, I say, of the very existence of singular things insofar as they are in God. (2p45s)

Here durational existence is contrasted with the very nature of existence, which strongly suggests that durational existence – regardless of whether the duration in question is short, long, or unlimited – is not real existence, or not the most important type of existence. As with other mere abstractions (2p40s1), it is the imagination that affords a view of things under a species of duration. Under a species of duration, existence is viewed as though it were a matter of occupying a particular part, or stretch, of time. In place of this confused view of things, reason affords a clear view under a species of eternity (2p44c2). Under a species of eternity, existence is the logical necessity with which an individual follows from God's nature (5p29s). According to Spinoza, "A thing is called necessary either by reason of its essence or by reason of its cause. For a thing's existence follows necessarily either from its essence and definition or from a given efficient cause" (1p33s1). Only God's existence follows from its essence and definition. The totality of God's existence

---

[16] Wolfson 1934 I, 366; Delahunty 1985, 285; Allison 1987, 66; Parchment 2000, 366–8; Nadler 2002a, 111; 2002b, 229. With these commentators, I accept the orthodox Platonic reading of Spinoza's view of eternity as timelessness. For an alternative, Aristotelian reading, see Donagan 1973, 241–58; 1988, 107–13; Kneale 1973, 227–40; Bennett 1984, 204–5; 1996, 76–8.

follows from God's essence. A finite thing's existence follows necessarily, not from its essence, but from a given efficient cause, namely, God (1p16, 1p25, 1p25c).

Though the total existence of a finite thing does not follow from its essence, this does not mean that the existences of all finite things are equal. One finite thing's existence can depend more on its own essence than another thing's existence depends on its own essence. A thing is more independent and less dependent the more its existence depends on its own essence. Striving, or power, to persevere in being is the actual essence of a thing (3p7). Greater power constitutes an existence that depends more on that power and less on the power of other things. Less power makes a more dependent existence, greater dependence on things other than that individual's own power. The nature of the relevant sort of power is clarified when we are told that

the intellect infers from the given definition of any thing a number of properties that really do follow necessarily from it (that is, from the very essence of the thing); and that it infers more properties the more the definition of the thing expresses reality, that is, the more reality the essence of the defined thing involves. But since the divine nature has absolutely infinite attributes (by d6), each of which also expresses an essence infinite in its own kind, from its necessity there must follow infinitely many things in infinite modes (i.e., everything which can fall under an infinite intellect), Q.E.D. (1p16d)

Properties follow necessarily from the essence of a thing. The more essence something has, the more properties follow from it. God's essence is infinite, and so infinite properties follow from it (1p16). Nothing exists that does not follow from God's essence (1p15). A finite thing's limited essence, by contrast, produces a limited number of properties (1p36, 3p7d).[17] As a result, not everything a finite thing undergoes follows necessarily from its essence alone (4p3). External things unavoidably contribute in some degree to a finite thing's existence (4p4). Its existence, unlike God's, is to some extent dependent on things other than its own essence.

Still, a finite thing strives to have a God-like existence, which is existence in the metaphysically rigorous sense of the term: a timeless, logically necessary existence. The more properties a thing has, the more of that thing that follows from its essence and, as a result, the more perfect it is. "For the perfection of things," according to Spinoza, "is to be judged solely from their nature and power; things are not more or less perfect because they please or offend men's senses, or because they are of use to, or are incompatible with, human nature" (1app). The *nature* of a thing is its essence. The *power* of a thing is the number of

---

[17] Garrett 2002, 139–40.

properties that follow from its essence. This constitutes a finite thing's proper function. A finite thing functions insofar as it produces properties or, what amounts to the same thing, insofar as effects follow from its essence alone. Having an essence from which a large number of effects follow makes someone better than a person whose essence is the source of fewer effects. It makes us better expressions of God's infinite power to exist (1p11s, 3p6d).

A finite number of properties follow from the essence of a finite individual. It is impossible for a finite thing to produce an infinite number of properties. No finite thing can be and act so that it never undergoes any change arising from the interference of things external to its essence (4p4). But though absolute perfection is impossible, some degree of perfection can be achieved.[18]

On this reading, to exist is to be eternal, and so a thing perseveres in being insofar as it is eternal. A thing is eternal insofar as it is the source of properties. Thus being a source of properties is the ultimate end by which to measure the utility of things. What makes something good is that it enables a person to be a source of properties. Something is bad in case it inhibits someone's power to be a source of properties.

Does this mean that perseverance in the ordinary sense of prolonging the duration of life is absent from Spinoza's theory? It is absent, I believe, from his theory of the good. Aside from his remarks concerning duration and perfection in 4pref, this is supported by 4p72, "A free man always acts honestly, not deceptively," and its scholium:

Suppose someone now asks: What if a man could save himself from the present danger of death by treachery? Would not the principle of preserving his own being recommend, without qualification, that he be treacherous? The reply to this is the same. If reason should recommend that, it would recommend it to all men. And so reason would recommend, without qualification, that men should make agreements to join forces and to have common laws only by deception – that is, that really they should have no common laws. This is absurd. (4p72s)

When it comes to a choice between deceit and continued durational existence versus honesty and the termination of durational existence, reason prescribes the latter pair. Existence, however, does not have to do

---

[18] Not only can perfection be achieved in some degree, but it is also the case that all people – indeed, all existing things – have some degree of perfection. In Ep19 Spinoza writes, "...it is indeed true that the godless express God's will in their fashion. But they are not on that account to be compared with the pious. For the more perfection a thing has, the more it has of godliness, and the more it expresses God's perfection. So since the pious have inestimably more perfection than the godless, their virtue cannot be compared with that of the godless" (C, 360; cf. 2p49cds, 4p45c2s).

with temporal duration. Existence in the metaphysically rigorous sense cannot be terminated through rational belief and action. On the contrary, rational belief and action are necessary and sufficient for genuine existence (5p38, 5p38d, 5p38s).[19]

Although someone's existence is no better than another's for having lasted over a greater period of time, it may still seem that Spinoza needs to allow that situations can arise in which it would be wise to suffer a present loss of eternity (i.e., a decrease in the power to produce properties) and prolong the duration of one's existence in order to make a larger gain in eternity in the future, thereby obtaining over the long run an overall net increase of eternity. One way of seeing how Spinoza may be able to make this allowance is through a commonsense distinction between what the exemplar, or ideal, of human nature would do in contrast with what someone should do who is trying to achieve the kind of life that the ideal represents.[20] Consider an analogy: what an ideally healthy person should do to maintain his health is not necessarily what someone should do to become healthy. The diet a healthy person needs, for example, to maintain his health is not necessarily the diet an unhealthy person needs to become healthy. Similarly, an ideally free person always acts honestly, but for someone who is not perfectly free, it may not always be good for him to be honest. In some circumstances staying alive long enough to become free, or more free, may override the value of a particular act of honesty.

A difficulty this exegetical maneuver faces, however, is the distinction between durational existence and eternal existence. *Existence* in

---

[19] Regarding Spinoza's view of power and self-preservation, Delahunty (1985, 226) remarks,

> All the same, there *is* a good reason to find Spinoza's theory inconsistent at this point also. In his view, man's power does not consist in being able to dominate other things and people, to keep them under his control; rather, "human power must be judged by strength of mind rather than by vigour of body", and hence those whose reason is most powerful are themselves most powerful (TP II, Section 11; Wernham trans., p. 275). . . . But the kind of power we must be after if we want to stay alive in a hostile world does not seem to be the power which consists in, or follows from, an enlarged understanding. . . . It is not so much that Spinoza goes wrong in saying that we must pursue more and more power in order to survive, as that he misdescribes the *sort* of power we must have more and more of (cf. Santayana, p. 148).

> If Spinoza is ultimately concerned with staying alive in a hostile world, Delahunty's objection carries considerable weight. But if the interpretation I am defending is correct, it is inaccurate to view Spinozistic power as intended for staying alive in a hostile world. Spinozistic power, on the reading I favor, is intended for making one's existence more knowable in an absolutely knowable world.

[20] Garrett 1990, 229; 1996, 292. Also see Garber 2004, 193–6.

the sense of duration (an interval of time) is a mere abstraction. *Existence* in the sense of eternity is genuine existence. Under what circumstances is it wise to suffer a loss of genuine existence to increase an abstraction in order to regain and add to genuine existence in a merely abstract future? It is not obvious that there are any such circumstances. Moreover, consider again the alleged analogy with health. If the contrast with the ideally healthy person is a person who is not healthy, this is not analogous to the contrast between Spinoza's ideally free person and a person who is not perfectly free. This is because, although no human being can be perfectly free, no human being can be perfectly unfree. All existing things express God's power (1p25c, 1p36d). A finite thing essentially is an expression of God's power (3p7d). So no finite thing exists without some effects following from its nature (1p36). It follows that every existing thing is free to some degree (1d7). All finite things are partially free. So the difference between the free man and someone who is partially free is analogous to a healthy person and someone who is somewhat healthy. Whatever preserves and increases the relevant state of the former can reasonably be expected to preserve and increase the like state of the latter. Also, whatever inhibits the relevant state of one is the sort thing that inhibits the like state of the other. It follows that the sort of thing that preserves and increases the freedom of the perfectly free man is the sort of thing that preserves and increases the freedom of the partially free man. Whatever inhibits the number of properties that follow from the free man's essence also inhibits the number of properties that follow from the partially free man's essence. Commonsense therefore does not supply a compelling reason to think that Spinoza is committed to the view that in some circumstances it would be wise to suffer a loss of genuine existence.

## 6. CONCLUSION

If the interpretation in this chapter is correct, it is possible to see how each of the ways of understanding Spinoza's theory of the good mentioned at the beginning captures an aspect of that theory. For example, Wolfson, Bennett, and Curley interpret Spinoza as holding that self-preservation is the good. There can be no question that such is the case. Perseverance in Spinoza's view is the key ingredient in the good, but this is perseverance in the sense of a timeless, logically necessary existence, an existence in which the effects a thing produces follow from its essence alone. Duration of existence is not part of what it means to persevere in being. Delahunty (1985, 227) is also correct in saying that "it is not mere life, but *activity*, that matters to Spinoza." Given what it means to act (3d2), an individual is more active the more there is that follows from his essence. An individual acts, in other words, insofar as he genuinely exists. Moreover, because to be free is to exist and act from the necessity of a thing's nature alone (1d7), Hampshire too is right in highlighting the central importance of freedom in Spinoza's view. The twofold nature of the good is rightly noted by Garrett, one aspect of which, as I have tried to show and as Nadler emphasizes, is understanding. The other is bodily activity.

In identifying the multiple strands woven together in the theory, Bidney's interpretation is the most complete of those mentioned. Self-preservation, virtue, understanding, and joy all turn out to be ingredients in the good. "Virtue," for Spinoza, means the same thing as "power," and by each he means the "very essence, or nature, of man, insofar as he has the power of bringing about certain things, which can be understood through the laws of his nature alone" (4d8). As with self-preservation, activity, and freedom, virtue is a matter of producing effects that follow from one's essence. Following tradition, Spinoza sometimes refers to such effects as "properties" (1p16d). A person's virtue increases as the total amount of his or her properties increases. It is also the case that the amount of joy a person experiences is proportional to the amount of properties he or she is the source of. Being the source of properties gives rise to joy (3p59). The highest joy, blessedness, is the love of God that accompanies contemplation and knowledge of oneself and one's dependence on God (5p36, 5p36d).

If there is a single thread that underlies and unites these diverse strands into a coherent whole, it is intelligibility. Earlier I suggested that, for Spinoza, to know is to be. But what underlies his thinking about the good is, it seems, the Parmenidean principle that to be is to be intelligible or, less ambiguously, to be is to be knowable. Something is *knowable* in case, and to the extent that, its existence follows from its essence. For Spinoza, no thing exists whose existence follows completely from its essence except God (1p14). No existence but God's, therefore, is an eternal truth (1p20c). That is, no existence but God's is, absolutely speaking, an eternal truth. So God alone is absolutely knowable. As Spinoza repeatedly tells us, the best life is one that participates most fully in God's nature (2p49cs, 4p45c2s, 4app31). The best life, then, is the most knowable one. The ultimate end is to realize one's nature as an eternal truth as far as possible.[21]

[21] I wish to thank Doug Anderson, Matthew Kisner, Olli Koistinen, Michael LeBuffe, Eugene Marshall, Jon Miller, and Alan Nelson for their helpful comments on earlier drafts of this paper.

# 12  The Power of Reason in Spinoza[1]

In the preface to Part 5 of the *Ethics* Spinoza promises to explain "the power of the mind, or of reason" and to "show, above all, how great its dominion over the affects is, and what kind of dominion it has for restraining and moderating them." This is an important task because of the ethical significance that Spinoza accords to reason. For example, Spinoza writes,

Acting absolutely from virtue is nothing else in us but acting, living, and preserving our being... by the guidance of reason. (4p24)

In other words, Spinoza identifies acting virtuously with acting rationally. Spinoza also identifies acting by the guidance of reason and freedom:

we... easily see what the difference is between a man who is led only by an affect, or by opinion, and one who is led by reason. For the former, whether he will or no, does those things he is most ignorant of, whereas the latter complies with no one's wishes but his own, and does only those things he knows to be the most important in life, and therefore desires very greatly. Hence, I call the former a slave, but the latter, a free man. (4p66s)

Moreover, Spinoza claims,

There is no singular thing in nature that is more useful to man than a man who lives according to the guidance of reason. (4p35c1)

According to Spinoza, this fact constitutes the rational foundation (and hence, owing to his identification of virtue and reason, the moral foundation) of society and political alliance: rational people are very useful to us and therefore it is in our interest to bind them to us by means of social and political alliances. It also provides us with a reason to be interested in the virtue and freedom of others. Because other people are most useful to us when they are rational, and to the extent that they are

[1] I would like to thank audiences at the NY/NJ Research Group on Early Modern Philosophy, McGill University, the 2008 Pacific APA, and Leiden University for many helpful comments on this paper.

258

rational they are *ipso facto* both virtuous and free, it is in our interest to promote the virtue and freedom of others. In other words, this fact forms part of the rational and moral basis of benevolence.

Being rational, and hence being virtuous and free, is not, for Spinoza, merely a matter of consistency, revising belief according to certain rules, or maximizing expected utility. It is a matter of loving the right objects. When someone loves external things like wealth, honor, or sensual pleasure, she is irrational, and many other passions spring from such irrational loves (TdIE; G II, 6). The problem with these external goods is that possession of them depends upon fortune and so love of them breeds insecurity and anxiety. As Spinoza writes,

For no one is disturbed or anxious concerning anything unless he loves it, nor do wrongs, suspicions, and enmities arise except from love for a thing which no one can really fully possess. (5p20s)

Reason countenances only love of something internal to us. More specifically, insofar as we are rational, we love only intellectual perfection. Spinoza writes,

In this life . . . it is especially useful to perfect, as far as we can, our intellect, or reason. In this one thing consists man's highest happiness, or blessedness. Indeed, blessedness is nothing but that satisfaction of mind that stems from the intuitive knowledge of God. But perfecting the intellect is nothing but understanding God, his attributes, and his actions, which follow from the necessity of his nature. So the ultimate end of the man who is led by reason, that is, his highest desire, by which he strives to moderate all the others, is that by which is led to conceive adequately both himself and all things which can fall under his understanding. (4app)

Unfortunately, reason is not the only force that motivates and guides our behavior. It is in competition with the passions, which often push us to act in ways that conflict with the dictates of reason. Clearly, then, if we wish to understand the conditions under which we can live free and virtuous lives, which are beneficial to both ourselves and our fellows, we will do well to understand the conditions under which reason can moderate and restrain the affects. Spinoza claims no innovations here. According to him, the remedies for the affects discussed in Part 5 are "known to everyone by experience." His aim is rather to provide a rational account of those remedies. Because it is better to be rational than not, it is better to have a rational account of the power of the mind over the passions than to know that power by mere experience.

In the preface to Part 5 of the *Ethics*, Spinoza wishes to make clear that he does not believe that the power of reason over the passions is absolute. It is not merely a matter of exercising our free will appropriately as, for example, the Stoics taught. Rather, there are conditions under which reason is more powerful than the passions and conditions under which the opposite is true. Furthermore, these conditions are not fully under our control and depend, at least in part, on fortune. Nevertheless, Spinoza's attitude toward the power of reason is fundamentally optimistic. He believes that, once the seed of reason is planted, there is a natural tendency for its power to grow relative to the power of the passions so that, assuming minimally favorable conditions, reason will eventually come to dominate. Spinoza describes his own moral and intellectual development as exhibiting this tendency:

And although in the beginning these intervals [of rationality] were rare, and lasted a very short time, nevertheless, after the true good became more and more known to me, the intervals became more frequent and longer – especially after I saw that the acquisition of money, sensual pleasure, and esteem are only obstacles so long as they are sought for their own sakes, and not as means to other things. (TdIE § 11; G II, 7–8)

The remedies for the passions discussed in Part 5 of the *Ethics* are supposed to be the mechanisms that explain this natural tendency toward greater rationality.

## I. SPINOZISTIC PSYCHOLOGY

Before the investigation of reason's power over the passions, it will be useful to set out some of the rudiments of Spinozistic psychology. According to Spinoza, a human being can be conceived in two ways: under the attribute of thought and under the attribute of extension (the principal attribute of body). Insofar as we conceive of a human being under the attribute of thought, we conceive of him or her as a mind. Insofar as we conceive of a human being under the attribute of extension, we conceive of him or her as a body. The human mind, according to Spinoza, is the complex idea that represents the human body (2p13). What about the external world? Doesn't it represent that too? Spinoza agrees that we have ideas that represent the world outside of us, but he believes that we do so in virtue of possessing ideas of parts of our bodies, the states of which express states of the external world. Whenever a part of the body is in a particular state because of the influence of an external cause, that state expresses that external cause. Thus in having an idea of such a part, we have an idea of something that expresses that external cause. The idea of that which expresses, Spinoza believes, also represents that which is expressed (2p16).

The human body is a complex individual made of parts that are themselves bodies (2p01). According to a doctrine that is often called "Spinoza's parallelism," for every body there is an idea that represents it and vice versa. Moreover, the order and connection of bodies is the same as the order and connection of ideas (2p7). So for every part of the body, there is a part of the mind (i.e., an idea) that represents that part of the body.[2] Alternatively, by dint of Spinoza's mind–body identity theory, every part of a human being can be conceived of as an idea or as a body (2p7s).

Another important element of Spinoza's psychology is his claim that the will and the intellect are one and the same thing (2p49c). By this he means that every idea has two dimensions: one representational and one conative or volitional. That is, every idea represents some body or bodies and every idea determines some action of the mind. In particular, it determines the mind to act as if its representational content were true. In other words, every idea both represents some state of affairs and affirms that it obtains. On this view, every idea is belief-like.[3] The actions of the mind produced by an idea are those which such a belief naturally produces given the desires of the agent.

This brings us to Spinoza's theory of desire. According to him, each finite thing strives [conatur] to persevere in its being (3p6). This striving or conatus is the essence of the finite thing. The essence of a thing determines its causal powers. So the conatus of each thing determines its causal powers. Each thing, insofar as it is in itself, produces those effects that conduce to its survival. Spinoza defines action in terms of causation: a thing acts insofar as it causes things to happen. So the conatus makes each thing, insofar as it is in itself, act in a way that conduces to its survival. That is, our conatus moves us to perform those actions of which we are capable and that would be conducive to our survival if the world were as our minds represent it.

In the preceding discussion of Spinoza's conatus doctrine, we have said that each thing strives to persevere in its being insofar as it is in itself. What does "insofar as it is in itself" [quantum in se est] mean?

---

[2] Does Spinoza mean to claim that everyone has, for example, an idea of every molecule in his or her pancreas? Yes, but, generally speaking, such ideas possess very little power to affect our mental life and thus intrude little if at all into our consciousness. See Garrett 2008.

[3] I say that they are belief-like rather than that they are beliefs because whether or not they play the psychological role associated with beliefs depends upon the content and power of other ideas contained in the mind. For example, if the mind contains other ideas opposed to a given idea i, and if they are collectively more powerful than i, then i will not guide the action of the agent. In other words, it will not play the belief-role.

What does it mean for one thing to "be in" or to "inhere in" something? The inherence relation is coextensive, for Spinoza, with causation.[4] So, insofar as something is in itself or inheres in itself, it is caused by itself. Only substances are, strictly speaking, caused by themselves, but modes can approximate self-causation to the extent that their existence and activity is not conditioned by external causes.[5] The more a finite mode's existence and activity is conditioned by external causes, the less it inheres in itself. Likewise, the less a finite mode's existence and activity are conditioned by external causes, the more it inheres in itself. Insofar as a finite mode's existence and activity are not conditioned by external causes, it will act in a self-preservative way.

But what can we say about the activity of finite modes insofar as they don't inhere in themselves, that is, insofar as external causes condition their existence and activity? To that extent, their activity reflects the *conatus* or essence of those external causes. Because each finite mode is influenced by external causes, many of its actions will be determined partially by its own nature and partially by the nature of its external causes (4p5). Consequently, the behaviors that externally caused ideas motivate will be partially self-preserving and partially directed to the benefit of the external modes that cause them. Because what helps others often harms oneself, externally caused ideas can easily motivate self-harming behaviors.

So now we know that the *conatus* doctrine says that, by its very essence, each thing, insofar as it is not influenced by external causes, will produce those effects of which it is capable and that conduce to its survival. Our next question is, what is survival? The answer derives from Spinoza's account of complex individuality. Let's start with Spinoza's account of the individuality of complex bodies, because Spinoza develops his account of complex individuality in terms of bodies. In virtue of the parallelism, we will easily be able to extend this account to the complex individuality of minds.

A complex individual body such as the human body comprises, according to Spinoza, a diversity of parts, each of which communicates its motion and rest to the others according to a fixed pattern (*ratio*).[6] A body is destroyed just in case its erstwhile parts no longer communicate their motions to each other according to the pattern that defines the complex body. A complex body survives just in case this pattern

---

4   Spinoza thinks that inherence is coextensive with conception (see the use of 1d3, 1d5, and 1a1 in 1p4d). And he thinks that conception and causation are coextensive (see 1a4 and 1p25d). These two together entail that inherence and causation are coextensive.

5   See Garrett 2002 and also Lin 2004.

6   Definition following axiom 2" of Part 2.

is maintained. So a complex body produces those effects of which it is capable and that conduce to the preservation of the pattern of motion and rest that defines it (3p6, 4d1, and 4p39).

Similarly, a complex individual idea such as the human mind comprises, according to Spinoza, a diversity of simpler ideas. Ideas, of course, don't move, and so Spinoza's account of their individuality cannot be in terms of their parts communicating their motions to each other according to a fixed pattern of motion and rest. There must be then some other kind of *psychological* pattern that ideas must realize in order for them to jointly constitute a single complex idea. Just what kind of psychological pattern is this? Spinoza's answer can be discerned in his word for pattern, "ratio," which in Latin means both pattern and reason. The mind strives to preserve its rationality. Rationality is the psychological pattern that defines the existence of the mind.

### 2. REASON AND PASSION

With the rudiments of Spinoza's psychology in place, we are now in a position to understand Spinoza's account of reason and the passions. Reason is, as I claimed above, a pattern obtaining between ideas. But is more than this. It also pertains to the character of the ideas themselves. In 4p26, Spinoza tells us that "the essence of reason is nothing but our mind insofar as it understands clearly and distinctly [*rationis essentia nihil aliud est quam mens nostra quatenus clare et distincte intelligit*]." I take this to be Spinoza's somewhat confusing way of saying that the mind is rational insofar as it clearly and distinctly understands. Clear and distinct understanding is the result of possessing adequate ideas. This is what Spinoza has in mind when he writes in 2d4, "By adequate idea I understand an idea which, insofar as it is considered in itself, without relation to an object, has all the properties, or intrinsic denominations of a true idea." Here Spinoza defines adequate ideas as those ideas that possess the intrinsic properties possessed by all and only true ideas. Those intrinsic properties are clarity and distinctness. So "the essence of reason is nothing but our mind insofar as it clearly and distinctly understands" means that the mind is rational insofar as it possesses adequate ideas.

We know from 2d4 that an idea is adequate just in case it is true, but this makes the characterization of rationality given in 4p26 quite puzzling. It would follow that rationality and truth are coextensive. This might appear to be an odd result. It would seem that people are frequently rational in believing falsehoods and irrational in believing truths. For example, Newton was no doubt rational in believing in his physics, although it was false, and the lucky and optimistic lottery

winner who believed that she would win prior to the drawing was irrational, although her belief was true. But these are not really counterex-
amples to Spinoza's claim. Spinoza's topic is reason itself apart from
any input from sense experience. We may deem it rational to believe
the testimony of the senses, but we do not come to believe it through
reason alone. In other words, it is sometimes rational to accept the deliv-
erances of faculties other than reason. Spinoza believed, as did many of
his epoch, that reason in itself is infallible and that whenever one commits an error in reasoning, inputs from the external environment – be
it in the form of sense experience, imagination, or some other kind of
external cause – are to blame. His justification for this belief can be
found in his account of adequate ideas.

To understand Spinoza's theory of adequate ideas, we must start with
his theory of ideas in general. Every idea is a mode of God insofar as he is
a thinking thing: an idea is God insofar as he thinks of this or that (2p2).
The human mind is, as discussed earlier, the idea of the human body. So
the human mind is an idea in the mind of God: the human mind is God
insofar as he thinks about the human body (2p11c). The human mind is
also complex; it is composed of many simpler ideas (2p15). Each of these
constituent ideas is also an idea in the mind of God. God is omniscient.
All of his ideas are adequate (2p32 and 2d4). But human minds are
prone to ignorance and error. Many of our ideas are inadequate. If each
of our ideas is numerically identical to one of God's ideas and God
has only adequate ideas, how can the human mind contain inadequate
ideas? The answer is that adequacy is a relation to a mind. Some ideas
that are adequate relative to God's mind are inadequate relative to a
human mind.[7] An idea is inadequate in the human mind just in case
God possesses that idea in virtue of possessing not only the idea that is
the human mind but also some other idea that is not part of the human
mind (2p28). An idea is adequate just in case God does not possess
it partially in virtue of possessing some idea other than the human
mind. What kind of ideas are in the human mind but not possessed by
God solely in virtue of possessing the idea that is the human mind?
For any finite mode, God is the cause of that mode not in virtue of his
absolute nature but rather in virtue of being affected by some other finite
mode (1p28). In other words, finite modes of God are caused by other
finite modes of God. So God does not possess any finite idea $i$ solely in
virtue of possessing $i$. That is, his possession of $i$ is not unconditional.
It is a condition on his possessing $i$ that he possesses infinitely many
finite ideas distinct from $i$ that form the causal chain that terminates

---

[7] This claim is forcefully defended in Della Rocca (1996a). My account of Spinoza's
theory of adequate ideas owes much to Della Rocca's treatment.

in $i$. If $i$ is also an idea in a human mind, then $i$ is not adequate relative to that mind. It would be adequate in the human mind if the human mind possessed the idea of the whole causal chain that terminates in $i$, but this is impossible, because that chain is infinite and the human mind is finite.

What this comes to in the end is that an idea is inadequate relative to the human mind just in case the human mind possesses that idea partially in virtue of causal inputs from its environment. An idea is adequate just in case the human mind possesses it independent of any causal inputs from the environment.

Given this account of adequacy, it would appear impossible for any human mind to possess any adequate idea. The human mind is finite; hence all of its constituent ideas are finite. God does not possess any finite idea unconditionally. Therefore, God possess every idea possessed by the human mind only insofar as he possesses infinitely many finite ideas not contained in the human mind. There are a number of interpretative and philosophical issues that surround this question. A comprehensive treatment of them lies outside of the scope of this paper. It will be useful, nevertheless, to say a few words about how Spinoza believes that we can possess adequate ideas.

According to Spinoza, the human mind is capable of possessing ideas of the common properties of things (2p38). All modes of a given attribute have something in common, that is, the attribute of which they are modes and the properties that follow from the nature of the attribute (2p13le2). (For example, motion and rest are properties that follow from the nature of the attribute of extension.) Are the ideas that represent these common properties adequate or inadequate in the human mind? First of all, God's possession of the idea of any attribute is unconditional, and his idea of any mode that follows unconditionally from the nature of the attribute is conditional only upon possessing the idea of the attribute. Now Spinoza believes that every mode possesses an idea of the attribute of which it is an attribute (2p38c). It does so only in virtue of its own nature, that is, in virtue of being a mode of its attribute. Consequently, the possession of the idea of the attributes of which one is a mode is not conditional upon anything outside oneself. So the ideas of the attributes of thought and extension must be adequate in the human mind. In other words, God would need to possess no idea other than the idea that constitutes, for example, the human mind in order to have an idea of the attribute of thought. Moreover, the idea of anything which follows from that attribute would also be adequate in the human mind. One need possess no idea other than the idea of the attribute, for example, of extension in order to possess the idea of motion and rest, which is something that follows from the nature of the attribute. Thus God's possession of the idea of the human body alone would entail his possession of the idea of motion and rest.

In addition to ideas of common properties, Spinoza believes that each mind contains an adequate idea of the eternal and infinite essence of God (2p45, 2p46, 2p47). This is because each thing, as a mode of God, inheres in God and so cannot be conceived without God. So the idea of each thing involves the idea of God, regardless of whether it is "considered as a part or as a whole," and so is adequate (2p46d). So every mind contains a spark of rationality insofar as it is endowed with an adequate idea of God's eternal and infinite essence. This is a surprising thesis. According to a widespread picture, no one, not even the wisest or most virtuous, can have any idea of God's essence in this life. Only after death is such knowledge possible. But according to Spinoza, not only the wise and virtuous possess this idea, but so do the fool and the knave. Indeed, so do rocks and insects! But Spinoza believes that in most minds, the power of this idea is very slight and, to the extent that it possesses any power at all, it is overwhelmed by the contrary force of various passions.[8] So, although an adequate idea of the essence of God is possessed by all, most are only dimly conscious of it and it does little to determine their thought and action.[9]

Moreover, the ideas that follow from an adequate idea are themselves adequate. The essences of singular things follow from the essence of God. So, because we have an adequate idea of God, if we deduce from that essence an idea of the essence of a singular thing, that idea too will be adequate. Likewise, any idea that we can deduce from the ideas of the common properties of things will also be adequate.

I stated earlier that Spinoza identifies rationality, virtue, and freedom. Here are his systematic grounds for doing so. Spinoza defines goodness as that which helps us persevere in our being (4d4). That which is good for each is that which helps him or her persevere in being. Goodness is thus a relative concept. Virtue is that state of character that most conduces to self-preservation (4p20). What follows from a thing's essence is always consistent with its continued existence (3p6). Destructive forces are always external. To the extent that anything performs self-destructive behaviors, this is only on account of the external causes of its states.

We have seen that Spinoza thinks that it is the essence of the mind to be rational. So rationality is the state that is most conducive to

---

[8] That is not to say that rocks and insects don't appear to think about God because they are so passionate. Rather, in them, the power of their ideas is so slight that they scarcely think at all.

[9] See Garrett 2008.

self-preservation, that is, is virtue (4p23 and 4p28). We are free so long as our actions follow from our natures alone and are not partially determined by an external force. So we are free to the extent that we are rational. Rational ideas are of common properties, God, and the things deduced from the ideas of those. So to have such ideas is to be virtuous and free. Because all things inhere in and are conceived through God, knowledge of God is the highest good. Such knowledge helps us know more and more things.

Passions are defined by Spinoza as inadequate ideas that register an increase or decrease in our power of acting (3p1 and 3p3). Inadequate ideas are those ideas that have inputs from the external environment. This definition resonates with the etymology of *"passione,"* the Latin word for passion, which derives from the verb "passio," which means to suffer or to undergo. Suffering and undergoing suggest passivity. According to Spinoza, we act when we are the cause of what we do. That is, the causes of our changes of state are within us. Insofar as we fall under the attribute of thought, the causes of what we do are entirely within us when they are adequate ideas. So we are passive when the causal chain that terminates in what we do leads outside of us to the external environment. In other words, we are passive when we suffer passions, that is, possess inadequate ideas.

It would be a mistake to identify passions with the kind of mental states typically denoted by the word "emotion." Passions, in Spinoza's terminology, include more than the kind of upheavals of jealousy, anger, fear, and the like with their concomitant physical flashes, flushes, and throbs, commonly associated with the term "emotion." Passions are also responsible for determining the ends of the less-than-rational agent. They enter into deliberation and planning in a way in which mere emotions might not. For example, the love of the empty and futile goods pursued by the ordinary person – honor, wealth, and sensual pleasure – is a matter of passion. Love of these things is not merely a feeling that washes over a person only to fade once calm resumes. Rather, love of these things structures the lives of those who pursue them. More violent and fleeting passions such as jealousy, shame, pride, and rage arise, typically because the pursuit of honor, wealth, or sensual pleasure has been hindered or helped.

To summarize Spinoza's view of the place of reason and passion in our lives: love of honor, wealth, money, or anything external is a passion that sets us off in pursuit of empty and futile things. To be sure, there are passions that do not depend upon love for external things, such as pain and sadness. But Spinoza thinks that love of external things is a particularly important source of passions in that they establish ends the pursuit of which generates further passions through its success or frustration (5p20s). The greatest happiness and virtue lies in giving up the desire for such things and living a life devoted to intellectual perfection, that is, pursuit of rational ideas. This pursuit revolves around the study of nature, including human nature, and – through the study of nature – intellectual love of God (5p15). But it is no easy thing to give up the love of honor, wealth, and pleasure. Such passions can be very powerful and, through that power, they can come to dominate the lives of those that they afflict. In the next section, I shall discuss Spinoza's views on the nature and extent of the power of the passions.

### 3. THE POWER OF PASSION OVER REASON

We are often torn between acting rationally – that is, virtuously and freely – and succumbing to our passions. Unfortunately, when such conflicts arise, frequently the passions triumph and we act against our better judgment.

As noted earlier, Spinoza has no patience for voluntaristic theories that hold that it is ultimately up to us whether to obey our passions or our rational ideas when they conflict. Whether reason or passion prevails depends entirely upon the relative power of the rational and passionate ideas at issue. What determines the power of an idea? The power of a rational idea is determined by its essence (3p7). The power of a passion is a function of the essence of the affected idea and the power of the external cause that affects it (4p5). These factors alone determine the power of an idea. If a rational idea is more powerful than a passion to which it is opposed, then it will restrain it. If, however, the passion is more powerful, it will overwhelm its rational rival. We have, in other words, no immediate control over whether we will be directed by our rational ideas or by our passions. The matter is decided by the differential powers of the ideas in question.

What is more, there is a psychological law that, under certain circumstances, can tilt the field to the advantage of passions over rational ideas opposed to them:

A desire which arises from true cognition of good and evil, insofar as this cognition concerns the future, can be quite easily restrained or extinguished by a desire for the pleasures of the moment. (4p16)

Spinoza here describes something familiar to all of us. Often we find ourselves in a situation where two incompatible courses of action present themselves to us. One of them would result in a greater overall benefit[10] than the other, but it requires that we wait. The second would result in a benefit that is inferior but can be enjoyed immediately. For example, such a choice might be faced by the student who must choose between conviviality now and failing the exam tomorrow or studying now and passing the exam tomorrow. Spinoza believes that the interval of time that we imagine separates us from the rewards we seek diminishes the power of our desire for it to motivate our action relative to desires whose satisfaction would be imminent or even merely closer. That imagined interval acts as a weight that impedes the expression of that desire in action. Even if our ideas of the more distant good are rational (that is, involve a true cognition of good and evil) and the desires for immediate gratification are irrational passions, this weight still counters the force of the desire for goods in the more distant future.

### 4. THE POWER OF REASON OVER THE PASSIONS

As we have seen, Spinoza has grounds for pessimism: Victory in the struggle between passion and reason depends upon the relative power of the rational ideas and passions in conflict. This in turn depends upon the internal resources of the agent and the power of the external forces that determine her passions. How they stack up is largely a product of fortune. What is more, as we have seen, there is a powerful psychological law that can easily favor passion over reason. And yet despite all this, Spinoza does not think that sometimes reason wins, sometimes it loses: it all comes down to how the cards are dealt. On the contrary, Spinoza thinks that, as described in the opening lines of the TdIE, where Spinoza putatively describes his own intellectual and moral development, there is a powerful tendency for reason, once its seed has taken root, to grow ever more powerful. In 5p20, Spinoza summarizes the remedies for the passions that he delineates in the preceding propositions. These are the mechanisms that explain this tendency. He writes:

From this it is clear that the power of the mind over the affects consists:

I. In the knowledge itself of the affects (see 5p4s);

II. In the fact that it separates the affects from the thoughts of an external cause, which we imagine confusedly (see 5p2 and 5p4s);

---

[10] That is, the benefit is greater, even discounting for the uncertainty of the future.

III. In the time by which the affections related to things we conceive confusedly, or in a mutilated way (see 5p7);

IV. In the multiplicity of causes by which affections related to common properties and to God are encouraged (see 5p9 and 5p11);

V. Finally, in the order by which the mind can order its affects and connect them to one another (see 5p10 and in addition 5p12, 5p13, and 5p14).

In what follows, I shall offer interpretations and evaluations of each of these five, plus an additional technique that Spinoza oddly passes over here, that is, understanding things as necessary.

### 4.1. In the Knowledge Itself of the Affects

In 5p3, Spinoza claims that

An affect which is a passion ceases to be a passion as soon as we form a clear and distinct idea of it.

This appears to state a version of the appealing idea that we can master our passions through self-knowledge. More specifically, coming to have knowledge of our passions allows us to defeat them. Indeed, various forms of psychotherapy seem to presume something very much like it. But what is the basis of its appeal and is it indeed so? Let us look at Spinoza's grounds for holding it: Passions are inadequate. Clear and distinct ideas are adequate. The idea of an idea, Spinoza seems to think, is not a different entity than the idea it represents (2p21, 2p21s, and 5p3d). No idea is both adequate and inadequate. So if we succeed in forming an adequate idea of a passion, Spinoza reasons, it ceases to be a passion. But how can we do so? An idea is inadequate just in case one of its causes is outside of the mind. An idea is adequate just in case all of its causes are inside of the mind. If an idea has a cause outside of the mind, is there anything I could do to change that? Of course not. As Bennett (1984, 336) puts the point, I could no more accomplish that than I could make myself a royal by changing who my parents are.

Perhaps what Spinoza has in mind is not an impossible change in an idea's causal origins but a change in the causes that currently sustain the existence of an idea.[11] This could be thought of in line with an idea acquiring new justification. For I might have an idea such as the idea of the fourth proportional number whose causal origins are outside of me – perhaps I acquired it from teachers who simply told me the

---

[11] Olli Koistinen (1999) attempts to defend Spinoza against Bennett's criticism in this way in his "Bennett on Spinoza's Metaphysical Psychotherapy," available at http://www.bu.edu/wcp/Papers/Mode/ModeKois.htm.

rule – and hence inadequate. Later I might derive the rule from axioms and hence acquire new justification. This new justification is the reason that I continue to believe it, so it is the cause of its continued existence although not of its coming into existence. Unfortunately, such an idea is still inadequate, on Spinoza's account of adequacy. Remember, an idea is adequate in the human mind just in case God's possession of the idea is not conditional upon God also possessing an idea not in the human mind (2p11c). But the existence of anything is conditional upon its causal origin and not just on the causes that currently sustain it. So, in this instance, God's possession of the idea of the fourth proportional number would still be conditional upon his having ideas outside of my mind, viz., his idea of my teachers' bodies. So the idea would not be adequate.

Spinoza tries to make the case that it is possible by pointing out that every affection of our bodies has properties in common with every other mode of extension (5p4d). I can only have adequate ideas of common properties. So if I conceive of a passive affect through the common properties of extension, then I will have an adequate idea of it. Yes, but it will be an idea numerically distinct from the passive affect. It must be distinct from it: it has different causes. The causes of the adequate idea of the passion will have causes entirely internal to me, whereas the passion will have some external causes. By Leibniz's law, they must be distinct.

But that there can be a rational idea of any passion does not provide us with any remedy for the passions. At most, it helps specify the parties to the conflict between reason and passion. It does not, however, give us any reason to think that reason enjoys any advantages in this conflict. And it certainly does not entail the kind of psychological alchemy described in 5p3 whereby leaden passion is transformed into golden reason.

You might think that it does indicate an advantage that reason has over the passions in that it guarantees that the mind can form a rational idea for every passion, whereas nothing guarantees that there can be a passion for every rational idea. This ensures that reason need never be outnumbered and holds out the possibility that its representatives will outnumber those of passion.[12] But the struggle between reason and passion is not decided by the relative number of rational ideas and passions. What matters is the aggregate power of the rational ideas compared to the aggregate power of the passions. The raw numbers are meaningless. Of course, if each individual rational idea and each passion had more or less the same amount of power, then whichever side had a numerical

---

[12] I owe this suggestion to Don Garrett.

advantage would likely have the edge. But there is no reason to assume that such parity obtains.

But what of the tenability of this claim independent of Spinoza's grounds for holding it? Whether or not it is true is surely an empirical matter, but there appears to be a plausible mechanism for it given the assumption that passions have a cognitive dimension, as Spinoza believes. Suppose a passion partially results from a poorly justified belief. For example, it is a tenet of many forms of cognitive therapy that depression is sometimes due to poorly justified negative beliefs. A person, for instance, might believe that no one at work likes her on the grounds that one person at work dislikes her, and this belief might contribute to depression. But the fact that one person doesn't like her is weak evidence for the belief that no one likes her. Reflection on her evidence might lead her to give up the belief that no one likes her and thus help alleviate her depression.

Although this might be effective in special cases, it is implausible to think that it generally is so. Many passions are not due to poorly justified beliefs, for example, love of sensual pleasure. In those cases, it does not appear that acquiring knowledge of them would help control them. For example, if I were to learn exactly how my love of sensual pleasure was a product of evolution by natural selection, I predict that my love of sensual pleasure would be undiminished.

### 4.2. In the Fact That It Separates the Affects from the Thought of an External Cause, Which We Imagine Confusedly

Love and hate are ideas that register an increase or decrease of power respectively accompanied by an idea of an external cause of this increase or decrease (3p13s). That is, when my power goes up or down and I believe that something external caused this change, then I will love or hate that external cause depending on the character of the change. If I separate my idea of the external cause from the affect, that is, the idea that registers the change in power, then I will no longer hate or love the external cause.

It may seem that this will not bring about any improvement in my condition. If you take the idea of an external cause away from love or hate, then it ceases to be love or hate. But it is joy or sadness. Bennett (1984, 333–5) thinks this is a problem for Spinoza. Isn't sadness just as bad as hate? It hurts just as badly, Spinoza would reply, but it isn't really as bad for you. To see why, let's look at the difference between love and joy. If you love wealth, honor, or sensual pleasure, you will likely make bad decisions. But if you can turn that love into objectless joy, then you benefit from the upsurge in power without being on the hook to wealth, honor, or pleasure. So you won't run around chasing external things to your own detriment. For similar reasons, sadness is better than hate. If I hate someone, that passion will push me to try to harm her (3p19). This in turn will cause her to hate me and make her try to do me even more harm (4p43). So my hate pushes me to do things that will ultimately result in more harm to me. Sadness has none of these consequences. So although the sadness is in itself just as bad as the hate from which it is derived, the harmful behavioral dispositions associated with the hate are disarmed when it is turned to mere sadness.

How is it possible to separate love or hate from the idea of an external cause? All of your passive affects really do have external causes. According to 1a4 and 2p16, you can't be in a state with an external cause without having an idea of that cause. So being affected by a passive affect entails having an idea of its external cause. How then can Spinoza recommend separating love and hate from the idea of its external cause? Spinoza says that once you have the idea of some external thing, you will continue to believe that the thing exists until you get ideas that are incompatible with the existence of that thing. One way of separating your hate from the idea of its external cause would be to have ideas that entail the nonexistence of the external cause – for example, if you form the belief that the external cause has been destroyed or that it has stopped hurting you. You can't just decide to have such beliefs, but you can increase the likelihood that you will have them if you can bring it about that they are true. That is, you increase the likelihood that you will believe that the external cause of your hate doesn't exist if you destroy it and you increase the likelihood that you will believe that the external cause of your hate no longer hurts you if you mollify it (for example, by repaying its hate with love). This of course, is not any kind of therapy, that is, changing one's emotional life through thought and talk. Rather, this is a matter of changing your emotional life by changing the world.

### 4.3. In the Time by Which the Affections Related to Things We Understand Surpass Those Related to Things We Conceive Confusedly, or in a Mutilated Way

Affects arising from reason are more powerful in the long run than passions for an object that the mind regards as absent. Every idea, in itself, represents its objects as present. The mind only regards an object $o$ as absent if it has ideas whose objects are incompatible with the presence of $o$ and these ideas are more powerful than any idea that represents $o$ (2p19). Thus we know that any passion for an object regarded as absent coexists with other more powerful ideas that restrain it. Whatever power of action a passion for an object regarded as absent may possess is reoriented and partially consumed by these other more powerful ideas. Rational ideas, on the contrary, represent the permanent and pervasive features of the world – the common properties of things, God's essence, and the essences of singular things. Nothing can be incompatible with the permanent and pervasive features of the world. So the mind never possesses ideas whose objects are incompatible with the present existence of the object of any rational idea. Thus, whereas passions directed toward objects regarded as absent must contend with rival ideas in virtue of which its object is considered absent, rational ideas never face similar competition.

Moreover, because rational ideas represent permanent and pervasive features, their objects are not subject to change. But, according to 5a1, when two contrary affects are present in the same subject, one or both of them must change until eventually they are no longer opposed. Because rational ideas represent unchanging things, any passion that is not reinvigorated by external causes must change in such a way as to eventually accommodate the rational idea.

We must be careful not to overstate the advantage that would accrue to reason in virtue of these factors. Ideas can oppose each other in ways that do not involve representing incompatible objects. So there may be ideas that are opposed to reason even if no idea can represent an object incompatible with the existence of the objects represented by rational ideas. For example, my passion for wealth is opposed to my rational ideas insofar as it motivates me to perform actions that lead me away from activities that would result in greater knowledge of God, whereas my rational ideas motivate me to perform those actions that would increase that knowledge. My passion for wealth does not represent an object incompatible with the permanent and pervasive features of the world. Rather, it motivates actions incompatible with the actions motivated by ideas that represent those features.

The advantage that reason enjoys is thus freedom from *a certain kind of opposition*, or opposition stemming from a particular source. But it is no more conceivable that reason should rule a finite mind unopposed than that a person should be so fortunate that the order of nature never brought her into contact with an external cause whose nature disagreed with her own (4p4). Thus there could very well be circumstances in which a rational idea faces more overall opposition than a passion for an object regarded as absent even though, unlike the passion, it faces no opposition from this particular source.

The upshot of this remedy is that every mind possesses an internal tendency toward rationality. The external environment intrudes upon my mind, with the result that I suffer passions that push me from the path recommended by reason. If, at that moment, the external world were to withdraw its interference, my mind would evolve in such a way that those passions would be eventually brought under the sway of reason. It is only on account of the continual renewal of the passions by external causes that this internal tendency toward rationality never comes to a permanent conclusion.

A number of features of Spinoza's account of reason's long-run advantage over passion are problematic. First, it appears that Spinoza here assumes that the only way that ideas can change is by alteration of their contents. That Spinoza believes this is clear from the fact that he explains why rational ideas cannot change by citing the fact that their objects are permanent and pervasive. But it would be much more natural to think that ideas adapt to each other, not only by alteration of their contents, but also by expressing their power of acting differently. Indeed, on other occasions, Spinoza seems to say just that. In particular, that ideas are capable of changing in this way is part of his account of akrasia. As noted earlier, according to Spinoza, each idea, in itself, represents its object as present. The mind only regards an object $o$ as absent if it possesses ideas the objects of which are incompatible with the present existence of $o$ and these ideas are collectively more powerful than the idea of $o$. The power of acting of the idea of $o$ is partially consumed by the conflict with its rivals and partially modified by their superior strength. That its power is partially consumed by this conflict explains why, *ceteris paribus*, passions for objects regarded as present are more powerful than passions for objects regarded as absent. That its power is modified explains why a desire for an object $o$ regarded as present motivates different actions than a desire for $o$ when it is regarded as absent. For example, my desire for food regarded as present will motivate me to eat, whereas my desire for food regarded as absent might motivate me to cook or head out to the store. The content of the idea is the same, but its power of acting is manifested differently in the different contexts.

But if this is so, then there is no reason to suppose that the conflict between rational ideas and passions toward objects regarded as absent will resolve itself by passions adapting themselves to passion, rather than by a process of mutual adaptation or even reason adapting itself to passion by manifesting its power of action differently. The fact that the passions in question are for objects regarded as absent does little to decide the matter. No doubt such passions waste some of their power contending with ideas whose objects are incompatible with the present existence of their object, regarded as absent. But this only shows that, *ceteris paribus*, they will be weaker than rational ideas. When *ceteris* isn't *paribus*, what determines the outcome of this struggle will be the relative strengths of the ideas in question. The strength of a rational idea is defined exclusively by the nature of the mind. The strength of a passion is a function of the nature of the mind and the nature of its external cause. If the external cause is powerful enough, the passion that it creates will be more powerful than any rational idea, even discounting for the strength it loses in its conflict with ideas whose objects are incompatible with the present existence of its object.

Moreover, 5a1, which provides a crucial premise of Spinoza's argument, is obscure. What is worse, every way of clarifying it seems to render it implausible. What is it for two ideas to cease to be contrary? Suppose I have two contrary ideas, one that pushes me to pursue wealth and one that pushes me to pursue love of family. Suppose that every action that will lead to greater wealth will prevent me from enjoying my family and suppose that every action that will allow me to enjoy my family will prevent me from simultaneously pursuing wealth. Under what conditions do these two passions cease to be contrary? When one of them ceases to determine my actions? When one of them ceases to exert any pull upon me, even pulls that fail to express themselves in action? When one of them is extinguished altogether? It is implausible that all mental conflict of this sort necessarily tends toward any of these. All of them are, of course, possible outcomes, but there are others as well. For example, I could devote myself to the pursuit of wealth while continuing to feel the pull of family, or even alternate between the two pursuits over the long run. Spinoza seems to want to believe that the intellectual love of God, once experienced, will grow and grow so that the only thing that prevents it from entirely consuming the mind is the fresh influx of external stimulation that produces and reinvigorates the passions. But if reason could gain control by this mechanism, then, by the same token, a mind innocent of intellectual love of God but driven by conflicting passions would, if unmolested by external causes, eventually resolve its internal differences and just one passion would hold sway. This assumes that conflict cannot be stable and must always move toward resolution. Why must this be so? Why cannot opposed forces achieve an equilibrium that does not afford any one of them a decisive victory?

### 4.4. In the Multiplicity of Causes by Which Affections Related to Common Properties or to God Are Encouraged

This remedy relates to how experience and association shape the train of thought. Spinoza believes that the world is such that we will more often have experiences that will call to mind rational ideas than experiences that encourage irrational ones. His account of this begins with the observation that experience can trigger further thoughts. For example, suppose I am out for a walk and I run into a lion. This experience will likely make me think about lions. It will "arouse and encourage" lion-thoughts. These might well include questions, such as "How could a lion wind up on Jersey Avenue?" or "I wonder what lions like to eat?" but they might also include thoughts not directly related to my experience. For example, I might dream about lions that night or I might remember half-forgotten facts about lions. In any event, my mind is likely to buzz with thoughts of lions.

Spinoza thinks that just as an encounter with a lion makes a person think about lions, so too does an encounter with anything whatsoever turn the mind to thoughts about those things that resemble it and the general qualities that account for that resemblance (2p18). In this putative fact about associational psychology, Spinoza sees an advantage for reason over passion. Everything exemplifies the common properties, so every encounter "arouses and invigorates" the common notions. Common notions are adequate ideas. Insofar as we possess adequate ideas and these ideas play an active role in our thinking, we are rational. So every encounter invigorates ideas that make us rational. Passions are for more specific kinds of objects, so only encounters with things that resemble those particular kinds of objects will arouse and invigorate the passions.

There is a serious problem with Spinoza's thinking here. Take the lion example again. When I encountered the lion, my thoughts about lions or the property of being a lion were invigorated. My thoughts about mammals or animals or living organisms or physical objects did not receive any such boost from my encounter. Any object exemplifies countless properties. Which ones will grip the mind? The salient ones. The ones that, for whatever reason, stand out and strike the mind as important or interesting or surprising. There are probably no true strict generalizations about what makes a feature stand out, but I would think that the opposite of 5p11, which Spinoza cites as the foundation of this remedy, tends to be true. *Ethics* 5p11 says that "As an image is related to more things, the more frequent it is, or the more often it flourishes, and the more often it engages the mind." On the contrary, what is typical, common, or normal is often overlooked. Although bodies are extended, encounters with bodies rarely make me think of the common properties of extended things. On the contrary, they usually make me think of the qualities that distinguish them from other bodies.

It might be objected that properties such as mass, charge, and position are possessed by all physical objects and are of considerable interest. Such properties are the modern scientific analogies of Spinoza's common properties. Doesn't the salience of these properties vindicate Spinoza's view?[13] No. These properties are of interest due to the fact that they are fundamental, not due to their ubiquity. Countless properties are ubiquitous. Only an elite few are fundamental. Spinoza's account does nothing to explain our interest in the fundamental, because if his account were correct we would be as interested in nonfundamental but ubiquitous properties as we are in fundamental properties.

### 4.5. In the Order by Which the Mind Can Order Its Affects and Connect Them to One Another

Here Spinoza expounds an advantage that reason enjoys over the passions that also depends upon the association of ideas. Ironically, this remedy highlights the way in which the association of ideas is an irrational mechanism. In 2p18, Spinoza tells us that if we have in the past experienced two things together, then if we subsequently perceive one of them we will automatically think of the other. For example, if in the past I experienced eaten a certain dish at my grandmother's house, then on a future occasion when I taste that dish again I will automatically think of my grandmother's house. In the unqualified way that Spinoza states this principle, 2p18 is implausible. Associations are not that easy to form. Such an association might be formed if the pairing made a suitably large impression on the subject for some reason or if the subject were exposed to the pairing many times. But it is certainly not the case that experience of two things together always forges an associative link. Nevertheless, we need not dwell on such worries because, as we shall see, the use to which Spinoza puts the principle could equally well rely upon a more qualified and plausible version of the principle.

Reason, if ever it does succeed in wresting control of the mind from the passions, knows that its rule is precarious. Powerful external forces that could reinvigorate the passions are never far away. But if reason's rule is long enough, a bulwark against these external forces can be established in the form of a set of associations that will resist the passions and even act as reason's surrogate in the event that the passions overwhelm it. Spinoza believes that reason can discover generalizations about what reason will guide us to do under specific circumstances, which he calls maxims of life. For example, Spinoza thinks that he has demonstrated that rational people respond to hate with love and do not repay it with hate (4p46s). Spinoza offers similar generalizations throughout Part 4 of the *Ethics*. If, in our dispassionate rational moments, we reflect frequently on these maxims of life and imagine scenarios in which passions

---

[13] This objection was urged on me by Don Garrett and Alison Laywine.

would drive us to violate them, then we can create an association between the maxim and the scenario. If we subsequently find ourselves in such a scenario, we need not count on the native power of our rational ideas to motivate us to conform to the maxims of life. The nonrational associative links may be powerful enough to enforce such conformity. For example, if a colleague has insulted me in a faculty meeting, I might respond irrationally by making an insulting remark in return. Later, when my anger has cooled and reason again prevails, I might undertake to reflect on the maxim of life that says that rational people repay hate with love and how my behavior violated that maxim. Reflecting long and hard in this way may form an associative link between scenarios in which I am insulted and the maxim. If I am successful, in the future, when I am insulted, I will immediately think of the maxim. Thinking about the maxim may well motivate me to act in conformity to it.

Of course, irrational people can also form associations. For example, if, in the above scenario, instead of retaliating with an insult of my own, I might have been bullied into backing down. Afterwards, still stinging from my humiliation, I might obsessively think about how bad it felt to be bullied and how I should have repaid my colleague with an insult. This could form an association between scenarios in which I am insulted and the irrational maxim, "Always insult those who insult you." Indeed there is no contradiction in supposing that I manage to forge both associations and so when I am insulted I simultaneously think of the rational and the irrational maxim.

Spinoza does not deny this. How then is the possibility of forming associative links a source of the power of reason over the passions? Because there is an asymmetry that favors reason over the passions. Association is an irrational mechanism that can be co-opted by reason. Associations forged by reason are like a fifth column among the irrational forces of the mind. By contrast, there are no rational mechanisms that can be co-opted by the passions.

### 4.6. Understanding Things as Necessary

Curiously omitted from Spinoza's list of techniques for moderating the passions in 5p20s is the technique that many readers of Spinoza associate most with his program for controlling the passions through reason: understanding things as necessary.

Spinoza believes that all truths are necessary (2p44). He believes that knowledge of this helps us free ourselves from bondage to the passions. He writes in 5p6,

Insofar as the mind understands all things as necessary, it has a great power over the affects, or is less acted on by them.

Why should this be so? One plausible line of reasoning begins with the observation that many of our passions are what Strawson (1962) would call reactive attitudes. Reactive attitudes are attitudes that presuppose participation in interpersonal relationships. Our reactive attitudes reflect the concern we have for the good, ill, or indifferent will that other people bear toward us. Many of the most pernicious of the passions that plague us are plausibly counted among the reactive attitudes. For example, envy, resentment, hatred, and anger are all reactive attitudes. Having reactive attitudes depends upon taking a certain stance toward the object of the attitudes or being in a certain frame of mind. Reactive attitudes are contrasted with objective attitudes. Objective attitudes are ones that derive from an effort to objectively understand the causes of the action. So, for example, blaming or resenting a thief involves reactive attitudes, whereas explaining the thief's larceny by reference to the poverty in which he or she grew up or his or her genetic makeup involves objective attitudes. If you understand things as necessary, then you realize that they are parts of causal chains that are themselves necessary. This is to take an objective stance toward things, and it is impossible to form reactive attitudes from within this standpoint.

This Strawsonian interpretation of 5p6 is bolstered by the fact that Spinoza contrasts understanding things as necessary with imagining something as free (5p5d). Whereas we have a greater power over the affects directed toward things that we understand to be necessary, affects toward things that we imagine to be free are the most powerful. Imagining something as free might be seen as a way of conceiving it as a personal and free agent, which is arguably a condition of adopting a reactive standpoint.

Nevertheless, the total evidence points decisively against the Strawsonian interpretation of 5p6. First, Spinoza does not treat this technique as having the limited scope that it would have on the Strawsonian interpretation. Reactive attitudes are a subset of the passions. So if understanding things as necessary gives us power over passions by forcing us to adopt an objective standpoint, it will not help moderate nonreactive passions. Many passions that play a large role in human life are not reactive. Fear, for example, is a significant passion, but it is not a reactive attitude. Fearing some danger does not presuppose that we are engaged in interpersonal relations with the object of our fear. I can fear an earthquake or a forest fire without anthropomorphizing it. Moreover, fear is compatible with thinking about what we fear objectively. I can, for example, study the causes of the fire objectively and still maintain my fear of it. If understanding things as necessary gives us power over the affects by requiring that we adopt the objective standpoint, then it will not help to mitigate fear. But Spinoza does not think that the power over the affects conferred by understanding things as necessary has such a limited scope. This is attested to by the statement of 5p6, which does not contain any qualifications on the affects over which understanding things as necessary gives us power. Moreover, the two affects that Spinoza cites in the scholium to 5p6 to illustrate this power over the passions, sadness over a lost good and pity, are not reactive attitudes. If I love wealth and I lose a portion of mine, then I will be sad. My sadness does not presuppose that I enter into interpersonal relations with the object of my sadness or have concern for the good, ill, or indifferent will that it bears me. In the case of wealth, such things are impossible. And as Bennett (1984, 341) points out, neither is pity a reactive attitude. Pity, for example, is a natural response to a sparrow with a broken wing. I need not anthropomorphize the sparrow in order to pity it. I need not imagine that the sparrow bears me any good or ill will. I need only note its suffering, which is perfectly compatible with thinking about it objectively.

What is more, the actual justification that Spinoza offers for 5p6 ultimately rests on an entirely different basis from the Strawsonian line discussed above. Spinoza claims that the reason that an affect is more powerful if we imagine the object toward which it is directed as free rather than understanding it to be necessary is that when we imagine it to be free, we imagine it to be unconditioned by external causes (5p5 and 3p49). By contrast, when we understand it to be necessary (assume that the object is finite), we understand that it is conditioned by an infinite chain of finite causes (5p6 and 1p28). Spinoza thinks that love or hate is diminished to the extent that we imagine that the joy that love involves or the sadness that hate involves has more than one cause. He appears to think that our love or hate is a fixed quantity that we distribute among the causes of our joy or sadness. If we understand a finite thing to be necessary, then we will understand that it has infinitely many causes. Our love or sadness will thus be divided among infinitely many objects. Assuming that our love or hate is finite, the amount of love or hate directed toward each cause will approach zero.

Unfortunately, it is implausible to think that love and hatred is a fixed quantity to be distributed among its causes.[14] For example, suppose that I hate Jones because I believe that he poisoned my dog. Now suppose that I learn that Jones did not act alone but had Smith as an accomplice. I will not hate Jones less upon learning this. I will likely now hate both Jones and Smith, each with the same intensity with which I once hated

---

[14] Here I am following Bennett 1984, 318.

Jones alone. For the same reasons, it does not follow that if I come to understand that the object of my hate was conditioned by an infinite chain of causes that I will hate each link of the chain with a portion of the quantity of hate that I initially had for the object. I could very well equally hate all of them with as much passion as I had for the original object of my hate alone.

## 5. CONCLUSION

In the end, the techniques for moderating the passions offered by Spinoza in Part 5 of the *Ethics* are not impressive. The only technique that appears workable is the one that involves habituating oneself to associate the true maxims of life with the circumstances in which they would be relevant. All of the others rest on dubious assumptions.

I do not think that Spinoza's failure here stems from any lack of argumentative skill. He is, rather, doomed to failure because the basic claim that he seeks to justify is false. Spinoza believes that acquiring knowledge will reorder our desires. Once we have tasted rational inquiry we will, little by little, lose our appetite for external goods such as wealth, honor, and pleasure. He does not claim that this is an inexorable progression, but he does think that there is a powerful natural tendency in this direction. The techniques discussed in Part 5 of the *Ethics* are meant to be the mechanisms by which this transformation occurs. But experience teaches that there is no such universal tendency. Many people who have attained a high degree of intellectual perfection and a large amount of knowledge of nature and our place in it still covet wealth, honor, and pleasure and experience no diminution in their love of these things as a result of their increased intellectual perfection. Naturally, scientists and philosophers tend to love wealth less than, for example, bankers. But this is likely less an effect of their erudition than a partial cause for their chosen vocation: it would be imprudent indeed to go into science or philosophy if what you really wanted out of life was lots and lots of money. But it does not appear that the learned love honor less than other people. And I would conjecture that they love pleasure no less than the average person. There is evidence that Spinoza himself placed little value on wealth, honor, and pleasure. Perhaps he mistakenly assumed that it was his intellectual perfection that made him so.

But let me be clear: in no way do I wish to deny the appeal of the kind of spirituality championed by Spinoza. Clearly, the study of nature can invoke awe and delight. And doubtless, in some fortunate individuals, this awe and delight can lead to the kind of satisfaction that makes less noble goods appear less attractive. But Spinoza's claims are far more sweeping. He believes that all knowledge has this effect on everyone. Because his account is meant to support this more universal claim, it sheds no light on the explanation of the more restricted, but much more plausible, claim that some kinds of knowledge has this effect on some people.

# 13 Spinoza on the Essence of the Human Body and the Part of the Mind That Is Eternal

The second half of *Ethics*, Part 5, presents Spinoza's theory of the participation of human minds in the eternal. Although this theory constitutes the culmination of the *Ethics*, it has often proven opaque to even its most attentive and penetrating readers. Edwin Curley has written candidly, "In spite of many years of study, I still do not feel that I understand this part of the *Ethics* at all adequately" (1988, 84). Jonathan Bennett memorably declared this part of the *Ethics* to be "an unmitigated and seemingly unmotivated disaster" and "rubbish which causes others to write rubbish" (1984, 357, 374).

Spinoza's central doctrines in this portion of the *Ethics* include the following:

1. There is in God an idea of the formal essence of each human body.
2. An idea of the formal essence of the human body remains after the destruction of the human body, and for this reason there is a part of the human mind that is eternal.
3. The wiser and more knowing one is, the greater is the part of one's mind that is eternal.

Each of these three central doctrines seems, on its face, to be inconsistent with the rest of Spinoza's philosophy; in fact, for each of the three doctrines, there are two different *ways* in which it seems inconsistent with the rest of his philosophy. The key to resolving these apparent inconsistencies lies in understanding Spinoza's theory of *formal essences* and its connection to his theories of intellection and consciousness. Accordingly, this essay takes up these three central claims in order, explaining in each case (i) why the claim must be attributed to Spinoza, (ii) why the claim seems difficult to reconcile with the rest of his philosophy, and (iii) how an understanding of his theory of formal essences can resolve the apparent inconsistencies.

## I. THE IDEA OF THE FORMAL ESSENCE OF THE BODY

The second half of Part 5 begins with the demonstration of two crucial and contrasting propositions:

The mind can neither imagine anything, nor recollect past things, except while the body endures. (5p21)

The Mind neither expresses the actual existence of its Body, nor conceives the Body's affections as actual, except while the Body endures (by 2p8c); consequently (by 2p26), it conceives no body as actually existing except while its body endures. Therefore, it can neither imagine anything (see the Definition of Imagination in 2p17s) nor recollect past things (see the Definition of Memory in 2p18s) except while the body endures, Q.E.D. (5p21d)

Nevertheless, in God there is necessarily an idea that expresses the essence of this or that human body, under a species of eternity. (5p22)

God is the cause, not only of the existence of this or that human Body, but also of its essence (by 1p25), which therefore must be conceived through the very essence of God (by 1a4), by a certain eternal necessity (by 1p16), and this concept must be in God (by 2p3), Q.E.D.[1] (5p22d)

It is clear from the demonstrations of these two consecutive propositions that Spinoza is invoking a distinction of some kind between the *actual existence* of a human body and the *formal essence* of a human body. The demonstration of 5p21 appeals to the corollary of 2p8, a proposition concerning the formal essences of "singular things [*res singulares*] that do not exist":[2]

The ideas of singular things, or of modes, that do not exist must be comprehended in God's infinite idea in the same way as the formal essences of the singular things, or modes, are contained in God's attributes. (2p8)

"Singular things" are defined in 2d7 as "things that are finite and have a determinate existence," and these include human beings. (Of course, the metaphysical status of all singular things in Spinoza's monistic metaphysics is as finite modes of the one substance, God; see 1p25c.) The corollary to 2p8 itself (from which Spinoza concludes that the mind "expresses actual existence" only while the body endures) goes on to

---

[1] All translations of Spinoza's writings are from C. However, I have employed "cognition" rather than Curley's "knowledge" as a translation for "*cognitio*," because Spinoza recognizes *cognitio* that is false and inadequate.

[2] Given the reference to "existence" in this definition, some explanation is needed of how Spinoza can then refer to "singular things that do not exist." Presumably, 2d7 is meant to indicate what kind of existence singular things have *if* they exist.

contrast what can be said of the ideas of singular things that do *not* exist with what can be said of the ideas of singular things that *do* exist:

> From this it follows that so long as singular things do not exist, except insofar as they are comprehended in God's attributes, their objective being, or ideas, do not exist except insofar as God's infinite idea exists. And when singular things are said to exist, not only insofar as they are comprehended in God's attributes, but insofar also as they are said to have duration, their ideas also involve the existence through which they are said to have duration. (2p8c)

Similarly, the demonstration of 5p22 appeals to 1p25, in which Spinoza sharply distinguishes between the *essence* and the *existence* of things in order to affirm that God is the cause of both:

> God is the efficient cause, not only of the existence of things, but also of their essence. (1p25)[3]

This use of the term "essence" (*essentia*) clearly refers to the *formal essence* (*essentia formalis*) of things. For although he later introduces (in 3p7 and 4p4) the separate and specialized notion of an "actual essence" (*essentia actualis*) of singular things – something identical to their striving to persevere in existence (i.e., *conatus* or appetite) – the actual essence of a thing exists only so long as the thing itself does, and is not properly contrasted with the thing's existence.[4]

---

[3] The demonstration of 1p25 reads,

> If you deny this, then God is not the cause of the essence of things; and so (by 1a4) the essence of things can be conceived without God. But (by 1p15) this is absurd. Therefore God is also the cause of the essence of things, Q.E.D.

[4] *Ethics* 2d2 states that "to the essence of any thing belongs that which, being given, the thing is necessarily posited and which, being taken away, the thing is necessarily taken away; or that without which the thing can neither be nor be conceived, and which can neither be nor be conceived without the thing." Because the *Ethics* specifically mentions two kinds of essences – *formal essences* and *actual essences* – there are two main interpretive alternatives with respect to 2d2. First, we may suppose that it defines only *one* of these two kinds of essences. Second, we may suppose that there is some generality or ambiguity in the definition that allows *both* kinds of essences to be different *species* of essence in accordance with the definition. The second option seems preferable. (Compare Locke 1975, who gives a general characterization of "essence," the specification of which allows things to have both a "real essence" and a "nominal essence.") For an essence can be given, and a thing can be "posited," in more than one way. Thus, an *actual essence* is something such that, when it is given as existing, the thing itself actually exists (i.e., is posited as existing). A *formal essence*, in contrast, is something such that (i) when it is given as existing, the thing itself is *possible* (i.e., is posited as possible); and (ii) when it is given *as instantiated*, the thing itself is posited as actual. Because a singular thing actually exists if and only if its actual essence does, we may also think of the actual essence of a singular thing as the *actualization* or instantiation of

Spinoza indicates (in 2p8, 2p8c, 1p33s1, and many other passages as well) that the reality or being of the formal essence of a singular thing – such as the formal essence of a human body – does not presuppose or entail the actual existence of that singular thing.[5] On the contrary, 2p8s compares nonexistent singular things whose essences are contained in God's attributes (i.e., thought and extension, as well as infinitely many unknown divine attributes) to actually undrawn or undelineated rectangles that are nevertheless contained within a circle (because points of the circle could constitute or determine their endpoints), even though the rectangles themselves could be said not to "exist" (at least not in the full-blooded sense in which drawn or delineated ones do).[6] On the other hand, he makes it equally clear, in many of the same passages, that the formal essence of a singular thing is *directly related* to the singular thing, and even provides a sense in which the singular thing itself can be said to have a kind of derivative being. (In 2p8c, for example, he writes of "singular things that do not exist, *except insofar as* they are comprehended in God's attributes. . . . ") Hence, Spinoza appears to regard the formal essence of a singular thing as somehow being or grounding the at-least-sometimes-unactualized *possibility* of the singular thing's existence – as noted by Alan Donagan (1973, 1988), R. J. Delahunty (1985), and Wallace Matson (1990). In this respect, they resemble Descartes's "true and immutable natures" of things or Leibnizian essences – unchanging forms that can be instantiated or exemplified by existing things, and without which those things would not even be so much as possible.

Yet this immediately raises two problems. The first problem arises from the fact that Spinoza endorses *necessitarianism* – that is, the

---

its existing formal essence, rendering the thing itself actual. Thus, the instantiation of the formal essence of a singular thing produces the singular thing *by* producing that singular thing's actual essence.

Spinoza's *Treatise on the Emendation of the Intellect* and his *Short Treatise on God, Man, and His Well-Being* also use the term "objective essence" (*essentia objectiva*), a term that does not occur in the *Ethics*. An objective essence is simply the idea of an essence (specifically, it seems, a formal essence), so that when an objective essence is given as existing, the formal essence of the thing is posited "objectively" – that is, in thought.

[5] In the unique case of God – who is of course infinite, and hence not a singular thing – essence alone *is* sufficient for existence, according to Spinoza. Indeed, God's essence and his existence are one and the same thing (1p20), for both are constituted precisely by the divine attributes themselves.

[6] Spinoza makes it clear that he intends this comparison only as a rough analogy, introducing it as follows: "If anyone wishes me to explain this further by an example, I will, of course, not be able to give one which adequately explains what I speak of here, since it is unique. Still I shall try as far as possible to illustrate the matter. . . ." Curley's footnote to the scholium in C provides a helpful explanation of the example and its accompanying diagram.

doctrine that whatever is possible is actual, and whatever is actual is necessary (see 1p16, 1p29, 1p33, 1p33s1, and 1p35d).[7] For if necessitarianism is true, then there *are* no genuinely unactualized possibilities for formal essences to be. The second problem arises from the fact that Spinoza endorses *parallelism* – that is, the doctrine that "the order and connection of ideas [of things] is the same as the order and connection of [those] things [themselves]" (2p7).[8] This doctrine requires at least that, whenever there is a thing that stands in various causal relations to other things, there is *also* an idea of that thing, standing in parallel causal relations to ideas of those other things, and vice versa.[9] It thus seems to entail that a thing and the idea of that thing must share the same status with respect to actual existence and nonactualized possibility: that is, either a thing and its idea must be actualized together or they must be nonactualized together, for otherwise one of the two "orders" – namely, things and their ideas – will fail to be parallel to the other in its ontological and causal structure.[10] Indeed, by the further *mode-identity doctrine* of 2p7s, any mode of extension is really *identical to* the idea of that mode (being merely expressions under different attributes of the same modal being). Yet as 5p22d makes clear, the idea in God that "expresses the essence of this or that human body" is just the idea *of* the essence of the human body; for this idea is described simply as constituting the conception of that essence. Hence, if the essence of this or that human body is merely an unactualized possibility, then so, it seems, is the idea of (i.e., the "idea expressing") the essence of that human body. Yet Spinoza disparages the idea that God has any "potential," as opposed to "actual," intellect (1p31s and 1p33s2), strongly suggesting that he would reject the notion that any mere possibilities of ideas ever remain unactualized in God. In any case, the mere unactualized possibility of an idea seems to be far less than what is required to support Spinoza's theory of the real eternality of a part of the human mind. Thus, it seems that both Spinoza's necessitarianism and his parallelism pose serious

---

[7] For a discussion of Spinoza's necessitarianism, see Garrett 1991.

[8] See Della Rocca 1996a for an excellent discussion of this central Spinozistic doctrine.

[9] It should be noted, of course, that for Spinoza the idea that is "of" a human body, in this sense, is its mind, and that the idea of any other singular thing is the "mind" of that singular thing. The sensory or imaginative idea that a human being has "of" an external object is not *the* idea of the object, in this sense, but is rather an idea of a state of the human being's own body, a state partially caused by the external object. See the *Ethics*, Part 2.

[10] Donagan (1973 and 1988, 194–200) argues that 2p7 must allow real ideas to correspond to merely possible things, and Matson (1990) agrees. Bennett (1984, 357–8) holds that this would violate the parallelism, and Delahunty (1985, 294–300) offers persuasive support for Bennett's verdict.

problems for the interpretation of formal essences of human bodies as at-least-sometimes-unrealized possibilities.

To resolve these two difficulties, we must clarify the ontological status of the formal essences of singular things and of the ideas that are *of* them. Spinoza strongly implies that formal essences are truly *something* in their own right: for example, 1p25d argues that essences must be conceived through (and hence caused by) God precisely because, by 1p15, *"whatever is"* must be conceived through God. But according to 1p4d, "there *is* nothing except substances and their affections" (emphasis added), and, by 1d3, the "affections" of a substance are simply its modes. Because only God is a substance (1p14), it follows that, in order to be counted among "whatever is," formal essences of singular things must be modes of God. This conclusion – that the formal essences of singular things are modes of God – is supported by the claim of 2p8 that these formal essences are "contained *in* the attributes" of God and by the corresponding claim of 5p22 that the idea of the essence of a human body is *"in* God." This is because whatever is *in* a substance – other than that substance itself – is by definition (1d5) a mode of that substance.[11]

Every mode (i.e., state, modification, aspect, affection) of God is either (i) *infinite* and eternal, following from God's "absolute nature," either immediately or via other infinite modes, and so pervasive throughout the attribute of which it is a mode (1p21–p23);[12] or (ii) *finite* and determinate (i.e., limited) in its existence, following with equal necessity from God but only as and when God is modified or affected by another finite mode (1p28d).[13] But if the formal essences of singular things are modes of God, they can hardly be finite modes. Because they have their own being or existence contained in the attributes of God regardless of when or whether the corresponding singular things themselves exist,

---

[11] *Ethics* 1d5 states, "By mode I understand the affections of a substance, or that which is in another through which it is also conceived." This relation of being "in" – *inherence*, we might call it – is absolutely central to Spinoza's metaphysics. As 1p4d and many other passages make clear, he regards "being in" and "being conceived through" as necessarily coextensive where inherence in a substance is concerned.

[12] Of course, even every infinite mode of an attribute is "limited" in one respect: it is not the attribute itself, nor is it identical to any other infinite mode of that attribute. I take it that this kind of "limitation" is perfectly compatible with the kind of eternity and pervasiveness that characterizes infinite modes. The infinity of infinite modes lies not in there being no *other* modes of the same attribute (because there obviously are), but rather in there being (as 1p21d puts it in application to the attribute of thought) "no Thought that does not constitute" the infinite mode – that is, in its pertaining pervasively to *all* of the attribute in question at all times, wherever it is found.

[13] For further discussion of the nature of infinite modes and of the way in which they follow (unlike finite modes) from "the absolute nature" of the attributes, see Garrett 1991.

it is hard to see why or how they could ever come into or go out of existence, as finite modes do. Their status as infinite modes is strongly confirmed in 5p23s by Spinoza's description of the parallel "idea, which expresses [i.e., is of] the essence of the body" as "a mode of think-ing... which is necessarily eternal." Outside the *Ethics*, too, Spinoza indicates that (formal) essences are eternal, immutable, and infinite, writing in *Short Treatise on God, Man, and His Well-Being* 1.1.2 that "the essences of things are from all eternity, and will remain immutable to all eternity" (C, 61) and in *Metaphysical Thoughts* I.iii that the "existence" of things depends on the "series and order of causes," whereas the "essence" of things "depends [only] on the eternal laws of nature" (C, 307).

The formal essence of a singular thing is thus not identical to the singular thing itself – for the singular thing, having "a finite and deter-minate existence" (by 2d7), is a finite mode, whereas its formal essence is an infinite mode. As we have already noted, the being of the for-mal essence of a singular thing is not alone sufficient for the singular thing's actual existence; instead, the singular thing, as a finite mode, *can* actually exist only – and also *must* actually exist – whenever and wherever there actually exist finite causes with the causal power to bring that singular thing into existence. As we have also noted, how-ever, the formal essences of singular things do somehow ground the actualizability of singular things themselves. From these various clues, we can infer what the formal essence of a singular thing must be: it is the omnipresent modification or aspect of an attribute of God that consists in the attribute's general capacity to accommodate – through the gen-eral laws of its nature as an attribute – the actual existence of a singular thing of the given specific structure whenever and wherever the series of actual finite causes should actually determine it to occur.[14] Although the singular thing itself can exist only for a limited duration, this general modification of the attribute constituting the thing's formal essence is permanent and pervasive and follows universally, via the general laws of nature, from the "absolute" or unqualified nature of the attribute itself – just as we would expect of an infinite mode. Although the for-mal essence of a singular thing is not *identical* to the singular thing, it

---

[14]  Matson (1990) rightly states that for Spinoza the "essences of 'nonexistent things'" must be "perfectly real, actual items" on the ground that "Spinoza has no truck with *mere* possibilities" (88); and he suggests, as I have here, that the "contain-ment" of a thing's essence in an attribute is equivalent to the attribute's laws not ruling out the actual existence of the thing (89). He does not, however, propose that formal essences are infinite modes; and he goes on to treat the idea "express-ing" the essence of the body as an *actual* idea strictly corresponding to a merely *possible* thing (89–90).

is nevertheless the essence "of" that singular thing, in the sense that the *instantiation of* that essence produces the singular thing itself.[15]

On the interpretation just offered, Spinoza's doctrine of formal essences is perfectly compatible with his necessitarianism. Because each formal essence is itself an infinite mode consisting in a permanent and pervasive feature of an attribute of God, following necessarily from that attribute's necessary nature, each such essence exists necessarily – as does the corresponding idea of that formal essence. Of course, it is true that the existence or nonexistence of a particular singular thing does not follow from the existence of its formal essence alone; and in this sense, the formal essence of a singular thing constitutes its actualizability without necessitating its actual existence. Nevertheless, for each particular point in what Spinoza calls "the order of nature" (*ordo naturae*), either the existence or the nonexistence of a given singular thing *is* fully necessitated at that point – by the infinite modes (including the formal essences of things)[16] *in concert with* the necessary infinite series of actual finite causes (see 1p33s1). Thus, whatever does not exist at a particular point in the order of nature is not, all things considered, within God's power to produce *at that point*; the actualization of its formal essence at that particular point is not, all things considered, possible.

The interpretation of formal essences just offered is also compatible with Spinoza's parallelism. For according to this interpretation, the formal essences of singular things are existing infinite modes in their own right – and so are the ideas of (i.e., the ideas "expressing") those formal

---

[15] By treating formal essences as infinite modes, Spinoza accounts for their being within the constraints of substance/mode metaphysics, according which everything that is, is either a substance or the mode of a substance; this is something that Descartes arguably failed to do with "true and immutable natures," which are not easily construed either as modes of extension or as modes of God's thought.

[16] Although formal essences are among the infinite modes, they do not exhaust them. Surely general and more specific laws of nature will also be infinite modes (Curley 1969; 1988, 47–8). It is also plausible to suppose that there will be more and less generic formal essences – e.g., a formal essence of mammal, a formal essence of human, and a formal essence of a particular human being – for the capacities of the attributes to support such beings are all different but omnipresent aspects of those attributes. Spinoza recognizes causal (i.e., explanatory) relations among infinite modes, and it is natural to suppose that laws of nature are prominent among the causes of formal essences, that more general laws are among the causes of more specific laws, and that more generic formal essences are among the causes of less specific formal essences. On the other hand, whatever violates the general laws of nature – for example, a perpetual motion machine, or a talking tree – will have no formal essence at all. It is not obvious that the formal essence of a particular individual could ever be so specific that another individual – say, a genetically identical twin – could not possibly coinstantiate it; however, nothing argued here depends on this.

essences. Singular things themselves, in contrast, are finite modes that exist for a limited duration – but so are the ideas of those singular things. In each case, the ontological status of an entity is precisely parallel to that of its corresponding idea.

## 2. THE ETERNAL PART OF THE MIND THAT REMAINS

*Ethics* 5p23 states, "The human mind cannot be absolutely destroyed with the body, but something of it remains which is eternal." According to the demonstration of this proposition, which cites 5p22 and 2p8c, this eternal "something" that remains "pertains to the essence of the human mind" and is "an idea which expresses the essence of the human body."[17] Furthermore, according to 5p38d and its scholium,[18] that which *remains* of the mind when the body perishes is also "a part of the human mind," a part that – as 5p39s and 5p40c reiterate – is eternal. Because,

---

[17] The full demonstration reads as follows:

> In God there is necessarily a concept, or idea, which expresses the essence of the human Body (by 5p22), an idea, therefore, which is necessarily something that pertains to the essence of the human Mind (by 2p13). But we do not attribute to the human Mind any duration that can be defined by time, except insofar as it expresses the actual existence of the Body, which is explained by duration, and can be defined by time, i.e. (by 2p8c), we do not attribute duration to it except while the Body endures. However, since what is conceived, with a certain eternal necessity, through God's essence itself (by 5p22) is nevertheless something, this something that pertains to the essence of the Mind will necessarily be eternal, Q.E.D. (5p23d)

> Just as a human mind is the idea of a human body, for Spinoza (2p13), so the idea of the formal essence of a human body is itself the formal essence of a human mind; this explains the reference in 5p23 itself to the eternal part of the mind as "pertaining to the essence of the human mind."

[18] These read,

> The Mind's essence consists in cognition (by 2p11); therefore, the more the Mind knows things by the second and third kind of cognition, the greater the part of it that remains (by 5p23 and 5p29), and consequently (by 5p37), the greater the part of it that is not touched by affects which are contrary to our nature, i.e., which (by 4p30) are evil. Therefore, the more the Mind understands things by the second and third kind of cognition, the greater the part of it that remains unharmed. . . . (5p38d)

> From this we understand what I touched on in 4p39s, and what I promised to explain in this Part, viz. that death is less harmful to us, the greater the Mind's clear and distinct cognition, and hence, the more the Mind loves God.

> Next, because (by 5p27) the highest satisfaction there can be arises from the third kind of cognition, it follows from this that the human Mind can be of such a nature that the part of the Mind which we have shown perishes with the body (see 5p21) is of no moment in relation to what remains. But I shall soon treat this more fully. (5p38s)

as we have seen, the idea "expressing the essence of the human body" in 5p22 is simply the idea of the essence of the human body, Spinoza clearly holds that the idea of the essence of a human body remains after the destruction of that human body and that, for this reason, there is a part of each human mind that is eternal.

However, this claim, too, is puzzling, and again in two different ways. First, Spinoza holds that the human mind just is the idea of the human body (2p13); so if there is some eternal part of the human *mind* that remains after the destruction of the *body*, then parallelism seems to require that there should likewise be an eternal part of the human *body* that remains after the destruction of the *mind*.[19] Yet how can there be a *part of the body* that is eternal? Second, it seems that an idea of the essence of the human body should constitute cognition *about* the essence of the human body. The so-called "Physical Digression" following 2p13s strongly suggests that this essence lies in or involves a certain "fixed pattern of motion and rest" that makes an extended singular thing what it is. Now, if an idea of the essence of the human body is the eternal part of the human mind, then it seems that cognition of the essence of the human body should be cognition that is somehow in the human mind. Yet human beings' cognition of their own distinctive fixed patterns of motion and rest seems highly limited, even for most of the very wise. In fact, according to 5p40c, the part of the mind that is eternal is "the intellect," which Spinoza identifies with the totality of one's intellectual ideas (see 2p48s and 2p49s); but it seems that relatively little of one's intellectual cognition concerns the pattern of motion and rest of one's own body. Thus, it seems that an idea of the formal essence of the human body does not have the right content to be or to explain the eternal part of the human mind.[20]

Once we have seen what the formal essence of the human body is, however, we are also in a position to see how that essence *can* constitute an eternal part of the human body, and hence how it can survive the destruction of the actually existing human mind. In order to appreciate this, consider first the part of the *mind* that is eternal. Spinoza states in 5p40c, "the eternal part of the Mind (by 5p23 and 5p29) is the intellect, through which alone we are said to act (by 3p3). But what we have shown to perish is the imagination (by 5p21), through which alone we are said to be acted on." As this suggests, the imagination consists, for Spinoza, of passive (and also inadequate) ideas (3p53d, 5p28d), which he calls "cognition [*cognitio*] of the first kind," whereas the intellect consists of active (and also adequate) ideas, which he calls "cognition of the second and third kinds." Together, the imagination and the intellect can be said

---

[19] Bennett (1984, 358–9) makes this point clearly.
[20] Bennett (1984, 359–63) and Allison (1990, 170–72) raise this objection.

to compose the mind, at least insofar as the mind has ideas.[21] In Part 2 of the *Ethics* (2p17–p31), Spinoza explains imagination as awareness of changing modifications (i.e., states or affections) of the actually existing body. Intellection, however, does not consist in the awareness of any changing modification of the actually existing body. Rather, according to 5p29, it occurs only insofar as the mind "conceives the body's essence under a species of eternity." Hence, in distinguishing the imagination and the intellect as parts of the mind, Spinoza also distinguishes two different objects of awareness: (i) the changing modifications of the actually existing human body and (ii) the formal essence of the human body. As his parallelism requires, Spinoza clearly includes among the parts of the human mind its *ideas of individual organs* constituting parts of the human body (2p15). But none of these ideas is itself the intellect or the (entire) imagination, which Spinoza also identifies as parts of the mind; and if the parts of the mind are not limited to ideas of spatially discrete parts of the body, then by parallelism, the parts of the body cannot be limited to its spatially discrete parts either. But if the parts of a body need not be limited to spatially discrete parts, then Spinoza is free to construe the formal essence of the human body as itself a part of the human body. For although it cannot be a spatially discrete part of the human body in the way that a particular organ is – as an infinite mode, it is an omnipresent aspect of extension, not limited in spatial extent – the formal essence of the human body is, nevertheless, *part of what must be present* at a particular time and place in order for the human body actually to exist there. *This* part of the human body, precisely because it is an infinite mode, will necessarily remain – there, and everywhere else as well – after the actually existing human body and its actually existing human mind are destroyed. This provides the solution to the first puzzle, concerning parallelism, about the eternal part of the mind.

Now, just as the formal essence of the human body is part of what must be present at a particular point in the order of nature for the human body to exist, so the idea of that essence is part of what must be present at a particular point in the order of nature for the human mind to exist. For according to 2p46, "the cognition of God's eternal and infinite essence which each idea involves is adequate and perfect," so that even the most inadequate imaginative ideas of the present affections of the body (5p45d, 5d47d) require some adequate cognition of God's attributes. But all "adequate" cognition is cognition of the second or third kind, for Spinoza, and thus constitutes intellection; and as we have seen, Spinoza

---

[21] See 2a3 and 2p11 on the primary role of ideas in constituting the mind.

holds that the existence of the intellect requires the conception of the essence of the body "under a species of eternity" (5p29).

In order to understand *how* Spinoza conceives the essence of the human body as required for all human intellection, however, we must briefly examine his explanations of how the second and third kinds of cognition – the intellectual kinds – are themselves possible. According to 2p40s2, we have cognition of the second kind through the "common notions and adequate ideas of the properties of things." As Spinoza explains in 2p38–p40, this means that we can have adequate ideas of properties, shared by our bodies and other bodies, that are "equally in the part and in the whole," and we can also have cognition of what follows from these properties. Cognition of the third kind, according to 2p40s2, "proceeds from an adequate idea of the formal essence of certain attributes of God to the adequate cognition of the essence of things." This third, and highest, kind of cognition is possible because *every* idea necessarily involves an adequate cognition of God's essence (2p45–p46; for example, cognition of what extension or thought is), the very cognition that is required to serve as the starting point for cognition of the third kind. In 5p31d Spinoza elaborates on this process:

The Mind conceives nothing under a species of eternity except insofar as it conceives its Body's essence under a species of eternity (by 5p29), i.e., (by 5p21 and 5p23), except insofar as it is eternal. So (by 5p30) insofar as it is eternal, it has cognition of God, cognition which is necessarily adequate (by 2p46). And therefore, the Mind, insofar as it is eternal, is capable of knowing all those things which can follow from this given cognition of God (by 2p40), i.e., of knowing things by the third kind of cognition....

All of the human mind's ideas, then, whether adequate or inadequate, are ideas of the human body (2p13). When it imagines, the human mind conceives affections or modifications of the body that are transitory and that depend on external causes, as well as on the nature of the body and the nature of its parts (2p17–p28). But all understanding requires some understanding of causes (1a4); hence, in conceiving these change-able affections of the actually existing body, the mind *also* conceives, though confusedly and inadequately, the external objects that are among their causes. In order to conceive these changeable affections at all, however, the mind must also conceive *something* of the unchanging formal essence of the human body, which is also among their causes and through which, together with more changeable local causal circumstances, they must be understood. Indeed, more generally, *any* human cognition that is not limited to the awareness of any *particular* time or place is cognition of this essence. But in conceiving something of the essence of one's human body, one conceives *ipso facto* something of the other infinite modes that are among its causes; and because at least some of these infinite modes – as pervasive modifications of a divine attribute – involve features that are equally in the part and in the whole, the mind's conception of them serves as the basis for cognition of the *second* kind.[22] Moreover, in conceiving something of the formal essence of the human body, one *also* conceives the nature of a divine attribute itself, and one thereby has the basis for cognition of the *third* kind.[23]

In this way, the awareness of one's own formal essence that necessarily results from the instantiation of that essence provides the conceptual materials on which the mind's cognitive power must operate in order to produce all of one's adequate cognition – that is, all the contents of the intellect. A human being's actually realized intellect may not contain highly conscious cognition of everything there is to know about the distinctive character of his or her own pattern of motion and rest – although such cognition is in principle attainable. But cognition "of" the formal essence of the human body is not limited to such cognition, for *all* one's cognition that is not limited to a particular perspective is cognition of pervasive features of nature *as they are manifested in* the formal essence of the human body. Just as all imaginative cognition (cognition of the first kind) constitutes cognition of *other* things only by being *first* cognition of some accidental states of the actually existing body, so all intellectual cognition (cognition of the second and third kinds) constitutes cognition of other things only by being *first* cognition concerning the formal essence of the human body. This constitutes the solution to the second puzzle, concerning content, about the eternal part of the mind.

### 3. WISDOM AND THE GROWTH OF THE ETERNAL PART OF THE MIND

Spinoza states in 5p39: "He who has a body capable of a great many things has a mind whose greatest part is eternal." In the scholium to

---

[22] *Ethics* 2p37 states that "What is common to all things and is equally in the part and in the whole, does not constitute the essence of any singular thing." As Antony Dugdale has pointed out to me, this raises the question of whether formal essences, even when conceived as infinite modes, can themselves be "common to all things and equally in the part and in the whole." But there is no requirement that *all* infinite modes be "common to all things" in the sense employed in Spinoza's account of the second kind of cognition. For although infinite modes are omnipresent, those that constitute the formal essences of singular things are not parts of or "common to" the actual existences of *other* singular things in addition to those whose formal essences they are.

[23] A very helpful account of the interrelation between the second and third kinds of cognition has recently been provided in Malinowski-Charles 2003.

this proposition, he remarks that human beings strive to change – "as much as our nature allows and assists" – from a state in which they do not meet this condition to a state in which they do meet it. He then characterizes the difference between these two states as a difference between having "a mind which considered solely in itself is conscious of almost nothing of itself, or of God, or of things" and having a mind "which considered only in itself is very much conscious of itself, and of God, and of things."[24] In the final scholium of the *Ethics*, he asserts specifically that the *ignorant* man "lives as if he knew neither himself, nor God, nor things; and as soon as he ceases to be acted on, he ceases to be"; whereas the *wise* man "insofar as he is considered as such . . . is by a certain eternal necessity, conscious of himself, and of God, and of things [and] he never ceases to be . . . " (5p42s; see also 5p31s). Spinoza also indicates in 5p40c that the intellect – which is, by this same corollary, the "eternal part" of the mind – can vary in extent. Thus, it is clear that he regards wisdom as directly correlated in degree with having a mind whose greater part is eternal.

Yet this final doctrine is puzzling as well, and again for two reasons. First, Spinoza regards human beings as more virtuous and hence (given his identification of virtue with understanding) as wiser than lower animals.[25] Moreover, he must surely regard human beings as wiser than

---

[24] The complete scholium reads:

> Because human Bodies are capable of a great many things, there is no doubt but what they can be of such a nature that they are related to Minds which have a great cognition of themselves and of God, and of which the greatest, or chief, part is eternal. So they hardly fear death.

> But for a clearer understanding of these things, we must note here that we live in continuous change, and that as we change for the better or worse, we are called happy or unhappy. For he who has passed from being an infant or child to being a corpse is called unhappy. On the other hand, if we pass the whole length of our life with a sound Mind in a sound Body, that is considered happiness. And really, he who, like an infant or child, has a Body capable of very few things, and very heavily dependent on external causes, has a Mind which considered solely in itself is conscious of almost nothing of itself, or of God, or of things. On the other hand, he who has a Body capable of a great many things, has a Mind which considered only in itself is very much conscious of itself, and of God, and of things.

> In this life, then, we strive especially that the infant's Body may change (as much as its nature allows and assists) into another, capable of a great many things and related to a Mind very much conscious of itself, of God, and of things. We strive, that is, that whatever is related to its memory or imagination is of hardly any moment in relation to the intellect (as I have already said in 5p38s). (5p39s)

[25] Thus, for example, he writes at 4p37s1, "Indeed, because the right of each one is defined by his virtue, or power, men have a far greater right against the lower animals than they have against men."

other singular things, such as rocks and trees. As we have seen, 5p23d claims that an idea of the formal essence of the human body is "the part of the human mind that is eternal." Yet there exists a formal essence for each singular thing, whether human or not; and hence, by the parallelism of 2p7, there also exists for each singular thing an idea *of* this essence. Because all singular things are equal in respect of having such an idea, it seems puzzling that they can differ in the extent to which a greater part of their minds is eternal.[26] Second, it seems that the formal essence of the human body, as an infinite mode, must be unchanging; and hence in the light of parallelism, it seems that an idea of the formal essence of the human body must remain exactly as unchanging as the formal essence of the human body itself. Thus, it seems hard to see how the part of the mind that is eternal could become greater or less even when one's wisdom increased or decreased.

To resolve these two difficulties, it is useful to draw two related distinctions. First, we must distinguish between (i) having an adequate idea of something by having an adequate idea of *some* feature (i.e., attribute, property, or affection) of the thing and (ii) having an adequate idea of something by having an adequate idea of *all* of its features. For example, Spinoza holds, as we have seen, that each human being has an adequate idea of God's essence insofar as God is extended;[27] and simply in having such an idea, each human being has *an* adequate idea of God. In fact, *any* adequate idea can be truly said to be an adequate idea "of God" at least in the sense that it adequately represents something about God. But no human idea represents God in all of God's aspects; for no human being has an idea of any divine attribute other than extension and thought, and it seems unlikely that any human being represents *all* of God's infinitely many finite modes.[28] Similarly, 5p4 affirms that "there is no affection of the Body of which we cannot form a clear and distinct concept" by conceiving properties that the affection shares with other things (5p4d), even though we as finite beings cannot understand any changing affection of the body in detail and completely through its specific causes.

---

[26] See Garber 2005, which draws attention to this difficulty and concludes that Spinoza is discussing two different kinds of eternity. It is significant in this regard that 5p23d cites 2p13 to show that "the idea expressing the essence" of the human body "pertains to the essence of the human mind." But the scholium to 2p13 notes that "the things we have shown so far are completely general and do not pertain more to man than to other individuals, all of which, though in different degrees, are nevertheless animate."

[27] Similarly, each human being, in conceiving of thought, has an adequate idea of the essence of God insofar as God is thinking.

[28] An idea that did so would be "the idea of God" described in 2p3 and 2p4.

Second, because the human mind is the idea of the human body and is itself in God, we must distinguish between the features of an idea *as it is in God* and the features of what is literally that very same idea *as it is in the mind of a singular thing* – that is, as Spinoza puts it, between ideas as they are in God *simpliciter* and as they are in God insofar as God has or constitutes the mind of a singular thing (2p11c). In particular, we must apply this distinction to an idea's degree of "power of thinking" (*cogitandi potentia*)[29] or "consciousness" (*conscientia*) – which Spinoza treats as identical, or at least coextensive.[30] Thus, an idea exists *in God* as part of God's infinite intellect, with sufficient power of thinking to produce, in fully conscious reality and perfection, all of the ideas that are its effects. In contrast, an idea actually exists *in the mind of a singular thing* only for as long as the singular thing exists, and it exerts within that mind a limited degree of power of thinking that reflects the singular thing's finite share of divine power (4p4d).

Because God's power of thinking is infinite, God's idea of every formal essence of every singular thing represents every aspect or property of that essence with a high degree of power of thinking. But it does not follow from this that a given singular thing will have sufficient power of thinking to possess, in full completeness, a similarly highly conscious idea of its own formal essence. On the contrary, a singular thing has power expressed under *any* attribute – including the attribute of thought – only to the extent that the singular thing approximates to the condition of causal self-sufficiency that is characteristic of a substance. (It has this self-sufficiency by having power to preserve itself – see 3p6 and the propositions that immediately follow it.[31]) Because some kinds of singular things necessarily approximate to this causal self-sufficiency less fully than do others, they necessarily also have less power of thinking.[32] The mind of a lower animal, for example, has ideas of imagination, and hence it has some intellectual cognition as well. Like a human being, it achieves this intellectual cognition by

[29]  "Power of thinking" is a fairly common term in Spinoza's writings, including the *Ethics* (2p1s, 2p7c, 2p21s, 2p49s, 3p2s, 3p11, 3p12d, 3p15d, and 3p28d). It designates "power of action" insofar as that power is expressed under the attribute of thought. Power of thinking is thus the power by which ideas produce other ideas.

[30]  I argue for this conclusion in Garrett 2008. One key piece of evidence is the strikingly parallel treatments of degrees of "excellence and reality" (which Spinoza regards as equivalent to power) at 2p13s and "consciousness" in 5p39s.

[31]  For more discussion of the ways in which singular things constitute finite approximations to a genuine substance, see Garrett 2002.

[32]  Singular things that less closely approximate a substance also have less of a genuine essence; and indeed, Spinoza writes of some things as having "more essence" than others (e.g., *Short Treatise* 1.2 and 2.26 and Ep19). See Garrett 2002 for further discussion of degrees of essence.

conceiving the essence of its body in the course of imagining. However, there is no reason to suppose, and every reason to deny, that the mind of an animal will attain a very highly conscious or complete cognition of the essence of its own body. And although Spinoza allows that all "things" have "minds" (3p1d), rocks and trees will have even less power of thinking than lower animals. Rocks, trees, animals, and humans can differ in the extent to which the greater parts of their minds are eternal, then, because they conceive the formal essences of their bodies more or less fully with greater or lesser power of thinking – that is, consciousness.

Very rudimentary singular things, such as rocks, may not undergo any significant increase or decrease in their power during the period of their actual existence. Human beings, in contrast, do undergo such changes, according to Spinoza (see 3p01): an increase in power is joy (*laetitia*), and a decrease in power is sadness (*tristitia*) (3p11s). Accordingly, a human mind's overall power to produce highly conscious adequate ideas from other adequate ideas can easily vary through time, as can the specific degree of power and consciousness of any individual idea within that mind (4p5–p18). Hence, the "proportion" of a human mind comprised by the intellect – that is, by the part of the mind that is eternal – can vary as well. The human intellect is eternal, for Spinoza, because whatever the human mind conceives adequately, it conceives by conceiving an eternal idea of the eternal formal essence of the human body, thereby incorporating an eternal idea into the human mind.

Thus, although the idea of the formal essence of the human body, *as it is in God*, is a comprehensive and highly conscious idea that undergoes no change, the intellectual life of a human being is a struggle to actualize within that human being's mind, as consciously as possible,[33] as much adequate cognition as possible of the formal essence of his or her body and of other things as they relate to, and are involved in, that formal essence. Fully achieving a complete and highly conscious cognition of everything that can be known about the essence of the human body would require that the formal essence of the human body be instantiated with very great power indeed.[34] How much power of thinking

---

[33] As 5p31s, 5p39s, and 5p42s all indicate, Spinoza thinks of intellectual progress in terms of achieving *consciousness* "of oneself, and of God, and of things." The order in which these objects are listed is no coincidental: because all intellection requires conceiving the essence of the human body, one becomes conscious of God and other things *through* becoming conscious of oneself; and because all adequate cognition of other things requires an adequate idea of the essence of God, one becomes conscious of other things through becoming conscious of God.

[34] Nevertheless, there is a sense in which the complete idea of the essence of the human body may be said to be already potentially in the human mind – indeed,

a person can actually exert on a particular occasion depends in part on favorable or unfavorable external circumstances. But to whatever extent human beings achieve more conscious adequate ideas, they have, to that extent, more fully appropriated into their own minds divine ideas that are eternal – and thereby made a *greater* part of their minds eternal.[35]

## 4. CONCLUSION

On the interpretation that I have proposed, the formal essence of a human body is a real infinite mode: the omnipresent (i.e., pervasive and permanent) modification of the attribute of extension that consists of its general capacity to accommodate and sustain – through the general laws of extension expressible as the laws of physics – the actual existence of a singular thing possessing a specific structure or nature whenever and wherever the series of actual finite causes mandates it. The formal essence of the human body thus *grounds* the actual existence of the finite human body, but it *necessitates* that existence only in concert with the infinite series of actual finite modes. Because the presence of the formal essence of a human body is required for the actual existence of a human body, this formal essence can be understood as a nonlocalized part of the human body. Furthermore, all intellection may be understood as deriving from the mind's idea of this formal essence – an idea that, as an infinite mode of thought, has an ontological status entirely parallel to that of the formal essence of the body. Although the idea expressing the essence of the human body exists as a complete and highly conscious idea in God, human beings must struggle, with

to constitute a kind of human potential intellect. Descartes famously held that certain ideas are already in the intellect innately even when they have not yet been consciously thought, on the ground that their content cannot be derived from the senses but only elicited from the intellect by thinking. Spinoza's view is in many ways similar, for he regularly implies (5p23d together with 5p38d and 5p38s) that *the* idea of the essence of the human body is already a part of the human mind, and he maintains that the various adequate ideas that this idea would involve can be *more* consciously actualized in the actually existing human mind through a sufficient exertion of power of thinking.

[35] *Ethics* 5p40s states that "our Mind, insofar as it understands, is an eternal mode of thinking, which is determined by another eternal mode of thinking, and this again by another, and so on, to infinity; so that together, they all constitute God's eternal and infinite intellect." I take this to mean that the human mind – like the "mind" of any singular thing – is a mode of thinking that is eternal *just insofar as* it understands, although the *inclusion* of this mode of thinking in the mind of an actually existing thing depends on the infinite chain of thinking causes producing the actually existing idea of that actually existing thing. The understanding contained in the ideas of all modes and their causes taken together constitutes the infinite intellect of God, as described in 2p4d, 2p11c, and 2p43s.

limited but varying power, to incorporate the various aspects of this idea into their actually existing minds with greater power and consciousness, just as they must struggle to instantiate more fully and powerfully the formal essence of their bodies. No matter what they do, of course, they cannot achieve *personal* immortality, with continuing sensation or memory. Their minds perish with their bodies – because these are identical – even though a *part* of each remains. But to the extent that they are successful in their struggle, Spinoza holds, human beings understand in the same way that God does. Indeed, they literally participate – for a period of duration – in God's own eternally conscious cognition, and they thereby achieve a mind the greater part of which is eternal.[36]

[36] I am grateful to Antony Dugdale, Charles Jarrett, Michael Della Rocca, Lee Rice, Alison Simmons, and Jonny Cottrell for helpful comments on earlier versions of this paper.

# Bibliography

BENEDICTUS DE SPINOZA(1632–77)

Spinoza. 1677a. *De Nagelate Schriften van B.d.S., als Zedekunst, Staatkunde, Verbetering van 't verstant, Brieven en antwoorden, uit verscheide talen in de Nederlandsche gebragt.* S.l. [Amsterdam]: s.n. [Rieuwertsz].

Spinoza. 1677b. *Opera Posthuma, quorum series post praefationemexhibetur.* S.l. [Amsterdam]: s.n. [Rieuwertsz]. Facsimile reprint: Benedictus de Spinoza, *Opera posthuma*, Amsterdam 1677, riproduzione fotografica integrale/complete photographic reproduction. A cura di Pina Totaro, prefazione di Filippo Mignini. Macerata: Quodlibet, 2008 (Spinozana: Fonti e studi per la storia dello spinozismo).

Spinoza. 1910. *Spinoza's Short Treatise on God, Man, and His Well-Being.* Translated and edited, with an introduction and commentary, A. Wolf. London: Adam and Charles Black.

Spinoza. 1914. *Benedicti De Spinoza Opera Quotquot Reperta Sunt.* Recognoverunt Vloten et Land, editio tertia. Hagae Comitum apud Martinum Nijhoff.

Spinoza. 1925. *Spinoza Opera.* 4 vols. Edited by Carl Gebhardt. Heidelberg: Carl Winters.

Spinoza. 1928. *The Correspondence of Spinoza.* Translated and edited by A. Wolf. London: Allen & Unwin.

Spinoza. 1985. *The Collected Works of Spinoza, Vol. I.* Translated and edited by E. M. Curley. Princeton: Princeton University Press.

Spinoza. 1986. *Korte Verhandeling van God, de mensch en deszelvs welstand/Breve trattato su Dio, l'uomo e il suo bene.* Edited and translated by F. Mignini. L'Aquila: Japadre.

Spinoza. 1992 [1977]. *Briefwisseling.* Translated and edited by F. Akkerman, H. G. Hubbeling, and A. G. Westerbrink. Amsterdam: Wereldbibliotheek.

Spinoza. 1995. *The Letters.* Translated by Samuel Shirley. Introduction and notes by Steven Barbone, Lee Rice, and Jacob Adler. Indianapolis: Hackett.

Spinoza. 2001. *Theological-Political Treatise.* Second edition. Translated by Samuel Shirley. Indianapolis: Hackett.

Spinoza. 2002. *Spinoza: The Complete Works.* Translated by Samuel Shirley, edited by Michael L. Morgan. Indianapolis: Hackett.

Spinoza. 2005. *Spinoza Œuvres*, general editor P.-F. Moreau. Paris: Presses Universitaires de France. Published so far: *Tractatus theologico-politicus/Traité théologico-politique*, edited by F. Akkerman, translated by J. Lagrée and P.-F. Moreau (1999); *Tractatus politicus/Traité politique*, edited by O. Proietti, translated by Ch. Ramond (2005).

Spinoza. *Treatise on the Emendation of the Intellect.* In *The Collected Works of Spinoza, Vol. I* and in Spinoza (2002).

Spinoza. *Descartes' "Principles of Philosophy."* In *The Collected Works of Spinoza, Vol. I* and in Spinoza (2002).

Spinoza. *Metaphysical Thoughts.* (Appendix to *Descartes' "Principles of Philosophy."*) In *The Collected Works of Spinoza, Vol. I* and in Spinoza (2002).

Spinoza. *Short Treatise on God, Man and His Well-Being.* In *The Collected Works of Spinoza, Vol. I* and in Spinoza (2002).

Spinoza. *The Ethics.* In *The Collected Works of Spinoza, Vol. I* and in Spinoza (2002).


OTHER SOURCES

Adams, M. M. 1986. "Universals in the Early Fourteenth Century." In *The Cambridge History of Later Medieval Philosophy*, edited by Norman Kretzman, 411–39. Cambridge: Cambridge University Press.

Akkerman, Fokke. 1980. *Studies in the Posthumous Works of Spinoza: On Style, Earliest Translation and Reception, Earliest and Modern Edition of Some Texts.* Ph.D. thesis, Groningen.

Akkerman, Fokke. 1991. "Leopold en Spinoza." In *Ontroering door het woord: Over J.H. Leopold*, edited by P. M. Th. Everard and H. Hartsuiker, 13–47. Groningen: Historische uitgeverij.

Akkerman, Fokke. 2003. Entry "Glazemaker." In van Bunge et al. (eds.) 2003, 331–4.

Allison, Henry. 1987. *Benedict de Spinoza: An Introduction.* Rev. ed. New Haven: Yale University Press.

Allison, Henry. 1990. "Spinoza's Doctrine of the Eternity of the Mind: Comments on Matson." In *Spinoza: Issues and Directions*, ed. Edwin Curley and Pierre-François Moreau, 96–101. Leiden: E. J. Brill.

Anderson, C. A. 1990. "Some Emendations of Gödel's Ontological Proof." *Faith and Philosophy* 7: 291–303.

Annas, Julia. 1993. *The Morality of Happiness.* Oxford: Oxford University Press.

Aristotle. 1984. *Categories.* Trans. J. L. Ackrill. In *The Complete Works of Aristotle.* The Revised Oxford Translation. Volume one, edited by Jonathan Barnes. Princeton: Princeton University Press.

Aristotle. 1984. *Metaphysics.* Trans. W. D. Ross. In *The Complete Works of Aristotle.* The Revised Oxford Translation. Volume two, edited by Jonathan Barnes. Princeton: Princeton University Press.

Arnauld, Antoine and Pierre Nicole. 1970. *La Logique ou l'art de penser, contenant, outre les règles communes, plusieurs observations nouvelles, propres à former le jugement.* Edited by L. Marin. Paris: Flammarion. (Text of 1683.)

Arndt, H. W. 1971. *Methodo scientifico pertractatum: Mos geometricus und Kalkülbegriff in der philosophischen Theorienbildung des 17. und 18. Jahrhunderts.* Berlin: De Gruyter.

Arndt, H. W. 1980. Entry "Methode (V)." In *Historisches Wörterbuch der Philosophie* 5, edited by J. Ritter and K. Gründer, 1313–23. Basel/Stuttgart: Schwabe.

Audié, Fabrice. 2005. *Spinoza et les mathématiques.* Second printing. Paris: Presses de l'Université Paris-Sorbonne.

Barbaras, Françoise. 2007. *Spinoza: La science mathématique du salut.* Paris: CNRS Éditions.

Bayle, Pierre. 1740. *Dictionnaire historique et critique.* Amsterdam: Chez P. Brunel.

Bayle, Pierre. 1965. *Historical and Critical Dictionary. Selections.* Translated by R. H. Popkin. The Library of Liberal Arts. Indianapolis: Bobbs-Merrill.

Bennett, Daniel. 1969. "The Divine Simplicity." *The Journal of Philosophy* 66: 628–37.

Bennett, Jonathan. 1984. *A Study of Spinoza's* Ethics. Cambridge: Cambridge University Press.

Bergson, Henri. 1934 [1911]. *La Pensée et le mouvant: Essais et conférences.* Fifth ed. Paris: Alcan.

Biasutti, Franco. 1979. *La dottrina della scienza in Spinoza.* Bologna: Pàtron.

Bidney, David. 1940. *The Psychology and Ethics of Spinoza: A Study in the History and Logic of Ideas.* New Haven: Yale University Press.

Bolton, M. B. 1985. "Spinoza on Cartesian Doubt." *Noûs* 19: 379–95.

Bredvold, Louis I. 1951. "The Invention of the Ethical Calculus." In *The Seventeenth Century: Studies in the History of English Thought and Literature from Bacon to Pope,* edited by R. F. Jones et al., 165–80. Stanford: Stanford University Press.

Brissoni, Armando. 2007. *Due cunicoli di Spinoza: L'infinito e il more geometrico.* Bivogni (RC): International AM Edizioni.

Brunschvicg, Léon. 1923. *Spinoza et ses contemporains.* Third ed. Paris: Alcan.

Brunschwig, Jacques. 1988. "La théorie stoïcienne du genre suprême et l'ontologie platonicienne." In *Matter and Metaphysics,* edited by Jonathan Barnes and Mario Mignucci, 19–127. Naples: Bibliopolis.

Brunt, N. A. 1955. *De wiskundige denkwijze in Spinoza's philosophie en in de moderne natuurkunde.* Mededelingen vanwege Het Spinozahuis, Vol. 12. Leiden: E. J. Brill.

Carnap, Rudolf. 1998. "The Value of Laws: Explanation and Prediction." Excerpted from *Philosophical Foundations of Physics* and reprinted in *Philosophy of Science: The Central Issues,* edited by Martin Curd and J. A. Cover, 678–84. New York: Norton.

Carr, Spencer. 1978. "Spinoza's Distinction between Rational and Intuitive Knowledge." *The Philosophical Review* 87: 241–52.

Carriero, John. 1991. "Spinoza's Views on Necessity in Historical Perspective." *Philosophical Topics* 19: 47–96.

Carriero, John. 1994. "On the Theological Roots of Spinoza's Argument for Monism." *Faith and Philosophy* 11: 626–44.

Carriero, John. 1995. "On the Relationship between Mode and Substance in Spinoza's Metaphysics." *Journal of the History of Philosophy* 33: 245–73.

Carriero, John. 2002. "Monism in Spinoza." In *Spinoza: Metaphysical Themes,* edited by Olli Koistinen and John Biro, 38–59. New York: Oxford University Press.

Carriero, John. 2005. "Spinoza on Final Causality." In *Oxford Studies in Early Modern Philosophy,* Vol. 2, edited by Daniel Garber and Steven Nadler, 105–47. Oxford: Clarendon Press.

Cassirer, Ernst. 1994 [1906–50]. *Das Erkenntnisproblem in der Philosophie und Wissenschaft der neueren Zeit.* Sonderausgabe. 4 vols. Darmstadt: Wissenschaftliche Buchgesellschaft.

Charlton, William. 1981. "Spinoza's Monism." *The Philosophical Review* 90: 503–29.

Chauvin, Etienne. 1692. *Lexicon rationale, sive Thesaurus philosophicus.* Rotterodami: vander Slaart.

Cicero. 1939. *De finibus bonorum et malorum.* Translated by H. Rackham. Cambridge, MA: Harvard University Press.

Cook, J. T. 1986. "Self-Knowledge as Self-Preservation?" In *Spinoza and the Sciences*, edited by Marjorie Grene and Debra Nails, 191–210. Dordrecht: Reidel.

Crane, J. K. and Ronald Sandler. 2005. "Identity and Distinction in Spinoza's *Ethics*." *Pacific Philosophical Quarterly* 86: 88–200.

Crapulli, Giovanni. 1969. *Mathesis universalis: Genesi di un'idea nel XVI secolo.* Rome: Edizioni dell'Ateneo.

Cross, Richard. 2005. *Duns Scotus on God.* Aldershot: Ashgate.

Curley, E. M. 1969. *Spinoza's Metaphysics: An Essay in Interpretation.* Cambridge: Harvard University Press.

Curley, E. M. 1973a. "Experience in Spinoza's Theory of Knowledge." In *Spinoza: A Collection of Critical Essays*, edited by Marjorie Grene, 25–59. Garden City, NY: Anchor Books.

Curley, Edwin. 1973b. "Spinoza's Moral Philosophy." In *Spinoza: A Collection of Critical Essays*, edited by Marjorie Grene, 354–76. Garden City, NY: Anchor Books.

Curley, Edwin. 1974. "Descartes, Spinoza and the Ethics of Belief." In *Spinoza: Essays in Interpretation*, edited by Maurice Mandelbaum and Eugene Freeman, 159–90. La Salle, IL: Open Court.

Curley, E. M. 1986. "Spinoza's Geometric Method." *Studia Spinozana* 2: 151–68.

Curley, E. M. 1988. *Behind the Geometrical Method: A Reading of Spinoza's* Ethics. Princeton: Princeton University Press.

Curley, Edwin. 1990. "On Bennett's Spinoza: The Issue of Teleology." In *Spinoza: Issues and Directions*, edited by Edwin Curley and Pierre-François Moreau, 39–52. Leiden: E. J. Brill.

Curley, E. M. 1994. "Spinoza on Truth." *The Australasian Journal of Philosophy* 72: 3–16.

Curley, Edwin and Gregory Walski. 1999. "Spinoza's Necessitarianism Reconsidered." In *New Essays on the Rationalists*, edited by R. J. Gennaro and Charles Huenemann, 241–62. Oxford: Oxford University Press.

Davidson, Donald. 1982. "How Is Weakness of the Will Possible?" In Donald Davidson, *Actions and Events*, 21–42. Oxford: Oxford University Press.

Davis, Richard. 2001. *The Metaphysics of Theism and Modality.* New York: Peter Lang.

De Angelis, Enrico. 1964a. "Il metodo geometrico da Cartesio a Spinoza." *Giornale critico della filosofia italiana* 43: 393–427.

De Angelis, Enrico. 1964b. *Il metodo geometrico nella filosofia del seicento.* Florence: Le Monnier.

De Dijn, Herman. 1971. *De epistemologie van Spinoza.* Ph.D. thesis, Leuven.

De Dijn, Herman. 1973. "Spinoza's geometrische methode van denken." *Tijdschrift voor filosofie* 35: 707–65.

De Dijn, Herman. 1974. "Historical Remarks on Spinoza's Theory of Definition." In *Spinoza on Knowing, Being and Freedom: Proceedings of the Spinoza Symposium at the International School for Philosophy in the Netherlands, Leusden, September 1973*, edited by J. G. van der Bend, 41–50. Assen: Van Gorcum.

De Dijn, Herman. 1975. *Methode en waarheid bij Spinoza.* Mededelingen vanwege Het Spinozahuis, vol. 35. Leiden: E. J. Brill.

De Dijn, Herman. 1978a. "Opnieuw over de geometrische methode van Spinoza." *Algemeen Nederlands Tijdschrift voor Wijsbegeerte* 70: 29–37.

De Dijn, Herman. 1978b. "*Tractatus politicus: More geometrico demonstratus?*" *Tijdschrift voor de Studie van de Verlichting* 6: 125–36.

De Dijn, Herman. 1983. "Adriaan Heereboord en het Nederlands cartesianisme." *Algemeen Nederlands Tijdschrift voor Wijsbegeerte* 75: 56–69.

De Dijn, Herman. 1986. "Conceptions of Philosophical Method in Spinoza: *Logica* and *mos geometricus.*" *Review of Metaphysics* 40: 55–87.

De la Court, Pieter. 1972. *The True Interest and Political Maxims of the Republic of Holland.* New York: Arno Press.

De Lucca, John. 1967. "Wolfson on Spinoza's Use of the *More geometrico.*" *Dialogue: Canadian Philosophical Review/Revue Canadienne de Philosophie* 6: 89–102.

De Vleeschauwer, H. J. 1932. "La Genèse de la méthode mathématique de Wolf: Contribution à l'histoire des idées au XVIIIᵉ siècle." *Revue Belge de Philologie et d'Histoire* 11, 651–77.

De Vleeschauwer, H. J. 1961. *More seu ordine geometrico demonstratum.* Pretoria: Mededelings van die Universiteit van Suid-Afrika.

De Vries, Matthias *et al.* (eds.). 1882–1998. *Woordenboek der Nederlandsche Taal.* The Hague.

Delahunty, R. J. 1985. *Spinoza.* London: Routledge and Kegan Paul.

Deleuze, Gilles. 1968. *Spinoza et le problème de l'expression.* Paris: Éditions de Minuit.

Deleuze, Gilles. 1981. *Spinoza: Philosophie pratique.* Paris: Éditions de Minuit.

Deleuze, Gilles. 1997 [1968]. *Expressionism in Philosophy: Spinoza.* Translated by M. Joughin. New York: Zone Books.

Della Rocca, Michael. 1996a. *Representation and the Mind–Body Problem in Spinoza.* New York: Oxford University Press.

Della Rocca, Michael. 1996b. "Spinoza's Metaphysical Psychology." In *The Cambridge Companion to Spinoza,* edited by Don Garrett, 192–266. Cambridge: Cambridge University Press.

Della Rocca, Michael. 2002. "Spinoza's Substance Monism." In *Spinoza: Metaphysical Themes,* edited by Olli Koistinen and John Biro, 11–37. New York: Oxford University Press.

Della Rocca, Michael. 2003. "The Power of an Idea: Spinoza's Critique of Pure Will." *Noûs* 37: 200–231.

Della Rocca, Michael. 2008. *Spinoza.* London: Routledge.

Descartes, René. 1985. *The Philosophical Writings of Descartes. Vols. I and II.* Translated by J. Cottingham, R. Stoothoff, and D. Murdoch. Cambridge: Cambridge University Press. Abbreviated as CSM.

Descartes, René. 1991. *The Philosophical Writings of Descartes. Vol. III.* Translated by J. Cottingham, R. Stoothoff, D. Murdoch, and A. Kenny. Cambridge: Cambridge University Press. Abbreviated as CSMK.

Descartes, René. 1996 [1897–1910]. *Œuvres,* publiées par Charles Adam et Paul Tannery, 12 Bde. Paris: Cerf; reprint (11 vols). Paris: Vrin. Abbreviated as AT.

Deveaux, Sherry. 2003. "The Divine Essence and the Conception of God in Spinoza." *Synthese* 135: 329–38.

Donagan, Alan. 1973. "Spinoza's Proof of Immortality." In *Spinoza: A Collection of Critical Essays,* edited by Marjorie Grene, 241–58. Garden City, NY: Anchor Books.

Donagan, Alan. 1988. *Spinoza.* Chicago: Chicago University Press.

Doney, Willis. 1990. "Gueroult on Spinoza's Proof of God's Existence." In *Spinoza: Issues and Directions,* edited by Edwin Curley and Pierre-François Moreau, 32–8. Leiden: E. J. Brill.

Duns Scotus, John. 1982. *A Treatise on God as First Principle.* Translated and edited by A. B. Wolter. Chicago: Franciscan Herald Press.

Dvns Scoti, Iohannis. 1968. *Quaestiones in lib. I. sententiarvm*, Lvgdvni 1639; reprograph. reprint Hildesheim: Olms. (= Opera Omnia V.2.)

Eisenberg, Paul. 1990. "On the Attributes and Their Alleged Independence of One Another: A Commentary on Spinoza's *Ethics* IP10." In *Spinoza: Issues and Directions*, edited by Edwin Curley and Pierre-François Moreau, 1–15. Leiden: E. J. Brill.

Emilsson, Eyjólfur. 1996. "Cognition and Its Object." In *The Cambridge Companion to Plotinus*, edited by Lloyd Gerson, 217–49. Cambridge: Cambridge University Press.

Engfer, Hans-Jürgen. 1982. *Philosophie als Analysis: Studien zur Entwicklung philosophischer Analysiskonzeptionen unter dem Einfluß mathematischer Methodenmodelle im 17. und frühen 18. Jahrhundert*. Stuttgart/Bad Canstatt: Frommann–Holzboog.

Euclid. 1956 [1908]. *The Thirteen Books of Euclid's Elements*, 3 vols. Translated and edited by Th. L. Heath. Reprint of the second ed. New York: Dover.

Feuerbach, Ludwig. 1847 [1833]. *Geschichte der neueren Philosophie*. Leipzig: Wigand.

Freudenthal, H. 1980. Entry "Methode (axiomatische)." In *Historisches Wörterbuch der Philosophie* 5, edited by J. Ritter and K. Gründer, 1336–41. Basel/Stuttgart: Schwabe.

Freudenthal, Jakob. 1899. *Die Lebensgeschichte Spinoza's in Quellenschriften, Urkunden und nichtamtlichen Nachrichten*. Leipzig: Von Veit.

Freudenthal, Jakob and Manfred Walther. 2006 [1899]. *Die Lebensgeschichte Spinozas*. Zweite, stark erweiterte und vollständig neu kommentierte Auflage der Ausgabe von Jakob Freudenthal 1899, mit einer Bibliographie herausgegeben von Manfred Walther unter Mitarbeit von Michael Czelinski. Band 1: Lebensbeschreibungen und Dokumente. Band 2: Kommentar. Stuttgart: Fromann-Holzboog.

Friedman, J. I. 1974. "Some Settheoretical Partition Theorems Suggested by the Structure of Spinoza's God." *Synthese* 27: 199–209.

Friedman, J. I. 1976. "The Universal Class has a Spinozistic Partitioning." *Synthese* 32: 403–18.

Friedman, J. I. 1978. "An Overview of Spinoza's *Ethics*." *Synthese* 37: 67–106.

Furley, David. 1999. "Cosmology." In *The Cambridge History of Hellenistic Philosophy*, edited by Keimpe Algra *et al.*, 432–51. Cambridge: Cambridge University Press.

Galilei, Galileo. 1964–6 [1890–1909]. *Le opere*. Edizione nazionale. 20 in 21 vols. Florence: Barbèra.

Garber, Daniel. 2004. "Dr. Fischelson's Dilemma: Spinoza on Freedom and Sociability." In *Spinoza on Reason and "Free Man,"* edited by Yirmiyahu Yovel and Gideon Segal. New York: Little Room Press.

Garber, Daniel. 2005. "'A Free Man Thinks of Nothing Less Than of Death': Spinoza on the Eternity of Mind." In *Early Modern Philosophy: Mind, Matter, and Metaphysics*, edited by Christia Mercer and Eileen O'Neill, 103–18. Oxford: Oxford University Press.

Garrett, A. V. 2003. *Meaning in Spinoza's Method*. Cambridge: Cambridge University Press.

Garrett, Don. 1979. "Spinoza's 'Ontological' Argument." *The Philosophical Review* 88: 198–223.

Garrett, Don. 1990a. "'A Free Man Always Acts Honestly, Not Deceptively': Freedom and the Good in Spinoza's *Ethics*." In *Spinoza: Issues and Directions*, edited by Edwin Curley and Pierre-François Moreau, 221–38. Leiden: E. J. Brill.

Garrett, Don. 1990b. "*Ethics* IP5: Shared Attributes and the Basis of Spinoza's Monism." In *Central Themes in Early Modern Philosophy: Essays Presented to Jonathan Bennett*, edited by J. A. Cover and Mark Kulstad, 69–107. Indianapolis: Hackett.

Garrett, Don. 1991. "Spinoza's Necessitarianism." In *God and Nature: Spinoza's Metaphysics. Papers Presented at the First Jerusalem Conference (Ethica I)*, edited by Yirmiyahu Yovel, 191–218. Leiden: E. J. Brill.

Garrett, Don. 1996. "Spinoza's Ethical Theory." In *The Cambridge Companion to Spinoza*, edited by Don Garrett, 267–314. Cambridge: Cambridge University Press.

Garrett, Don. 2002. "Spinoza's *Conatus* Argument." In *Spinoza: Metaphysical Themes*, edited by Olli Koistinen and John Biro, 127–58. New York: Oxford University Press.

Garrett, Don. 2008. "Representation and Consciousness in Spinoza's Naturalistic Theory of the Imagination." In *Interpreting Spinoza: Critical Essays*, edited by Charlie Huenemann, 4–25. Cambridge: Cambridge University Press.

Geach, P. T. 1965. "Assertion." *The Philosophical Review* 74: 449–65.

Gerritsen, Johan. 2005. "Printing Spinoza – Some Questions." In Akkerman and Steenbakkers 2005, 251–62.

Gilbert, N. W. 1960. *Renaissance Concepts of Method*. New York: Columbia University Press.

Goudriaan, Aza. 1999. *Philosophische Gotteserkenntnis bei Suárez und Descartes im Zusammenhang mit der niederländischen Theologie des 17. Jahrhunderts*. Leiden: E. J. Brill.

Graeser, Andreas. 1991. "Stoische Philosophie bei Spinoza." *Revue Internationale de Philosophie* 45: 336–46.

Grajewski, M. J. 1944. *The Formal Distinction of Duns Scotus: A Study in Metaphysics*. Washington, DC: Catholic University of America Press.

Gueroult, Martial. 1968. *Spinoza I. Dieu (Ethique, I)*. Paris: Aubier-Montaigne.

Gueroult, Martial. 1970 [1960]. "Le *Cogito* et l'ordre des axiomes métaphysiques dans les *Principia philosophiae cartesianae* de Spinoza" In Gueroult, *Études sur Descartes, Spinoza, Malebranche et Leibniz*, 64–78. Hildesheim: Olms.

Gueroult, Martial. 1974. *Spinoza II. L'Âme (Ethique, II)*. Paris: Aubier-Montaigne.

Gueroult, Martial. 1977. "Le *Spinoza* de Martial Gueroult." *Revue Philosophique de la France et de l'Étranger* 167: 285–302.

Hacking, Ian. 1999. *The Social Construction of What?* Cambridge, MA: Harvard University Press.

Hampshire, Stuart. 1962. *Spinoza*. Rev. ed. Baltimore: Pelican-Penguin.

Hampshire, Stuart. 1983. "Two Theories of Morality." In Hampshire, *Morality and Conflict*, 10–68. Cambridge, MA: Harvard University Press.

Harrington, James. 1992. *The Commonwealth of Oceana*. Edited by J. G. A. Pocock. Cambridge: Cambridge University Press.

Hegel, G. W. F. 1985 (1832). *Wissenschaft der Logik* I, hg. v. F. Hogemann und W. Jaeschke. Hamburg: Meiner. (= Gesammelte Werke Bd. 21.)

Henninger, M. G. 1989. *Relations: Medieval Theories 1250–1325*. Oxford: Clarendon Press.

Hobbes, Thomas. 1994 [1651]. *Leviathan*. Indianapolis: Hackett.

Hoffman, Paul. 1991. "Three Dualist Theories of the Passions." *Philosophical Topics* 19: 153–200.

Honnefelder, Ludger. 2005. *Duns Scotus*. Munich: Beck.

Hubbeling, H. G. 1967. "Spinoza's metafysica in verband met zijn methode." *Wijsgerig Perspectief* 8: 77–91.

Hubbeling, H. G. 1977a. "La Méthode axiomatique de Spinoza et la définition du concept de Dieu." *Raison Présente* no. 43, 25–36.

Hubbeling, H. G. 1977b. "The Development of Spinoza's Axiomatic (Geometric) Method: The Reconstructed Geometric Proof of the Second Letter of Spinoza's Correspondence and Its Relation to Earlier and Later Versions." *Revue internationale de philosophie* 31, 53–68.

Hubbeling, H. G. 1980. "Spinoza comme précurseur du reconstructivisme logique dans son livre sur Descartes." *Studia Leibnitiana* 12: 88–95.

Hubbeling, H. G. 1983. "Arnold Geulincx, origineel vertegenwoordiger van het cartesio-spinozisme." *Algemeen Nederlands Tijdschrift voor Wijsbegeerte* 75: 70–80.

Huenemann, Charles. 1999. "The Necessity of Finite Modes and Geometrical Containment in Spinoza's Metaphysics." In *New Essays on the Rationalists*, edited by R. J. Gennaro and Charles Huenemann, 224–40. Oxford: Oxford University Press.

Hume, David. 1998 [1751]. *An Enquiry Concerning the Principles of Morals*. Edited by T. L. Beauchamp. Oxford: Oxford University Press.

Inwood, Brad. 1995. "Review of Julia Annas, *The Morality of Happiness*." *Ancient Philosophy* 15: 647–65.

Inwood, Brad and L. P. Gerson (eds. and transls.). 1997. *Hellenistic Philosophy*, second ed. Indianapolis: Hackett.

Iribarren, Isabel. 2002. "The Scotist Background in Hervaeus Natalis's Interpretation of Thomism." *The Thomist* 66: 607–27.

Iwanicki, Joseph. 1933. *Leibniz et les démonstrations mathématiques de l'existence de Dieu*. Strasbourg: Librairie Universitaire d'Alsace. Ph.D. thesis, Strasbourg.

James, Susan. 1993. "Spinoza the Stoic." In *The Rise of Modern Philosophy*, edited by Tom Sorrell, 289–316. Oxford: Oxford University Press.

James, William. 1978 [1895]. "The Knowing of Things Together." Reprinted in *Essays in Philosophy*, edited by F. H. Burkhardt and I. K. Skrupskelis. Cambridge, MA: Harvard University Press.

Jarrett, Charles. 1977a. "Some Remarks on the 'Objective' and 'Subjective' Interpretations of the Attributes." *Inquiry* 20: 447–56.

Jarrett, Charles. 1977b. "The Concepts of Substance and Mode in Spinoza." *Philosophia* 7: 83–105.

Jarrett, Charles. 1978. "The Logical Structure of Spinoza's *Ethics*, Part I." *Synthese* 37: 15–65.

Jarrett, Charles. 2007. *Spinoza: A Guide for the Perplexed*. London and New York: Continuum.

Joachim, H. H. 1901. *A Study of the Ethics of Spinoza: Ethica ordine geometrico demonstrata*. Oxford: Clarendon Press.

Kaplan, Francis. 1998. *L'Éthique de Spinoza et la méthode géométrique: Introduction à la lecture de Spinoza*. Paris: Flammarion.

Kennington, Richard. 1980. "Analytic and Synthetic Methods in Spinoza's *Ethics*." In *The Philosophy of Baruch Spinoza*, edited by Richard Kennington. Washington, DC: The Catholic University of American Press.

Kline, M. 1972. *Mathematical Thought from Ancient to Modern Times*. New York: Oxford University Press.

Kneale, Martha. 1973. "Eternity and Sempiternity." In *Spinoza: A Collection of Critical Essays*, edited by Marjorie Grene, 227–40. Garden City, NY: Anchor Books.

Koistinen, Olli. 1991. *On the Metaphysics of Spinoza's* Ethics. Reports from the Department of Theoretical Philosophy. Turku: University of Turku.

Koistinen, Olli. 1993. "Individual Essences in Individuation." In *Good Reason: Essays Dedicated to Risto Hilpinen*, edited by Olli Koistinen and Juha Räikkä, 139–49. Turku: University of Turku.

Koistinen, Olli. 2002. "Causation in Spinoza." In *Spinoza: Metaphysical Themes*, edited by Olli Koistinen and John Biro, 60–72. New York: Oxford University Press.

Koistinen, Olli. 2003. "Spinoza's Proof of Necessitarianism." *Philosophy and Phenomenological Research* 67: 283–310.

Kulstad, M. A. 1996. "Spinoza's Demonstration of Monism: A New Line of Defense." In *History of Philosophy Quarterly* 13: 299–316.

Land, J. P. N. 1882. "Over de uitgaven en den text der Ethica van Spinoza." In *Verslagen en Mededeelingen der Koninklijke Akademie van Wetenschappen, Afdeeling Letterkunde*, Tweede Reeks, Elfde Deel, 4–24. Amsterdam: Muller.

LeBuffe, Michael. 2004. "Why Spinoza Tells People to Try to Preserve Their Being." *Archiv für Geschichte der Philosophie* 86: 119–45.

LeBuffe, Michael. 2005. "Spinoza's *Summum Bonum*." *The Pacific Philosophical Quarterly* 86: 243–66.

Leftow, Brian. 1990. "Is God an Abstract Object?" *Noûs* 24: 581–98.

Leibniz, G. W. 1969. *Gottfried Wilhelm Leibniz: Philosophical Papers and Letters*, second ed. Translated and edited by L. E. Loemker. Dordrecht: Reidel.

Leibniz, G. W. 1989a. *G. W. Leibniz: Philosophical Essays*. Translated and edited by Roger Ariew and Daniel Garber. Indianapolis: Hackett.

Leibniz, G. W. 1989b. "Two Sects of Naturalists." In Leibniz 1989a.

Leibniz, G. W. 1999. *Sämtliche Schriften und Briefe*, hrsg. v. d. Berlin-Brandenburgischen Akad. d. Wiss. zu Berlin und d. Akad. d. Wiss. in Göttingen, VI, 4, Berlin.

Lennon, T. M. 2005. "The Rationalist Conception of Substance." In *A Companion to Rationalism*, edited by Alan Nelson, 12–30. Malden, MA: Blackwell Publishing.

Leopold, J. H. 1902. *Ad Spinozae Opera posthuma*. The Hague: Nijhoff.

Leopold, J. H. 2005. "Le Langage de Spinoza et sa pratique du discourse." Translated by Michelle Beyssade. In Akkerman and Steenbakkers (eds.) 2005, 9–33. [French translation of Leopold 1902, 1–37.]

Lin, Martin. 2004. "Spinoza's Metaphysics of Desire: The Demonstration of IIIP6." *Archiv für Geschichte der Philosophie* 86: 21–55.

Lin, Martin. 2006. "Teleology and Human Action in Spinoza." *Philosophical Review* 115: 317–54.

Locke, John. 1975. *An Essay Concerning Human Understanding*. Ed. P. H. Nidditch. Oxford: Oxford University Press.

Long, A. A. and D. N. Sedley (eds. and transls.). 1987. *The Hellenistic Philosophers*, Vols. 1–2. Cambridge: Cambridge University Press.

Long, A. A. 1986. *Hellenistic Philosophy*, second ed. Berkeley and Los Angeles: University of California Press.

Long, A. A. 2003. "Stoicism in the Philosophical Tradition: Spinoza, Lipsius, Butler." In *Hellenistic and Early Modern Philosophy*, ed. Jon Miller and Brad Inwood, 17–29. Cambridge: Cambridge University Press.

Machiavelli, Niccolo. 1996 [1531]. *Discourses on Livy*. Translated by H. C. Mansfield and Nathan Tarcov. Chicago: University of Chicago Press.

Malinowski-Charles, Syliane. 2003. "The Circle of Adequate Knowledge: Notes on Reason and Intuition in Spinoza." In *Oxford Studies in Early Modern Philosophy*, Vol. 1, edited by Daniel Garber and Steven Nadler, 139–63. Oxford: Clarendon Press.

Mann, W. E. 1982. "Divine Simplicity." *Religious Studies* 18: 451–71.

Mark, T. C. 1975. "*Ordine geometrica demonstrata*: Spinoza's Use of the Axiomatic Method." *The Review of Metaphysics* 29: 263–86.

Matheron, Alexandre. 1988 [1969]. *Individu et communauté chez Spinoza*. Nouvelle éd. Paris: Minuit.

Matheron, Alexandre. 1994a. "Ideas of Ideas and Certainty in the *Tractatus de Intellectus Emendatione* and in the *Ethics*." Translated by Jonathan Bennett. In *Spinoza on Knowledge and the Human Mind*. Vol. 2 of *Spinoza by the Year 2000*, edited by Yirmiyahu Yovel, 83–91. Leiden: E. J. Brill.

Matheron, Alexandre. 1994b. "Le moment stoïcien de l'Éthique de Spinoza." In *Le Stoïcisme aux XVIe et XVIIe siècles*, edited by Pierre-François Moreau, 302–16. Caen: Presses Universitaires de Caen.

Matson, Wallace. 1990. "Body Essence and Mind Eternity in Spinoza." In *Spinoza: Issues and Directions*, edited Edwin Curley and Pierre-François Moreau, 82–95. Leiden: E. J. Brill.

McKeon, Richard. 1930. "Causation and the Geometric Method in the Philosophy of Spinoza." *The Philosophical Review* 39: 178–89, 275–96.

Menn, Stephen. 1998. *Descartes and Augustine*. Cambridge: Cambridge University Press.

Mercer, Christia. 2001. *Leibniz's Metaphysics: Its Origins and Development*. Cambridge: Cambridge University Press.

Meyer, Lodewijk. 1666. *Philosophia S. Scripturæ interpres: exercitatio paradoxa, in quâ veram philosophiam infallibilem S. Literas interpretandi normam esse apodicticè demonstratur, & discrepantes ab hâc sententiæ expenduntur, ac refelluntur.* Eleutheropoli [ = Amsterdam], s.n. [Rieuwertsz].

Miller, Jon. 2003a. "Spinoza and the Concept of a Law of Nature." *History of Philosophy Quarterly* 20: 257–76.

Miller, Jon. 2003b. "Stoics, Grotius and Spinoza on Moral Deliberation." In *Hellenistic and Early Modern Philosophy*, edited by Jon Miller and Brad Inwood, 116–40. Cambridge: Cambridge University Press.

Miller, Jon. 2005. "Spinoza's Axiology." In *Oxford Studies in Early Modern Philosophy*, Vol. 2, edited by Daniel Garber and Steven Nadler, 149–72. Oxford: Clarendon Press.

Mommsen, Theodore and Paul Krueger (eds.). 1985. *Digest of Justinian*. Translated by Alan Watson. 4 vols. Philadelphia: University of Pennsylvania Press.

Moorman, R. H. 1943. "The Influence of Mathematics on the Philosophy of Spinoza." *National Mathematics Magazine* 18: 108–15.

Moreau, Pierre-François. 1990. "Concorde et sociabilité dans la *Korte Verhandeling*." In *Dio, l'uomo, la libertà: Studi sul* Breve Tratatto *di Spinoza*, edited by Filippo Mignini, 375–9. L'Aquila: Japadre.

Morris, T. V. 1987. "On God and Man: A View of Divine Simplicity." In *Anselmian Explorations: Essays in Philosophical Theology*, 98–123. Notre Dame: University of Notre Dame Press.

Nadler, Steven. 2002a. "Eternity and Immortality in Spinoza's *Ethics*." *Midwest Studies in Philosophy* 26: 224–44.

Nadler, Steven. 2002b. *Spinoza's Heresy: Immortality and the Jewish Mind*. Oxford: Clarendon Press.

Nadler, Steven. 2006. *Spinoza's Ethics: An Introduction*. Cambridge: Cambridge University Press.

Nadler, Steven. 2008. "'Whatever Is, Is in God': Substance and Things in Spinoza's Metaphysics." In *Interpreting Spinoza: Critical Essays*, edited by Charlie Huenemann, 53–70. Cambridge: Cambridge University Press.

Neu, Jerome. 1978. *Emotion, Thought, and Therapy*. Berkeley: University of California Press.

Nietzsche, Friedrich. 1886. *Jenseits von Gut und Böse. Vorspiel einer Philosophie der Zukunft*. Leipzig: C. G. Naumann.

Noone, T. B. 1999. "La distinction formelle dans l'école scotiste." *Revue des Sciences philosophiques et théologiques* 83: 53–72.

Parchment, Steven. 2000. "The Mind's Eternity in Spinoza's *Ethics*." *Journal of the History of Philosophy* 38: 349–83.

Parkinson, G. H. R. 1964. *Spinoza's Theory of Knowledge*. Oxford: Clarendon Press.

Parrochia, Daniel. 1993. *La Raison systématique: Essai d'une morphologie des systèmes philosophiques*. Paris: Vrin.

Pauen, Michael. 2002. *Grundprobleme der Philosophie des Geistes. Eine Einführung*. Frankfurt am Main: Fischer.

Pauen, Michael. 2003. "Vorläufer der Identitätstheorie? Über das Verhältnis Spinozas zu neueren Varianten des Monismus." *Studia Spinozana* 14: 34–55.

Perzanowski, Jerzy. 1991. "Ontological Arguments II: Cartesian and Leibnizian." In *Handbook of Metaphysics and Ontology*, Vol. 2, edited by Hans Burkhardt and Barry Smith, 625–33. Munich: Philosophia.

Petry, Michael. 1986. "The Early Reception of the Calculus in the Netherlands." *Studia Leibnitiana*, Sonderheft 14: *300 Jahre 'Nova methodus' von G. W. Leibniz (1684–1984)*, edited by A. Heinekamp, 202–31. Stuttgart: Franz Steiner.

Plantinga, Alvin. 1980. *Does God Have a Nature?* Milwaukee: Marquette University Press.

Plato. 1997. *Plato: Complete Works*, edited by J. M. Cooper. Indianapolis: Hackett.

Prins, J. 1988. "De oorsprong en betekenis van Hobbes' geometrische methodenideaal." *Tijdschrift voor Filosofie* 50: 248–71.

Prokhovnik, Raia. 2004. *Spinoza and Dutch Republicanism*. Basingstoke: Palgrave Macmillan.

Radner, Daisie. 1971. "Spinoza's Theory of Ideas." *The Philosophical Review* 80: 338–59.

Rice, L. C. 1974. "Methodology and Modality in the First Part of Spinoza's *Ethics*." In *Spinoza on Knowing, Being and Freedom: Proceedings of the Spinoza Symposium at the International School for Philosophy in the Netherlands, Leusden, September 1973*, edited by J. G. van der Bend, 144–55. Assen: Van Gorcum.

Risse, Wilhelm. 1962. "Mathematik und Kombinatorik in der Logik der Renaissance." *Archiv für Philosophie* 11: 187–206.

Risse, Wilhelm. 1970. *Die Logik der Neuzeit*, Vol. 2: *1640–1780*. Stuttgart/Bad Canstatt: Frommann-Holzboog.

Robinet, André. 1980. "Modèle géométrique et critique informatique dans le discours spinozien." *Studia Leibnitiana* 12: 96–113.

Röd, Wolfgang. 1970. *Geometrischer Geist und Naturrecht: methodengeschichtliche Untersuchungen zur Staatsphilosophie im 17. und 18. Jahrhundert*. Bayerische

Akademie der Wissenschaften, Philosophisch-historische Klasse, Abhandlungen, NS vol. 70. Munich: Bayerische Akademie der Wissenschaften/Beck, 1970.

Röd, Wolfgang. 1992. *Der Gott der reinen Vernunft: Die Auseinandersetzung um den ontologischen Gottesbeweis von Anselm bis Hegel*. Munich: Beck.

Rogers, K. A. 2000. *Perfect Being Theology*. Edinburgh: Edinburgh University Press.

Rorty, A. O. 1996. "The Two Faces of Stoicism: Rousseau and Freud." *Journal of the History of Philosophy* 34: 335–56.

Rousset, Bernard. 1985. "Éléments et hypothèses pour une analyse des rédactions successives de Éthique IV." *Cahiers Spinoza* 5: 129–45.

Rousset, Bernard. 1988. "La Première Éthique: Méthode et perspective." *Archives de Philosophie* 51: 75–98.

Saccaro del Buffa Battisti, Giuseppa. 1990. "La dimostrazione dell'esistenza di Dio dall'abbozzo del 1661 e dalla *Korte verhandeling* al 'De Deo.'" In *Dio, l'uomo, la libertà: Studi sul Breve Tratatto di Spinoza*, edited by Filippo Mignini, 95–118. L'Aquila: Japadre.

Savan, David. 1986. "Spinoza: Scientist and Theorist of Scientific Method." In *Spinoza and the Sciences*, edited by Marjorie Grene and Debra Nails, 95–121. Dordrecht: Reidel.

Scarpellini, Costante. 1954. "Il matematismo spinoziano." *Rivista di Filosofia Neoscolastica* 46: 36–55.

Schildknecht, Christiane. 1990. *Philosophische Masken: Literarische Formen der Philosophie bei Platon, Descartes, Wolff und Lichtenberg*. Stuttgart: Metzler.

Scholz, J. 1863. "Über die geometrische Methode in der Ethik des Spinoza." *Jahresbericht über die Stadtschule [ . . . ] zu Spremberg*: 3–17.

Schuhmann, Karl. 1985. "Geometrie und Philosophie bei Thomas Hobbes." *Philosophisches Jahrbuch* 92: 161–77.

Schuhmann, Karl. 2004 [1987]. "Methodenfragen bei Spinoza und Hobbes: Zum Problem des Einflusses." In Karl Schuhmann, *Selected Papers on Renaissance Philosophy and on Thomas Hobbes*, edited by P. Steenbakkers and C. Leijenhorst, 45–71. Dordrecht: Kluwer Academic.

Schüling, Hermann. 1969. *Die Geschichte der axiomatischen Methode im 16. und beginnenden 17. Jahrhundert: Wandlung der Wissenschaftsauffassung*. Hildesheim/New York: Olms.

Scott, Jonathan. 2002. "Classical Republicanism in Seventeenth-Century England and the Netherlands." In *Republicanism: A Shared European Heritage*, Vol. 1, *Republicanism and Constitutionalism in Early Modern Europe*, edited by Martin Van Gelderen and Quentin Skinner, 61–84. Cambridge: Cambridge University Press.

Searle, John. 1992. *The Rediscovery of the Mind*. Cambridge, MA: MIT Press.

Sedley, David. 1999. "Hellenistic Physics and Metaphysics." In *The Cambridge History of Hellenistic Philosophy*, edited by Keimpe Algra, Jonathan Barnes, Jaap Mansfeld, and Malcolm Schofield, 355–411. Cambridge: Cambridge University Press.

Shmueli, Efraim. 1980. "The Geometrical Method, Personal Caution and the Idea of Tolerance." In *Spinoza: New Perspectives*, edited by R. W. Shahan and J. I. Biro, second printing, 197–215. Norman: University of Oklahoma Press.

Sider, Theodore. 2001. *Four Dimensionalism*. Oxford: Oxford University Press.

Skirry, Justin. 2004. "Descartes's Conceptual Distinction and Its Ontological Import." *Journal of the History of Philosophy* 42: 121–44.

Sobel, J. H. 1987. "Gödel's Ontological Proof." In *On Being and Saying: Essays for R. L. Cartwright*, edited by J. J. Thomson, 241–61. Cambridge, MA: MIT Press.

Sobel, J. H. 2004. *Logic and Theism: Arguments for and against Beliefs in God*. Cambridge: Cambridge University Press.

Staal, Frits. 1986 [1963]. "Euclides en Pānini: Twee methodische richtlijnen voor de filosofie." In Frits Staal, *Over zin en onzin in filosofie, religie en wetenscha*, 77–115. Amsterdam: Meulenhoff.

Staal, Frits. 1988. "Euclid and Pānini." In Frits Staal, *Universals: Studies in Indian Logic and Linguistics*, 143–59. Chicago: University of Chicago Press.

Steenbakkers, Piet. 1994. *Spinoza's Ethica from Manuscript to Print: Studies on Text, Form and Related Topics*. Ph.D. thesis, Groningen. Assen: Van Gorcum.

Steenbakkers, Piet. 1997. "Purisme et gloses marginales dans le traduction néerlandaise de 1677 de l'*Ethica*." In *Spinoziana: Ricerche di terminologia filosofica e critica testuale*, edited by P. Totaro, 233–47. Rome: Olschki.

Steenbakkers, Piet. 2003a. Entry "Bouwmeester." In van Bunge et al., (eds.) 2003, 144–6.

Steenbakkers, Piet. 2003b. Entry "Meyer." In van Bunge et al. (eds.) 2003, 694–9.

Steenbakkers, Piet. 2004. "Spinoza on the Imagination." In *The Scope of Imagination: Between Medieval and Modern Times*, edited by L. Nauta and D. Pätzold, 175–94. Leuven: Peeters.

Steenbakkers, Piet. 2007. "Les Éditions de Spinoza en Allemagne au XIX$^e$ siècle." In *Spinoza au XIX$^e$ siècle*, edited by A. Tosel, P.-F. Moreau, and J. Salem, 21–32. Paris: Publications de la Sorbonne.

Steenbakkers, Piet. Forthcoming. "The Text of Spinoza's *Tractatus Theologico-Politicus*." In *Spinoza's Theological-Political Treatise: A Critical Guide*, edited by Yitzhak Melamed and Michael Rosenthal. Cambridge: Cambridge University Press.

Steinberg, Diane. 1998. "Method and the Structure of Knowledge in Spinoza." *Pacific Philosophical Quarterly* 79: 152–69.

Steinberg, Diane. 2000. *On Spinoza*. Belmont, CA: Wadsworth.

Steinberg, Diane. 2005. "Belief, Affirmation, and the Doctrine of *Conatus* in Spinoza." *The Southern Journal of Philosophy* 43: 147–58.

Steup, Matthias. 1989. "BonJour's Anti-Foundationalist Argument." In *The Current State of the Coherence Theory*, edited by J. W. Bender, 188–99. Dordrecht: Kluwer Academic.

Strauss, Leo. 1965. *Spinoza's Critique of Religion*. Translated by E. M. Sinclair. New York: Schocken Books.

Strawson, Peter. 1962. "Freedom and Resentment." *Proceedings of the British Academy* 48: 1–25.

Swinburne, Richard. 1997. *The Evolution of the Soul*. Oxford: Clarendon Press.

Thomas Aquinas. 1981. *Summa Theologiae*. Translated by the English Dominicans. New York: Christian Classics.

Tonelli, Giorgio. 1959. "Der Streit über die mathematische Methode in der Philosophie in der ersten Hälfte des 18. Jahrhunderts und die Entstehung von Kants Schrift über die 'Deutlichkeit.'" *Archiv für Philosophie* 9: 37–66.

Tonelli, Giorgio. 1976. "Analysis and Synthesis in XXVIIIth Century Philosophy Prior to Kant." *Archiv für Begriffsgeschichte* 20: 178–213.

van Bunge, Wiep. 1990. *Johannes Bredenburg (1643–1691): Een Rotterdamse collegiant in de ban van Spinoza*. Ph.D. thesis, Rotterdam.

van Bunge, Wiep. 2003a. Entry "Balling." In van Bunge et al. (eds.) 2003, 45–7.

van Bunge, Wiep. 2003b. Entry "Jelles." In van Bunge et al. (eds.) 2003, 492–4.

van Bunge, Wiep, Henri Krop, Bart Leeuwenburgh, Han van Ruler, Paul Schuurman, and Michiel Wielema (eds.). 2003. *The Dictionary of Seventeenth and Eighteenth-Century Dutch Philosophers*. Bristol: Thoemmes.

Van Gelderen, Martin. 1992. *The Political Thought of the Dutch Revolt 1555–1590*. Cambridge: Cambridge University Press.

Vermij, Rienk. 1991. *Secularisering en natuurwetenschap in de zeventiende en achttiende eeuw: Bernard Nieuwentijt*. Ph.D. thesis, Utrecht. Amsterdam: Rodopi.

Viljanen, Valtteri. 2008a. "On the Derivation and Meaning of Spinoza's *Conatus* Doctrine." In *Oxford Studies in Early Modern Philosophy*, Vol. 4, edited by Daniel Garber and Steven Nadler, 89–112. Oxford: Clarendon Press.

Viljanen, Valtteri. 2008b. "Spinoza's Essentialist Model of Causation." *Inquiry* 51: 412–37.

Visser, Piet. 2003. Entry "Rieuwertsz." In van Bunge et al. (eds.) 2003, 841–5.

Von Dunin Borkowski, Stanislaus. 1910. *De junge De Spinoza: Leben und Werdegang im Lichte der Weltphilosophie*. Münster i.W.: Aschendorff.

Voss, Stephen. 1981. "How Spinoza Enumerated the Affects." *Archiv für Geschichte der Philosophie* 63: 167–79.

Voss, Stephen. 1993. "On the Authority of the *Passiones Animae*." *Archiv für Geschichte der Philosophie* 75: 160–78.

Walker, R. C. S. 1989. *The Coherence Theory of Truth*. London: Routledge.

Wartofsky, Marx. 1973. "Action and Passion: Spinoza's Construction of a Scientific Psychology." In *Spinoza: A Collection of Critical Essays*, edited by Marjorie Grene, 329–53. Garden City, NY: Anchor Books.

Whitrow, G. J. 1988. "Why Did Mathematics Begin to Take Off in the Sixteenth Century?" In *Mathematics from Manuscript to Print 1300–1600*, edited by C. Hay, 264–9. Oxford: Oxford University Press.

Wilson, M. D. 1978. *Descartes*. London: Routledge & Kegan Paul.

Wilson, M. D. 1991. "Spinoza's Causal Axiom (*Ethics* I, Axiom 4)." In *God and Nature: Spinoza's Metaphysics*, edited by Yirmiyahu Yovel, 133–60. Leiden: E. J. Brill.

Wilson, M. D. 1999. "Objects, Ideas, and 'Minds': Comments on Spinoza's Theory of Mind." In *Wilson, Ideas and Mechanism: Essays on Early Modern Philosophy*, 126–40. Princeton: Princeton University Press.

Wolf, A. 1974 [1927]. "Spinoza's Conception of the Attributes of Substance." In *Studies in Spinoza: Critical and Interpretive Essays*, edited by S. P. Kashap, 16–27. Berkeley: University of California Press.

Wolfson, H. A. 1934. *The Philosophy of Spinoza: Unfolding the Latent Processes of His Reasoning*. Two volumes in one. Cambridge, MA: Harvard University Press.

Yovel, Yirmiyahu. 1999. "Transcending Mere Survival: From *Conatus* to *Conatus Intelligendi*." In *Desire and Affect: Spinoza as Psychologist*, edited by Yirmiyahu Yovel, 45–61. New York: Little Room Press.

# Index